Hope for the Autism Spectrum

of related interest

Dyslogic Syndrome
Why Millions of Kids are "Hyper", Attention-Disordered, Learning Disabled,
Depressed, Aggressive, Defiant, or Violent – and What We Can Do About It
Bernard Rimland
ISBN 978 1 84310 877 1

Autism Heroes
Portraits of Families Meeting the Challenge
Barbara Firestone, Ph.D.
Forewords by Teddi Cole and Gary Cole and Catherine Lord, Ph.D.
Photographs by Joe Buissink
ISBN 978 1 84310 837 5

Families of Adults with Autism
Stories and Advice for the Next Generation
Edited by Jane Johnson and Anne Van Rensselaer
Foreword by Stephen Edelson, Autism Research Institute, San Diego
ISBN 978 1 84310 885 6

The Complete Guide to Asperger's Syndrome
Tony Attwood
ISBN 978 1 84310 495 7 (hardback)
ISBN 978 1 84310 669 2 (paperback)

Sally Kirk Foreword by Elizabeth Mumper, MD

Hope for the Autism Spectrum

A Mother and Son Journey of Insight and Biomedical Intervention

Graphics Design by Allan Kirchhoff

Jessica Kingsley Publishers
London and Philadelphia

ARI Parent Ratings of Behavioral Effects of Biomedical Interventions (Appendix B) printed
with permission from The Autism Research Institute.

First published in 2008
by Jessica Kingsley Publishers
116 Pentonville Road
London N1 9JB, UK
and
400 Market Street, Suite 400
Philadelphia, PA 19106, USA

www.jkp.com

Library of Congress Cataloging in Publication Data
A CIP catalog record for this book is available from the Library of Congress

British Library Cataloguing in Publication Data
A CIP catalogue record for this book is available from the British Library

ISBN 978 1 84310 894 8

Printed and bound in the United States by
Thomson-Shore, Inc.

To every child on the autism spectrum
and the people who love them

Part of this book's proceeds are donated to the Autism Research Institute which is superb at identifying and funding research that makes a difference *today*.

Disclaimer

This book is intended as information, *not* medical advice. The author is not even a doctor for crying out loud. In other words, do not take this information as medical advice or as a substitute for a discussion with a doctor. Medical information and recommendations are frequent subjects of debate. They are also likely to change over time. This is *especially* true in the field of biomedical intervention in autism which is growing and changing rapidly. This book will become out-of-date, but Chapter 29 identifies other resources for keeping current over time. There are also many other sources of detailed medical information, including your doctor, the manufacturer's package insert and website, and the U.S. Food and Drug Administration website at www.FDA.gov. Furthermore, the information presented in this book is not all-inclusive. Full discussion of the approved applications, usefulness, side effects, risks, monitoring, drug interactions, etc. of medications and other agents described in this book is beyond its scope. The book is fat enough as it is. Also note that not all the medications and other agents discussed in this text have U.S. Food and Drug Administration approval for use in children, or for some of the applications that they are commonly used for.

Contents

Foreword

Autism has become a public health emergency. While experts debate how much of the increase in autism-spectrum diagnoses is due to overdiagnosis, diagnostic substitution, or changing diagnostic criteria, clinicians, teachers, and parents notice that something has happened to this generation of children, and that more children with neurodevelopmental impairments are in their offices, classrooms, and neighborhoods.

I am a general pediatrician, who was teaching pediatrics to family medicine residents when I noticed in the mid-1990s that children seemed sicker than before: more eczema, more allergies, more asthma, more childhood diabetes, more ADHD, and more autism. In Virginia, where I work, autism increased eleven-fold and ADHD sixty-six-fold in a fifteen-year period. Even writing off half of those diagnoses as overzealous or erroneous, something terrible seems to be happening to our best and brightest children.

During my training in pediatrics at the University of Virginia, we were taught the mantra of Dr. Birdsong, instrumental in the establishment of the university's pediatric department, admonishing us to "look at the baby and listen to the mama." Everyone benefits from being able to tell their story and be heard. Yet parents of children with autism-spectrum disorders tell surprisingly similar stories about their experiences seeking medical help: that their concerns were minimized, that the mothers were treated as if they were crazy, and that their doctors seemed to lack the skills or time to help them. Their perception is that their doctors did not listen to them, which, if true, would violate one of the cardinal rules of pediatrics: first take a careful history. The wisdom of the great clinicians who valued their patients' stories included their realization that, by listening carefully, they not only served their patients well, but enriched their own experience as healers.

Listening to parents tell their stories about children who were meeting developmental milestones and seemed to be happy before suddenly "slipping away into their own world" made me very curious and worried about what was happening. During the last decade, I have met many amazing clinicians, parents, and patients who have enriched my personal and professional life beyond all expectations. They, too, were intrigued and concerned about what was happening to this generation of children.

As extraordinarily bright and dedicated parents saw their children lost to autism, they began unique journeys to figure out what was wrong and how to get their children back. One should not underestimate the power of parental tenacity, strengthened through the millennia and dedicated to ensuring their children's well-being. Parents who were exhausted from the demands of raising a child (or several children) with autism turned to their computers in the wee hours of the morning and did their own research. Parents brought skills from their professional life to the service of the autism community: nurses researched potential environmental triggers for autism, lawyers constructed cases for vaccine court, marketing executives worked on autism awareness campaigns, fundraisers raised money for research, researchers changed the focus of their scientific investigations, and physicians opened practices dedicated to children with autism.

Our autism paradigm has shifted. Originally considered a psychiatric disorder caused by refrigerator mothers, autism was later considered a static encephalopathy, genetically determined, immutable, and not treatable. The new paradigm considers the interaction between genetics and environment, the integration of body and brain, and the impact of metabolic and inflammatory conditions on neurologic function. With this shift, exciting opportunities for intervention emerge. As medical problems are systematically evaluated and addressed, some of us are fortunate enough to witness children, who were "in there" all along, emerge with stunning language and social interactions, inspiring those involved in their care.

In this book, an extraordinary mother recounts the story of her own child with autism, then shares lessons she learned in order to benefit other children and families. She translates data about medical problems into easy-to-understand information that families find helpful; she shares strategies for safe interventions that families can begin on their own. Her emphasis on the value of good nutrition and special diets chosen for the individual patient provides an avenue empowering parents to work towards recovering their children.

It is crucial for the families of children with autism to realize that there are treatments that can alleviate the pain from which many children with autism suffer. It is vital that medical professionals apply basic clinical skills to aid these amazing children. It is imperative for the research establishment to give priority to treatment-oriented research that is likely to help children now who are affected by autism spectrum disorders.

At the entrance of the Rimland Center at eye level is a plaque that carries the essence of our message: "listen to the parents." Listen to Sally speaking in these pages for the children who have lost their voices.

Dr. Elizabeth Mumper
Medical Director of the Autism Research Institute
and founder of the Rimland Center

Many Thanks for Making This Book Possible

I thank my dear husband, Rich, who was initially quite skeptical of biomedical intervention, yet evolved into a great advocate as he saw the improvements in our son, Will. I deeply appreciate his flexibility and his bolstering wave of support and enthusiasm for this book, even saying, "We will publish it ourselves if we have to!" He and our sons Allan, Will, and Lucas have patiently endured my time "in the tower," as they call it, an upstairs storage room where my PC and biomedical books are tucked away.

But we did not have to publish ourselves thanks to the insight of Jessica Kingsley Publishers who recognized that this book would make an important difference for many. It was a pleasure working with Jessica Kingsley and production editor Lisa Clark whose talents and enthusiastic efforts sculpted better explanations into these pages.

I also owe a great debt to some extremely busy people at the Autism Research Institute and Defeat Autism Now! They did not know me from the man in the moon yet were willing to lend me an ear. They offered help either by making connections for me or by reviewing my manuscript for medical or technical accuracy. They include Steve Edelson, PhD; Elizabeth Mumper, MD; and Jon Pangborn, PhD.

My dad, Wayne Stallard, who despite being poked fun at in this book, has been my most avid reader. His practical, candid comments were a great asset and reassurance. And there have been others—family, friends, and acquaintances—who have helped more than they can know with their reading and encouragement. They include my mother (Nancy Stallard) and sisters (Ginnie Pollen and Laura Kavanaugh), who also supplied entertaining, true-life tales I could craft to my purposes throughout these pages. Other invaluable supporters have each made their own unique contributions, including Marcia Dersch, Diana Fischer, Eileen Abbott, Patrick Kavanaugh, Elizabeth Libbey Stallard, and Kathleen Bush with her big, yellow dog. Thank you to each and every one.

Yet, my son, Will, deserves the grandest "Thank you!" for his willingness to let the whole world peek into his personal life in the hope of helping others. His only comments upon reading the text were "It is interesting" and "I am okay with it"—simple and to the point. It took depth for him to recognize that this book is not really about him or me.

Rather, this book is about you. You and your special someone. Helping you is the guiding force behind every word.

Why This Book Was Written and Who Is Behind It

I am the mother of a child on the autism spectrum. In writing this book, I hope to help you avoid some of the pitfalls that have riddled our journey and offer shortcuts to a better life for you and your child. Whether you are a parent, teacher, therapist, medical provider, or other interested individual, I wish to challenge your thinking on many fronts and stir you to thoughtful introspection.

Biomedical intervention has rewarded us richly with the most Wow! improvement my son, Will, has ever enjoyed. You can bet I will be explaining it and emphasizing its value, for I have witnessed, quite convincingly, that health problems are at the heart of autism-spectrum disorders. By offering easy-to-understand explanations of biomedical problems, their causes, and treatments, I hope to empower you to help your child. It is vital for those of us living (and sometimes dangling) on the autism spectrum to know that we can confront it. Though biomedical intervention does not work for everyone, it works for many. We can use it to improve health, brain function, and behaviors in our special someone. It is up to us to seize the opportunity and transform knowledge and hope into reality.

Who am I? Well, I was a little girl who grew up in the Hoosier state (Indiana) just outside Chicago, Illinois. I was surrounded by my parents, big brother, two little sisters, and a menagerie of pets. When grown, I attended Purdue University for a computer science degree. Then, I married my high-school sweetheart, Rich, who was graduating from Purdue as a mechanical engineer.

Rich and I worked locally for a few years before moving to the tippy toe of the state, near Evansville, Indiana. While working there, we earned masters degrees in business and then launched our personal "Operation Family Plan." That is where this book begins. Operation Family Plan yielded three fine little boys: Allan, Will, and Lucas. Known as "the LAW" (**L**ucas, **A**llan, **W**ill), they taught us many things and took us down more avenues than we ever imagined at the outset.

Our middle son, Will, was a healthy baby who regressed onto the autism spectrum around 18–24 months of age. Our family has journeyed with him down many uncharted paths, certainly new and foreign to us. There have been many twists and turns, ups and downs along the way. We have all grown and changed through the years of our journey. It has been a family affair.

Today, Allan is 16 (a teenager, yipes!); Will is 14 (another teenager, double yipes!); and Lucas is galloping up behind at 11. Rich manages an industrial plant and enjoys running, golfing, and fishing. As for me, I worked full time until Allan was about one. Then I switched to part-time work which has dwindled over the years. Now, I only occasionally connect from home to the computers at work. Otherwise, I manage the home front, spending much effort on meeting Will's needs. I have poured over countless books and materials on autism. As an audience member at innumerable conferences, presentations, meetings, and classes, I have taken notes and probed with inquiries. I ponder and analyze, scrutinize and question, experiment and reflect. I have worked extensively with Will in biomedical, therapeutic, educational, and social activities. Will himself has taken an active role in scores of organized social and physical programs, educational extras, and therapy sessions. Of all theseendeavors, Will's most rapid and obvious progress came from biomedical intervention.

I have learned so much along our journey. That is what I hope to share with you. If you and your child can avoid some of our bad turns and enjoy some shortcuts, my writing this book will have been worthwhile. If you examine your attitudes and gain some insights, these will be a double bonus.

And so, our story begins.

Our family (Back row: Sally and Rich. Front row: Allan (16), Will (14), and Lucas (12).)

Chapter 1

What Is This Book about Anyway?

There is hope. Your life and your child's life can be better. This book is about improving your lives through learning to understand your child's mind *and* body—and then acting on what you find. A journey on the autism spectrum has its hazards and godsends. These pages give you shortcuts to the godsends while steering you clear of the hazards. Valuable insights and information await you if you know someone with:

o   attention deficit disorder (ADD)

o   attention deficit hyperactivity disorder (ADHD)

o   pervasive developmental disorder (PDD)

o   Asperger's syndrome (AS)

o   high-functioning autism (HFA)

o   autism.

This book is also an invaluable resource for parents whose children do *not* have an autism-spectrum diagnosis but experience sensory or motor problems or perhaps issues with mental ability, aggression, or anxiety. These are conditions that can precede an eventual autism-spectrum diagnosis.

But take heart. Parents can prevent such a course of decline by learning about the biomedical problems that lead to decline and by taking action to intervene. Parents make a powerful difference. Do not be a spectator of your child's condition. Be a crucial, intervening player who turns the tide in your child's favor. My fervent hope is that this book can help you keep your child off the autism spectrum by improving his worrisome behaviors and symptoms. (Incidentally, for the sake of readability, I'll be using only the pronouns *he* or *his* when referring to a child on the autism spectrum since three out of four children with autism are boys.)[1]

Though originally intended for parents and family members, this book also has much to offer teachers, therapists, and medical professionals, as well as teens and adults with an autism-spectrum diagnosis themselves.

So let's get on with improving your lives. We'll talk *mind* first, then *body*.

UNDERSTANDING THE MIND ON THE AUTISM SPECTRUM

Learning to understand your child's mind is key to being able to help him and help yourself. Understanding is transforming. When you see the world as your child sees it, his behaviors make perfect sense. The blessing of understanding is that it leads to empathy and compassion. It melts frustration and exasperation into genuine respect, whole-hearted support, and even admiration. The impact it has on your relationship is profound. Understanding gets you and your child on the same team, working together to face the challenges. It makes all the difference in the world. In addition, when you understand where your child is coming from, you can be much more effective at helping him. The goal is not to *change* your child per se. Rather, it is to remove obstacles wherever they exist and offer support wherever it is needed. Give your child his best shot at being the happiest, healthiest, and most successful version of *himself.*

These pages offer some new perspectives and ideas you may not have considered before. There are also practical suggestions to help improve your relationship with your child, as well as the relationships you and your child have with your child's "typical" siblings. Guidance for problems with anxiety, meltdowns, and social skills are included as well. Getting a better life for you and your child requires self-education. Congratulations! You already started that when you cracked open this book. And by the time you are done, you will have numerous recommendations for other valuable resources of meaningful ideas, information, and support.

Speaking of support, you need emotional support too. Sharing our family's journey is meant to help encourage and validate you, as well as offer another perspective for you to consider. Never forget that your emotional health is crucial. If you go off the deep end, you can't help anyone (and besides, it feels lousy), so who needs it? Your sanity is an essential ingredient for you to succeed on behalf of your child. Family and friends are important sources of support and will be discussed. Other support resources will be recommended as well.

WHY SHOULD WE UNDERSTAND THE BODY?

It is important to recognize that the diagnosis of an autism-spectrum disorder is currently based purely on *behaviors*. Unfortunately, this diagnosis says little

about the potential underlying medical causes of those behaviors. For example, if I bite my brother (a behavior), it could mean I am angry at him, or it could mean I have rabies. Which is it? To know the true source of my behavior, you have to take a closer look. Let's say you find out that I actually have rabies. Do you prescribe a medication to suppress the biting behavior? Or do you treat the rabies (the root cause)? Obviously, you treat the rabies because that will relieve the physical ailment behind the biting, as well as the biting behavior itself.

Prescribing medication to improve attention or to reduce anxiety or aggression in a child on the autism spectrum is not necessarily bad. It may be essential, but you should recognize that it is also superficial, so you cannot stop there. You have to look beyond the physical manifestations for possible underlying medical causes. Too often people (including medical professionals) do not search for the medical underpinnings of autistic behaviors. They shrug off behaviors and even physical symptoms as "just part of the disorder." Don't believe it. The only Wow! kind of improvement my son has ever enjoyed came from identifying and treating his underlying *biomedical* issues, not his *behavioral* ones. An entire chapter of this book is devoted to the Wow!—that is, the before and after difference of the first 21 months of biomedical treatment (Chapter 14). This boon of progress was especially incredible since it followed many years of intense effort and striving while falling ever further behind. Though educational and therapeutic efforts have been helpful, their success was rather limited until they had a healthier body and mind to work with.

UNDERSTANDING THE BODY ON THE AUTISM SPECTRUM

Though the mind is important, it is the body that is so often overlooked on the autism spectrum. We miss many opportunities to improve brain function and autistic behaviors when we concentrate only on the mind and do not recognize underlying issues in the body. When helping a child, it is critical that we understand these physical issues. Through understanding, we are propelled to a position of power to intervene and improve health, brain function, and behaviors.

A generous portion of this book is devoted to descriptions of physical problems that are common on the autism spectrum. Though these problems are not always obvious at the surface, once we know what to look for, we can recognize them. These clues from our child help us solve his riddle. By understanding the problems and how they came to be, we can see that the treatments make a great deal of sense. They are safe and effective and have helped many who have gone before us. Several chapters discuss various treatments in ample detail.

Since every child is unique, each responds to biomedical intervention in his own way. Some children make wonderful progress and even lose their autism-spectrum diagnosis. Videos of recovered autistic children can be viewed at www.autism.com. A larger group of children, like my son, make major progress but still remain somewhere along the spectrum. Sadly, there is also a small group that makes little or no progress.[2] Younger children tend to respond better and faster than older ones. The optimum age to begin treatment is between ages 18 months and 5 years. Yet, older children and even adults can improve, some remarkably.[3] My son, who started biomedical treatment at age 11, is living proof of that. So when it comes to treatment, it is better late than never.

If you are not already familiar with biomedical intervention, you will be particularly interested in Chapter 16, "A Foundation for Understanding Biomedical Issues and Treatments in Autism." This chapter explores current-day thinking on autism's causes and treatments. It also offers the biomedical point of view and approach to treatment. Subsequent chapters discuss physical problems in fundamental body chemistry, the digestive tract, and the immune system, as well as effective interventions to address them. Through these chapters, you will learn what physical and behavioral signs to look for in your child. For many, the crux of autism originates in problems of body chemistry, a subject presented in Chapter 17. By treating the physical problems that underlie autistic behaviors, you can alleviate the symptoms of autism. Autism is treatable—and even preventable in many cases.

When undergoing biomedical treatment, it is certainly an asset to have a doctor who is well versed in biomedical intervention. Yet, there are *many* interventions you can introduce on your own. Do not underestimate how much *you* can help your child. This book can help guide you and also point you toward resources of more in-depth professional information.

NOW YOU KNOW WHAT THIS BOOK IS ABOUT

This book is about hope—real and tangible hope. Its purpose is to improve your quality of life and that of your child through understanding what is really going on in his mind and body. Understanding is power—power to help your child and yourself. Understanding takes you to a place where problems transform into opportunities. Seize the opportunities. Act on them. For you, they offer less stress, more sanity, and a sense of being in control and having influence. They also offer you an improved relationship with your child and more rewards in parenting.

For your child, the opportunities are even greater. What would it mean to him if he could be truly understood, respected, and encouraged? And what if he could enjoy improved health, brain function, emotional stability, and behaviors? What would all these mean to his happiness, clarity of mind, self-esteem, and social pleasures?

A better life can happen. I have seen it with my own eyes, and I am only one of a multitude. Know that it is possible and may be within your grasp. You can transform understanding into opportunities and opportunities into reality. Yes, there is hope. You can find it and put it to work for you and your child.

A special word to parents of newly diagnosed children: *diagnosis* is a dreadful word, really. It can feel like an unchanging, heavy cloud permanently stationed over the heads of you and your child. That is absolutely not true. Since my son's first diagnosis several years ago, he has improved tremendously —sometimes at a crawl, sometimes by leaps and bounds, and sometimes he has moved backwards. If nothing else, know that there can be considerable improvement, and you can help make it happen. Being your child's parent makes you the best person in all the world to help him. Do not let a diagnosis be a life sentence; take it on as the beginning of a journey toward improvement and a happier life for you and your child. Though at times the journey can get discouraging, the soul of a parent is resilient beyond comprehension. It has always given me the strength to go even when my "goer" was gone. And though the journey may not be easy, there is something significant and indispensable at the core of the relationship between a parent and a child. You have that *something*. For starters, that is all you need.

NOTES

1. Pangborn and Baker 2005, p. 1:11.
2. McCandless 2007, p. 67.
3. Ibid., p. 11.

Part 1

OUR YEARS OF SEARCHING

Chapter 2

All Is Well

DAYS OF BLISS

In August 1993, my husband Rich and I were blessed with a robust bundle of great joy. Will was beautiful and bubbles of mirth came gurgling up inside as I heard his first cries and could see he was healthy. Rich phoned everyone on the call list to report that Will was here, weighing in at 7 pounds, 2 ounces, and stretching to 20 and ¾ inches. Our two-year-old son, Allan, wore his "big brother" pin with pride, though he was skeptical that this new baby was such a good idea.

The pregnancy had been normal and quite comfortable as pregnancies go. I am really lucky that way. I never knew what morning sickness felt like, and everything from blood pressure to blood sugar to ankles always stayed A-okay for me. Not that the increasingly large and crowding tenant sitting on my innards was easy street, but I have no horror stories to tell. On the other hand, I make up for it at delivery time. Allan's delivery had been the kind with a gazillion hours of labor and an emergency C-section in the end. The doctor called it "failure to progress," which is just a fancy way of saying I flunked delivery. Okay, fine, I can accept that. I do not usually like to admit failure but, in this case, I was just incredibly relieved to get my beautiful baby out safely. So when it came time to decide Will's form of delivery, "repeat C-section" had a lovely ring to it for some reason. Anyway, Will's C-section and hospital stay went perfectly fine, and we went home in the usual course of time.

Will was an exceptionally happy and easy baby. He was a good eater and a good sleeper. When he did get upset, he was easily pacified. This same pleasant, sunny personality continued as he grew into a toddler.

ON A FIRST NAME BASIS WITH THE PEDIATRICIAN

Now, I am a very good mommy, and whenever it comes to health issues, I am Johnny-on-the-Spot. Will never missed a well-baby checkup or an infant vaccine per the mandatory schedule. Whenever we suspected a germ was afoot in our little treasure, we packed him off to the doctor's office, usually coming home with antibiotics.

When Will was two months old, I returned to work three days a week. We really liked our daycare center, albeit a den of iniquity for germs. It does not matter how much one sanitizes; eight babies in a room all day are bound to cough, sneeze, and slobber each other into the doctor's office. Will had his share of ear infections and thrush (egads! What are those white patches in my baby's mouth?). And, of course, there is the insidious pinkeye that is so contagious. I swear you can catch it just by looking at someone who has it. Once it would get in the family, pinkeye went round and round like a blurring merry-go-round. When it came to children in my house, childhood infections just seemed to go with the territory. All my kids caught them, over and over again, though only Will had a lot of thrush. It was just something you deal with and make the best of, right? All the parents of young children that we knew were stuck in the same revolving door to the doctor to get antibiotics until the kids hit three or so.

Will had the unusual hitch of having a hernia at four months old. What's with that? Babies do no heavy lifting. It made me a bit anxious for my little baby to have surgery. Okay, okay, so I was *extremely* anxious. In fact, I bawled shamelessly all the way down the hospital hallway to the surgery room, where the sympathetic nurse offered some reassuring words and then locked me out. Sometimes, you just cannot suck it up. Anyway, Will did amazingly well, never even flinched or acted like the incision hurt. What a champ!

Furthermore, Will was our only child to have episodes of chronic diarrhea, episodes that would last for weeks. The pediatrician called it "chronic toddler diarrhea" and assured us it would go away which it did eventually.

SOME MILESTONES—THINGS SEEM OKAY

Will started smiling at around four-to-five weeks. I was told that was advanced. Yes, my son would be a genius. He had a particularly gorgeous smile with huge dimples and bright eyes. Of course, every mother thinks her baby has the most beautiful smile. And you know what? They are *all* right.

Will's first words started around his first birthday (uh-oh, bye, dog, duck—I know you were dying to know what they were). Will commando crawled at eight months and walked around 15 months, a little late by the book. However, that was exactly what his big brother did, so I did not sweat it. Besides, I really prefer a late walker. They cannot get into nearly as much stuff when they are floor bound. I was perfectly happy to let my sister Laura have the Tarzan baby who walked at seven months and could climb to the top of any counter using the tippy tops of drawers for stepping stones. She was welcome to the "danger, danger, go directly to danger" baby who needed heroic acts of rescue hundreds of times a day. Because of my dear nephew, every chair in her house was on its side until someone needed to sit in it. Whenever a chair was vacated, it was promptly returned to the floor. All doors were shut. Every baby-safe mechanism known to man was not only in her house but voraciously tested each day by her wee one. Sometimes that is what parents have to deal with. It gave me sweet memories of my late walkers every time I visited my dear nephew.

When Will was 16 months old, I wrote of him in our Christmas letter, "Will is intrigued with his big brother, is constantly pointing at everything, and makes an art form of dinner-tray finger painting and hair a-la-food." Going back to watch family videos of this time, I can see there were coordination and attention issues. At the time, however, his development seemed normal to us, and we had no reason to expect that it would not continue that way.

GATHERING CLOUDS

Our first concerns about Will's well-being started when he was somewhere between 18 months and two years of age. He walked with an unusual gait and lost his balance easily. I remember seeing a friend's daughter who was about Will's age. This little girl climbed on top of a coffee table and stood straight up without using her hands. Will's balance was nowhere close to this. The contrast was startling, and I felt my first pang of "could something be *wrong*?" I am not a fingernail-biter but I was thinking of becoming one. That first realization was only the beginning of our autism-spectrum "journey."

A TEST I WISH WE HAD

Since that day nine years ago, a simple psychological test has since been developed for 18-month-olds that is valuable for predicting autism-spectrum disorders. It is called the Childhood Autism Test or CHAT and was designed for pediatricians to use at the 18-month well-baby checkup. Frankly, it is easy enough for a parent to do on his or her own, perhaps with the aid of someone the child does not know. Any cause for concern should prompt a doctor visit. The CHAT is a two-part test consisting of nine yes-or-no questions for the parent and five easy observational tests for the pediatrician. The questions for the parent are along the lines of "Does your child ever use his index finger to point to ask for something?" and "Does your child enjoy being swung, bounced on your knee, etc.?" The observational tests for the pediatrician include such tasks as "During the appointment, has the child made eye contact with you?" The test questions and observational tasks can be found on www.AutismNDI.com and other Web sites by doing a search on "Childhood Autism Test."[1]

If this simple and reliable test had been available when I first worried about Will's development, I may have gotten him on the right track sooner.

NOTE

1. Seroussi 2002, pp. 218–19. The questions and tasks are also listed in Hamilton (2000), pp. 43–46.

Chapter 3

It Started with Motor Delay

A TRAUMATIC EXPERIENCE

I pointed out Will's Charlie-Chaplin style of walking to the pediatrician at his two-year well-baby checkup. The resulting hip and leg x-rays showed nothing amiss structurally. I returned promptly in six months as instructed. The walk had not changed, and the doctor thought Will's fine motor skills appeared delayed as well. Now, this was getting scary, and I do not like scary, not even in movies.

The pediatrician ordered a complete evaluation by physical, occupational, and speech therapists. The results shook me to my very core. My precious Will had significant delays. I was stunned. It was incomprehensible to think that this pleasant, loving toddler would always have to work twice as hard as everybody else to accomplish the same task. The playing field would not be even. There was no explanation for the delays; they just were. I felt a deep, throbbing ache that would not go away. Life should be fair to such a sweet little boy. But it was not, and I was crushed. Nevertheless, I had to pull myself together for Will. My personal pep talk went something like this: "Okay, Sal. Get a grip. It is not the end of the world. Nobody is dying here. You do not always get what you want. So what? Just make the best of it. With therapy, Will can catch up. He may never even remember having been behind. Pull yourself together and dive in headlong. When the going gets tough, the tough get going. So what, you feel like a bucket of mush? That is immaterial. It is hustle time."

If you are living in a traumatic-experience chapter of your journey right now, I really feel for you. It is a very ugly chapter. But, if it is any consolation, keep in mind that it is relatively short lived and you *will* get used to the idea. The mushroom cloud will settle, and you will adjust. There are still good days ahead. Take whatever psychological time you need to get over the shock and then move on. Remember that this is a journey. Do not be duped into thinking that the first diagnosis is an end-all. Will has actually been through three diagnoses over the years and may have more to go. There have been other significant findings and events along the way as well. That is good news because, with each step, you gain knowledge that empowers you to help your child. Do not let that first medical report create an upheaval. It obviously needs to get your attention but keep in mind that it might be an incomplete or even wrong assessment of your child. Whatever it is, recognize it is only a starting point. You are only on the *Go* square of the parent Monopoly board. You have many spaces yet to land on, each yielding its secrets for help, treatments, and the removal of obstacles.

I THINK I CAN, I THINK I CAN...

Will's motor delays qualified him for our state's early-childhood-education pre-school. Weekly physical therapy (the gross motor), occupational therapy (fine motor), and speech therapy were included as part of the Monday–Friday morning preschool. It was a wonderful program whose educated and talented employees helped Will work on many specific skills in language, cognition, self-help, and social and emotional areas. And it was all free of charge to us. Early intervention is critical, and the preschool educators knew it—God bless Indiana!

We felt that, for success in school, it was particularly important to get Will's fingers agile. They would need to write and cut and manipulate. Without good dexterity, how would Will ever crumple up paper for spit wads when the teacher was not looking? Okay, so maybe not for that purpose, but OT was essential just the same. OT is short for occupational therapy. See, I was catching onto the lingo already. To get an extra dose of OT, we took Will to a private occupational therapist for a bonus weekly session. When preschool was out in the summer, we paid for the therapies ourselves. We were trying to propel Will into high-speed catch-up mode.

Through therapists and preschool teachers, I was plunged into a mysterious yet interesting world where words and concepts like *sensory integration*, *proprioception*, and *vestibular system* swirled around. I bought therapy gizmos and had Will opening button boards to get his after-dinner snacks. His glasses and bowls were replaced by funky ones with built-in straws. Plus, I started putting shaving cream on the bathtub walls. Mom has really lost it now. People at the grocery undoubtedly wondered, "Why is that lady insisting that itty-bitty boy struggle alone against the arduous entry doors?"

I felt all these interventions helped Will from falling further behind his peers motor-wise. However, they did not "catch him up." At least he seemed to be doing well otherwise. His attention span for learning was good. He knew shapes, animals, and some colors. He got along well with other toddlers and did not have any problems eating or sleeping. Will would bring us a constant stream of books to read to him. Besides books, he was also an enthusiastic animal lover, who loved trips to the zoo and subjected our poor, patient dogs to many zealous bear hugs. Later, he discovered videos, and we really had to work to keep him involved in more enriching endeavors. Batman was a huge hero at our house. All normal amusements for a little tyke.

Chapter 4

The Plot Thickens

SOMETHING IS AFOOT

Do you know that uneasy feeling you get when your child does something that doesn't seem quite right? Well, I got one of those feelings. Then I got a few more. Expressing my concerns to the pediatrician only received a shoulder shrug. I got the impression he did not think there was anything to do about it. So, I just kept watching and tried to quiet my fears. But they would not be quieted. As time went on and my uneasiness mounted, I built my case. I gathered examples of Will's actions that would prove to the doctor that Will was indeed struggling and in need of close professional scrutiny of some sort. Granted, it is hard to know when enough is enough; but, in hindsight, I believe I took longer than necessary to build my case. It was not as if I were going to the Supreme Court. A little evidence is all you really need to go to your doctor or to a different doctor and insist on an evaluation or a referral. Don't wait around.

OVERRELYING ON DOCTORS

This is probably a good place to mention that you should not blindly rely on your doctor. That person is not the only doctor around, and not all doctors give the same advice. I know that seems self-evident but, when thinking about this time period, I have to admit that I overrelied on my pediatrician. When he shrugged his shoulders, I figured nothing could be done. We were just unlucky and would have to get used to the idea, kind of like we had gotten used to not knowing why Will had motor delay. In 1996, the Internet wasn't what it is today. And it didn't occur to me to go looking for answers anyplace except at my doctor's office. I thought about shopping around for another doctor but didn't see any more hopeful options. And it never occurred to me to go "out of network" on my insurance, though I could have afforded it.

What limited me was my own way of thinking. I assumed my doctor had extensive knowledge and experience and was well aware of everything going on in pediatrics. Though that may be unrealistic, it is what I thought. After all, my doctor had been to college for umpteen years studying the body and brain, right? As I saw it, doctors—in general—saw patients every day who had the kinds of problems Will was having. They "practiced" on them constantly and would know if something worked. Didn't doctors read medical journals and attend conferences, too? I considered them well-informed and on the leading edge. What did I know by comparison? Nothing. Oh, I lied. I did take Psych 101 in college. So I knew a little brain stuff, but that was mostly about rat mazes and salivating dogs, not very helpful to Will's situation. Otherwise, my medical and psychological know-how was limited to first-aid classes and TV specials. Who was I to pass judgment on my doctor's learned opinion?

Furthermore, I assumed that, if children like Will were being helped (sometimes significantly) by measures outside my doctor's area of expertise, my doctor would know about it. Don't count on it. Doctors are only human. I can understand not wanting to read dry medical journals on a Saturday night. In addition, even if your doctor has heard of other supposedly successful measures, he or she may not be open-minded to them and will not recommend them to you. After all, there is merit in caution, and doctors are generally a conservative bunch. If these other measures are considered "alternative," your doctor may be waiting for them to gain broader acceptance before mentioning them to patients. Personally, I would rather get word of potential help than a shoulder shrug; but, hey, I am not everybody.

MY CASE IS MORE THAN READY

Anyway, by the time Will was nearing four years old, I was frantic. He was still drooling like a young toddler, and his potty training was at ground zero. Will seemed to have no warning of when he "had to go" and was as surprised by accidents as everybody else. Another alarming behavior was that, when given a choice, Will would always select the last option offered, even if I immediately restated the question, simply flipping the order of the choices. His attention and concentration had disintegrated significantly, and it was scaring the gajeebies out of me. Though talkative and able to respond to direct questions, he was completely unable to carry on a conversation. In addition, he could only comment on what was going on right now, this minute. The past was a gray, fuzzy place of uncertainty, too difficult to retrieve from memory. Moreover, multitask instructions seldom saw completion. For instance, a directive like "go to the bathroom" could not be carried out. Instead, I had to stand over him and give each instruction as he completed the last: "Put up the seat." "Pull down your pants." "Go potty." Also quite disconcerting was how he sometimes asked how to get to a certain room in our house. And, no, we did not live in a castle. Motor delay had been one thing, but intellectual issues were on a new plane of terror. I stormed the pediatrician's office in a panic. It was a no-brainer for him to make a referral to a pediatric neurologist.

I must pause a moment to point out that, at that time, I did not believe this precious little person could ever be independent. What is important to know is that today as I look at my 14-year-old marvel, I see independence is possible. So wherever you are in your journey, keep that in mind. Don't call it quits. You do not have to "be realistic and accept the facts," as though the situation were etched in stone. It is the future, for crying out loud. Nobody knows what it holds. In my experience, very much progress can be made between now and then.

THE CURE—OR SO WE THOUGHT

You will have to indulge me here in a little hero worship. I am entitled to it, as you will see. Besides, there are real, live, flesh-and-blood heroes out there, you know. We have been lucky enough to meet some. This particular pediatric neurologist was one of them. His name is listed in Appendix A alongside some of Will's other would-be future heroes. This fellow probably did not suspect he was a hero, but he was just the same. There we were—an anxious, earnest bundle of apprehension and fear treading into unknown territory, the realm of the specialist. It was a momentous appointment for us. I was dreading what he might say. He truly held our world in his hands.

Now, he looked like a regular guy, but he just so happened to have done his residency in a sleep clinic. So, his standard set of opening questions started with sleep. Well, we knew we had no issues there. Will was a phenomenal sleeper. We told the good doctor that Will was a dream to put to bed and that he slept 12 hours a night. He even still took naps. Does he snore? Oh well, yes, like the Three Stooges. But so does his...er, uh, his...one of his parents. So we figure he gets it honestly. Does he roll around when he sleeps? Oh, heavens, yes. He rolls around all over the place. You cannot possibly sleep with him the way he Kung-Fu punches all night. Why do you ask? Attention problems? Oh, yes, and here are some examples...

By the end of our interview, we were exhilarated with hope. The doctor definitely suspected Will had a sleep problem that could be causing his symptoms. Something was obstructing Will's airway as he fell into the deeper levels of sleep. The snoring was the flapping sounds of a crowded airway trying to rasp air in and out. As Will's air supply shrank, he had to rouse himself somewhat, thus the rolling and moving—not enough to wake him but enough to increase the air supply. As a substitute for quality sleep, he was forced to settle for quantity. That was why he slept so much. Why, the poor kid was a walking zombie! If you have ever stayed up all night and on through the next day, you know the fog that settles in your brain. Robotically, you stumble through the motions of the day seemingly from a distance. I marveled at how such a little kid could possibly have been doing this day after day after day. Rich and I were very excited. Maybe this was the source of all Will's difficulties. It certainly sounded logical and promising.

An overnight sleep study was conducted in which Will slept at the hospital, his head covered in little suction cups attached to cords. The results clearly showed sleep apnea, a sleep disorder in which a person repeatedly stops breathing or breathes shallowly for brief periods during sleep. The episodes can occur as often as 300 times a night, impairing sleep quality and reducing the level of oxygen in the blood. A second test was performed at the hospital with Will under anesthetic. This time a tiny camera on the end of a tube was slipped up Will's nose and down his throat. Sounds gross, but it was actually fascinating. I watched the associated TV screen reveal what the camera saw as it wormed along the airway. During this simulated deep sleep, the airway was collapsing around the tonsils and adenoids. What the heck are adenoids? No matter. Just some unnecessary stuff that hangs by the tonsils. Since they and the tonsils were causing Will's "obstructive sleep apnea" we could do without them. It would be ten years before I learned that children with autism have a higher rate of obstructive sleep apnea.[1] The plan of action was sweet and simple. Get the culprits out of there and end their reign of harm. And so we did, or perhaps I should say a surgeon did.

The effect was immediate and powerful. Will stopped drooling and picking the last choice offered. Within a couple of weeks, he was talking in longer sentences and following multitask instructions. *There was progress in potty training!* We were thrilled by his quantum improvement in attention, memory, and use of logic. Only a few weeks after surgery, Will was initiating and carrying on conversations. He could even describe past events. His therapists were telling us that he was more willing to try activities and much more successful doing them than before. Talk about removing obstacles. This was gargantuan. It was like lifting a glacier off his back. The hero doctor estimated Will would be caught up to peers in 6–12 months. We were ecstatic. Will was featured in the hospital's magazine and got five minutes of fame on the 6 o'clock news. All was good in the world again. Oh, and by the way, we had three boys by that time. Our newest arrival, Lucas, was 18 months old and a charming knockout. With older and younger brothers to bolster him, Will would be pushing the limits in no time.

TROUBLE IN PARADISE

You can imagine our distress when, seven months after surgery, we began seeing regression. Will's potty training, which had been mastered for months, began to falter. He tired easily, and his physical endurance was on the wane. His dinner conversation became unrelated to the topic at the table. Batman was Will's incessant theme no matter what new topic we tried to introduce. Will talked constantly and loudly, even when others were speaking, often repeating the same things over and over. It was frightening how focused he was becoming on his own world; he was taking less notice of ours. His rate of learning slowed noticeably, and he became increasingly distractible. His preschool teacher was voicing concerns about attention deficit. One day she even got in his face and repeated his name three or four times before receiving a response. On her final attempt, he had jumped in surprise—startled, as though she had sneaked up and clanged pot lids. All this was a blazing cry for more intervention, but what? In alarm, we raced back to the hero doctor. Maybe the sleep apnea was back somehow. The good doctor did another sleep study, but the sleep department was intact. He referred us to a child psychiatrist.

MY FIRST PRESENTATION AS CASE MANAGER

I knew this appointment with the psychiatrist would not be a simple one. The solutions to Will's problems were not as obvious as stitches or a plaster cast. A greater degree of involvement and input was needed on my part. So, I carefully typed up a list of concerns that was as brief and succinct as possible. It is part of the role of being a case manager for a child. You need to present a complete and accurate, yet concise, picture of relevant information, so the professional can assess and treat your child properly. If you put some careful thought up-front to what the doctor needs to know, you will not forget to relay important information since it is right in front of you on paper. Otherwise, if you go to a doctor with a vague, half-complete description of the issues in your mind, you are likely to come out with a vague, half-complete diagnosis or treatment plan. And what good is that? Besides, what you write is also an excellent record of the issues at that point in time. You and your doctor may find such documentation valuable in the future as memories fade. I have found my past writings helpful for purposes I could never have anticipated at the time I wrote them.

In my document, I put our greatest concern in emphasized lettering: *It is so difficult to direct Will's attention. Even when he pays attention, his comprehension and memory are usually poor.* Four bullets followed, each supported by a few examples to illustrate the problem clearly.

ENTER STAGE LEFT—CHILD PSYCHIATRIST

I wish I could say that, having done my homework, we met with great success; however, no such luck this time. The psychiatrist spent a neat little hour of his day ignoring my carefully devised list, despite the several references I kept making to it. Instead, he persisted in asking us about numerous bizarre behaviors that Will did not exhibit. If Will spent hours every day lining up toys in rigid orders, I would have put it on my list, all right? Something I have since learned is that these professionals work *for you*. You are paying them, and they should discuss what you wish to discuss. Of course, you already know that I overrelied on doctors back then. So, I waited patiently for the psychiatrist to finish his left-field questions and get to my list. Well, surprise, surprise—he never got to my list. But he felt we should come back in three months to discuss this some more. Yeah, right, and we are eating snakes for dinner tonight. No, it was evident that this guy could not help us even if he went to college for a million years. He did not know how to *listen*. We paid the exorbitant bill and never returned. That is the way it goes sometimes. It is a shame that you cannot know ahead of time if an effort will be successful. Expect some wrong turns along your journey. The good news is that sometimes you land on Free Parking when the pot is loaded.

Yet questions remained. Do we try a different psychiatrist? If so, who? We had no way of knowing who might be able to help us. If the hero doctor thought this was a good psychiatrist, then was there any point in trying to see another? Maybe this was not a good route at all. What to do? What to do?

REGRESSION FADES

As we stewed over our next steps, Will mysteriously began to improve at a modest rate. The period of regression, which had lasted five months, began to fade away. We will never know why it came or why it receded. In its wake, I recognized that the obstructive sleep apnea was not the "end-all" we had believed—a sobering realization indeed.

NOTE

1. Jepson and Johnson 2007, pp. 174–75.

Chapter 5

Living with the Wrong Diagnosis: ADHD

LIFE IN A PINBALL MACHINE CALLED ADHD

So, we had no luck with the hero doctor or the child psychiatrist. We bided our time. After a few months, Will's preschool teacher asked the school psychologist to take a turn. I will call him "Dr. School." He administered several tests to Will with two basic conclusions. One was that Will was ready academically for regular kindergarten. That was good news. The second conclusion was a diagnosis of attention deficit hyperactivity disorder (ADHD), a developmental disorder consisting of difficulties with attention span, impulse control, and hyperactivity. ADHD has a little brother, ADD (attention deficit disorder), which mirrors it except for the hyperactivity component. I agreed with the ADD part of Will's diagnosis, but I could not see the "H." As far as I could tell, Will was not hyperactive at all. Quite the opposite, really: he lacked energy. Since Dr. School was recommending medication for Will's attention problem, I really wanted to be cautious. The idea of drugging my kid grated against my grain. I certainly respected Dr. School and his opinions, but I just had to check out that "H." I took Will to a private child psychologist, "Dr. Private," as I'll call him. He seemed thorough and also very good at explaining his tests and conclusions to me. I liked that. In the end, Dr. Private agreed with Dr. School. The diagnosis remained ADHD, and the recommendation was medication. I figured if you can't beat 'em, join 'em. It was time to give attention medication a try.

I GUESS THE DOCS WERE RIGHT

By this time it was 1998, and Will was five-and-a-half. Trying medication was rocky at first as we experimented to get the right dose of a drug called Adderall. Dosing is not governed by weight but rather by each individual's response to the drug. Too much made Will irritable…and everyone else through a domino effect. Once we got past the dosing issue, we could see that the medication really did help Will focus. There was a tricky balance between maximizing the level of attention and minimizing the side effect of irritation. Okay, so I was a believer. I guess Will really did have ADHD after all. Now it was time for some self-education. Bring on the books, magazines, and articles about ADHD. I needed to find out what this was all about. Of all the materials I read, I found the best to be a book called *Taking Charge of ADHD* by Russell A. Barkley. It helped me to understand Will's struggles with attention and how to best deal with them.

A SNEAK PREVIEW

Will would remain on varying doses of Adderall for the next nine years. Much of that time I considered the medication an indispensable support. However, after seeing Will's improvements on biomedical treatment beginning at age 11, I began to hope that maybe *someday* he would not need that daily dose of Adderall. Occasionally I would try taking him off of it, but that trial never lasted more than a day. I didn't have the endurance for it. Also, Rich noticed each time, remarking, "What is up with Will?" Will would lose focus and talk incessantly, even when others were talking. His coordination was noticeably clumsy, as he bumped into people and objects. Though he was down to 15mg a day, he still seemed to need the Adderall. However, three years after biomedical treatment began, I was able to remove the drug without being able to tell any difference. Rich didn't notice either, and there were no poor reports from school. We went without Adderall for seven months, though later decided it was worthwhile to use on school days for an edge in attention in class. My boy was getting better. Yet, those days were a long way off. Back then, I was still groping through material on ADHD for answers. Unfortunately, it didn't always add up.

SOMETHING SEEMED FISHY, BUT WHAT COULD I DO?

None of the ADHD literature I read mentioned motor delay. If anything, children with ADHD were over-motor enabled, not under. Now, didn't that seem odd? There were no sensory integration issues with this diagnosis either. Yet Will was hypersensitive to haircuts and nail trimmings, as well as certain textures and sounds. And why would someone who was sensitive to sound talk so loudly? Nor did ADHD explain Will's fleeting eye contact. And what about his poor social habits like interrupting or forcing the conversation topic to his favorite? Will would ramble eternal, one-sided monologues about his beloved interests. No notice was taken of the other person's boredom in facial expression, body language, or tone of voice. Unlike typical conversation, this was no exchange of ideas. You could not even squeeze in a syllable. And what was it with these favorite subjects anyway? They went beyond favorites; they were obsessions. They followed in sequence over the years from Batman to dinosaurs to Legos. They were all-consuming and devoured Will's thoughts entirely, leaving no room for anything else. Then there was this issue of Will being down right belligerent at times. How could he mysteriously morph into such a discontented child when his personality had been all smiles only a few years before? Furthermore, it took Will three-to-five seconds to respond to a question or request. It was as though his thinking was in slow motion. As I helped him with homework over the next few years, I noticed strange recall behavior. On Saturday, he could not work a math problem for all the Legos in Texas. Then, on Sunday, with no intervening instruction, he could whiz through the whole math assignment with ease. At times, he seemed able to think; but at other times he would cry out in frustration, "My brain is not working!" Inconsistency was his trademark. I was perplexed, annoyed, and exasperated—and that was on a good day. On a bad day, I might be angry, panicked, or depressed, never a pretty sight.

In years previous, I had soaked up books, articles, and TV shows on parenting. It was a refreshing change of pace from the usual menu of Winnie-the-Pooh and Sesame Street. The crown jewels of all my efforts were two books: *It's Not Fair, Jeremy Spencer's Parents Let Him Stay Up All Night!: A Guide to the Tougher Parts of Parenting* by Anthony E. Wolf and *Siblings Without Rivalry: How to Help Your Children Live Together so You Can Live Too* by Adele Faber and Elaine Mazlish. Since my nightstand was already cluttered with reading, I listened to them on audio in the car on the way to work.

Via my self-education efforts, I came to believe I possessed pretty good parenting skills. My boys were fairly easy to manage and were often complimented on their behavior. They played well together and were generally a pleasure to have around. But life had been growing rough for Will (and correspondingly for the rest of us). The typical good-parenting techniques became less and less successful. Certainly, his attention problems could contribute to his behavior, but, still, it just did not seem right. He got extreme at times, even hysterical. He would work himself into a state, and it was anyone's guess where it had come from or where it was going. These emotional hijackings were like a tide of intense, overwhelming emotion. Once unleashed, they mounted to tsunami proportions. I had never seen anything like it. I tried various techniques, some recommended by the experts and others just out of desperation. Surely something would bring him around. The weird part was that Will did not seem to have control of himself at these times. He would lose his composure and could not retrieve it even for himself, let alone anyone else.

Not only did the ADHD literature fail to explain Will's emotional instability, it didn't account for why he was such a homebody either. He seemed tortured to be away from the comfort zone of his house and bedroom. Family outings stressed and upset him, everything from a couple of hours at a fair to a camping weekend with relatives. Outings were great stuff, from our point of view. Why did he ask to go home, and then brood and ostracize himself when we did not? Why couldn't he just relax and enjoy himself?

Motor delay, hypersensitivity to sound and texture, social skill deficits, obsessive interests, belligerent moods, and hysterical, uncontrollable crying—these behaviors were a complete, unfathomable riddle to us. Poor kid, living life with the clueless. No doubt we were a complete, unfathomable riddle to him as well. He probably wondered why we did not understand him or help him. But, alas, none of the ADHD literature I read addressed these sorts of problems. Though the attention part of the diagnosis fit, it seemed a very incomplete portrait of Will. Yet it was all we had.

WANTING MORE

It would be over two years before the ADHD diagnosis was overturned, and Asperger's syndrome (AS) was put in its place. During the intervening time, Will always had appropriate supports and therapy in the public-school system. That was all well and good, but I wanted more. Such interventions helped Will be his best within his limitations, but I wanted the burden of those limitations removed. I wanted to get another glacier off my little boy. But how? I looked in many places with the resources I could find. I pursued several fruitless avenues too discouraging to mention. It is a downtrodden feeling to strike out hopefully after some bright prospect, only to conclude it was a fiasco in the end. But what is a parent to do? You search. If something seems promising, you try it. There are no guarantees except that you will be down some bucks in the end—sometimes a lot of bucks. Yes, it is disheartening, but still you have to try. It would be *so* worth it if something worked. You see your child in need, and that ache to help compels you onward.

A MOTHER'S ACHE

When our children get hurt, we come in to kiss the bump and make it "all better." That is what moms do, right? We have to. The buck stops with us. But what if we cannot make it better? And what if our child is *seriously* hurting yet we cannot fix it? We cry. We ache. We are restless, agitated, and sometimes desperate, always searching for a way to make it "all better." I have always been a determined sort, but Will's disadvantages gave rise to a whole new form of determination. I wanted so badly for him to have the same opportunities as everyone else, to help him in any way that made sense. My sister Laura once remarked on my efforts over the years. She likened me to a salmon, swimming up the white-water rapids to spawn. I never stop, cannot stop. The exertion and pain of the journey are immaterial to the magnitude of its purpose. That is what moms do. Similarly, Rich has said that I am unrelenting when it comes to Will. If that is so, it is because I can be no other way. The ache will always drive me as long as Will needs assistance and as long as there are promising and sensible possibilities to try. Will has made tremendous gains from ages 2 to 14. It is a great credit to his efforts and to mine. We are a team, and we draw closer to a day when he will not need such vigilance and support. Though the ache has lessened as Will has improved, it is still there. It becomes acute at times when he struggles and lessens at times he succeeds. I may not like the ache, but it has served a vital function on the road toward Will's becoming the best version of himself.

Enough about me. Let's talk about you. So there you sit, reading a book about the autism spectrum. You could be doing chores around the house, catching up at the office, sleeping, fishing, or riding a roller coaster. But no. There you sit, reading this book. Hmm. So what does that tell me about you, fellow salmon? You must know someone who needs your help. And I have an idea you are the perfect person for the job. You are your child's champion and hero.

And, no, not every attempt to help will be successful, but still you have to try. No one has perfect foresight or will make the right decision every time. Take, for instance, the day my dad thought it would be funny to toss our calico cat into the tub with me and my little sister Laura. It was not his best idea. One moment we were splashing merrily. The next, we were clawed up one end and down the other by a riotous, unwelcome visitor in desperate search of dry land. Some-where amid our screams, Dad reconsidered the wisdom of his deed. He opened the sliding glass door. A flash of calico rocketed from my shoulder and vapor-ized down the hallway. No, definitely not Dad's best idea.

So not every idea will be a winner in hindsight. You can only do your best. Every child is unique, and human understanding of the issues is so limited that what works for one may not work for another. Predicting which individuals will respond to which interventions can be a roll of the dice. That pretty much guar-antees that you will try some dead-end avenues, dead-end for your individual child anyway. I have always been blessed that Rich went along with my ideas whether he bought into them or not. And he never threw my failures up in my face.

MEANWHILE, WE LAUNCHED OPERATION "REGULAR KINDERGARTEN"

Will started regular kindergarten in the public school with speech therapy as his only special support. I took pains to meet his teacher and provide summary information about ADHD. She had been teaching for years, and I got the impression she thought she already knew everything she needed to know. Her biggest concern was that Will got his medication early enough each morning so that it took effect by class time. With that, we muddled through the days as best we could. Mid-way through the school year, we moved out of state for Rich's job transfer. In my last conversation with the teacher, she asked if she could be frank. She said Will was doing perfectly fine, and I just needed to quit being such a worrier. I got off the phone elated. This was fantastic news. Some of the behaviors I considered off-beat for a six-year-old were actually in the normal range! Fabulous! Unfortunately, as it turned out, she was wrong. Maybe she just was not very observant. Maybe she did not care. Or perhaps she had an unusual definition of the normal range. Whatever the explanation, my elation was soon squelched.

Will was not in the new out-of-state school two weeks when I got a call from his teacher. She wanted to meet with me. She had "concerns." Uh-oh. I did not like the sound of that. What could she be talking about?—Will had been "doing perfectly fine." Well, we met. Darn it anyhow, she saw the same behaviors I saw and was on the same wavelength of misgiving that I was. Will was antisocial with classmates and strong-willed and obstinate with her, despite the fact he adored her. So much for my elation! The neat part was that this wonderful, caring teacher not only recognized Will's issues, but she was not put off by them. She hung tough and was always on his side, bless her heart.

FIRST GRADE: ANXIETY RUNNING AMUCK

Will was blessed with another caring and dedicated teacher the next school year—thank goodness, since it was to be a very rough year. I think I drove this dear lady a little crazy at first as I relayed Will's history and warned her of his, shall we say, peculiarities. She had years of experience and probably felt confident she could handle whatever arose. What is it with these overprotective mothers anyway? They think they are the only ones in the world who ever had a kid. This all changed with Will's first classroom meltdown. We are not talking a few tears here. We are talking nuclear-reactor meltdown. He was fine one moment (or so she thought). The next moment she turned around to find him crying, blubbering, and unable to tell her what was wrong. He remained inconsolable for quite some time. She had never seen anything so sudden and intense and prolonged before. Being such a caring person, she was quite alarmed. Her voice on the phone to me was high-pitched and panicked. She described the event as though it was shocking. I guess to her it was. Hmm. But wasn't this what I had warned her of? Guess she thought I had been exaggerating, the poor dear. I would live to repeat this experience with several teachers in the years to come. Like déjà vu, I would warn, they would pacify, soon my phone would ring, a high, squeaky voice would be on the other end talking fast in great earnest, they would describe this *most* unusual behavior. Was I missing something here? This *was* usual behavior. Had I not told them so? I never understood why nobody believed me up front. But as much as the scenario repeated, it must be natural human behavior of some sort. Anyway, that was okay. They could not say I had not warned them. There is more than one way to break in a teacher, eh?

I will call Will's first-grade teacher "Teacher First." By year's end, she told me in all sincerity that Will was the "enigma of her career," a championship title I would rather have left for another. During the year, she called me often for advice and support and to compare notes. She kept me informed of meltdowns and other issues of importance. It was obvious that she truly studied Will's behaviors and struggles and racked her brain and education for ideas to help him. She acted as if Will was *her* kid. I could not have asked for a more sensitive and devoted ally.

This dear soul tried everything, and Will benefited from her pains (as much as he was able). Understanding math concepts was an issue for him. Teacher First pulled everything out of her bag of tricks. She tried various hands-on learning toys, and she put funny little dots on the numbers themselves. Seemed odd to me but I guess that is the sort of thing teachers learn in teacher school. All things considered, however, it was the recurring meltdowns that were so frightening. The frequency of Will's meltdowns gave Teacher First a crash course of on-the-job training in meltdowns. She got better at recognizing the subtle, early-warning signs of a meltdown's gathering clouds. It is a tall order to notice anything subtle about a single child when you have a classroom full of children; however, Will made it worth her while. Teacher First also became more adept at heading off an approaching meltdown. Unfortunately, it was not always possible. And once launched, a meltdown and its subsequent aftermath to regain composure seemed an eternity, both to her and to Will. Sometimes Will managed to hold himself together at school. But the instant he stepped into the "safe place" of the car at pick-up time, he cut loose into full-scale meltdown. That was not the response I had bargained for with my greeting of "So nice to see you sweetie. How was your day?" Oh, well. Time again to call Teacher First to see if we could piece together the trauma de jour. We would always glean some new knowledge to aid us in our quest to avoid Will's triggers. He was not learning to handle them, but we were.

MELTDOWN MANIA

Will lived at such a heightened state of anxiety that a seemingly miniscule event could send him plummeting over the cliff's edge. It reminded me of when I was anxious about my mother being in the hospital. She was weak and could hardly walk. A test showed her blood count was way down. More tests were in progress. What would the doctors find? It could be something terrifying or not. It turned out to be the "not," thank heavens. But, for those few days, the undercurrent of worry kept my engine running at a high level of anxiety. The small glitches of life that I normally weathered with ease sent me into a tizzy, at least internally. Yet, I was experiencing a normal reaction to a known stressor. The perplexing thing about Will was how he could be in a perpetual state of high anxiety. He was a little kid, for crying out loud. What do little kids have to worry about?

Furthermore, once the anxiety was triggered, Will simply did not have the ability to let go of the pain. He kept reliving the anguish as though it had just happened, sometimes for 30 to 45 minutes. Sure, children get upset about things. They cry and shout. They call names and stamp their feet. They take back their ball and hit their classmate. Not ideal behavior, perhaps, but certainly within the realm of normal. At some point, no matter how vile the offense, they rein in their feelings and behavior, and get on with life. Yet, at this time in Will's life, he simply did not have the self-control to pull himself together. It was beyond his capability, though he needed and wanted it desperately. When a meltdown finally burned itself out, Will was exhausted. He remained fragile for the next few hours, sometimes for the rest of the day.

MELTDOWNS ON THE HOME FRONT

Though less frequent, meltdowns occurred at home as well. Will treasured alone time in his bedroom playing Bionicles, a plastic building toy similar to their more famous cousin Legos. However, Bionicles include hip joints and gears to give the gift of movable limbs. The constructed results are masked creatures resembling robots with built-in weapons and special powers. *Very* cool. A book series dubs each Bionicle character with a name and full range of super powers, vulnerabilities, and motivations. Will memorized all the facts and could spout them readily for any admiring Bionicle fan. He was (and still is) a gifted builder.

He would spend hours building creatures and staging their mighty battles of good against evil. You would not call this an obsession, would you? Nah.

When it came to Bionicles, Will was a perfectionist; his fascinating fun could morph into a nightmare on an unlucky day. For example, one time he flew from his room exclaiming in earnest that he could not find the orange mask for a particular Bionicle creature. He pleaded frantically that I find it for him. Several thoughts crossed my mind:

- I don't know what I am looking for.
- If the highly motivated Will has not found the orange mask, I surely cannot.
- Will's bedroom is a huge bone yard of Bionicle pieces. Searching for any one piece is like hunting for a needle in ten haystacks.
- Why doesn't he just settle for one of the other 15 million masks in his room? Any of them would do.

However, I was too well seasoned to say any of these rational comments out loud. I was not that stupid. Instead, I considered the various relaxation techniques we had been practicing. Perhaps now would be a good time to try one, maybe a simple one. It turned out I was stupid after all, megastupid. My suggestion to take a few, slow, deep breaths launched Will from frantic to hysterical. Obviously, Mommy was a complete imbecile. What would possess her to stop and breathe when the world was collapsing? Inconceivable! His self-destruct button had been pushed. Believe me, I was in his bedroom in a nanosecond, tearing the place apart for anything orange. Thank heavens, Will soon spotted the orange mask, the "Holy Grail." I must admit I was pretty darn happy to see it myself. This would always be Will's reaction in the moment of crisis. My attempts to teach him self-control were repeatedly flops. Episodes such as these left me angry and exasperated.

Another vivid meltdown is emblazoned in my memory. One day I forgot to warn Will that Lucas had gymnastics after school. Typically, Will seemed to feel that, after a day battling through school, he must go directly home. I tried to honor this need and was generally careful to warn him of any variance. But, alas, I am not perfect and inevitably slipped up one day. When I picked the boys up after school and mentioned gymnastics, Will immediately went into tears. I assured him I had brought Bionicles to play with while he waited and that we would be home in no time. Nope, this did not cut it. I could tell from the continuing flow of tears and constant kicking into the back of my seat that I had committed an unforgivable sin and would pay dearly for it. From Will's perspective, he desperately needed alone-time in his room. He had struggled all day in the stormy sea of school, head barely bobbing above the crashing waves. Now the sweet safety of the shore was in sight. Just when he felt the blessed grains of sand beneath his toes, I pulled him back out to sea.

However, my point of view was quite different. I fumed with clenched teeth, feeling that he had no business making such a huge deal of a short detour. He would have gone to gymnastics whether I had given advance warning or not. This should not be the cataclysmic event he was turning it into. We were truly ready to strangle each other by the end of gymnastics, each wondering what planet the other had come from and wishing they would go back.

And so was the nature of meltdowns. At any time, often without warning, I might turn around to discover those all-too-familiar, desperate, urgent eyes fixed in Will's expression. The sight would send a big ball plunging into the pit of my stomach. Here we go again. In pure dread of the coming moments, I would drop whatever I was doing to focus on the emergency at hand. If I managed to maneuver Will safely around all the out-of-proportion hazards, we could avert disaster, and I would enjoy a profound sense of relief. That was the best I could hope for. If not, I was in for an experience akin to being dragged by one foot through the woods tied to a spooked horse. There was no telling what might happen or when it would end. The meltdowns were particularly taxing if anyone outside the immediate family was present. The embarrassment, frustration, and exasperation of public ordeals were draining and kept me on edge and wary. Yet, it seemed there was never any choice but to face each wave when it came and struggle to keep our heads above water.

Part 2

OUR YEARS OF UNDERSTANDING

Chapter 6

Getting the Right Diagnosis: Asperger's Syndrome

TEACHER FIRST'S IDEA

Teacher First's deep concern mirrored mine, at times even exceeded it. She was growing more desperate during the second half of the school year. Perhaps she felt she had tried everything and was still not succeeding. The meltdowns were too unpredictable, too intense, and too long-lasting for her to accept. She urged me—no, she pushed me—to take Will to the highly regarded Children's Hospital at the state capital for an evaluation. I had not heard of this place. What could be so magical about it? We had already been to so many places it seemed, but Teacher First was emphatic. If she thought some sort of breakthrough was possible by seeing yet another doctor, I was more than willing to try.

A CAREFUL REVIEW BY A TALENTED TEAM

It was a couple of months before our scheduled appointment finally arrived. Will was nearly eight years old when we strode into the James L. Dennis Developmental Center, a part of the Department of Pediatrics at the University of Arkansas for Medical Sciences, in Little Rock, Arkansas. I was quite unsuspecting of the profound impact the day's result would have on our future. Lucky us, though. More heroes were turning up.

I was pleasantly disarmed by what I found inside the "examination room." This was not the typical rushed appointment where you sit on a cold, plastic, straight-backed chair. You know the kind. You are shuffled from one room to another. A doctor focuses on a clipboard as he jots notes that you know cannot possibly capture the essence of all you have said. Or perhaps the doctor writes

furiously but never looks at you until the drill is over, and it is time to poke and prod. No, the nature of this encounter was entirely different. The room was large; it had couches, comfortable ones. A team of four specialists from varying disciplines lounged calmly. I carefully settled onto the edge of a cushion and tried to get used to this unprecedented, relaxed atmosphere. Will played on the floor. The specialists introduced themselves and explained the format for our time together. First, they would cover some general information with me. Then they would take turns interviewing me and testing Will. Next, as Will and I went to lunch, they would convene to discuss their findings. Through their exchange, a consensus diagnosis would be settled upon. After lunch, a presentation of the test results and the diagnosis with all its supporting reasons would be made. And as if that were not enough, they would devise recommendations for me and Will's pediatrician to follow up on. Their approach was thoughtful and comprehensive. It was precisely the evaluation I desperately wanted, had I ever dared to dream it existed.

I began to feel optimistic as I answered their initial questions, which were presented in a very relaxed, genuinely interested style. They gave their full attention; there was no indication they had anything else to do but focus on Will and me. I was amazed that they did not appear surprised or at a loss by anything I told them. Could it be they had heard of such behaviors before? Could it be they knew what to do about them, besides just suffer? Maybe, just maybe, this would lead somewhere meaningful.

A TREMENDOUS RELIEF

As promised, we reconvened after lunch. I perched on the edge of my couch cushion awaiting the verdict. Each specialist reviewed his or her findings in turn. A diagnosis of Asperger's syndrome (AS) was delivered. Huh? What kind of a word is that? Surely they had made it up. But, no, they were sincere. They went on to explain many facets of AS and how Will's behaviors and test results placed him squarely under its umbrella. Everything they said about AS fit Will like his shadow.

It was a tremendous relief. Now I finally knew what I was dealing with. Best of all, I was not the first on the planet to deal with it. Others had come before who could provide information, insights, and advice. Ah, yes, this was a good day indeed. It was to be a real turning point because I would finally quit banging my head (and Will's) against the incomplete diagnosis of ADHD, a diagnosis that did not address our most painful problems. I could stop searching for answers where only incomplete ones existed. In fairness to those who diagnosed Will's original ADHD, I must note that his condition had deteriorated

considerably over time. Yet I could not help feeling that the signs of AS had been present back then: the coordination and cognitive issues, not just the inattention. Perhaps ADHD was better known among professionals at the time Will was first diagnosed. Who knows? At any rate, a reassessment had certainly been in order. For when you live with a child on the autism spectrum, it is a tremendous help if you can understand him. If you know where he's coming from and what challenges he faces, you are much more effective in helping him and in dealing with his problems. So, it's important to make sure to educate yourself about any diagnosis you are given. Does it really fit your child? After all, you are the expert on this little being. You will know if the diagnosis makes sense or not. Sure, there is variation among individuals within any diagnosis, but you will be able to tell if your child is in range or not.

Thank goodness Teacher First knew where to send us and insisted that we go. The evaluation team sent me off with several articles and print-outs of Internet pages. The information described AS and made suggestions for dealing with its strengths and challenges. Later, a 13-page document summarizing the day's evaluation and its recommendations made its way to my mailbox. Teacher First cried when I relayed the news, but I assured her it was a breakthrough. A new dawn was lighting up our sky.

ANXIETY MEDICATION

After Will's evaluation and AS diagnosis, I was off to the pediatrician for the anxiety medication recommended by the team. Will's doctor reviewed the team's evaluation and thoughtfully considered my request. He hesitated. "Do you really feel medication is necessary?" he asked. As much as I disliked the idea of further drugging my son, I responded without delay. "One of us has to get an anxiety drug. It is him or me. Oh, and if it is me, then his teacher needs a prescription too." The doctor promptly picked up his pharmacy pad and started scribbling. He was a smart man. Desperate mothers are not a force to reckon with if it can be avoided.

By the time Will was finally on the anxiety medication, the school year was nearly over. The more significant pressures of school had abated. Unfortunately, Teacher First did not have an opportunity to observe the medicated Will in the typical school setting.

Next came the easy-going days of summer break. Will's meltdowns mostly stopped. His personality was the same, but now he could handle normal, everyday demands much better. We saw no side effects of the medication. We crossed our fingers and hoped it would last. The team had made several other recommendations in terms of training and therapy. Of those I was able to pursue, the anxiety medication made the most noticeable impact.

A SNEAK PREVIEW

The anxiety medication was Buspar, and Will would remain on varying doses of it for nearly five years. Many of those years I considered it a lifeline, not a cure but indispensable nonetheless. However, after about a year and a half of biomedical intervention, I began to question its value. Will's volatile mood had stabilized. There were no meltdowns and, even when upset, Will maintained self-control. The spinning hurricane was dissipating over the solid ground of improved physical health. Maybe the Buspar was no longer necessary. Dare I stop it? I felt like a soldier with post-traumatic stress syndrome contemplating a return to the front. I delayed, but all signs pointed to the obvious. I was giving Will a crutch he no longer needed. I squinted my eyes shut, crossed my fingers, and took the plunge. There was no splash. No teachers called or emailed. I cracked one eye open. Still no splash. Home life remained unchanged. I opened both eyes and lifted my head to look around. A couple of months went by. Still no splash. Hmm. Cool. Way cool.

Chapter 7

Asperger's Syndrome and the Autism Spectrum

WHAT IS ASPERGER'S SYNDROME?

Asperger's syndrome (AS) was first described in 1944 by an Austrian pediatrician, Dr. Hans Asperger. The official diagnostic criteria for AS centers on impairments in two areas:[1]

1. *Social impairments.* These may include lack of eye contact and poor use of nonverbal skills such as facial expression, body language, and gestures. Children with AS may not recognize social cues or reciprocate in social and emotional exchanges. In addition, they may have trouble establishing age-appropriate relationships with peers.

2. *Restrictive interests and behaviors.* These can refer to special interests that are excessively intense. In addition, the child may have a strong preference for routine, consistency, and predictability.

A child does not have to exhibit all these characteristics to be given the AS diagnosis; however, he must have traits that fall in both of the two areas.

Other conditions may coexist with AS such as seizures and sensory sensitivity to textures, sound, taste, smells, or visual stimulation (such as fluorescent lighting). Also, one AS child might have low tolerance for pain while another has high tolerance. Low muscle tone may be present, a condition that limits gross and fine motor skills. In addition to having impairments in visual processing and discrimination, the child may appear clumsy and get lost easily. Visually based fine motor skills like handwriting and shoe-tying can be difficult.

Though fluent in speech, the child may struggle with the art of conversation. He may be more interested in merely having an audience than in an exchange. Furthermore, his style of speaking may conjure the image of a little professor. Literal interpretation of words is common, which makes sarcasm, humor, and figurative language confusing. For example, if the AS child hears it is raining cats and dogs, he might look skyward expecting to see cats and dogs tumbling from the heavens. Such phrases must be taught; they are not intuitive for children with AS. Also, an inability to recognize that other people have different perspectives and background knowledge can muddle communication and make other people's behavior mystifying to the AS child.

Problem solving and flexible thinking are often replaced by rigid rules and habits that govern behavior and reactions to situations. This makes it hard to integrate and apply recent learning and experiences to new settings. The child falls back on old modes of behavior and responding whether they work well or not. This inability to adapt dynamically to changing circumstances, coupled with a world of unexpected events, can be confusing and unsettling at best, frightening and overwhelming at worst.

Moreover, controlling and expressing emotions may be difficult. When under stress, the child reacts emotionally rather than logically. This may explain why newly learned behaviors are hard to put into practice. Time management and organizational skills can be trouble spots, as well. It can also be difficult to organize information in memory and recall it in a coherent, structured manner. This can make mental-processing speed appear slow and can also cause written composition to be a struggle.

Fortunately, children with AS often possess admirable traits. They tend to be honest, follow rules, and have a strong sense of fairness. You know where they stand because they are typically frank and forthright. They are devoted friends and enjoy a distinct sense of humor. Their intelligence is in the normal range, and their desire to learn is a valuable strength. Rote learning and fact memorization are areas where they can excel.[2]

THE AS WAY OF THINKING

Children with AS perceive situations differently. It is important to recognize that their way of thinking is different, not defective. *Asperger's…What Does It Mean to Me?* by Catherine Faherty has a beautiful way of illustrating this point. The text is a workbook that teaches self-awareness and life lessons to children with AS and high-functioning autism. It begins by having the child identify his strengths and talents. It goes on to introduce AS as simply "another thing about me." The explanation, written in first person, goes something like this: Most people do not have AS, but some do. I am one who does, but I am not alone. There are people all over the world who have AS. It is invisible and sometimes causes my brain to work differently from the brains of people who do not have it. My AS brain is like a computer with an AS operating system. People without

AS have a "plain" operating system. That is why we have trouble understanding each other's point of view sometimes. We look at situations differently, just as computers with different operating systems do. Neither is good or bad. They are just different.[3] This is a valuable and stabilizing perspective for the AS child to recognize. It also helps us "plain" folks maintain an appropriate and necessary level of respect for the AS child's way of thinking.

I made a heading of "AS" and drew a small group of stick figures (since I am such a gifted artist). I put Will's name on one of the figures. Then I drew a larger group of figures under the heading "plain." Some of these figures I labeled "Mom," "Dad," "Allan," "Lucas," and "teacher." I told Will that each group should make an effort to understand the other group's way of thinking. In real life, however, some of the "plain" people will not make the effort. Still, it is to his advantage to learn how the plain group thinks since there are so many of them. I explained that he and I were going through the workbook together for two reasons. One was so he could learn the plain people's way of thinking; that understanding would make it easier to get along with them. The other reason was so I could learn Will's AS way of thinking. Will seemed eager to be understood. He made a good teacher. At the same time, I wanted him to gain insights about himself and us plain folks, too. He already knew he was different from others. He recognized surprise or confusion in people's responses to him. Also, he did not understand why others acted as they did. His insecurity and self-consciousness were clues to me that he feared something was truly wrong with him.

The AS explanation came as a relief. He latched onto it because it gave him a tangible reason for the differences between himself and others. The knowledge freed him to accept himself, whether others did or not. Neither way of thinking and feeling was crazy, just different. He was A-okay.

AS AND THE AUTISM SPECTRUM

AS holds a place on the autism spectrum, as shown in Figure 7.1. At the far right of the spectrum scale lies classical autism, the most acute form where symptoms are more numerous and severe. Next lies high-functioning autism (HFA) and then AS where the number and severity of behaviors are diluted. Pervasive developmental disorder (PDD) comes next, followed by ADD and ADHD on the far left.[4] There are many who would disagree with placement of ADD and ADHD on the autism spectrum. Yet I must side with those who do place them there. Admittedly, I am not qualified to participate in any scholarly debate on the subject. However, as a parent who watched her child deteriorate from one diagnosis (ADHD) to the next (AS) in the blink of less than three years, AS seemed merely a continuation of ADHD—more behaviors, more intense.

Furthermore, the biomedical interventions to be discussed later in this book span the spectrum of Figure 7.1 without regard to the lines drawn by psychiatric diagnoses. Thus, the same interventions may apply as readily to a child with ADHD as to one with classical autism.

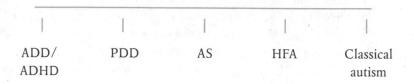

Figure 7.1 The autism spectrum

Around 18–24 months of age, Will had edged onto the autism spectrum. Over time, I watched helplessly as he slipped further and further toward classical autism: more behaviors, more severe in their expression. However, with bio-medical intervention, I have seen him slide back toward less severe behaviors. He is still Will, but the number of behaviors and their intensity has declined sub-stantially. Since biomedical treatment began, he is *more* Will and *less* autism. He has become freer to be himself and less at the mercy of his biomedical woes. Today, he is still on the spectrum but at a much happier spot. It is my fervent hope that perhaps someday he may ease off the spectrum entirely. Only time will tell. I sometimes worry that he was too old when treatment began. Had some developmental windows of opportunity already closed? I do not know. Nobody does. But I will not let that discourage me or sway me from my charted course.

ONSET TIMING OF AUTISM

A child can develop autism en utero or up through 3 years of age. So, for some, autism is present at birth (early-onset autism). For others, development appears normal until later, usually around 12–24 months of age. At that point, the child's development regresses into autism (regressive autism). Before 1990, regressive autism after age 1 accounted for about one-third of autism cases in children; the remainder of children were autistic from birth. Beginning in the 1980s, however, an unexpected reversal occurred. While both types of autism increased, regressive autism increased at a substantially higher rate. Now over two-thirds of children with autism regressed into it after age 2; that leaves less than one-third of the cases to early-onset autism.[5] One must wonder why that happened. Something is up, but what?

A DISTURBING INCREASE IN THE RATE OF AUTISM

Think of the 1950s when Dwight D. Eisenhower was president. Television had become the dominant form of mass media. And Rosa Parks refused to give up her seat on a public bus in Montgomery, Alabama. At that time, autism was exceedingly rare, only one or two in 10,000 births.[6] Now fast forward to the early 1980s. President Ronald Reagan had declared war on drugs. People were stampeding stores for Cabbage Patch dolls, and teenagers were mesmerized by Pac-Man at the arcades. By that time, the incidence of autism had risen to about one in 2,000 children.[7] Today, the United States Center for Disease Control (CDC) sets the rate of autism-spectrum disorders at one in 150 children.[8] It has become more commonplace than multiple sclerosis, cystic fibrosis, or childhood cancer.[9] Can you comprehend the enormity of that increase? That is saying that a mere 25 years ago, only one child in 2,000 had autism. Today, it is 13 in 2,000, a 13-fold increase of epidemic proportion. The U.S. government has often tried to dismiss the epidemic, saying that it is merely better diagnosing and wider public awareness of autism that has caused the rate to appear inflated.[10] Certainly some portion of the increase could be explained away in this manner, but not all of it. Even that portion accounted for, an epidemic remains.

Let us apply a little, thoughtful common sense by contrasting your child-hood to today's. When I was a kid, there were no children in my neighborhood with ADHD, PDD, AS, or autism. They would have stood out, just like they do today. Their inattention, meltdowns, obsessions, and certainly nonverbal or self-injurious behavior could not have gone unnoticed in a neighborhood game of duck, duck, goose. I never saw such children in the grocery, at church, or at school. All the way through high school, I never laid eyes on a special-education bus or knew of any programs for such children. At school, I never saw a line of children outside the nurse's office to get their daily medication. My parents never discussed newspaper articles with dire forecasts of how aid for such children was burdening the country's educational, health, and welfare systems.

Contrast that setting of not-so-long-ago to that of recent times. As an adult, I have known children in my Indiana, Arkansas, and Virginia neighborhoods who had obvious "problems." They are easy to spot, even from a distance. I have witnessed behaviors like hyperactivity, unexplained screaming, blatant social faux pas, and out-of-proportion upsets. Nope, never saw anything like that when I was a kid. My children's schools in all three states have had special programs, at least for the more severely affected children on the spectrum.

Special-ed buses are not an uncommon sight. And I have been startled to see a long line of children filing into the nurse's office before school to get their "meds." Parents do not drug their kids for fun; there must be a need. Something is going on. I see articles in the paper and hear on the news about the struggles over funding for children with autism-spectrum disorders.

So is there an epidemic or have we just gotten better at diagnosing these days? It does not take a genius to recognize when something is wrong. I can see it plainly with my own eyes. Yes, there is an epidemic. People can quibble over the precise numbers, but the epidemic cannot be explained away.

Now, let us flip this logic and look at the rate of autism from another angle. Pretend the rate of autism has always been one in 150. If so, that was the rate in the mid-1980s, but we did not know it because the children back then did not get diagnosed. So, where are all the autistic adults today? With today's diagnostics, they would be diagnosed by now. I should see them at the grocery, on the sidewalk, and at family reunions. But I do not. I should hear their voices in the Walmart or see them rocking on benches in the park. I should know at least some nonverbal adults. Yet I do not. The number of autistic adults is still relatively small, even with today's diagnostics and public awareness.[11] This fact leads me to conclude that there were not one in 150 children with autism in the mid-1980s. That seems self-evident. By most accounts, autism is considered an epidemic.[12]

ARE GENETICS TO BLAME?

Some people claim that autism is strongly genetic. Certainly, genes play a role, but they cannot cause an epidemic in a measly 20 years. True, genes mutate or change from one generation to the next. That is how the necks of giraffes evolved to such a length. But it did not happen in the blink of 20 years, by any stretch of the imagination. The rate of genetic diseases is only expected to increase about 1 percent per hundred years.[13] A "genetic epidemic" is really a contradiction of terms. Besides, how many autistic people do you know that have children? If autism is purely a genetic disorder and people with autism do not reproduce, then shouldn't autism be heading toward extinction? It certainly is not doing that.

No, something in addition to mutating genes is going on. But what? Alas, I am getting ahead of my story. It is time to get back to our journey.

NOTES

1. American Psychiatric Association 1994, pp. 75–77.
2. Attwood 2006, pp. 6–7; Grandin *et al.* 2006, pp. 90–91; Myles and Southwick 1999, pp. 1–23; Stewart 2002, pp. 19–27, 46, 49–51, 64, 68.
3. Faherty 2000, pp. 11–12.
4. McCandless 2007, pp. 1–2, 16–17; Bock and Stauth 2007, pp. 100–103.
5. Grandin *et al.* 2006, p. 88; Cave with Mitchell 2001, p. 64.
6. Pangborn and Baker 2005, p. vii.
7. Edelson 2006c, pp. 69–70.
8. Center for Disease Control and Prevention 2008a.
9. Kirby 2005, p. 17.
10. Ibid., p. 146.
11. Edelson 2006c, pp. 69–70.
12. Kirby 2005, p. xiii.
13. Edelson 2006c, p. 69.

Chapter 8

A New Footing

ON THE AS TRAIL

The evaluation team from the Children's Hospital in Little Rock had given me a Web site (www.tonyattwood.com.au) for more information about AS. Tony Attwood, PhD, is an Australian clinical psychologist who specializes in AS. He has written several books and is a popular speaker at conferences around the U.S.

As I read about AS from the Web site and other sources, I could see that the diagnosis fit Will like a peeling fits an orange. Sure, AS had some traits and variations that Will did not possess. However, Will exhibited no behaviors outside the AS domain. The literature answered my great question: "What is going on here?" Descriptions and explanations of behaviors were given. Internal thought processes of AS were hypothesized and explored. I gained perspective and appreciation for Will's challenges. The material offered sympathy and support for the parent experience. My emotions and feelings were affirmed and bolstered. Ah, yes, and the advice was the sweetest of all. Learning the hard way by experience had not suited my temperament or energies. So the spoon-feeding of wisdom from those who had worked with many AS children was a lavish banquet. These experts knew the pitfalls to avoid and techniques for success. Their practical advice enhanced our lives, bless their hearts.

ALONE ON A DESERTED ISLAND

You know, it is easy enough to read books and accept that there are other children besides yours who have AS. You sincerely believe they exist, of course. Why else would there be such a wealth of literature about them, right? In spite of this, the existence of these children was a little remote and theoretical for me because, in my small town, I did not actually know of anyone with an AS diagnosis. Hardly anybody, including those in the educational system, had ever heard of AS. The few who recognized the word did not know what it was. I was the educator for teachers and medical providers alike. My belief in the existence of another AS child was kind of like a child's belief in Santa Claus. The child is pretty sure he is real, but never actually sees him go by in his sleigh. Not that this lack of AS proof bothered me, mind you. However, sometimes you do not realize a need is going unmet until it is satisfied. Funny how that works.

MY FIRST CONFERENCE

An innocent-looking flyer showed up in my mailbox one day, announcing an upcoming three-day conference about AS in Dallas, Texas. Hmm. Imagine that: a whole conference about nothing but AS. Seems odd for a syndrome that so few people have ever heard of. Oh, and look, the whole first day is devoted to Dr. Tony Attwood, the one whose Web site was recommended by the evaluation team. Plus, there are two additional days of numerous other speakers on various AS topics. Well, that does it. One way or another I am going.

Dr. Attwood drew a crowd of about a thousand people on the first day of the conference. According to the show of hands, the vast majority were parents. As I sat in this throng, a mere one of hundreds, I delighted in an upwelling sense of support and encouragement. It was true; I was not alone. There *were* other parents whose children had the AS diagnosis. Sure I had believed that before, but now I saw it with my eyes. There really was a Santa Claus.

Another highlight speaker for me was Jeanette McAfee, MD, a mother of an AS daughter. She talked about social skills, a tough area for Will. He wanted friends desperately and was very friendly. Yet he did not understand basic social interaction well enough to make and keep friends. Dr. McAfee had written a curriculum, *Navigating the Social World*, for teaching social skills to children with AS and high-functioning autism. The book was on sale in the lobby, along with a host of other good AS books. You can guess who took one home. Each program in the curriculum had specific goals and step-by-step instructions. It was very detailed and precisely what I needed as a study tool for Will.

Another sizable benefit of the conference was the opportunity to swap experiences with other parents around the lunch table. Their stories made me acutely appreciate that Will did not have the aggression problems some of their children did. I wanted to hurry home and hug my little pacifist.

I have been to other conferences and workshops since, but none has had the impact of that first one. Life is like that for us humans. The first time we do anything always seems to be the most exciting. We are funny like that. I enjoyed finding the rest of the fold and hearing the stories of my comrades. The books on sale in the lobby were a blessing, a shortcut to quality AS reading. I left with a feeling of understanding and empowerment. I had learned I was not the victim;

Will was. Now I had a direction and a plan. I was off the deserted island and what a blessing it was. A conference has a living dimension to it that you cannot get out of a book.

MY TRANSFORMATION

I had been learning a great deal about AS since Will's diagnosis. It dramatically changed my whole concept of him. In this new light, I no longer saw him as someone whose purpose in life was to drive me crazy. He was not making this up. It was his reality, and he had little power to influence it. His challenges were formidable, yet he faced them as best he could. In truth, he was a hero to be genuinely admired and valued for all he accomplished. He lived within constraints that were out of his control, and I must recognize and respect those constraints and support him wholeheartedly.

My transformed attitude had a profound impact on our relationship. Now I was on Will's side. We were a team. I did not need to insulate myself from him anymore. There would still be challenges, but we could work through them together. Finally, I had some understanding of where he was coming from. It made all the difference in the world. Will undoubtedly noticed that his mother was more accepting and respectful toward him. Her patience was now genuine and encouraging, whereas before it had been forced and cloaked in undertones of "get with it!" I hope Will came to feel that my purpose in life was not to drive him crazy either.

APPRECIATION OF AS THROUGH THE EYES OF MIGRAINE

Many years before, I had my first migraine headache. Though migraines are a lousy lot, there is one good thing I can say about them. Having them granted me a valuable insight into what it might be like to have AS.

In the early years of my migraines, no medications seemed effective to prevent or abort the attacks. Back then, a migraine episode went something like this. As I felt the first ominous twinges of migraine in my head, my energy level dropped. A slow fog began to creep into my mind. I had a vague sense of a growing distance between me and the world around me. My range of facial and voice expressions shrank as my focus became more and more internal. As I slipped further into the migraine's grasp, I cared less and less about the din of events and people around me. Though I trudged on, my usual fortitude to withstand even minor frustration and setbacks abandoned me. It was easy to get angry or upset—just ask my poor kids and husband. Along with my self-control, my ability to think and focus ebbed away. It became increasingly difficult to plan my next task or even do simple addition. My brain was not working. To follow a conversation was not worth the exertion; it took too much effort to concentrate on the other person's comment and formulate a response.

Then, there were the sensory distortions. Sounds and light took on a new dimension of pain. Bright lights and rays of sunshine felt like shards of glass stabbing through my eyes and making my head reel. Loud and even average-volume noises would slam into my skull and ricochet off the walls within. The sounds were paralyzing as they set off monstrous throbbing sensations in my brain. I was less Sally and more my migraine, preoccupied and consumed in the prison of my body.

Oh, sure, I would push onward and make myself keep going…for a while. But the inevitable always came, the crash-and-burn scene where I had to shroud myself away for 10–12 hours in sleep. Migraines taught me that you cannot force yourself to do something just because you want to. That was a new experience for someone who had always thought she could accomplish anything if she just pushed hard enough.

Granted, migraines and AS are not the same condition. However, comparing the internal experiences was intriguing for me. My altered reality when beset by a migraine gave me a personal, first-hand glimpse at what living with AS might be like. For me, the parallel furnished a hearty appreciation for what Will was up against. Just as it was not my choice to lose concentration, thinking speed, and sensory stability during a migraine, it was not his choice to lose them with AS. Our resulting losses of self-control and social skills were understandable.

I recalled those homework sessions when an exasperated Will would cry out, "My brain is not working!" At the time, I thought he was being obstinate and evasive. Instead, he was being perfectly honest. His brain really was not working, just as mine did not when smothered by migraine. At other times Will would get angry and demand, "What is the answer?" Apparently, he felt taunted. From his point of view, I knew the answer and was withholding it just to torture him; pretty nasty, huh? After learning about AS, I could understand why he had been angry. But back then I was only baffled. Here I had just shown him how to work a certain type of math problem. How could he not know how to repeat the steps to solve a similar one? And he was mad at me besides? Our perspectives were irreconcilable. But now it all made sense. The emotional outbursts, the flawed social interactions, the seclusion and inflexibility, the sensory distortions—they all made sense. The blessing is that understanding leads to empathy and compassion. I was finally getting it.

Chapter 9

Food for Thought

A STARTING PLACE

There are many good AS books, but one that was particularly helpful to me was *Helping a Child with Nonverbal Learning Disorder or Asperger's Syndrome* by Kathryn Stewart, PhD. It is excellent at describing the various strengths and challenges that AS poses to the child. Then building on those strengths and challenges, the book offers a treasure-trove of interventions and teaching opportunities to help the child be successful.

My approach to get the most from an information-packed book like this one is to use a highlighter the first time I read it. I highlight any point that I want to review again later. Once I finish the book, I might go back and reread the highlighting, pulling out what I want to put into practice. Perhaps, I will make a note in my calendar to reread the highlighting again in six months to refresh my memory and keep me on course. Marking particularly important sections with sticky notes can also be useful. Of course, I would not have to do this if my mental notes would just stay where I put them, but they have a pesky habit of blowing away to the lost corners of my mind. So, occasional refreshers of marked pages and highlighting come in very handy.

A GODSEND BOOK ON MELTDOWNS

Many children on the autism spectrum have serious problems with anger or anxiety. Brenda Smith Myles and Jack Southwick wrote an outstanding book called *Asperger Syndrome and Difficult Moments: Practical Solutions for Tantrums, Rage, and Meltdowns.* This indispensable resource was my meltdown bible for years. Its information is not only applicable to those with AS but also many others along the autism spectrum.

This book is *not* about the child whose parents can avoid meltdowns via discipline or giving choices and structure. It is not about the child who throws a tantrum to get his way. No, all those situations imply that the child has control of himself. He is thinking and reasoning. Even though a tantrum may look out of control, in these instances it is really a thought-based act, with a motive and an objective. Ah, yes, and plenty of drama for effect but that is just an extra bonus.

Rather, this book on meltdowns is about those children who literally lose control of themselves. When triggered, they may rage and become aggressive or destructive. Or they may simply wash away in a flood of tears and sobbing. Such children are like a driver losing control of a runaway stagecoach. Overcome by their powerful emotions, they are dragged off recklessly in every direction. The rational part of them is taken hostage, jostled and thrown about in the driver's seat. They try desperately to rein in the stampeding emotions, yet they are powerless to control them. Like a helpless onlooker, they frantically pray that they do not plummet over a cliff into the gorge below. There is no choice but to be jerked along, eyes the size of the wagon wheels themselves. It is frightening for them to endure and frightening for us to witness. I always felt like the junior cowboy making a mad dash across the prairie to catch up to the raging stagecoach. I had to cut it off at the pass, right? But half the time I just got trampled. Think of this book as a field guide for the junior cowboy.

My favorite part of the Myles and Southwick book is its analysis of what the authors call the "rage cycle," which consists of three stages: rumbling, rage, and recovery. In the rumbling stage, the child exhibits subtle, early-warning signs of stress; these are unique to each child. For Will, his eyes took on an intense, anxious appearance. It was very subtle, dangerously so. If he were talking, his voice kicked up an octave, and his neck muscles went taut. These signs were a bit more noticeable than the anxious eyes. The authors emphasize the crucial importance of recognizing the rumbling stage since the child still has some self-control at this point. More intervention options exist in this stage. If you play your cards right, you may be able to avert, or at least curtail, the rage stage. The book gives many helpful intervention suggestions of what to do and what not to do. It is up to you to determine which techniques work best with your particular child. I found that the rumbling stage was the optimal time to find out what was troubling Will while he could still talk. I had to act quickly. Often, removing him from the situation in a nonpunitive way was the most effective course of action.

However, sometimes I did not recognize the rumbling in time, or my efforts at curbing it failed. Then it was time to batten down the hatches as we were sucked into the swirling rage stage. Again, *Asperger Syndrome and Difficult Moments* offers several helpful suggestions. A valuable one for us was that I modeled calm; Will had enough charged emotion for both of us plus an entire Super Bowl crowd. I must be his inverse, the epitome of a soothing shore of gently lapping waves. Calm, relaxed, in control, and capable. Of course, it was a total act. I was always keyed up and frantic during meltdowns, but that was only on the inside. Outside I was the picture of serenity. I should have won an Academy Award for any one of my many remarkable performances.

Another effective strategy for us during the rage stage was *not* to discuss the problem. I never tried to reason with Will or explain anything to him at this time. That would be like spewing gasoline on a fire; I know because I saw other people attempt it. Will's rational side was simply not available for discussion; it was a hostage, remember? What he needed was to be reassured that everything would be all right in the end. My job was to offer support, respect, and comfort. I kept my comments very limited and brief, but I acknowledged the problem and made a blanket statement that it would be taken care of—no details. Even when I did not know what the problem was, I still emphasized to him that, whatever it was, it would be okay. That was it. The less said, the better.

In Will's case, refocusing his attention away from the problem was also important. I would give a directive like "Forget about xyz. All you have to do right now is get back in control." For some children, giving an order like that while they are upset might ignite a bad reaction. But in Will's case, he *wanted* someone to take charge and provide direction for his rampaging horse team. Refocusing not only distracted him from perpetually reliving the pain of his problem, but it also gave him something constructive to do. As he calmed himself down, he was accomplishing something important, something he could feel good about. And he desperately needed to feel good. I would congratulate him on his incremental successes and encourage him to continue his efforts. Giving Will an order during the rage stage had been my own idea. I have found it best to use the advice of any book as a guide and to make adaptations to fit my unique situation.

The rage stage was also a planning time for me. It gave me time to strategize about the problem and figure out what to do when Will reached the recovery stage. No doubt, he would be exhausted and fragile. He would feel bad that he had lost control. We did not want to risk a boomerang back to the rage stage, so good nursing was important during recovery. Again, Myles and Southwick offer guidance.

Will was not ready to reenter life where he had left off. So restorative activities were key for him. At school, he might read in the nurse's office until he was ready to return to class. At home, quiet time alone in his room usually worked best. His room was never a punitive place; it was a safe haven. All the things he loved were there: books, Legos, Bionicles. Interaction with others was out; it was simply too taxing, except maybe for a dog. Dogs have always been one of this boy's best friends. The unconditional love and acceptance of big, brown eyes and a waggy tail healed a million woes. There is no better listener. Will calls our dogs a "portable fan club." Wherever he goes, there they are. He says, "It is so nice to have somebody who is always so glad to see you." He's right. They have helped ease many a meltdown for him. In fact, I needed a little recovery time myself after meltdowns, so a dog to sooth my emotions was good for me, too.

Until Will felt completely back to normal, we never discussed the meltdown. It might be hours or the next day before I would bring it up, if at all. Even then, the meltdown itself was not the topic of discussion, other than, perhaps, to compliment him on some aspect of how he handled it. What we talked about were topics that could help prevent future meltdowns. After all, prevention is the best intervention. In fact, *Asperger Syndrome and Difficult Moments* devotes an entire chapter to its prevention strategies.

One aspect of prevention is aimed at the child by teaching him social and behavioral skills. It is also important to teach him ways to interpret social situations. The other aspect of prevention is to restructure the environment so the child is less apt to encounter triggering situations. The authors present various suggestions for restructuring.

SOCIAL SKILLS FUN WITH VIDEOS

I found several of Myles and Southwick's prevention ideas helpful, but two were our favorites. Our first favorite was learning social skills with videos. The wonderful "pause" button on the remote let us freeze a person's facial expression or body posture so we could discuss its features and the feelings behind it. Beyond studying facial expressions and body language, there was much to learn about human interaction, people's perspectives, and their motivations and reactions. What a person thinks and what he says and how he acts are often different. After all, people are not like dogs who always let you know where you stand. If a dog dislikes you, he lets you know it. If he loves you, you know that, too. What you see is what you get. It can be a refreshing way to relate after an uncertain day in the complicated world of human social nuances. But alas, we are humans so learning our subtle and confusing ways is a must.

Our favorite TV series was *Gilligan's Island*. Seven stereotypical people are stranded on a tropical island. Among others, there is a greedy millionaire, a fame-starved actress, and the blundering first mate Gilligan, who messes up every opportunity to be rescued. Their wide variety of exaggerated facial expressions and gestures made perfect teaching aides. Story lines are simple yet encompass numerous examples of human interaction. Being able to show that what people say is not necessarily what they mean is an important life lesson. Watching the show's characters try to manipulate each other yielded valuable examples of ulterior motives and the concept of being "conned." AS children tend to take language literally at face value. And being honest themselves, they tend to project that honesty onto others, deserved or not. Their black-and-white thinking creates a good guy—bad guy categorization of people. Such traits make them vulnerable in the hard-knocks world of human interaction. Will benefited from seeing each castaway not as good or bad, but as a unique blend of characteristics, like real people. Each is capable of being good or bad depending on the circumstances. Again, the pause button, which allows you to ask questions and discuss the action, is a fantastic tool. In this way, we explored the motivations and thought processes of the various characters, as well as the intricacies of their interactions. In addition, I transformed Allan, Will, and Lucas into actors to role play scenes with simple props.

Gilligan's innumerable blunders also taught Will that people can make mistakes and that mistakes can be funny. The person can still be a likable, good person of value. Mistakes do not have to be humiliating catastrophes that end life as we know it. That kind of thinking is what meltdowns are made of. We must fight that mindset at every twist and turn. Finally, the crowning glory of a show like *Gilligan's Island* is that it is entertaining. For my boys, it was learning by belly laugh.

LUNCH BUNCH

Another of the meltdown book's suggestions for rage cycle prevention was lunch bunch, our second favorite technique. It is geared for success in the school setting. I asked Will's teacher to recommend two classmates who would make good lunch partners for him. One day a week I went to school, and the four of us ate lunch together. To promote a festive atmosphere, I would take a special snack. Recess time found us alone in a room playing a board game or cards. The kids became friends—a support every school child needs. It was also an opportunity for us to practice social skills. Will's friends enjoyed the special treatment and expressed genuine disappointment if lunch bunch got cancelled for some reason. In addition, lunch bunch let me observe Will in a school–peer setting. I would make mental notes of topics we needed to discuss later.

During a different school year, the teacher asked the class each week who wanted to join us for lunch. Many hands would go up which really bolstered Will's sense that he was liked by his classmates. Either Will or the teacher would select our two lunch comrades for that day.

THE TALE OF THE LITTLE GIRL AND THE DAD WHO COULD FIX ANYTHING

The following tale introduces an important concept that is the topic of the rest of this chapter. Ready? Here goes.

There once was a little girl…okay, it was me. And I had this big, beautiful, hard-plastic doll named Debbie. Now, one day Debbie took a ride on the back of my best friend's bike. Don't ask me why. It seemed like a good idea at the time. Unfortunately, Debbie did not know how to ride, and she fell off. One of her legs caught in the spokes of the back wheel. Tragically, this pretty much yanked off poor Debbie's leg.

But never fear. My dad could fix anything. So, off I went in search of Dad to reattach Debbie's leg and make it good as new. But when I asked Dad, he made the ridiculous statement that he could not fix her. Now that made absolutely no sense. As I have already said, Dad could fix anything. Dad must not *want* to fix her. He was just being mean, so unlike Dad who was usually such a nice guy. Why would he do this to his little girl? I repeatedly tried to persuade Dad to change his mind and fix Debbie. No doubt I made quite a nuisance of myself, but Dad would not be persuaded. He just kept giving me silly responses like, "She is made of hard plastic. That is not something you can fix. Once broken, it stays that way." I tried to make helpful suggestions in case Dad was just momentarily low on brain power. "You could glue her, Dad. Or maybe tape her." Dad insisted it would not work; the leg would fall off again. All his comments bounced off me as though completely irrelevant. "Come on, Dad," I thought. "You can fix anything. Why won't you fix poor, pitiful Debbie? You could fix her *if* you wanted to." But I did not tell him that. Instead I just kept pleading, and dear ol' Dad kept giving the same silly responses. Finally, he said them loud enough that I knew I had better stop.

It would be years before I ever figured out why Dad had not fixed Debbie. Funny that it was for the exact reasons he had told me. Their meaning had completely escaped me at the time. Too bad Dad was not a mind-reader and could know my flawed premise, the premise that said he could fix anything. Then he could have addressed the premise. *That* would have meant something to me. He could have said, "Dads *cannot* fix everything, you little knothead!" Surprised, I would have exclaimed, "What? Are you sure about that?" "Yes! I am sure. Quite sure." "Oh. Well, okay. I didn't know that." With that new revelation of knowledge, all the other things he said would have had meaning to me. I would have understood and quit driving him nuts—maybe.

Before I let this go, let us take it one step further. Say that my dad asked various child psychologists to explain my behavior. They may have provided many a worthy insight for Dad. He may have experimented with other responses to my repeated request. Yet the learned psychologists may still not have hit upon the premise. Perhaps, just perhaps, the best bet would have been to ask my best friend. Being a little girl, she would implicitly have known that dads can fix anything. No doubt, she thought her dad could. Of course, she thought her dad was better looking than my dad which was utterly ridiculous. He had huge, bushy eyebrows and…uh, well I guess that is another story. The whole purpose of this diversion is to make the point that you can listen to the experts all you want. It can be very worthwhile. They have studied many children with your child's diagnosis and have first-rate knowledge to share with you. But if you could actually get inside of the head of someone with AS, now *that* would be something. You could learn the true premises. You may learn you have been addressing the wrong premises all along. Why be a broken recording, repeating the same words to the edge of your sanity, saying words that only have meaning to you, but mean nothing to the person you are directing them to? Hmm. Now there is an interesting possibility.

WHAT CAN A 13-YEAR-OLD KID KNOW, ANYHOW?

Some of the best insights I ever gained came from a 13-year-old boy with AS. This exceptionally introspective and articulate individual, Luke Jackson, wrote a book he entitled *Freaks, Geeks and Asperger Syndrome: A User Guide to Adolescence*. In his book, he offers many valuable insights into the inner workings of the AS mind, simply by stating what, to him, is obvious. It is a book of advice or, as he calls it, a user guide to adolescence. His audience is parents, teachers, those with AS, and more. I found his chapters on fixations, language, school, friendships, and socializing particularly enlightening.

For example, in his "Fascinations and Fixations" chapter, Luke discusses obsessions, or what he prefers to call "specialist subjects." He explains that, when he is thinking of his specialist subject, he can be so overwhelmed with excitement that he simply *must* talk about it. He confesses that this may appear selfish but that the urge is very hard to overcome. Apparently, he often doesn't.

When I read this, a huge, blinding light bulb went on in my head. I could not believe it. I had always thought that, when Will embarked on a long-winded monologue, the problem was that he could not read the other person's bored expression, so he rambled on. He was missing the flashing *boredom* sign written on the other person's face. If I could just teach him to recognize the cues, then he would curtail the monologue, right? So, all this time I had been putting Will through the ropes to learn to interpret facial expressions, a tactic recommended by the experts, after all. Goodness only knows the time we had spent. Will was always able to identify and imitate expressions in practice, even the complex ones. Yet, in an actual situation, when he was monologuing, he hardly ever "recognized" boredom and cut his comments short. This exasperated me. So what did I do? I kept going over and over facial clues, body posture, and tone of voice. Granted, having me for a mom is no picnic, but I thought the solution had to be there, right? While Will continued giving me the right answers in practice, he did not put them into real life. How bewildering! Kind of how Dad must have felt about my incessant pleading for Debbie's repair.

Reading Luke Jackson's perspective was a revelation. Could it be that all this time I had been completely missing the true premise? Maybe the premise was not about recognizing boredom at all. Maybe the real premise was this: "I am having way too much fun here to give a care about anyone's measly boredom." Hmm. One behavior. But two entirely different potential explanations for it. This could be a breakthrough. The facial clues were mastered, and pointing them out during actual situations had never made any lasting impression. So why was I still banging my head against that wall? Instead, I should try saying something like, "Will, you are usually very polite. I know you love talking about your favorite topic, but it is impolite to keep talking when you see the other person is bored. A bored person will not want to be your friend." Then, I should give a concrete limit on how long or how many sentences are in the realm of polite. At that point, I might have him switch to a topic the other person might be interested in. Who knows, maybe such an approach might just do the trick. It is certainly worth a try. And to think I got the idea from some 13-year-old kid with spiky hair. Who'd a thot it?

Oh, and just one other point about *Freaks, Geeks and Asperger Syndrome*. Be prepared to accept some valid criticism of the peculiarities of us non-AS people. Luke really enlightens you to appreciate his perspectives. Such appreciation leads to understanding, respect, and admiration.

THE PREMISE IS KEY

So, in addressing any issue, the trick is to unearth the true premise. It is tempting to concentrate on the problem behavior itself rather than its underlying motivation. But we must resist. For example, if we focus on aggression (a behavior), we will devise an entirely different set of interventions than if we focus on the root cause of the behavior—anxiety perhaps, though that depends on the individual. When our interventions for the behavior (aggression) don't work, we scratch our heads and wonder. But maybe we did not need aggression interventions at all. What we needed to address was the anxiety. If you are ever to understand and appreciate AS, you must be able to see beyond the behavior to its motivation.

Aim your efforts at the source motivator and not at the behavior. When you help a child solve his *real* problem, the behavior will take care of itself.

There are many ways to sleuth out a premise. You can ask your special child. Brainstorm ideas of your own. Bounce the question off your child's teachers or other people. Seek out the many books written by the experts or individuals with AS. The secret is in there somewhere.

The ironic thing is that the person with AS probably needs just as many resources to understand us. I can always tell by what Will says or how he responds to me that I have done something that makes no sense to him. That is my cue to explain my rationale or point of view. It may seem odd or foreign to him, but at least there is a chance we can come to understand each other. We are different people with different ways of thinking. We just need some thoughtful, reconciling communication to get us in sync.

Chapter 10

Friends and Family

SUPPORT OF FRIENDS AND FAMILY

Wherever you are in your journey, you need support, every little bit you can get. The road is too rough to ride out alone. At times, you need a lot of support, while, at other times, you can get by with less, but you do need some.

My family and friends have been indispensable resources for expressing my worries, theories, and initiatives. They fill a critical void. They not only listen but offer their interest and ask thoughtful questions. They explore ideas with me and provide a wealth of knowledge from their diverse backgrounds. If they ever think I am crazy, they do not say it. Instead, they validate and affirm, empathize and encourage. Their support is precisely what I need to solidify my thinking, ease my mind, and nourish my soul. I tend to be a self-reliant, independent critter. But when it comes to core issues like my children, I have found that nurturing resources in family and friends are not only a matter of solace but of survival. Without them, there have been times I would have been bashed to splinters among the jagged rocks.

So, develop and nurture your relationships. Seek out new ones if necessary. You do not need numerous confidants, just a golden few. Some may have children with special needs, but that is not a requirement. If your child takes part in any special programs at school, a soccer field, or elsewhere, try to get to know the other parents. Also, consider a place of worship; they often have small study groups broken into categories like single parents and married couples. Why not join or start one for parents of children with special needs? Autism organizations are a good place to look as well. You have so much in common with those folks; it is easy to strike a chord. You will find it helpful to tap their knowledge of the educational system, health care, community offerings, and a myriad of other relevant topics. Plus, it can be very rewarding when you help them. Before you reach a crisis point, connect with support groups and services; it is one of the best things you can do for yourself and your family.[1]

Consider electronic friends as well. A very helpful benefit of one autism group I joined is a group email list. Members can send an email to the list asking any sort of question about the school system, local medical providers, or playgroups. You name it, and they ask it. Any member can reply to the list; that way everyone learns. Often information about world or local events relevant to autism also appears. We are eyes and ears for each other. Even if this organization did nothing else, the email group alone would be worthwhile. If you are not able to locate such a group, try starting one by word of mouth.

Only one word of caution about family and friends. Try not to drain them dry. If you are like me, in your ardor to help your child, you run the risk of going overboard. It is hard not to, not when you care so much and see such need. My family and friends may guess otherwise, but I do try to curb my discussions. I do not want them to cringe when they see me coming for fear I will ramble on. It can be a tricky balance to meet your needs and respect theirs.

CONTRIBUTIONS OF SIBLINGS

Siblings (sibs) make unique contributions not available from anyone else. Holding an unsentimental view of each other, they offer no-nonsense feedback that is direct, honest, and blunt. Say you talk too much or too loud. Sibs will reprimand you point-blank. Invade their personal space, and they give you a ready shove out of it. When they do not want to play, they tell you to get lost. No bones about it. Sibs possess the power to mold and shape, build and destroy. Their company combats a world of boredom. Their rejection compels introspection. Either way, their interaction is one of the best tools for learning real-world social rules. Will has benefited tremendously from Allan and Lucas's on-the-job training in social skills—a little heavy handed at times, perhaps, but that is the way of sibs. In truth, each of the three has benefited from the others in innumerable ways. We have had foster children, as well, who have contributed to the social training of childhood. It is the day in and day out, constant, and inescapable nature of togetherness that exerts the best and worst from everyone. It challenges the individual to define who he is and why. Trial by fire, so to speak. It is why kids can fight like cats when young and grow up to be best friends, for there is nothing worse they can do to each other than they have already done.

It is a very enlightening exercise to set your children down with pencil and paper (assuming they are old enough to write; if not, make an oral exercise of it). On the paper, write a few simple questions for each child to answer about each of his siblings. Examples: "What are Mortimer's strengths?" "In what area(s) does he have room for improvement?" "What do you like best about Mortimer?"

"What could he do to improve your relationship?" Their responses (including those between typical sibs) can be surprising and insightful additions to the parent perspective. They are probably more reliable, practical, and down to earth than our own.

OPEN COMMUNICATIONS BETWEEN PARENT AND CHILD

Typical siblings have unique challenges regarding the sib with special needs. As a parent, it is critical to recognize that how kids perceive the weaknesses of their siblings is strongly influenced by how their parents perceive and interpret them. That is even true whether the sib has special needs or not. Certainly, we all have weaknesses of one sort or another. It is important that parents provide children with age-appropriate information. We should also communicate openly and offer our perspective with each child about important issues.

Listening to your kids and making opportunities for them to express their feelings privately make them feel loved and special. Individualized, focused attention goes a long way. They will have thoughts and concerns you could never anticipate. You will miss the chance to address those concerns if you do not seek them out. For example, once during a move out of state, I was careful to reassure the kids that everything valuable was moving with us: the family, the pets, and all the toys and books. I was surprised when one of them voiced concern about if the new house had electricity. Huh? In a thousand years of contemplation, I would never have guessed the electricity was on anyone's mind. Heavens, what did they think? We were moving into a teepee? But, yes, indeed sweetie, the new house will have electricity and running water and flush toilets and heating and air conditioning. You name it. It will be there. So you have got to ask; you cannot always guess what goes on in their creative minds of unique perspective.

One of the best times I have found for making private conversation is tuck-in time. Kids never want to go to bed. Even the child who does not tell you squat during the day is more than willing to chat at bedtime. Riding around in the car is another perfect time as you are both a captive audience. A special meal or outing with just one child is also a golden opportunity to kick back and converse in a relaxed atmosphere.

TOUGH STUFF BETWEEN PARENTS AND "TYPICAL" SIBS

I have difficulty being objective when one of Will's typical sibs has a conflict with him. During a conflict, my gut reaction is to protect Will since he seems vulnerable. I have found, however, that protecting Will intensifies the conflict because, rather than being an impartial peacemaker, I have taken a stand of my own. As a parent, you need to be prepared to face some bad feelings and resentment from typical sibs without responding emotionally. At least at first, I like to pretend I am an unrelated third party who has no part in the situation. It gives me a level of detachment and objectivity while my initial role is simply to listen and understand. My typical child needs to know I am truly paying attention, respecting his perceptions, and trying to see his point of view. At times, it helps to pretend I *am* him so I can appreciate his perspective better. Sometimes I need to ask questions to delve beyond his words to the essence of the hurt. Once I think I understand, I can step back into my skin. Perhaps some of my own observations and interpretations should be expressed. Some of the time we can resolve the issue right then. Other times we need to go a step further and brainstorm problem-solving ideas. I may end up with action items, or maybe he does. We may need to inform or involve another person. Whatever we have to do, it is worth it. Sibling relationships are valuable.

Sometimes criticism may be directed at you. But try to look at it as an opportunity. I do not claim to be perfect, and maybe a step in that direction would be an improvement. I should be able to accept and evaluate feedback with an open mind. Sibs often feel that their special-needs sib can "get away with murder." I readily remember a time that really caught me off-guard. Allan had told me it was not fair that he and Lucas got in trouble right away when they did not do as they were told. Will, on the other hand, never got in trouble for disregarding my directives. I had to admit that there was some truth to what he said. My philosophy had always been that I tell a child to do something once, maybe twice, but that was it. Then I moved into action. I do not think a mother should have to repeat herself over and over. Kids have ears and brains, and I expect them to respond. Maybe I missed my calling as a drill sergeant, but that is how I operate. It keeps me happy, and I think it builds character or some such virtue in my children. However, what Allan said about my letting Will slide on this rule was true. Given Will's issues with inattention and distractibility, I would repeat myself. Even when I did act, it was prodding in nature rather than punitive. At first, I felt Allan did not understand the situation. Fair treatment does not always mean the same treatment. I felt the additional patience for Will was warranted. Though I explained my reasoning, Allan remained firm. He claimed Will was more capable than I was giving him credit for and that he should get in trouble just like everybody else. Hmm. Could he be right about that? Surely not. I discussed it with Rich who supported Allan's observations and opinions. I gave it some more thought and then made an experiment of it. I treated Will "like everybody else." It turned out he was as capable as Allan had forecasted, just lax because he had been getting away with it. Allan was absolutely right, the little booger. My consolation is that I am now one step closer to perfect.

An even more difficult issue to deal with is when siblings direct hurtful words and actions at the special-needs sib who seems vulnerable. It is upsetting, but a parent must resist the urge to suppress the siblings' feelings. The feelings must be addressed but not stifled because quelled feelings do not go away; they go underground and resurface in even less desirable ways. Working through such problems is thorny. It takes a lot of thought and care, soul-searching, and best guesses to work out a plan to improve a situation. There are no easy answers. For times like that, I found it helpful to reread my highlighting in a book I mentioned earlier in Chapter 5, *Siblings Without Rivalry* by Adele Faber and Elaine Mazlish.

FOCUS ON SIMILARITIES, NOT DIFFERENCES

Keeping in mind the influence you possess, try to focus your typical children's attention on how their special-needs sib is *like* them, not different from them. For instance, take the child who is slap happy and making up not-funny jokes for his displeased sib. This is an opportunity for you to provide the sib with your observations and interpretation. Take him aside, and ask him *why* he thinks the special-needs sib does that. Listen carefully to his thoughts without criticism. Build on what he says with a "similar-to-him" vantage point. Your comments might go something like this. "You know, I wonder if your sib is trying to get you to like him. Do you ever want people to like you?" Here you can discuss a time the sib wanted to make a friend. Ask him what he did to try to gain the friendship. Did it work? How did he feel? Go on to suggest that, "Maybe your sib is trying to entertain you, to make you think he is a fun guy. Perhaps he is trying to get you to like him. Agreed, he goes overboard and is not being very successful. I will address that with him. However, can you understand why he behaves like that?" You have presented a perspective of the behavior that is not only accurate but constructive, not destructive. It makes for a healthier sibling relationship if the sib can identify with the child rather than view him as just plain weird or defective.

Furthermore, go on to brainstorm problem-solving ideas. What could the sib do in this situation to improve the objectionable behavior? Perhaps, the sib's original response to the child was "Shut up!" That may have vented some irritation but hardly addressed the heart of the problem. A more helpful, coaching-style response might be for the sib to reply with practical information. Possibilities may include, "You are not being funny. I would rather talk about xyz." Or "I do not like made-up jokes. They are not funny. Tell me one you heard at school." Or "There is a joke book on my bedroom bookshelf. Go get it and read me some real jokes. I do not like made-up jokes." Just about anything would secure a better outcome than the original "Shut up!"

OUTSIDE SUPPORT FOR "TYPICAL" SIBS

It helps sibs if they can spend some time with others who have a special-needs sib of their own. For like us, sibs need support, too. Allan and Lucas have enjoyed a valuable worldwide program near us called Sibshops that is just for the sibs of children with special needs (www.SiblingSupport.org/sibshops). There, they play games, make crafts, eat snacks, and talk about various aspects of having a special-needs sib. Such a program affords a chance for kids to spend time with children who truly understand and appreciate their perspective. The kids can express their frustrations, learn from each other, and stop feeling so alone.

MOTHER PERFECT

Many moons ago, I read in a book somewhere that, for self-evaluation, men compare their performance to the performance of people around them. Women, on the other hand, measure themselves against a standard of perfection, an ideal that may not exist in real human beings. I never like generalizations, but it was beneficial for me to realize that there are different methods to assess one's accomplishments. Before that, I had never questioned whether I should compare myself to Mother Perfect. Who is she? Well, she is my imaginary yard stick. Mother Perfect has unlimited time, boundless energy, eternal patience, profound wisdom, and no needs or interests of her own; she does not even get PMS—that is how perfect she is. Her only flaw—not for my children, but for me—is that she is a terrible nag, forever critical and disparaging no matter what phenomenal feat I might accomplish. Her drawbacks are certainly not worth the motivational impetus she provides. Allowing Mother Perfect to be my inner voice is not only unrealistic and self-defeating but plain stupid, don't you think? What sense does it make to appraise one's self against a criterion that is not even real, a figment of the imagination? I still do not compare myself to other people as my measuring stick, but I should at least be realistic and fair to a well-meaning, hard-working parent like me. I give others a break; why not myself?

Thus, having recognized Mother Perfect for what she is, I have dispatched her many times. In my mind's eye, I have launched her into outer space, shoved her out of a high-speed vehicle, fed her Drano, and pitched her over the edge of a cliff. She has an annoying habit of cropping back up in my inner voice sometimes; I simply must ship her off again because she is a discouraging, impractical, never-satisfied whiner. Who wants to take advice from somebody like that? Not me. I hope you have no nasty, judgmental Mother or Father Perfects about your household. If you do, send them packing. They are a drain on your life force, your worst enemy.

BEING FAIR TO "TYPICAL" SIBS AND MEETING THEIR NEEDS

The unrealistic mandates set forth by Mother Perfect are not the only self-imposed ideas that can hamper a parent's happiness and effectiveness. There is also the commonly held belief that to be "fair" to our children, we must treat them all the "same." Imposing this requirement on ourselves proves especially unsatisfactory when a child with special needs is involved. Consider the amount of energy, effort, and time we spend with (and for) each of our children. Hands down, a child with special needs requires more. It would be easy for me to put myself down for not giving my typical children as much of my time as I do my special-needs child. But is the "fairness equals sameness" rule really the best measure? I don't think so. As a parent I need to be fair, but that doesn't necessarily mean same or equal treatment. Wouldn't "meeting each child's needs" be a better guide? I should give each child what *he* needs, which is not necessarily the same as what his siblings need. Here is an example to make the point clear. Lucas choked on an orange two different times last year, scaring the living gajeebies out of me. Both times I gave him the Heimlich maneuver and dislodged the oranges. Now if *fair* treatment meant *equal* treatment, I would also have had to give Allan and Will the Heimlich. But obviously, that would have been foolish since they were not choking. They did not need it. And surely I should not feel guilty about not giving them one just because Lucas got one. The bottom line is that my time and effort are based on need. Some needs can be satisfied with less time and effort; others more. Yet, as long as I am meeting each child's unique needs whatever those might be, I get an A+ rating.

Besides, each of my typical children could count on me if he became a special-needs child. I would run the race for him, too. He can thank his lucky stars he does not have that need. Sure, my typical children are left to their own devices more than if I had extra time on my hands. But that is not all bad. In leaving them on their own, I am fostering more self-reliance and independence than the anal, compulsive Mother Perfect would foster. For those things that are important, I am there. Do I not listen to their woes and offer concern and support? Have I not tutored homework, chauffeured for activities, and hosted birthday parties? If I earn a dollar, does it not translate into good things for them? Indeed, it does. Plus, they hear my voice cheering at their sporting and academic events. They have seen me as room parent, soccer manager, and school fundraising queen dressed in a wacky outfit of cereal boxes. I have an idea if you sat down and started a list of your good deeds, you would find it extensive. You must give yourself credit for each and every item on your list. Do not allow an inner voice to discount your accomplishments with a "yes, but." For that is the voice of Mother Perfect, and we all know that chic is completely out of touch with reality.

Another point to consider is that your children have never been raised by anyone else, certainly not by Mother Perfect. So they have no comparison point, no preconceived notions like the ones you may have erected in your mind. Unless you are telling them all the things you think they are missing, they are blissfully ignorant. They think they are doing just fine under your competent stewardship.

One of Rich's extraordinarily supportive practices is that he regularly tells our children how incredibly lucky they are to have me as their mom. He not only supplies them with details of my inflated virtues but leads them in theatrics like cheering, standing ovations, and bowing to me. Yes, it is kooky, but we all have fun with it. I, for one, am grateful for the opposing challenge to the obnoxious voice of Mother Perfect. But, best of all, it has the wonderful effect of brainwashing the children. In such a case, reality is not even relevant; the kids accept Rich's view implicitly. They often make supportive comments to me when he is not even present. So, if you do not already have the cheerleader you deserve, find one. If you have to, make a deal with him or her in exchange. Oh, I am only kidding, of course. Well, maybe. A bowing crowd at your feet is worth a few favors.

MAKING SIBS FEEL SPECIAL

You can even run your own ad campaign by emphasizing your good works to your children yourself. Though, in truth, the goal is to make them feel special. For instance, if I bring my children some favorite item from the grocery, I make a grandiose announcement: "You have *the* most fabulous mother on this planet. She must love you to the ends of the universe and back. She has been thinking what a fine son you are. Can you possibly imagine what I have in this bag for you?" His eyes light up because he knows something special is about to happen and he is going to like it. It may only be grapes or ice cream or some luxury I do not buy often, but he will be happy. What is important is that he knows his goddess of a mother has been thinking sweet thoughts of him. It sends a clear message that he is loved and treasured. That is what it is all about, isn't it? It meets every child's first, most critical need. So what would make your child feel

special? A coveted book from the library? The scheduling of an outing or a visit from a friend? The possibilities are endless. Enjoy.

A custom that I feel has been very beneficial for both me and my typical children is to carve out some time to do something special with each one alone. It does not even have to be that often, maybe just once a month. Depending on their age, I have picked an activity we can both enjoy. When they were smaller, it was something active like miniature golf, bowling, or a library program. It is just a time to be together, to make each child know he is special. Nothing momentous has to happen. I just want to send the message that I love him, value him, and am interested to know what is on his mind. As they have gotten older and can converse more, I have gone to eating lunch with them at school, having carried in a meal of their choosing. Or perhaps I take one of them to a restaurant or ice cream store. Just he and I, staying in touch. It is such a pleasure what you learn from them when the hubbub and interplay of family life is not there to distract you both.

NOTE

1.   Martin 2006, p. 122.

Chapter 11

Back to Our Story

A LOW PROFILE THROUGH SECOND GRADE

When Will started second grade, the teacher and I met so she would not be blind-sided by any surprises. I left her with a written letter of relevant history and information about Will, as well as the most effective techniques for dealing with meltdowns. As issues arose, she would have a ready resource to refer to. She also knew I was available to help.

By and large, the school year went rather smoothly. Will got upset sometimes, but meltdowns at school were rare. The few school-induced meltdowns he had waited for the car ride home. The teacher did not know my phone number by heart; it was a year of reprieve. The wrestling match with math continued, so now there was special support. Yet, overall it was a calm year.

THIRD GRADE SHOWS PROMISE

Third grade started out as Will's best grade ever. His teacher was one Allan had had before and I had great faith in her. Though I had given her my usual letter, we did not meet until the end of the first grading period; I was getting lax. When we did get together, Rich and I were pleased that she not only had my letter in hand but had highlighted portions of it. Yes, Will was definitely in good hands. She worked well with Will on both the academic and emotional fronts. His grades were the best they had ever been, though math remained pesky. Written composition began to emerge as a trouble spot; it was the organizing and structuring of ideas into a related, cohesive line of thought that was hard for him. But Will was doing well. As the months went by, I began to feel that meltdowns were relics of the past.

MOVING? THIRD GRADE GOES TO POT

About half way through third grade, a job transfer opportunity in Virginia arose for Rich. Moving out of state? How hard could that be? We were soon to find out. As relocation plans became eminent, Will had his first meltdown of the school year. More followed in rapid succession. Then meltdowns started cropping up at home. I had been working all along on transition reassurances; Will said he was looking forward to the move. But there was no doubt that the flashing lights and wailing sirens of red alert had been triggered. They spelled emotional catastrophe for all of us. To no avail, Will's doctor increased the dosage of his anxiety medication. The meltdowns continued same as before. We had no choice but to take down the sails and ride out the storm.

THE CAVALRY RUSHES IN

I had hoped that, once the move was over, Will would not feel so much pressure. Silly me. Too much was new and daunting. Will got two new teachers in Virginia, a special-education teacher for math and a general-education teacher for everything else. He gave them both a crash course in meltdowns, sometimes more than one a day, and, oh, how they lasted. It was an all-time low for the poor little guy. He was an extremely stressed-out kid, completely overwhelmed by everyday life. His teachers had never seen anything like him before. Fortunately, they were an experienced and compassionate team. Though they did not understand his pain, they were very sympathetic and turned themselves inside out to accommodate him. Once again, we were blessed with teachers who went the extra mile. They were a credit to their profession and their humanity.

Come to think of it, we have almost always had good experiences with teachers. I credit Will in large part for this. When not caught up in anxiety, his classroom behavior was exemplary. In fact, he had collected several "Behavior Hall of Fame" awards at his previous school. On the flip side, when he was anxious, his urgent cry for help was evident. Teachers would react with concern and were eager to assist. However, if Will had been one to express his anxiety with aggressive or destructive behavior, I fear it would have been much harder for the teachers to recognize his underlying need and offer sympathy and support. It is difficult to see need behind aggression and destruction. I feel for those children whose need is just as great as Will's but whose method of expression tends to mask and distract from the underlying need.

Despite the fallout of the move, it was a blessing. In Virginia, the school system was prepared for autism. Will's teachers immediately contacted a member of the county's autism support staff. This person was trained in autism and could provide professional advice to the teachers as situations arose. She also held a meeting with Will's therapists and teachers including those in art, library, music, and physical education. She discussed Will's needs with them and made suggestions of how they could best meet those needs. Tailored documentation was provided for future reference. The autism support resource also went to Will's classroom for a discussion with the children, not about Will but about acceptance. She discussed differences among people and how each person is unique and has special gifts to offer. I was certainly still involved in Will's school scene but was no longer the sole resource anymore. It was a welcomed gift.

MAN OVERBOARD! THROW A LIFE RING!

The response from the teachers and autism resource had been stellar. However, the autism resource supported several schools, so she was not always available when the teachers needed her. I cannot imagine how a lone teacher tries to teach class when consuming issues with a single child repeatedly arise. It was never easy for them, but they were adjusting. As the months passed, they became more skilled at recognizing approaching meltdowns and heading them off, or weathering them if they had to. Though meltdowns became less frequent, they were still common occurrences. Will's emotional state was fragile and unpredictable. The teachers and school administration recognized that the need was greater than they could support long term. They had a man overboard. They went searching for a life ring.

The school system had an AS/high-functioning autism program centralized at one of the elementary schools. That program became the life ring. School representatives met with us and the teachers. A decision was made for Will to attend the program for fourth grade. We broke for the summer. Will took advantage of the math and writing classes offered in summer school (another new-town bonus opportunity). Though it was a little rocky, the shortened school days made it bearable.

HOMEWORK

For Will and me, the most grueling part of our relationship had always been homework, grueling by its nature and frequency. An ordeal on his "on days," it put us over the brink on his "off days." Having been a driven student myself, I stressed too much when he forgot facts he had known the day before. If he could not grasp a math concept, I would fret inside as if it were a calamity. We often felt trapped in a deadlock. On the one hand, we had work we must do; and on the other hand, we could not do it, try as we might. Ramming our heads against the homework wall would not topple it.

My intensity was a big part of our homework problem. Emotionally I could not simply let homework be homework and nothing more. I had to blow it all out of proportion. As we arduously plodded along, my inner voice ran amuck. "Will, if you cannot understand this math problem, how can you get a passing grade? Then what? What about high school? College? Getting a job and being independent? What if you decide girls do not have cooties after all? How can you get a girl if you cannot do this math problem?" Yes, I was a freak, but I could not seem to help it. Too much of my heart belonged to this little boy. I wanted so badly for him to succeed. I scoured the AS literature for homework techniques and applied them as best I could. Yet, a profound sense of dread still lurked in my gut when the backpack came home. Would there be many assignments? Was Will having an "on" or "off" day? Would I end up in tears again after he left the homework table?

Now, as you might imagine, doing homework with the psycho mom was no picnic for Will either. He was forever asking, "Are we almost done?" I thought I was patient and encouraging, but he undoubtedly sensed the undercurrents. The whole homework scene was an endurance contest for both of us, a test of stamina, determination, and grit. Worst of all, it strained our relationship. I just wanted to be mom, to do the loving, care-taking, kiss-my-boo-boos role, not the pushy, oppositional taskmaster role. Yet we were trapped in a recurring, never-ending struggle that was draining both of us daily.

A GRAND ALLY

The best investment we ever made in my sanity and Will's was a homework tutor. I will call this blessed human being "Tutor Dear." She had been Will's math teacher in third grade, and has been a grand ally to us both ever since. Since she had spent several months in the trenches with Will during a very difficult time in his life, she knew him well and understood how to coach him best. Not only was she a well-educated, experienced special-education teacher, but she was used to kids forgetting things; that did not faze her. She accepted it; indeed, she *expected* it. She simply retaught the material as if it was no big deal. I was in awe. Moreover, to her, homework was limited only to the scope of today; she did not throw in college, future girl friends, and the kitchen sink. How did she do that? Could it be *I* was weird? Well, I guess I already admitted to that.

Tutor Dear and Will have done homework together Monday through Thursday from fourth grade on. She worries more over his grades than I do. You would think they were her grades. In a sense, I guess they are. She has certainly contributed to Will's academic success. He adores her and places a high value on what she says and how she does things. He is very motivated to finish his homework during their hour together. Heaven forbid having to wrap up at home with Godzilla mom. Besides, now I do everything the wrong way. He is emphatic we do homework strictly according to the methods of the all-wise, all-knowing Tutor Dear. Will and I both regard her as his second mom. She knows him so well, cares about him so much, and offers a continuity over time that has always been lost as teachers and support staff swap out each year. Ah, yes. Life was good. I could hear the birds singing again. I was free to just be mom. That was enough for me.

TAKE A DEEP BREATH—HERE COMES FOURTH GRADE

We had not known any details of what the AS program would be like. Just before school started, Will, Rich, and I waded cautiously into the new school for a sneak preview. As luck would have it, we thought we had died and gone to heaven. There was an onsite, autism-trained teacher who Will shared with only a few other students. She had her own classroom that even contained a "quiet spot" room for escape during meltdowns. Will would see her for one-on-one math instruction daily and have ready access to her whenever he needed her. Otherwise, he was in a general-education class with one of the program's aides. The aide assisted him when his attention lagged, his anxiety was roused, or he needed extra instruction. Such close monitoring enabled problems to be addressed at the start. The aide could take Will out of class for a moment or even back to the autism classroom and teacher if necessary. It looked like a perfect fit; it was. The supports in Will's school environment increased so dramatically that he rolled into fourth grade with ease. He even met his best friend there, a boy in the program at the next grade up. Life was good. Will had not been able to accommodate his world before, so his world had changed to accommodate him. For the time being, it was necessary. He was able to be productive and successful. Meltdowns were limited. And you know who was singing Hallelujah.

AUTISM RESOURCES

Our move to the outskirts of a big city (Richmond, Virginia) afforded wonderful opportunities. We never dreamed of the tailor-made AS program for Will in the small town we had moved from. Furthermore, every time I turned around, I discovered other autism supports and resources in the community. I actually had to pick and choose because there was not time for them all. It was a terrific "problem" to have.

The best local resource I found was the Autism Society of America (ASA). Founded in 1965 by Bernard Rimland, PhD, ASA is the oldest and largest grassroots autism organization in the U.S. It provides information and education, supports research, and advocates for services in the autism community. At the chapter near me in central Virginia, presentations on autism-related topics are given at monthly meetings while child care is provided. Occasionally, meetings break out into discussion groups, so parents can learn from each other regarding designated topics. Available at each meeting is a wide variety of pamphlets and flyers collected from outside resources. Books and videos can be borrowed from the lending library. This chapter also offers special-interest groups such as biomedical treatment and AS, which meet monthly. Even if I were not able to attend any meetings, I would still be a local ASA member just to get the chapter's monthly newsletter. The newsletter gives notice of upcoming workshops and conferences in the region. Descriptions and contact information for other relevant local support groups also appear. In addition, autism news concerning the state and federal governments are reported, as well as chapter activities.

ASA has been a vital link between us and numerous other offerings in the community. Everything we have done can somehow be traced back to ASA, whether it is a group I joined; a conference, class, or presentation I attended; or an autism activity Will enjoyed. ASA has a network of chapters across the U.S. Their Web site (www.autism-society.org) can be used to locate the chapter nearest you. I truly hope there is one close by. Do not be surprised if your local chapter is different from the one described here. Much depends on the individual volunteers involved in each chapter and the financial resources available to them.

Having learned about so many resources, I wish I could go back and visit the me of a few years ago in my small town. Back then, I had felt so isolated from the autism community, its knowledge and support. Now I can see that it did not have to be that way. If I could visit my old self, I would tell me to contact the nearest chapter of ASA, even though it was an impractical distance away. The chapter may have a newsletter or other offerings I could take advantage of from home. That would be a place to start.

I would also tell me to subscribe to the *Autism/Asperger's Digest Magazine*, an easy-to-read periodical full of helpful information that covers many aspects of living on the spectrum. Every time that magazine appears in my mailbox, I am reminded that there is a whole world of people out there living lives parallel to mine. I can learn so much from them and feel their support even from a distance. A face-to-face meeting would be nice; but, hey, you have to take what you can get.

Furthermore, I could go one step further. Having participated in an email group and other autism organizations, I would not feel so apprehensive about starting an activity of my own in my small town. Other parents could be found through contacting schools and offices of medical, psychological, and therapy providers. There had to be other parents somewhere; I just needed to flush them out. If I wanted to hold meetings, I could get ideas for speakers and topics from reviewing ASA meeting agendas; for example, old newsletters from my chapter are available online at www.asacv.org. Even an autism book club would make a good setting to meet people and exchange ideas and knowledge. It would not have to be anything big or fancy, just some means to make a connection.

Part 3

A PIVOTAL DISCOVERY: BIOMEDICAL INTERVENTION

Chapter 12

Hello, Biomedical Intervention!

A SPRINGBOARD TO A WHOLE NEW WORLD

Before one meeting of the Autism Society of America, I was perusing the table of flyers and information pamphlets. An interesting flyer about an upcoming conference lay humbly among the others. Its front cover said "Defeat Autism Now!" Whew! Now that was a bold statement. I liked the idea, but it was an alien concept since I was much more familiar with the notion of "ravaged by autism." We lived on the defense, not the offense. Yet such a claim merited a closer look.

The flyer invited doctors, nurses, and parents to attend a conference. It addressed parents, stating:

> If you are a parent, you will gain insights into some of the physiological issues that may be contributing to, or in some cases causing, your child's autistic symptoms. Physical problems like diarrhea, constipation, food allergies, yeast overgrowth, nutrient deficiencies, and high mercury or lead levels can all play a role in preventing your child from reaching his or her full potential. Listen closely as other parents and experts in the field of biomedical interventions for autism relay information on underlying causes, and more importantly, safe and effective treatments for your child.

The comment about diarrhea and constipation startled me. I had never heard of them in relation to the autistic population before. Heavens, yes, Will had peculiar, alternating bouts of one or the other from time to time. His encounters were bothersome but not severe, at least not since he had been a toddler (I am sure Will just loves to have this written of him! Mothers really are awful creatures.). Anyway, I was fascinated by the possibility that there could be underlying medical problems that could be treated. Particularly exciting was the possibility that Will's AS symptoms might be alleviated as a result. I was very cautious, however, about letting myself entertain that idea too much. I had been burned too many times by potentialities that panned out to nothing but money from my wallet and energy from my hopes and dreams.

There was also one obvious point of confusion for me. If safe and effective medical treatments for autism existed, why had I never heard of them before? We had lived in three different states across the Midwest, South, and East Coast with a new array of pediatricians, specialists, and therapists at each location. Surely someone would have clued me in.

I hesitated. Maybe the people at Defeat Autism Now! were just out to make a quick buck off vulnerable saps like me. Could it be that their treatments were not effective or, worse yet, not safe? Perhaps they were some sort of off-beat radicals doing experimental procedures. The flyer described the conference speakers. They were highly qualified professionals from prestigious medical facilities and universities. Even the parent speakers were authors and founders of organizations, not a schmuck in the bunch. I decided it was at least worth investigating.

Aside from the diarrhea and constipation mentioned in the flyer, I did not suspect that Will had any of the other physical problems listed. However, time would reveal that he had them all and more (except for high levels of lead). As the future unfolded, I would come to understand how these physical problems evolved into being. Best of all, biomedical interventions would make dramatic improvements in Will's mood, anxiety-coping, attention, mental-processing speed, social skills, and more. I did not know it yet, but I had found a fire that would melt another glacier off my son.

BIOMEDICAL CONFERENCE, HERE I COME!

The spring 2004 Defeat Autism Now! conference was in Washington, D.C. That was within driving distance of where I lived. Being one who gets lost in my own driveway, I was apprehensive about wading into the wilds of the District of Columbia. Nonetheless, I took heart (and a global-positioning system) and shoved off for a one-day taste of the four-day conference. True to the flyer's word, I was "exposed to world-renowned university researchers and medical doctors of diverse backgrounds at the forefront of effective treatment interventions for children with autism." The speakers were extremely knowledgeable, and their approach was rigorously scientific. They insisted on scientific method, peer-review validation, and repeatable research findings. Even in the question/answer sessions, speakers stuck to the facts of specific research or clinical studies, with no embellishing or guessing. It was quite clear they knew what they were talking about and had the evidence to back it up. There was also an open admission that some information was not known and that more research was needed.

As an added bonus, the speakers' overall nature was extremely committed, highly motivated, and very compassionate. Several physicians and researchers were parents or grandparents of children on the spectrum, who had tried traditional treatment methods and found them unsatisfactory. So, they left the comfortable couch of conventional, mainstream thinking in search of truly effective ways to help their kids. They joined forces with Defeat Autism Now! and added their knowledge and subsequent experience with the biomedical approach to Defeat Autism Now!'s knowledge base. Safety was paramount. It was comforting to know that parent-physicians were doing these interventions on their own children.

Oddly enough, these people were not radicals—certainly not in their scientific rigor and insistence on safety. In many ways, they were conservative—with one major difference: they were willing to think outside the box. Though conservatives, they were not conformists. They did not conform to typical mainstream beliefs about autism. I had always heard a consistent message from my many medical providers. They told me the only treatments for AS were medications to suppress symptoms, used in conjunction with therapy and special training. Defeat Autism Now! believed that underlying medical causes of autistic behaviors could be identified and treated; with treatment, those behaviors could be alleviated in many cases. The organization also endorsed therapy and training in conjunction with the medical treatments. Hmm. So maybe Defeat Autism Now! really was radical after all, radical in its beliefs though not in its unrelenting, scientific approach.

I was impressed. The style of Defeat Autism Now! had tremendous appeal. It was tantalizing to see the gains many of its patients had made. Of course, the proof would have to be found at home. Leaving the conference, I knew I wanted Will seen for medical testing by a doctor familiar with the Defeat Autism Now! approach. This was one stone I could not leave unturned. Many biomedical interventions can be done without a doctor, but, for me, it was the course I was most comfortable with and was able to afford. At the time, I knew so little about biomedical intervention that I had zero confidence that I could do any of it alone. Had I known what to read and continued attending conferences (at least the free ones online), my knowledge and confidence would have grown. I would have seen there was a great deal I could do on my own—not all of it, but a lot. However, at the time, I did not know how to self-educate and was frightened by the idea of "experimenting" on my son. As it turns out, the excellent resources I will mention in the coming chapters would have eased my concerns tremendously. Yes, it was new and foreign. Indeed, it would have been a step into uncharted territory where I could not overrely on a doctor, a definite character departure for me since I am a very conservative person. Just the same, I could have done much of it. I am happy with the route I took, but I want you to know there are other options.

WHERE DID DEFEAT AUTISM NOW! COME FROM, ANYWAY?

Knowing a little of the origins and history of Defeat Autism Now! helps one appreciate its diverse expertise, sound research, safety emphasis, and strong desire to help our children. This organization has mobilized these attributes into one body of thought, attitude, and action. It also gives easy access of its resources to parents and professionals.

The tale begins in March of 1956 with the birth of Mark Rimland, a baby boy with autism. In those days, autism was exceedingly rare, only one or two in 10,000 births.[1] It was definitely the "good old days" in that regard. Unfortunately, professional opinion at the time blamed a child's autism on cold "refrigerator" mothering. Can you imagine a doctor flinging such an accusation in your face? Here you are, the desperate parent, panicked and hysterical over your precious child's affliction, and the doctor condemns you with the guilt trip of being the cause of it? Inconceivable. Today that seems lunacy, but at the time it was conventional wisdom. So much for convention.

Mark's father, Bernard Rimland, PhD, set out on a quest to find every scrap of knowledge ever published in any language about autism. It was a daunting, mammoth task in the days before the Internet, copy machines, and word processors. In the end, Dr. Rimland published a landmark book called *Infantile Autism: The Syndrome and its Implications for a Neural Theory of Behavior*. The volume earned the Century Award in 1964 and dissolved the abominable belief of mainstream medicine that autism was an emotional disorder caused by detached mothering. The publication successfully argued that autism instead stems from biological causes requiring biomedical treatments. Such avenues of treatment must be sought out and explored. Due to the publicity resulting from the book, Dr. Rimland was flooded with communications from parents who were successfully experimenting with megadoses of vitamins. Moreover, research scientists, interested in investigating the ideas discussed in the book, were also in touch. Thus, a movement was launched that would swell into a worldwide communication network of parents, researchers, and physicians, with Dr. Rimland at its center.

In 1965, Dr. Rimland founded the Autism Society of America as a national forum to keep parents abreast of new and important developments in autism.

Two years later in 1967 he founded another nonprofit organization, the Autism Research Institute (ARI). ARI's central theme is that autism is treatable. It primarily devotes itself to conducting autism research and disseminating results of worldwide research to parents and professionals around the globe. The research concentrates on the causes of autism and methods of preventing, diagnosing, and treating it. Furthermore, where obstacles involving autism prevention or treatment exist, ARI strives to remove them. For example, in the early days when various specialty medical tests were not available commercially, ARI founded a lab to make them available. When vitamins and supplements tailored to the autistic population did not exist, ARI recruited a vitamin manufacturer to fill the void. ARI's Web site (www.autism.com) has a plethora of information and resources relating to various aspects of autism.[2]

DEFEAT AUTISM NOW! COMES ON THE SCENE

Dr. Rimland and two highly accomplished associates joined forces in 1994 to create Defeat Autism Now! These three founders were Sidney Baker, MD (a 1964 Yale graduate), Jon Pangborn, PhD (father of a son with autism and a biochemist), and Dr. Rimland. Their vision was to accelerate the growth of knowledge about the safest and most effective treatment options for autism and speed dissemination of this information to families of autistic children as well as to professionals. They recognized that, in the typical world, medical advancement is painfully slow; sometimes it takes decades for a safe and effective treatment to achieve widespread use. The founders felt much could be done *now* to help autistic children. Who could afford to wait for decades?

For the first think-tank conference, physicians and scientists with special knowledge in autism research and treatment were invited to convene. About 30 experts from the U.S. and Europe assembled. Their disciplines included psychiatry, neurology, immunology, allergy, biochemistry, genetics, and gastroenterology, among others. That is a lot of expertise in one place working cooperatively on a single problem, an ideal tactic for assaulting the complex puzzle of autism.

The experts reached consensus on the most useful approaches and safe treatments. In addition, they wanted the best ideas and practices of the group written down so their knowledge could be shared with physicians and parents far and wide. To meet this need, a document, which grew into a book, *Autism: Effective Biomedical Treatments*, was written by two of the founders, Dr. Pangborn and Dr. Baker. Over the years as knowledge grew through university and clinical research, the book has been revised to incorporate new ideas and refinements from subsequent think-tank conferences. It is an indispensable tool for physicians and parents using biomedical treatments. Due to the complex nature of the subject matter, it is not always easy reading. However, it is the bible of biomedical intervention in autism, containing valuable information covering the gamut from battling constipation to getting a child to sleep. A treatment approach is outlined, and numerous conditions and interventions in autism are described. In essence, the book is a treatment guide. The purpose and interpretation of laboratory tests are also explained. The last section is a useful resource about nutritional supplements in autism, right down to dosages, safety cautions, and more. Sure, there is some biochemistry in there that might cross your eyes. But if biochemistry is not your cup of tea, you can skip over it. The book can be ordered on ARI's Web site (www.autism.com) or at www.amazon.com.

In addition to think-tank conferences, there are open-to-the-public conferences like the one I attended. A large conference is held on the East Coast of the U.S. each spring and on the West Coast each fall. Mini-conferences are interspersed during the year as well. The ARI Web site carries news of upcoming conferences. It also offers speaker presentations from past conferences, complete with audio and video, that can be viewed on a home computer for free. In addition, these presentations are available for purchase on DVD, audio CD, and MP3 disks. Furthermore, a conference syllabus is published for each major conference and can be ordered from the Web site's store. Syllabuses include presentation slides and speaker articles that contain a great deal of useful information for attendees and nonattendees alike. There is also training for doctors and nurses about how to implement the biomedical approach to autism. Moreover, speakers from Defeat Autism Now! have published valuable books to teach and guide. Many can be ordered from the ARI Web site's store. Some are available in many languages.

Over time, the founders' vision has materialized. Defeat Autism Now! is a highly effective organization. Much is being done *now* to help autistic children. I am always surprised at how much new information appears at each conference. The turnaround to get recent knowledge into the hands of families and medical providers is amazingly fast. Defeat Autism Now! is solving the riddles of safe and effective medical treatments for autism. As a result, children are getting better.

At one conference Dr. Rimland was encouraging people to have an attitude he called *marapoia*. Nobody knew what it was. Well, for starters, you know what paranoia is, that inner voice that says, "Someone is out to get me." Marapoia, on the other hand, says, "Someone is out to *help* me." Dr. Rimland, the spirit of ARI and Defeat Autism Now!, was indeed out to help us. He remained the dedicated director of ARI for nearly 40 years until his death in November 2006. With his departure, the autism world lost a giant. ARI's associate director, Stephen

Edelson, PhD, a 30-year friend and co-worker of Dr. Rimland who shared his vision and carries his torch, is now ARI's director.[3] ARI and Defeat Autism Now! continue to offer a cornucopia of resources, many of which are free, to those of us living on or near the autism spectrum. As you will see, they have helped Will and me tremendously.

NOTES

1. Pangborn and Baker 2005, p.vii.
2. Ibid., pp.vii–ix.
3. Edelson 2006b, p. 1; Edelson 2006a, p.3.

Chapter 13

We Started Biomedical Intervention

MAKING THE FIRST APPOINTMENT

To find a doctor for Will, I went to the Autism Research Institute (ARI) Web site (www.autism.com). Practitioners worldwide who use the Defeat Autism Now! approach can request to be listed there. Basic information is provided about each practitioner such as address, phone number, and biomedical training and offerings. I selected a doctor near me whom I will dub "Dr. Biomedical," and an appointment was set for June of 2004. I was told to expect a packet in the mail that would include an intake form to collect Will's history. No problem. I had had plenty of experience with intake forms in my day. Same-ol', same-ol'.

THE INTAKE FORM

The intake form turned out to be anything but same-ol'. It was the longest, most detailed history ever requested on Will. You would have thought he were running for president and needed to be scrutinized before being placed on the ticket. There was page after page of questions that covered the gamut from developmental milestones to bowel habits, dental work, and antibiotic use. It went on and on. How bizarre!

Dr. Biomedical was a glutton for information. I was used to doctors who flitted over my summaries of information about Will. Each time we had moved, I made an orientation appointment with the pediatrician to acquaint him with Will's history because I felt it was important for the doctor to know Will's past in order to treat him in the coming years. Yet, the doctors never acted as if Will's background of problems was relevant to the present. In their search for a specific ailment, they honed in on a few details, excluding everything else. Each visit was treated as an entirely separate incident, independent of all other visits. An ear infection today. A yeast infection called thrush mouth next week. Chronic diarrhea later yet. Sharp abdominal pains? Well, come back if they continue. Time was never taken to reflect over the long, ongoing saga, to look for connections among the myriad of problems. In retrospect, it is easy to see that such a limited approach could never solve the complex puzzles of the autism spectrum. The body is more than the sum of its isolated parts: it is a whole, interrelated system where problems in one place can affect other places, even the brain. Excluding the hero doctor who blew the whistle on Will's obstructive sleep apnea, Will's various pediatricians, pediatric neurologists, and psychiatrists did not approach autism from a holistic perspective. They focused only on behaviors and on the brain; their scope did not extend to factors beyond. They were devoted to suppression rather than resolution of problems.

To Dr. Biomedical, my high-level summaries would have been painfully lacking in detail. She seemed to thrive on details, details about *everything*, the *whole* picture. How odd. How pleasantly odd. As it turns out, that is the standard Defeat Autism Now! approach. Hmm. How thorough, how promising, and how hopeful.

FIRST APPOINTMENT WITH DR. BIOMEDICAL

When our June 2004 appointment arrived, Will had just finished fourth grade and was approaching his eleventh birthday. As we met Dr. Biomedical, she reviewed the intake form and gave Will a physical exam. She asked us some questions. Each scrap of information seemed to harbor clues for her in a game of hide and seek. She deemed which tests made sense for Will based on her analysis of what she saw; the tests included blood, urine, stool, and hair. She stated she would be in contact as the results came in and also determined which vitamins and supplements to get underway. Not a single prescription was offered that day. How unusual. Was there more to medicine than a prescription pad? Dr. Biomedical also recommended a book. Otherwise, we were to come back in three months to touch base. Well, we were out of the starting gate…and going in the right direction, I hoped.

HARBORING DOUBTS

I had grown up thinking vitamins were a sideline to health. They are a part of the "eat-right-exercise-and-get-plenty-of-sleep" mumbo-jumbo that doctors recite. Yeah, yeah, everyone's heard it. We mostly just nod our heads and then go our merry ways doing whatever we want. It seems nobody pays much attention to vitamins until he is sick, diseased, or old. Humans are weird that way, bless our silly little souls. Anyway, all Dr. Biomedical's emphasis on high-grade vitamins, minerals, and supplements was making me nervous. How could mere vitamins make a dent in the serious problems we faced? It seemed like trying to fix a broken bone with a bandaid.

Furthermore, I had grown up believing milk was the healthiest food on earth. At the conference, speakers had asserted that milk was a potential trouble-maker for many autistic children. Also, certain other foods, commonly consid-ered healthy, fell suspect. This information struck me as nutritional profanity.

And what about the tests Dr. Biomedical had ordered? There were so many. Was that excessive? And were they the right ones? How did I know if she was playing in the center field of Defeat Autism Now! and not in left field?

Thus crept in the doubts. My firmly set jaw of resolve petered into some-thing more akin to chattering teeth. Please don't let this doctor be a quack. I am paying too much money for that. Besides, my husband will lose all faith in my judgment if this is a farce; I simply cannot endure it.

COMBATING DOUBTS

I kept reminding myself that this was not just a single doctor flapping all alone in the wind. Defeat Autism Now! was a worldwide movement, much bigger than any one person. But what really calmed my fears as I waited for news of Will's test results was self-education. I read the book Dr. Biomedical had suggested: *Children with Starving Brains: A Medical Treatment Guide for Autism Spectrum Disorder* by Jaquelyn McCandless, MD. The author is a grandmother of a girl with autism and has had extensive medical experience applying biomedical treatment to children on the spectrum. She was also very active in Defeat Autism Now! Her book discussed possible medical causes of autism and the biomedical treatments that address those causes. Moreover, it was a detailed treatment guide for parents and physicians.

Also, as luck would have it, a comforting article about biomedical testing in autism arrived in my mailbox right on cue. My friend, the *Autism/Asperger's Digest Magazine*, contained an article discussing some of the key biomedical tests available and how to decide which were most appropriate for a person on the spectrum.[1] The article's author, William Shaw, PhD, had an impressive educa-tional and professional history. His advice for test recommendations was based on his ten years of experience as director of a laboratory that specialized in met-abolic and nutritional testing, particularly in autism. His lab, the Great Plains Laboratory, had done more testing for people on the spectrum than any other place in the world. He also had personal experience with his teenage stepdaugh-ter who had severe autism. I was very curious to see how Dr. Shaw's test recommendations compared to what Dr. Biomedical was doing for Will. The comparison was a pretty good match, which boosted my confidence in the doctor I had chosen.

Dr. McCandless' book and Dr. Shaw's article reaffirmed to me the rational basis of medical conditions in autism. They bolstered my spirits and transformed my doubts into hopes. I crossed my fingers and waited.

OUR FIRST TEST RESULT: MILK ALLERGY

The first test result to come in was about milk sensitivity. Dr. Biomedical recommended cutting out all milk products from Will's diet and using other foods and supplements to compensate for the nutritional loss. It was not a true allergy in the sense that it caused immediate respiratory distress or skin reaction. I would have noticed that. Rather it was a sensitivity that his body apparently had. Well, that was news to me, but I was committed to giving this a fair shot. So, I got familiar with all the alias names for milk that I might find listed as ingredients on food packaging. A later chapter will describe this intervention as the "casein-free diet." I talked to Will about it, and he reluctantly went dairy-free.

After about seven-to-ten days, I was startled to notice that Will's typical four-to-five second delay time in responding to questions or requests had vanished. I did a double-take and started drilling him with question after question about anything I could think of, even math facts. Will repeatedly answered the questions immediately without a delay. How could this be? Where did the delay go? Some mysterious fog in his brain had lifted. But how? Milk cannot do that, but, somehow, it did. I was thrilled, yet completely confused. I had spent years training myself to wait patiently for a response from Will without hurriedly repeating the question or raising my voice. The delay was something I had had to accept. Yet I had just learned that I did *not* have to accept it. We could *fix* it. What a revelation! If I could have done a handspring without killing myself, I would have done a dozen.

No amount of medication, therapy, or special education could ever have done this. As said by Sidney Baker, MD, in *Autism: Effective Biomedical Treatments*, "If you are sitting on a tack, it takes a lot of behavioral therapy to help you sit still."[2] Defeat Autism Now! is all for behavioral therapy, but, if there is a tack, behavioral therapy may not be the best way to remove it. Milk was obviously one of Will's tacks. With it removed, he was able to respond much better to therapeutic and educational efforts.

Through the ban on milk, Will's static, narrow range of only three interests expanded to five almost overnight, an event way out of the norm. He also started participating more in dinner conversation, rather than always forcing it to his favorite subjects. He could also converse on a wider range of topics than before.

How could taking some vitamins and giving up milk possibly evoke such improvement? The encouraging response was exciting. My taste buds were whetted, and I was hooked. Anticipation of other bits of heaven riveted my attention and mobilized my energies on biomedical treatment, and it has ever since. Now, I was on a quest to find all Will's tacks and figure out how to remove them.

OUR APPROACH TO BIOMEDICAL PROBLEMS

In the end, Will's test results revealed several issues: gut problems, heavy-metal overload, zinc deficiency, and milk sensitivity. Other food sensitivities were also discovered. These sensitivities, however, would only be temporary if we played our cards right. There was also a potential problem in body chemistry with something called the methionine cycle. You think I made up that word, don't you? But, honest, that really is its name. Anyway, many of these were complicated problems that would take time and care to resolve. In fact, we are still working on some of them to this day. Ah, but the payoffs make it very worthwhile. For us, confronting biomedical problems has been like fighting a war on many fronts. That strategy is typical for children on the spectrum. The body has many complex systems, each with potential for things to go wrong.

We visit Dr. Biomedical once every 3–6 months, depending on the interventions she is doing. Even with her guidance, I have been very involved in Will's treatments. I feel a need to self-educate about the causes and biomedical interventions in autism. Paying careful attention to the details of Will's behavior and bodily functions has been important, too. Once I have knowledge of treatments and observations of Will, then I can generate treatment ideas that address his symptoms. In between doctor appointments, we stay busy carrying out Dr. Biomedical's suggestions and running trials of my own.

I also have had to be patient; ugh! I find that hard. Sometimes improvements happen quickly, but often they take time. I know patience is a virtue, but what good is it really? Somebody tell me that. Wouldn't I just love some convenient magic pill or genie in a lamp to resolve all the issues at once. Ah, but that is only in my dreams. In the real world, patience must suffice in their place.

We have found that improvements sometimes come in spurts: sometimes, they come slowly, while occasionally, there are setbacks. Overall we make progress, a far cry from the pre-Defeat-Autism-Now! days of constant worry and struggle, forever fearful of sliding down the slippery slope. It has not been easy, but as you will see, the payoffs have been significant.

NOTES

1. Shaw 2004, pp. 8–12.
2. Pangborn and Baker 2005, p. 1:9.

Chapter 14

The Wow! of Biomedical Intervention

PAYOFFS OF BIOMEDICAL TREATMENT FOR WILL

Our goal has never been to change Will but rather to empower him, to remove the obstacles that made it hard for him to be his best self. Thanks to biomedical treatment, today's Will is a much happier, healthier, and more competent version of himself. Neither maturity nor any other explanation could account for such rapid progress in such a short time after many years of struggling and falling behind. Since I am the "Will expert," I was the first to notice the changes, but, over time, more people commented on Will's gains. House guests who had not seen him for a few months were particularly surprised. These affirmations and unsolicited ones from teachers, therapists, and Tutor Dear have warmed my spirit and bolstered my commitment to biomedical intervention.

Do not ask me how treating Will's seemingly unrelated medical problems evoked such strides in his behaviors and development. Brain–body relationships are not fully understood. I am thankful I do not have to understand all the science to enjoy the benefits. Lucky me. Lucky Will. We have treated body chemistry, gut issues, vitamin and mineral deficiencies, heavy-metal overload, and other problems. Later chapters will describe these common problems in children on the spectrum, as well as their treatments.

Since every child is unique, each responds to biomedical intervention in his own way. Many have even recovered. Think of recovery from autism as you would think of recovery from a car accident. It doesn't necessarily mean you are left without any trace of injury. You may still have a limp or a scar, yet you are able to get back to living a happy, normal life. *That* is recovery.[1] Videos of recovered autistic children can be viewed on the ARI Web site (www.autism.com) in a variety of languages. Though I had to watch these videos with a box of tissues, they were inspiring and well made. One of them even won the coveted Gold Remi Award at the 2005 International Film Festival.[2] Though many children recover, a larger group of children—like Will—make major progress yet still remain somewhere on the spectrum. At least, this has been the finding of Dr. McCandless, author of *Children with Starving Brains,* in her extensive experience. Even so, what would it mean if your child could at least be potty-trained or able to sleep through the night? Or what if his aggression or anxiety could lose its edge? Unfortunately, Dr. McCandless has found that there is also a small group of children who make little or no progress on biomedical intervention.[3]

Response to specific interventions varies from child to child. Some of those that helped Will may not be as effective for another child. The opposite is also true. Medical expertise is not to the point where it can always predict which children will respond and which will not to any given treatment. Often, the only way to find out is to give it a try. Response depends on several factors, including each child's genetic makeup and the length of time the problems have persisted. Younger children tend to respond better and faster than older ones. The optimum age to begin treatment is between ages 18 months and 5 years. Yet, older children and even adults can improve, some remarkably so.[4] Will, who was 11 when biomedical intervention began, is living proof of that. So, when it comes to treatment, it is better late than never.

We enjoyed our most rapid gains in the first 18 months of treatment. It has been similar to the experience of trying to lose weight where the first five pounds came off faster and more easily than the next five. Early on in our bio-medical trial, Will's improvements were more noticeable and exciting. After about 21 months, though, we started to hit plateaus, just like people trying to lose weight. Each successive pound was a harder battle to win. Will's gains became more subtle, and the time between them lengthened. Since then, there have even been some setbacks, just as dieters experience. Yet we have regained the ground we lost and have continued to move forward. At this time, we are still making innovations in Will's biomedical supports, though his rate of improvement is now more akin to the normal rate of development in children. The rest of this chapter contrasts the Will "before" biomedical treatment with the Will "after" the first 21 months of treatment. It covers a time that carried Will through fifth grade and about half of sixth grade.

LEVEL OF HAPPINESS

The improvement in Will's quality of life has been the most precious gem of all. The before-Will was often an unhappy child, tending to be cross and complaining, not to mention acting out nightmarish meltdowns. He was insecure and overly sensitive; almost paranoid at times, he perceived insult even when none was intended. Whether figment or fact, a perceived insult ignited him to rage and tears. Forever afraid of embarrassment, he would crucify himself with humiliation if he thought he had fallen short. Will was easily frustrated and unwilling to try new things. His only reprieve occurred when immersed in his narrow, obsessive interest in building toys like Bionicles.

The after-Will is an amazing contrast. His typical state is pleasant, smiling, and positive. Better yet, he is sweet and loving. He adores jokes and enjoys his own unique sense of humor. Fostered by his new competencies, self-confidence and self-esteem have taken a foothold. Defensiveness has yielded to being more at peace with himself. A willingness to try new things prevails, and he is not as easily discouraged by difficulty as he had been.

ANXIETY AND SELF-CONTROL

The second best blessing of biomedical treatment has been Will's shrinking anxiety and increased self-control. The before-Will was on daily doses of decidedly necessary anxiety medication. He tended to be tense and high-strung, seemingly on guard for some unseen danger. His parallel in nature was the nervous zebra, forever wary of a lion stalking the herd or a crocodile haunting the water hole. We had no lions or crocodiles around our house. What was it that made him so anxious? Why was fight or flight the order of the day?

Events large, small, and even miniscule could ignite a meltdown; even I found him hard to predict sometimes. If not circumvented in its rumbling stage, a meltdown spiraled into uncontrollable sobbing, and often Will could not talk. The only successful method of dealing with a meltdown was to table its cause and focus Will on regaining control. Dispelling the meltdown's energy and emotion had to happen first. Addressing its cause or trying to reason with Will was usually a grave mistake. Once the stormy seas began to subside, recovery could last 30–45 minutes. For hours afterward, Will's emotional state might remain tenuous and fragile, a ready target for a subsequent meltdown. The disruption to family life was taxing. I played the coach trying to ease Will through each new self-imposed crisis. The role left me an edgy, weary version of myself, yet I could contrive no route of escape. For Will, daily immersion in obsessive interests was a critical outlet to ease pent-up anxiety.

I feel very sorry for the anxiety-ridden Will of old. What goaded him to react as he did when it was apparently not his nature? Biomedical treatments are freeing him to be who he wants to be. The after-Will is considerably more relaxed and playful. No meltdowns have punctuated the landscape for many months. Will can get upset occasionally, but the character of the upset is dramatically different from the old-day meltdowns. For one, now there is a legitimate reason when he is upset. Furthermore, self-control is not lost; he does not fall apart. Rather than being distraught and helpless as he once was, now he is angry or annoyed, reactions more appropriate to the situation. He voices his viewpoint and stands up for himself. He can be reasoned with and participate in problem solving. Once a resolution is reached, he can take a deep breath and go on. If he is really angry, his emotional state may be fragile for a couple of hours at most. And this is without any anxiety medication. The contrast is night and day. Will's success in anxiety-coping has been remarkable. It has also been a tremendous relief for his coach.

TRANSITIONS

Transitions used to be a real trouble spot for Will. He needed to be forewarned in the morning of coming events that afternoon or evening. When I forgot to forewarn, there was usually retribution to pay. Will would be angry and sulk. He could not seem to have fun even at an event he normally would have enjoyed. He appeared determined to stay miserable. There was a genuine need for time to adjust mentally to upcoming transitions.

The after-Will can roll with the flow much more easily. The anger and sulking are gone. He may not like the event compared to his previous plans for the time, but he can cope. A groan or complaint may be voiced, but then he is good to go. Often he takes a book along to make the best of it.

ATTENTION AND AWARENESS

Will demonstrated to me that attention is the pivotal gear that turns many coveted mental functions. If the battle of attention is won, the other functions surrender peacefully. They include memory, recall, comprehension, and social skills. A person who is alert and aware of the world around him becomes more capable of these advanced functions. Attention is the key to unlock them.

Inattentiveness was one of the most disconcerting traits of the before-Will and had been for a very long time. Too often, he would sit and stare into space, with no expression and no movement, simply checked out for minutes on end. At such times, waving a hand in front of his eyes might not break the stupor. Speaking to him, even saying his name, might not rouse him. If I raised my voice loudly, poor Will would jump out of his skin as though I had tiptoed from behind and blasted a trumpet. A gentle touch on the shoulder would also break the seeming hypnosis and was much better since it did not scare him to death. But what could cause such episodes? People should never be like that, unless perhaps briefly on a Monday morning before their coffee.

Also odd was how Will's level of attention mysteriously waxed and waned throughout the day, without identifiable rhyme or reason to it. In retrospect, I suspect it was something he had eaten. Perhaps milk or some other food he was sensitive to had flooded his consciousness with fog.

The after-Will still has some inattention problems when doing homework or sitting in a class he finds uninteresting. Otherwise, serious inattention is nowhere to be found. At home, he is always occupied and engaged. What a treasure to have a more attentive version of Will, as well as all the trimmings that go with it like improved memory, recall, comprehension, and social skills.

MEMORY AND RECALL

The before-Will lived only in the present. He could tell me the color of his pants but not whether his teacher had been at school that day. Most questions about the past, even the recent past, were met with "I don't know." At other times, he would provide an absent-minded "yes" or "no" answer, but I could never trust it to be accurate. Surely the information was filed somewhere in his head. Could he just not find it? Or was it too difficult to concentrate long enough to search for it? I could never tell. Tutor Dear and I communicated directly with Will's teachers since Will could not play the middleman. Through everyone's efforts, Will could learn his school work. Yet, after an entire year in fourth grade, he did not know his aides' names. Furthermore, if a child said "Hi" in a store, he could not tell me the child's name or how the child knew him. The incredible enigma of Will was that, for topics of interest to him, his memory and recall were extraordinary; in these instances, he had a photographic memory and could recite long texts from books word for word.

The after-Will can recall events from times back when I did not think he was attentive enough to catalog the knowledge. This is very encouraging and exciting; those years in the fog were not a complete loss to him as I had feared. Apparently, Will was picking up information even when it did not appear so. The "I-don't-know" answer is no longer the standard; he often gives accurate answers to my questions. At school, he is bombarded by names of people to remember, and he remembers them! There are seven periods of teachers, aides, support personnel, and classmates; he even calls the custodian by name. Who is this kid, anyway? He is certainly not the kid I knew before biomedical intervention.

This new Will sometimes worries about getting his homework done; that is a first. He tells me of upcoming school events that he is excited about and has asked me to sign papers or send money to school. For a kid who lived only in the present less than two years ago, he now can recall the past and think of the future as well. He can file information (memory) and pull it out (recall) more readily than ever before.

COMPREHENSION

Some things used to seem hopeless, like teaching Will to wear his pants frontwards and having the heel of his sock match the heel of his foot. It did not matter how many ways I explained it, there was still only a 50/50 chance he would have it right the next day. Scouring my mind and reference sources, I searched for the elusive trick that would make these kinds of things click for Will. Maybe if I just put the right twist on my explanation or presented it from a new angle, he would understand. Yet I was like a broken audio recording, repeating myself in one form or another over and over. The next day would come, and my chance for success was still only 50/50. The futility of the effort was demoralizing, so I finally gave up. The explanations petered out and were replaced by directives like "Turn your sock around." It was not what I had hoped for, but it got the job done.

After biomedical treatment was in swing, Will's comprehension improved. I decided to tackle these age-old problems. I showed him *once* about the pants and the sock. He got it. He puts them on correctly to this day, with only occasional errors. You may not be able to appreciate the feat that this was, but, believe me, it was big. Also, Will used to play alone in his bedroom a great deal. He did not join his brothers for board games, cards, computer games, or PlayStation. After he was in treatment, I started noticing how much more time he was spending with his brothers, joining their games and vying for time on the computer and Playstation. His new-found level of comprehension enabled him to play; now the games were fun for him, rather than confusing and frustrating. The biomedical interventions were clearing the fog out of his brain so the smart little feller inside could strut his stuff. After about 11 months of biomedical treatment, Tutor Dear told me Will was "grasping math concepts better this year than last." To gain an edge in math was front-page news.

MENTAL-PROCESSING SPEED

The before-Will almost always had a four-to-five second delay in responding to questions or requests. He had had that problem for years. Also, when people asked him a question, I often felt pressure to answer for him because of that uncomfortable delay time or unreliability of his answers.

After Dr. Biomedical took Will off milk products, the delay disappeared. I suspect other interventions have helped as well. Will still sometimes exhibits a delay at school or when doing homework, but not in any other settings. I do not rush in to answer questions for him any more either. He can answer for himself.

CONSISTENCY

One of the trademarks of the before-Will was inconsistency, on every level from mood and attention to memory, recall, and comprehension. Sometimes he was "with it" and sometimes he was not. We were never sure what to expect. Very confusing to me was that a homework fact known yesterday might be lost today but would resurface in his brain tomorrow. The after-Will is much more consistent and predictable on all fronts. Again, I wonder if what he ate was influencing his abilities.

SOCIAL SKILLS

Eye contact: Eye contact is fundamental to human interaction. But how does one *teach* it? It is so innate, almost like breathing. To the before-Will, I habitually gave explanations and reminders about eye contact. However, the success rate remained hit and miss. It was also difficult for Will to look at a camera for photos. So often in my snapshots, he is looking off, has a blank expression, or is smiling in an unnatural way, with closed eyes. I always took numerous pictures, even of the same pose, in the hope that one might be good. Kodak film made a mint off me in the days before digital cameras.

With the after-Will, it is unusual for me to see an error in eye contact. For the most part, the whole issue gradually melted away during the first six months of intervention. Will began to appreciate the subtle mysteries of eye contact and changed his behavior accordingly. The only lack of eye contact I see in the after-Will occurs sometimes when he is not comfortable with the other person. Oh, and now I can get a good photo of him in only one or two tries.

Conversation: The natural volley, back and forth, of conversation was an elusive skill for the before-Will. It seemed too difficult for him to concentrate on what the other person said and then formulate a response. As a result, there was no real conversation. In its place were two forms of pseudo-conversation. One was, in truth, a question-and-answer drill. When I needed information from Will, I would ask him a question, and he would answer. The back-and-forth mechanics of conversation were there, yet it was not the pleasant, flowing exchange of ideas between people as conversation is intended. It had some functional value but lacked satisfaction on both sides.

The other form of pseudo-conversation was the long monologue. Will would talk at *great* length about one of his favorite subjects. The other person's interests, signs of boredom, or lack of eye contact were irrelevant. For Will, a monologue was much easier than a true conversation. It eliminated the requirement to take new ideas from the other person and integrate them with his own thoughts before devising a response. Being an expert on his favorite subjects, he never ran dry of words. Like a captain, he would sail on for long periods alienating many a seaworthy listener. Attempts on the part of others to mutiny and change topics failed. The ship's captain would steer the ship back on his desired course. This even continued when the crew was engaged in other conversations of their own. When this was pointed out, Will felt bad and turned his face down. He knew better, but, bless his heart, he could not help it. He wanted so badly to be involved, yet remained an outsider, isolated and very lonely.

The after-Will can still stage a monologue at times but nothing like before. Monologues occur much less often and are easier to curb, and Will can accept a change of topic. The need for question-and-answer drills has tapered off; discussions more akin to true conversation are taking place. Life at the dinner table has improved significantly. Will stopped forcing his own agenda and began following the topics of the table. "Off topic" comments are rare. He generally seeks out eye contact before talking and does not usually talk to someone already engaged in conversation. The after-Will even initiates conversations like "How was your day, Mom?" I had *never* heard that before. What a warm, sunny feeling it gives.

Humor. The after-Will understands humor better now than he did before biomedical treatment. He no longer retells a joke to the same person. He has also learned to rely on joke books, rather than make up jokes of his own.

RANGE OF INTERESTS

For years, Will always had an obsessive interest in only one or two things at a time. There were the Batman years starting in toddlerhood. Batman eventually gave way to the dinosaur years and a relatively short stint of Speed Racer for several months. These yielded to Legos, our dogs, and finally to Bionicles. Each fixation seemed to consume all Will's thoughts, speech, and free time. They were his reasons for being. It is great to have passions, but not to the exclusion of everything else.

Since biomedical intervention, Will's range of interests have mushroomed in quantity and are more normal in their intensity. He still has fun with the dogs and Bionicles, but they are no longer the only game in town. On any given day, he may also be seen reading, playing cards, walking the dog, or battling Dungeons & Dragons miniatures with his brothers. He plays computer and Playstation games and enjoys certain TV shows. He can always be counted on for any group activity. It used to be that, when he and his brothers went to a neighbor boy's house to play, Will would shoot directly to the boy's bedroom to play Legos for the duration of the visit, regardless of what the others were doing. The after-Will does not go off by himself anymore. Now he joins in with everyone else, no matter what they are doing.

Also new is that Will can get interested in a topic for only a brief period of a week or two; he never used to do that. Yet, learning Spanish and state capitals each enjoyed a short but shining moment in the limelight. It reminded me of when I was a kid and my sister Laura chased after butterflies nonstop for two weeks one summer. She envisioned amassing the ultimate butterfly collection of all time, at least until some other passing fancy sparkled before her eyes. It is healthy to have a lot of varied interests, both long- and short-lived. Fortunately for Will, he now enjoys many more of the pleasures of boyhood, so much so that I doubt he would even meet the "restrictive interests and behaviors" requirement for the AS diagnosis anymore.

COORDINATION AND BALANCE

I do not remember the last time Will knocked over his glass at dinner, a frustratingly common event of the past. He also often used to get hurt by tripping, slipping, or banging into objects. These problems occur much less frequently now. I no longer need to hold his hand to steady him when he crosses a log or walks atop a short wall. These are tasks he used to avoid for fear of falling. Now he seeks them out and enjoys them. His body has become a gratifying tool he can direct, rather than a tenuous, halting puppet on strings that can only be influenced, not controlled.

PHYSICAL ENDURANCE

Will used to fatigue very easily. A typical day at school seemed to wear him out. When he got home, he only wanted to play quietly in his room at some stationary activity. He was seldom physically active and hardly ever played outside. At the end of the day, he would collapse into bed as if it was a welcomed friend.

This new kid is seldom tired. At bedtime, he moans and groans with a shower of pleas to stay up and play. He will put the dog on a leash and play tug-of-war with her as she tries to drag him down the path. Furthermore, Will is ever ready to accept an invitation to join group activities. He regularly joins his

brothers in an outdoor game of four-square, which involves bouncing a large ball to other players in chalk-drawn squares. He even enjoys building up a sweat as he dashes around the yard in an exciting battle of soaker guns. Getting completely soaked with water does not bother him; that is exceptionally odd in light of days gone by. He can even take a blast of water in the face and keep playing, an event that would have sent the before-Will screaming indoors. This new Will has stamina and can push himself. He seems to feel good and it shows.

SENSORY SENSITIVITY AND PAIN TOLERANCE

Can you imagine what it must be like to live in a body that distorts the way you experience the world? A body that escalates the hubbub of the school cafeteria to a resounding roar, straining your nerves to the point of frenzy? A body that amplifies a simple bang on the knee into an intense, throbbing explosion? What kind of body sends a message of revulsion in place of the pleasing sensation of finger paints or shaving cream? How could a body be so confused that it garbles and warps signals even to its own anguish and torment? I cannot imagine living in such a body. Observing the before-Will was glimpse enough for me.

Particularly when Will was younger, the sounds of a Civil War reenactment, a cowboy showdown, or fireworks display would absolutely terrify him. Though he coped better as he got older, he was still overly alarmed by loud noises, especially if they were unexpected. It was not unusual for him to wear ear plugs to avert agitation in the school cafeteria and during assemblies. Yet, he talked so loudly himself at the dinner table that we had to shout our request to talk more softly. Ironically, at school he sometimes whispered too quietly to be heard. You might say his volume regulator was broken.

Furthermore, he defied his therapist's attempts to get his fingers into shaving cream or pudding. A thoughtful classmate substituted her hand to paint his Christmas t-shirt at school. There were times Will had to be in bed asleep before I could clip his nails or trim his hair. You can imagine how good those haircuts looked. Moreover, Will's pain tolerance was low; the smallest bump could put him in tears. The sting of a yellow jacket at a festival once sent him wailing for 45 minutes until exhaustion overtook him. Poor little guy. He was confounded by his own body's bewildering feedback to sensations.

The after-Will can rely on his senses and trust what his body tells him. He went through all of sixth grade without using his ear plugs once. Loud or unexpected sounds do not disturb him excessively. Voice regulation is the only remnant of old, and even it is not so commonplace or extreme as it once was. Now Will can take a bump or a bang without undue consequence. It has emboldened him to leave his old comfort zone of minimal physical activity.

Will's body has transformed from adversary to ally. It has become a much more pleasant place in which to live.

SCHOOL GRADES AND HOMEWORK

Though the before-Will was generally a B student, the after-Will gets more As and fewer Cs. More importantly, his new-found capacities enabled him to handle the increased work load and level of complexity of each new school year. Without them, chances are he would have gotten in over his head.

Though Tutor Dear guides Will through most homework, I get the weekend shift. With the before-Will, a homework session felt like a wrestling match to both of us. I dragged my opponent through each and every problem or question, one by one. Especially in math, Will struggled with concepts and multi-step problems. And he could seldom reason his way through story problems. Simple addition facts were hard for him to remember, and the buttons on a calculator could be distracting. The after-Will has a memory and can problem-solve much better than previously. He can do more complex math, even with equations that require multiple steps. Though Will can still make mistakes, he is not at a complete loss as he often used to be.

With the before-Will, I especially dreaded written composition. It was so hard for Will to focus on a big chunk of ideas and organize them that he chose to fight tooth and nail instead. He claimed it was a complete injustice that he ever be forced to write about something that did not interest him, so he only wanted to complain rather than write, even though I did the actual typing. And because he hated the whole ordeal so much, he only wanted to write his composition *once*. None of this mumbo jumbo about a rough draft, editing, and final copy for him. According to the edicts of Will, you write the dumb thing once and be done with it. Anything more was an immoral injustice. Besides, it was a stupid assignment in the first place. So Will would complain and argue, while I tried redirecting him to the task at hand. I felt more like a lion tamer than a homework assistant. No doubt Will felt as if I were holding him down to pull out every single one of his teeth. Not exactly what you call quality time.

With the after-Will, Tutor Dear and I are still quite involved to make sure Will gets his homework done. Yet Will does more of it on his own without constant assistance and prodding. He can study or do worksheets by himself with us only being involved for review. Though he can get frustrated with writing assignments at times, there are no arguments, immoral injustices, or tears. He is much more competent and thus willing to buckle down and do the work.

MOTION SICKNESS

I had always thought a person's tendency toward motion sickness was innate and fixed, which shows all I know. Will did not have any specific treatment aimed at curing this problem, yet there is no denying that biomedical intervention has had a profound influence on his long-held problem with motion sickness.

Even at 3 and 4 years old, Will could not ride in the back bench of a van, at least not without spewing like a mini volcanic eruption. We learned this the hard way, as you might imagine. One memorable family vacation to Yellowstone National Park comes to mind. Leaving the campsites, we crammed into a van with extended family members. Will ended up on the back bench. Everybody, look for buffalo! Old Faithful, here we come! Why wasn't Will excited? He even began crying but would not answer our inquiries about why. Oh well, we are almost there. He will be fine once he gets out of this stuffy, cramped van. The instant the gear shift went into park, my doting sister Ginnie rescued her tearful, pitiful nephew. Holding him, she stood snuggling him in the parking lot. It was a touching scene…until he gushed down *inside* her shirt. There was no missing the symbolism between Will and the blasting geyser of Old Faithful in the background. My mother, who missed her calling as a fast-acting news reporter, thought to snap a photo. Captured for all time was a vivid image of Ginnie hunched forward in horror, her dangly earrings glistening in the sunshine. She is eternally grateful the photo does not appear in this book. Ah, vacation memories. But no lasting harm was done. The incident did not deter Ginnie from a career working with children as a physical therapist. And it clued us in to Will's issue with motion sickness.

Then there is the mode of transportation known as the big, yellow school bus. Even perched in the front seat, poor Will had a long-standing tradition of motion sickness starting in preschool. Since details on this topic do not make pleasant dinner conversation, let us fast forward several years. Will had barely been in biomedical treatment for three months when fifth grade began. The afternoon ride home went fine. It was that morning ride to school with a fresh breakfast down the hatch that caused trouble. The first half of the school year, Will typically threw up on the bus once or twice a week. By the second half, following the identical bus route, Will was achieving three-to-four weeks between throw ups. That was a significant improvement—just ask the bus driver.

In sixth grade, the route was somewhat shorter. Will did not throw up for such a long time that he got cocky. He started sitting in any seat he wanted and even reading books, a sure-fire way to get sick on a bus. Seven months passed before his first breakfast landed on the bus floor. I can only shake my head bewildered (and tickled pink). The days are over of toting extra clothes to school; of warning bus drivers, school nurses, and teachers; of reminding Will to get out his plastic bag if he felt nauseous. And that is not to mention my having to face the knotted plastic bag of spoiled clothes that came home after school. Now life is good; I live like a queen.

TODAY

This chapter described the impact of the first 21 months of biomedical treatment. Since that time, another 21 months have passed. In every respect, Will has continued to improve and mature. The only exception is a recent minor setback in motion sickness due to an intervention that is necessary nevertheless. My hopes for Will's future include further gains in attention, conversation, and organizational skills, as well as self-management and time management. In three-and-a-half years of biomedical treatment, he has come light years from where he once was. As Will's height shoots past mine and I see him making his own way more and more, I feel he's going to be okay. He had a very rough start in this world, but there are many joys for him here after all.

NOTES

1.   Edelson 2007a, p. 3.
2.   Pangborn 2006c, p. 32.
3.   McCandless 2007, p. 67.
4.   Ibid., p. 11.

Chapter 15

Life Goes On

FIFTH GRADE: OUR FIRST YEAR OF BIOMEDICAL TREATMENT

Fifth grade was an exciting year and a trying year. Will had barely been in biomedical treatment for three months when school began. The autism teacher of the previous year had left and was replaced by a new one. With apprehension, I learned that this new teacher did not have prior experience with children on the spectrum or with grade-school-age children. Oh, boy! I hoped this would not be a step back to the years of teaching the teacher. Will really needed expertise beyond mine. But I tried to be optimistic. As it turned out, we were lucky, very lucky. The new teacher was a natural and quite intuitive. She befriended Will and laughed at his jokes. She even got him a joke calendar to share after their math sessions together. When it came to his attention problems, she had the patience of Job. Plus, she gave careful thought to Will's behaviors and difficulties and responded with insightful action. In the end, she was an ideal person with whom to spend our first year of biomedical intervention. Throughout the year, she bolstered me with emails and phone calls as Will's various improvements caught her eye. The feedback was exciting and a powerful affirmation to my own observations at home.

The year had its meltdown challenges, however. After the relative calm of fourth grade, I was lulled into believing that our move to Virginia was the only real culprit in Will's earlier upheaval. With that major trigger out of the way and the supportive environment of the AS program, I believed Will could cope with typical daily stress. To my dismay, I was to discover it was not quite that simple. For one thing, Will had really enjoyed having a best friend in the program the year before. But now the friend had moved on to middle school, and Will felt the loss keenly. Also, as his sense of awareness increased with biomedical treatment, he became vulnerable to new worries that had not entered his consciousness before.

Though meltdowns were not nearly as frequent as those during the move of the third-grade year, they still reared their thorny heads often enough. I was even called to school to get Will on four memorable occasions. Once in the car, Will would unleash a deluge of emotion that was worse than any I had ever witnessed. These meltdowns truly frightened me—yes, even me, an old hand at weathering the pelting gales of meltdown. Like category 5 tornadoes, they touched down explosively. Will did not wash away in a flood of tears as he used to. He was in control enough to talk, a promising development, I suppose. However, the intensity and destructive force of the emotion he expressed in words were frightening. I am not a timid person, but those meltdowns rattled my cage severely. Like a tidal wave, they went way over my head. Will found himself in counseling at the children's hospital faster than you could say 911. However, in the end, it was not the counseling that seemed to make a difference. Rather, it seemed that continued improvements in Will's biomedical health were what correlated to his increasing ability to harness and control his emotions.

During the final grading period of the school year, Will did not have a single full-scale meltdown. Of this period, the autism teacher wrote that, when Will was in the rumbling stage, he was able to say what was bothering him and then work toward a solution. The rage stage of the meltdown was averted. Though progress had come in many forms over the course of the year, none was as significant for Will as this achievement.

SIXTH GRADE: A MOTHER'S DREAD OF MIDDLE SCHOOL

I was scared stiff of sixth grade. Will had improved much in the previous year, but the massive, looming changes of middle school unnerved me. The school building was an old high school with two, large, hodge-podge additions to accommodate a student body of over 1,500 children. Despite the additions, it was still so cramped that numerous classroom trailers had been squeezed in back of the school. I recalled Will getting lost in the simple layout of his third-grade elementary school. How would he possibly find his way around this maze of hallways that resembled the tubes and tunnels of a hamster cage? Besides, back in grade school, kids lined up and filed off together everywhere they went. Not so in middle school. When the bell rang there, kids swarmed into the halls like bees off in every direction to search for nectar. For Will, trying to find his way amid such a jostling, noisy mob of kids was a sure-fire recipe for disaster. Somewhere amid the mayhem, his best friend would be lurking. But what were the chances of Will seeing him? My apprehension escalated the more I thought about life in middle school. Will's sheltered world of only a couple of teachers was about to explode into a kaleidoscope of seven. His cozy little life with the same familiar 20 classmates would burgeon into seven different arrays of children, one for each class period. And as if that were not enough, every single face would be brand new. Will's old classmates were zoned for a different school, and he had been the only fifth-grader in the AS program. How could the Will I knew manage so much transition at once?

Flashbacks of old times zipped through my mind until my head reeled. I made dire predictions of frightening meltdowns in this new setting. In the past, I had sometimes underestimated Will's anxiety level, but never had I overestimated it. So I took issue with the school system to get Will an ever-present aide to ease the transitions, watch for meltdowns, and try to diffuse them. Before the department heads of the school system, I read notes from Will's previous teachers and aides as testimony to support my predictions of peril. I described Will's reaction to our move during third grade. Moreover, I asserted that the transition to third grade was less severe than that of middle school. All my arguments were based firmly on the sound logic of Will's historical past performance. And even though the aide for the coming year was granted, I was still haunted by visions of out-of-control meltdowns, replays of former days. Sure, the biomedical gains had been far-reaching, but I doubted they could save us from such an enormous onslaught of change.

So, I equipped all the new teachers with my phone number, email address, and "Guide to Will" document. No doubt, they thought I could use a tranquilizer, maybe even a few shock treatments. But, hey, I had been on this shore before. I knew D-Day was coming, whether they did or not. The fateful first day of school eventually arrived. I popped myself an antacid and put Will on the bus (just kidding about the antacid actually). But if I had thought it would help, I undoubtedly would have taken a handful.

Well, you know what happened? *Nothing!* The kid went to school, and he did fine! There were no phone calls, no meltdowns, nothing. I couldn't believe it. After all my warnings and calamitous forecasts, after all my cries of "wolf" that rang up and down and all around the school system, the kid was *fine!* Come on now, aide or no aide, my kid would not be fine in the face of such massive change. Sure, the autism teacher was very talented and experienced and had a brother of her own with AS. But, still, who the heck was this kid who answered to the name of Will? Some body snatcher had stolen my son away and was hiding him somewhere, the boy I thought I knew. But, no, Will was fine. He really was. Fabulously, wonderfully fine. Unfortunately, I, on the other hand, looked like the village idiot. No doubt the whole school system and every teacher now had me pegged somewhere between a compulsive liar and a nut case. But that was okay. It was magnificent, really. If Will was happy, then so was I. I could live with a bad reputation. It was better than having been right, I can tell you that much.

Issues came up through the course of the year, but nothing monumental. I was never called to school for a single meltdown. It was a relative picnic. Will got angry or annoyed sometimes with the behaviors of some of the other boys in the program, but his feelings were justifiable. Some of those behaviors would have upset anyone. I could always appreciate Will's point of view. The autism teacher and speech therapist would work conscientiously with Will and the other students involved. Furthermore, the school had a talented psychologist who really connected with Will. They met regularly, and he provided Will with some new perspectives and approaches for dealing with difficult situations. Will listened to him and took what he said to heart. This had never happened before. The before-Will had never been able to apply his knowledge in the heat of the moment. Now he could. Will navigated the entire school year without a single event I would classify as meltdown. We spent the year focusing on academics and social skills. It was a year of many successes. Will was my hero.

SEVENTH GRADE: A ROCKY START

Will's digestive tract problems with bad gut flora were flaring as the school year began. We spent an entire month that fall coping with "die-off reaction," a topic discussed in a future chapter. There was even one major meltdown that pulled me to school to get him. That had not happened since fifth grade. But winning the gut battles were well worth it. Will's behaviors and abilities improved once we got gut flora back under control.

A GLIMPSE FROM THE SCHOOL NURSE'S POINT OF VIEW

On a crisp winter morning, I stopped by the school clinic to drop off Will's lunch vitamins. The nurse paused a moment to describe to me what she obviously thought was a very cute story, about how Will had asked her where to get tickets for the school dance, his first. He was embarrassed and hurried to assure her he was going with a friend. Heaven forbid anyone think he was taking a *girl*. "Will's progress has been remarkable," she mused. Then she relayed another incident about something she'd asked him to do for her. "If I had asked him to do that last year in sixth grade, he couldn't have done it," she exclaimed. Then she repeated, "His progress has been remarkable." I thanked her and stumbled back out to my car in the parking lot. As I pulled away, eyes brimming with tears, I smiled to myself and replayed her words several times. She had said *remarkable*. I beamed. This dear lady had known Will for a year and a half. In that short time, having only casual contact, she had seen *remarkable* progress. I kept repeating her words to myself, savoring the pleasure. A tear spilled down my cheek as I swelled with the sweet taste of success. All my effort had been worth it. Yes, indeed, it had, all the diets, time, energy, money, and heartache. Life was good, so very good. Actually, it was *remarkable*. God bless the school nurse for her sincere, unsolicited affirmation. It was a treasure to my spirit that day. Some of Rich's famed chocolate chip cookies were definitely in her future.

A PERSPECTIVE FROM THE SCHOOL PSYCHOLOGIST

Back at the beginning of sixth grade when Will had started middle school, I got a call from the school psychologist. He had just met Will for the first time and didn't know what to make of him. "Help!" he exclaimed. Will would barely talk to him and sat in a chair with his legs over his head. No doubt visions of retirement were playing through the incredulous man's head. The best tip I offered that day was to play a card game, Uno, with Will to break the ice. Thus began a ritual for them that worked like magic. They became fast friends. Will opened up and highly valued (and applied) insights from his card-wielding buddy. Together, they weathered several bumpy rides with success. One special day in the spring of Will's seventh-grade year, the psychologist emailed me. "Will and I are having too much fun!!" he wrote. "We don't play games any more—just talk. I can't believe this is the same student who came in my office a year and a half ago!"[1]

A TIDBIT FROM WILL'S AUTISM TEACHER

Nearing the end of seventh grade, I received another heart-warming email. This time it was from one of the autism teachers, describing an incident in which Will had started "ranting" on a "soap box," an apt description no doubt. In the past, once upset, Will had a hard time recovering and moving on. Now that had changed. The teacher wrote, "He did regain composure and handled the rest of the day just fine. Last year, he probably would have wanted to/needed to come home. Yet another marked improvement on his part…I was impressed!"[2] As for me, I danced a jig. Go, Will!

EIGHTH GRADE IS COMING: A BOLD STEP IN MATH

Math had always been Will's most difficult subject by far. Since the early grades, it was his only pull-out class. A teacher worked with him either one-on-one or with up to four students. Yet, at the close of Will's seventh-grade year, I received the most startling email from his autism/math teacher. She thought Will was doing well enough that he could move to a regular math class (with support) for eighth grade. I quite nearly wet my pants. This was *big, really big.* I remembered back to a day a couple of years earlier when Will was in fifth grade. I had gone to school to observe him. At the time, Will had been on biomedical intervention for a few months. I was hopeful to see improvement. The one-on-one math teacher asked Will to work a simple problem on the page and then sat back to see if he could do it. Will was not only unable to work the problem but wandered about the page seeming to work parts of different problems without even realizing it. I left school that day with a very heavy heart. Will's math future seemed quite bleak. Now, with a couple more years of biomedical intervention under his belt, this same student was moving to a regular math class—to do *algebra* of all things. I was amazed and at the same time leery. We settled on a class in which half the students needed extra help so were given a second teacher in the classroom to assist them. Though there have been some bumps along the way, Will has managed. He brought home a C+ for the first grading period—not bad for a kid who couldn't even stay on the same problem a couple of years earlier.

TREASURED DEVELOPMENTS

When Will comes home from school now, he often tells me tidbits about his day, something funny or interesting that happened. He *never* used to do that. Before, we were like two isolated lives bumping along together through the tunnel of time, but now Will shares some of his thoughts and feelings. More and more we connect and our conversations are rewarding. He even said something sarcastic the other day. Will who always took words so literally and never recognized sarcasm said something sarcastic. What a contradiction—and a delight! Moveover, this kid who had always been so impossible to rush now has an emerging sense of urgency not to miss the school bus. I have even been chided a couple of times for not being ready by the very one whom I used to prod relentlessly through each and every step of his morning routine. We still have a ways to go in self-management, but this is a beginning. Even six months ago, Will could not keep track of which day of the week it was; it was like a blind spot for him. Though he knew the names and order of the days, they did not seem to hold any meaning. Often in the mornings, he would ask if it was a school day as though the weekday–weekend routine was completely random to him. And telling him "Today is Tuesday" or "Yesterday was Friday" did not answer his question about school. Yet *now* Will usually knows which day of the week it is. On a recent Sunday night, he even thought to set his alarm to wake himself for school on Monday morning. I was in disbelief. This new-found awareness gives his life predictability. In terms of being able to manage himself, it is a significant, fundamental advance. In addition, Will's school recently introduced us to an innovative idea in self management. The school provided Will with a hand-held electronic device just like the ones many people use at work to track their appointments and to give them reminder beeps when they need to go to meetings. Will makes an entry in the device so it will beep him later when the time is right to do a particular task. At school, he may have it remind him to turn in an assignment, write down homework, return a library book, or go to a club meeting. It has been helpful at home as well for prompting him through his morning routine to get ready for school. Will loves the independence and sense of control this tool offers him. More than once he has exclaimed that "it makes me feel so powerful!" He is advancing in other ways too. I have seen Will run on the treadmill while operating the hand controls for a Playstation game. I doubt I could even do that. And to think this is the same boy who would trip and fall backward walking across a flat floor. Life is good, very good—and getting better.

SCHOOL FRIENDS

In the early elementary years of school, Will spent his recesses on the play-ground glued to a book, thereby shutting out all social contact. For the most part, I "arranged" friends for him back then. Later when he entered the autism program in fourth grade, he made friends with a boy in the program. They were tight and still are. A couple of years later, he made another friend in the program. But then, starting in seventh grade and continuing into eighth, Will made some friends outside the program *on his own*. And a couple were even *girls*, of all things. Now what was I to think about that? I had accepted the first one as an irregular-ity, but now there was another. I heard about being lab partners, sitting at school assemblies together, walking in the halls, and eating lunch together. They were swapping stories and sharing interests. Holy cow! What was going on here? Will even arranged to meet one girl at a school dance and was invited to come watch another at her band concert. The next thing I knew, he was calling her on the phone. Then, she even called him. I had never dared to dream these dreams. Yet here they are, becoming reality. A warm mix of delight, amazement, and pride wells up inside me whenever I think of Will's increasing ability to fit in. Now I do not have to live forever so Will can have a friend. He can enjoy relationships on his own. And I can rest in peace.

FOCUS ON STRENGTHS

Albert Einstein is not world-famous because he focused on his deficits. Sure, he could have had tidy hair, but what good is that to the world of science? Likewise, with AS, skills are uneven. Parents have a natural desire to zero in on the weak areas. Support, training, and therapy for these areas are a good idea, a great idea. But do not overlook your child's strong suits. Herein lies the greatest opportunities for his enjoyment, self-esteem, self-confidence, and success. His future career will probably fall in an area of expertise, not weakness.

For example, Will is a master builder. He had long been a fanatical enthusiast of Legos. He could build from directions with ease and erect elaborate structures free-hand as well. Later, he expanded into the more complicated realm of Bionicles. He can assemble them, even brand new ones, with surprising speed. I am told by his brothers that he only needs the directions the first time he constructs a Bionicle; subsequent rebuilds are done from memory. Quite impressive, so his brothers say. And we are talking about a lot of pieces here, often up to 200 or 400. So, building expertise is a definite strength Will can focus on. It not only offers entertainment and fosters self-esteem and confidence but may have future career implications as well. Maybe machinery design or maintenance? Architectural design or drafting? Building construction? Who knows, but there are many practical applications for this skill.

Will could capitalize on his excellent memory as well, albeit a selective memory. Think of the Harry Potter books, a series that spawned an unwavering tradition at our house. As each new book was published, my husband Rich would slip off to the store at some odd hour of the night, returning triumphantly with his prize. As morning dawned, he would hold up his crown jewel before the riveted, enthusiastic eyes of his offspring. Like the Pied Piper, he and his magical book lead a procession of would-be listeners to the appointed reading spot. As Rich read aloud for hours on end, his spectators sat entranced, dangling on his every word. Any interruption such as a call to dinner was assailed by a gale of moans and groans, pleas and bargains, even from the grownup in the crowd. Between readings, the treasured book was soundly hidden away since not one boy could be trusted not to sneak a peek. If you have ever read a Harry Potter book, you know that each is a masterfully woven tale of numerous personalities, perpetual crisis moments, intricate webs of detail, and challenging vocabulary. And each book builds on the saga of the earlier ones. At times, it is easy to lose track of the precise scenario of earlier events that lead to the current crisis. So, occasionally, Rich would pause to query who could explain some past portion of detail. Will would invariably supply the intricate string of missing pieces. As he recounted past events, sometimes even from earlier books, glimmers of recall would dawn on his audience. In awe, they would slowly begin to nod their heads in agreement. "Ah, yes. That's how it happened." Such a memory is an outstanding, *marketable* strength. Will shines with potential, perhaps to be a brilliant professor, albeit an absent-minded one possibly.

Will is also an exceptionally avid reader. He has good comprehension and can read fast. In sixth grade, his school library offered a wonderful program known as Battle of the Books. Participating sixth- and seventh-graders were given a list of 28 books to read during the school year. Near year's end, teams were formed and competitions were held. Will was one of the few who read every book on the list. At competition time, each child had a buzzer and would race to hit it first in answer to the questions. Once the buzzer was pressed, only three seconds were allowed before points would be deducted. Will's silly mother was apprehensive. Would Will get too excited and hit his buzzer when he had no answer? Could he keep up with his classmates and spit out his answers in time? Oh, ye of little faith! Will knocked their socks off. In the first competition, he scored more than any single player, sixth- or seventh-grader alike. His rapid-fire buzzing and prompt, accurate responses dazzled his mother into disbelief. This kid had 28 books crammed into his head. It could have been a muddled mess in there. But, no, Will was shooting out facts, often before the reading of the question was finished. He was quick and sharp. His mom, on the other hand, was apparently a blockhead—oh, but a very, very proud blockhead she was. Tears of pride and delight welled up in my eyes. That is *my* boy. He had fun and was as pleased as could be with his performance. News of it would be bandied about throughout the family, extended family, teachers, and support members, plus any friends or neighbors I could latch onto to give a blow-by-blow description. Will would receive numerous accolades all around. So who knows? He might be an author some day. An editor? A paralegal? What other professions use fast readers with good comprehension? Only time will tell where this strength may lead.

Much to Will's thrill, we attended a "meet-the-author" book signing by Anthony Horowitz, author of the popular Alex Rider, teenage spy, book series. At the time, a motion picture of his first book, *Stormbreaker*, was soon to hit the box office. Yes, this was big, and my Alex Rider fan was beaming with excitement. A woman in the audience asked this famed author why he had started writing. Anthony Horowitz promptly replied that it was because he was not good at anything else. He detailed how bad he had always been at everything in school, even woodworking. Every report his parents ever received from his teachers was dismal. His only talent was spinning yarns. He emphasized to the audience that you only have to be good at one thing. He said that some kids are good at 20 or 30, but you really only have to be good at one. He assured every child in the audience that he or she was good at one thing at least. The man was absolutely right. Will leaned over to me and whispered, "This is heaven."

So do not concentrate on your child's shortcomings. Acknowledge and work on them, yes. But focus on the strengths. Consider your child's talents and ponder ways to capitalize on them. It is the strength of one's strengths that wins the game. Who cares if Einstein's hair was a mess when he had the theory of relativity to offer?

NOTES

1.   Kenneth Roach, email dated 1 March 2007.
2.   Sarah Bristow, email dated 29 April 2007.

Part 4

BIOMEDICAL PROBLEMS AND INTERVENTIONS OF THE AUTISM SPECTRUM

Chapter 16

A Foundation for Understanding Biomedical Issues and Treatments in Autism

THIS CHAPTER'S INTENT

Welcome to the orientation chapter about the biomedical approach to autism. Later chapters will explore specific biomedical problems found in autism, as well as safe and effective treatments to address them. But before diving in, it is helpful to have some background knowledge. This chapter will clarify various ideas of current-day thinking on autism's causes and treatments and will offer a perspective for understanding the biomedical approach. You will find it particularly helpful if you are new to biomedical intervention or wary of it, as I once was.

WHY THE MAINSTREAM COMMUNITY IS SKEPTICAL OF BIOMEDICAL TREATMENT

The first published description of autism was made by the child psychiatrist Leo Kanner in 1943. Though he documented signs of problems in the immune systems and digestive tracts of the children he described, his emphasis on their behavioral observations pegged autism as a psychiatric illness, and it is still considered as such today.[1] Envision a thick, heavy volume. The title etched on its cover is *Diagnostic and Statistical Manual of Mental Disorders*. Alas, you have discovered today's highly regarded professional reference for the diagnosis of mental and behavioral disorders (a great book to curl up with on a Saturday night, no doubt). Autism, AS, PDD, and ADD/ADHD appear in this manual. Their

129

existence there limits their scope of treatment. After all, if autism is truly a *mental* disorder, only mental treatments make sense, not *medical* ones. So, mainstream minds limit autism treatment to psychiatric medications and behavioral therapies. Thus, you have the proverbial box that keeps otherwise intelligent and creative minds from probing beyond its confining walls. Run medical tests for autism? How absurd! We are dealing with a mental disorder here, right? Unfortunately, mainstream thinking is trapped in a mindset that does not allow it to consider seriously otherwise scientifically sound evidence.

Surely any open-minded person who took an honest look at the Defeat Autism Now! approach could not resist the sensibility of it all; its basis in sound scientific and clinical research and the dramatic improvement in autistic behaviors that many children enjoy when their biomedical conditions are treated. Yet you may hear attacks against biomedical treatment, even vehement ones perhaps, because some people can see only what they believe and are unable to believe what they see. To them, I can say only one thing, a quote from Jeff Bradstreet, MD, when he spoke at the October 2005 Defeat Autism Now! conference. He quoted a Chinese proverb, "The person who says it cannot be done should not interrupt the person doing it." Makes sense to me. Why guard beliefs of the past when breakthroughs are under our noses? I look forward to the day when mainstream thinking incorporates what Defeat Autism Now! has to offer.

FIRST SCHOOL OF THOUGHT

Today, there are two opposing schools of thought about what causes autism and how to treat it. One school, just discussed as mainstream, says autism is a strongly genetic, brain-based disorder. The most likely treatments to help include psychiatric drugs and behavioral and educational therapies.[2]

This was the only school I ever heard of before I met Defeat Austim Now! In Will's case, what always confused me about the genetic aspect of this theory was that no one in Will's family tree had been known to exhibit autism-spectrum behaviors. So where did Will get his autism gene(s)? And none of our practitioners could offer us a genetic test to help clarify Will's genetic link to the autism spectrum. We were just supposed to assume that a genetic flaw existed somewhere. And just another point to add to my confusion, most genetic disorders had easily recognizable facial or body features, e.g., Down's syndrome, Fragile X syndrome, and Williams syndrome. But where were such features in this genetic disorder called autism?

I could find no satisfactory explanations to resolve these puzzling points. There was nothing to do but wait for continuing efforts in genetics research to uncover the answers. The study of genetics has indeed commanded the bulk of money spent on autism research over the last 20–30 years. However, this research has been unable to peg a specific gene-carrying chromosome as the primary culprit in autism. True, family and twin studies showed that hereditary factors played a role, but how big a role? Depending on the study, identical twins both have autism 40–90 percent of the time. But why isn't it 100 percent? They have the identical genes, don't they? Therefore, shouldn't it be impossible for only one twin to have a genetic disorder? It made me wonder. Could it be that, in some cases of autism, genes are not the sole cause? Could environmental influences be playing a role?[3] If that were true, it opened the door to the possibility that the slipping and sliding backward of Will's development around 18 months of age was due to environmental pressures.

But, back then, this idea did not occur to me. I just kept trying to make sense of the gene explanation of autism, though it seemed confusing and incomplete. But what did I know about such things? I was no scientist. I accepted the strongly genetic basis for autism for lack of any better ideas. After all, the medical profession was endorsing this theory, and they ought to know what they are talking about, right? Their message was clear. Genes are preordained; they are your fate. Autism, therefore, is just a severe case of bad luck. So, do not bother looking for solutions; instead, make do the best you can. Your only options are to suppress symptoms with drugs if possible and provide extra support with special education and therapy. End of story.

For me, this school's mindset placed blinders on my thinking. No treatments were considered outside psychiatric drugs or educational and therapeutic activities. I did not take a hard look at some of Will's seemingly unrelated physical issues, and it never crossed my mind to probe for other sources of intervention. My attitude became one of acceptance, inaction, cross-my-fingers-and-hope-for-the-best. Being trapped in such a position of helplessness, I focused my efforts on trying to understand Will's world and how to make our two worlds coexist as peaceably as possible. It was a worthwhile objective, indeed, yet incomplete and inadequate. I lost precious time in the holding pattern of this school of thought. Illness is the body's plea for change; it is not a time to be idle.

SECOND SCHOOL OF THOUGHT

The second school believes that genes do not dictate outcome as much as they create varying degrees of vulnerability to environmental influences. In other words, genes set the stage, but they do not define destiny. If certain factors from the environment emerge on a genetically vulnerable stage, health problems may result in various parts or processes in the body, health problems that can impact the brain. They can occur before birth, during infancy, or in early childhood. Interventions that restore health to the injured body parts or processes not only heal these areas but also in turn enhance brain function and behaviors. The bottom line is that autism is not a brain disorder, but rather a disorder that *affects* the brain. For a child with autism, particularly one who regressed or lost skills he once possessed, it is likely that environmental factors have caused injury.[4]

Consider the alarming increase in the rate of autism and the very slow rate of change in genetic factors. Also reflect on the dramatic upsurge in the number of cases of regressive autism compared to those of early-onset autism. It only makes sense that environmental influences have taken on a greater role in today's world, accounting for a large portion of our current plague of autism-spectrum disorders. Environmental causes will be discussed in the coming chapters.

As for Will and me, we gained some advantages from the psychiatric medications of the first school of thought. However, their benefits were limited and superficial. What enabled us to lay claim to substantial gains that were sustained was following the guidance of the second school and treating the whole body.

If I were drowning in a pool, psychiatric medications are like a pill that enables me to keep treading water. Biomedical intervention, on the other hand, is like pulling the plug on the pool so I can eventually stand. The water might still reach my neck, waist, or ankles. If I am really fortunate, I will stand on dry ground. Regardless, the difference between swimming and standing is enormous. With the first school, we were always treading water, feeling helpless and on the defense. With the other school of thought, we have taken a position of power to make informed decisions and improve our lives.

SO WHAT IS THE DEAL WITH GENES, ANYWAY?

Certainly, there are some traits that genes dictate. For example, if my genes say I will have hazel eyes, poof! I have hazel eyes. No amount of environmental influence will change the expression of my genes for eye color. Similarly, there are some purely genetic causes of autism. Forgive my use of such big words, but adenylosuccinate lyase deficiency is a genetic condition that guarantees autistic symptoms. There are Fragile X syndrome, Rett syndrome, Angelman syndrome, and others as well. However, such purely genetic sources of autism are rare.[5]

More often, genes do not mandate outcome but instead merely *predispose* a person to a particular outcome. For example, suppose a hereditary condition is prevalent in my family tree. For fun, let's call it the dreaded Fimquat disease. I may well carry a gene for Fimquat. Therefore, my doctor tells me I am at increased risk of developing this condition. *Risk* is the key word here. The doctor did not say I would definitely fall victim to the family curse. No, the Fimquat gene is not my fate. It does, however, set the stage, a vulnerable stage, upon which Fimquat *could* make an appearance. Luckily, as in many hereditary conditions, I can influence the expression of this gene with certain lifestyle practices that minimize my risk. Let's say the risk factors for Fimquat are smoking, high-fat foods, and being female. I cannot do anything about being female, but I can still stack the deck in my favor by eliminating the environmental triggers I can control. Furthermore, in the case of Fimquat, I can further reduce my chances by taking an aspirin a day and eating lots of fruits, vegetables, and Girl Scout cookies. As a result of my efforts, I may never develop Fimquat, despite the presence of its gene. My story has a happy ending because, due to favorable environmental influences, the gene did not express itself.

Could autism also be a disorder that may or may not be expressed depending on factors in the environment? Could it be that genes set the stage for vulnerability or resistance and that environmental factors determine what plays out? For example, being male increases a child's chance of developing an autism-spectrum disorder. Obviously, however, autism is not the fate of every male. Furthermore, children on the spectrum often have a family history of what is called an "autoimmune" disorder. This term *autoimmune* means that a body's immune system mistakenly attacks the body itself. We usually think of germs as causing injury, but, in this case, it is the body's own immune system that is the unwitting culprit. Autoimmune disorders such as rheumatoid arthritis, insulin-dependent diabetes (Type I), psoriasis, hypothyroid disease, lupus, and rheumatic fever are significantly higher in the family histories of autism-spectrum children than in typical children.[6] Research published in the *Journal of Child Neurology* in 1999 found that children were twice as likely to have autism if two or more family members suffered from an autoimmune disorder. They were 5.5 times more likely if three or more family members had autoimmune disorders. The most vulnerable children were those whose mothers had an autoimmune disorder. These children were 8.8 times more likely to have autism.[7] The coming chapters will discuss several impairments in the immune systems of children on the spectrum. Such impairments can play a major role in the physical problems these children experience. Yet, not all children with family histories of a fragile immune system develop an autism-spectrum disorder. Why some do and others do not may have a lot to do with environmental factors.

In summary, sometimes genes dictate outcome, but other times they merely set the stage where a multitude of different scenarios could unfold depending on the environment. So were Will's genes the main reason he slipped onto the spectrum around 2 years of age? I do not believe so. He has the same genes today that he had back at the depths of his woes. Yet, the difference in his capabilities are night and day. I cannot help but wonder whether if, rather than accepting the first school of thought, I had known to implement biomedical intervention at Will's first signs of trouble, we could have been spared time on the spectrum altogether. After what I have witnessed these last few years, I truly believe the answer is "definitely yes."

IS AUTISM BRAIN-BASED?

When we think about autism, the brain is our central focus of concern; but, though our concern is brain-based, does that mean autism itself is brain-based? Are problems in the brain the sole cause of autistic behaviors? Therefore, are interventions that target the brain our only hope of improving behaviors?

Consider the story of a 6-year-old boy who is the son of friends of ours. They were living in Germany when the boy toured a museum during a school fieldtrip. Later, grinning mischievously, he told his mother that he had seen *naked* statues in the museum. Hmm, he wondered. Now *what* was she going to say about that?! Maintaining a casual air, his mother queried whether the statues were boys or girls. Her son was taken aback. Flustered, he sputtered that he did not know because the statues did not have any heads. Hmm. Maybe he was missing something here. Perhaps he did not know as much about boys and girls as he thought he did. To him, the answer to the question lay in the head, the length of the hair. Looking elsewhere in the human anatomy provided no hints.

Likewise, does the answer to autism lie in the head alone, in the brain? Or can other body parts harbor clues? By intervening in these other parts, can the brain be influenced? These are fascinating questions that cut to the heart of biomedical intervention.

A REVISED CONCEPT OF A PERSON ON THE SPECTRUM

As I shifted my thinking from the ideology of the first school to that of the second, my concept of Will changed dramatically. I stopped thinking of him as a mystery, a puzzle that could not be solved. Instead, I began to view him as someone who was not *physically* well. The implications were huge. I had not noticed poor health initially, but who knows what I might find if I were to dig a little deeper? This new outlook was enlightening and empowering. It reminded me of getting my first pair of eyeglasses. Suddenly, there was so much more to see and investigate that I had never noticed before. That is how it was when I first looked at Will through my new eyeglasses of the second school. Now isn't that odd? In reality, nothing had actually changed: not Will, not his behaviors—nothing. Only how I looked at the situation was different. Suddenly, there were numerous opportunities where there had been so few only a moment before.

As a result, I found myself asking questions I never would have considered as a student of the first school. For example, how do you take care of someone whose health is compromised and vulnerable? Think of elderly family members. For starters, you become more careful about what they eat and how much they eat. Maybe you ask them to supplement their diet with vitamins and minerals. In addition, you protect them from germs and other exposures that do not ordinarily concern you. This new way of looking at autism made ideas that had seemed foreign to me initially now seem quite sensible and logical.

LOGICAL ADAPTATIONS TO ACCOMMODATE AN UNDERLYING PROBLEM

When I was an adherent of the first school, I used to observe unusual behaviors and dismiss them as just one of those mysteries of the spectrum. But with my new eyeglasses, I reopened many investigations. I started asking if it were possible that some of those behaviors were actually reasonable adaptations a child makes to accommodate an underlying problem. For example, Will often used to look at an object from the corner of his eye rather than focusing on it directly with both eyes, which seemed a peculiar way of trying to see something. On an impulse, when Will was in third grade, I had asked the school psychologist about it. The psychologist did not have an explanation but had observed that same behavior in many children on the spectrum. Hmm. Well, then at least it is "normal" spectrum behavior. I took some comfort in that, and let it go for years.

Later, the second school of thought would push me to ask *why* a person might try to focus sideways. Quit discounting the behavior on the grounds that the person doing it is on the spectrum. Simply consider what would make a "normal" person act in this way. A visual processing problem, perhaps? I was lucky. Mary Megson, MD, of Defeat Autism Now! had already researched this issue for me. It boiled down to this. Many of these children have a legitimate visual perception problem that makes it difficult for them to get a clear picture of an object by looking directly at it. However, a child could successfully bypass the problem by turning the eye sideways; then the desired image falls on an off-center portion of the retina where the cones are closest together. Dr. Megson's research went a step further. She found that she could stop the need to glance sideways by giving children a specific form of vitamin A found in cod liver oil. Who'd a thot it? Well, cod liver oil did the trick for Will. He does not glance sideways any more. Once again, I am a believer in biomedical intervention.[8]

So what other behaviors might be logical adaptations to ease the effects of an underlying problem? What about those famous spectrum children who eat very little or are picky eaters? Well, what would make a "normal" person not want to eat? Come on, we are humans. We love to eat. There has got to be a good reason when we stop eating. Well, I can think of times I avoided food, even of times that just the thought of food turned my stomach. Perhaps I had the flu or a sore throat. Is it possible these children have gastrointestinal problems for which avoiding food is a perfect strategy to minimize discomfort? Several coming chapters are devoted to gut problems that are common on the spectrum. So there is merit in considering whether a gut issue plays a role in being a picky eater.

Let's ask another question. If a child resists food, could it be his throat hurts from the burning pains of reflux? A child that has endured pain for a long time may not even suspect it does not belong there. He may not realize it is something to mention. This may be particularly worth investigating in a nonverbal child who cannot tell you he feels pain.

Let's keep brainstorming for picky-eater ideas. Could the child be constipated? Nobody with backed-up plumbing wants to throw more food on top of the mess. In such a case, only a child's favorite foods could tempt him. It would make sense.

One last question, just for kicks. What if food did not have much flavor? That would make it easy to refuse. Some children obtain improvement in both appetite and sense of taste when given zinc. This may be due to zinc's presence in a saliva protein that plays a major role in our sense of taste.[9]

Each of the questions posed here relates to physical problems commonly found in children on the autism spectrum. There may be other good questions to consider as well. The point is that you have to start asking questions, for, until a question is posed, there is no hope of finding a solution.

The list of issues to consider goes on and on. What about those famous 40–80 percent of children with autism who do not (or, is it *cannot?*) sleep at night?[10] Make a list of your child's unusual behaviors and start generating lists of reasons a "normal" person might be forced to act that way.

WHAT IS A PSYCHIATRIC DIAGNOSIS AND WHAT DOES IT DO FOR YOU?

A psychiatric diagnosis is based on behaviors. Observing behaviors is a relatively subjective means of classification compared to a blood test, for example. But there are no blood tests for autism-spectrum disorders, no clear-cut and definitive means of assigning diagnoses. So, we do the best we can with what we've got—observable behaviors. We set standards that define and group behaviors very specifically, in the hope of reducing ambiguity and minimizing subjectivity. That is the purpose of the volume *Diagnostic and Statistical Manual of Mental Disorders*, mentioned at the beginning of the chapter. Using this standard, a professional tries to fit a child's behaviors within the umbrella of allowable behaviors for a given diagnosis. There are rules that govern a match. In essence, a psychiatric diagnosis is a *behavioral* definition of a child. If you get a chance to see the manual, it is intriguing to read what characteristic behaviors and rules define the diagnosis your child has been given. Even reading about related diagnoses is interesting because you can see the reason that your child did not fit into one of them.

In truth, a diagnosis is a relatively broad classification, not a precise definition. An individual child will probably not exhibit all the behaviors allowed within his designated diagnosis. That is okay. As long as the key requirements of the diagnosis are met, it fits him. The broad nature of a diagnosis accounts for the wide behavioral variance you sometimes see among children within the same diagnosis. Think of a diagnosis as a parking lot. In the parking lot for trucks *any* kind of truck can park. There will be pickups, garbage trucks, toy trucks, and semi-trucks—a lot of variance—but still all trucks.

Having an accurate psychiatric diagnosis can be helpful in many ways. It made a huge difference in my understanding of Will's world once he had an accurate diagnosis. I quit trying to cram Will, a square peg, into the round hole of ADHD. Once I started learning about AS, his accurate diagnosis, I was able to understand him much better. I could interpret and predict his behaviors with significantly greater accuracy and could also deal with those behaviors more successfully. A diagnosis is also very important when navigating the educational system. Will has enjoyed numerous extra supports in school on account of having a diagnosis because laws exist that afford special treatment for people with disabilities.

WHAT ARE THE LIMITATIONS OF A PSYCHIATRIC DIAGNOSIS?

A diagnosis has its limitations. While it answers the question of *what* a child does, it does not explain *why* he does it. So, if I want to know the reason a toddler bit his brother (a behavior), the toddler's diagnosis (say, "biting disorder") will not tell me. Was the toddler retaliating against his brother (cause for biting: anger)? Maybe he was defending himself (cause: fear). Did he think a button on his brother's shirt was candy (cause: mistaken identity)? Perhaps he was teething and trying to relieve his gums (cause: pain). If we keep going, we could even suggest he has rabies (cause: disease). Each of these potential explanations has an entirely different cause. Having an accurate psychiatric diagnosis will not tell us which one is right or, more importantly, what to do about it.

In the case of the biting toddler, effective treatment is entirely dependent on the cause behind the behavior. Would reassuring a child with rabies stop him from biting? No. Would disciplining a fearful child do the trick? 'Fraid not. In this example, there are numerous, different potential treatments that run the gamut. Mismatches of treatments to causes will result in continued biting behavior. Even if we have an accurate behavioral diagnosis for the toddler, we still do not know what treatment will be effective. And *that* is what we are really interested in. Who cares what the diagnosis is when the toddler's brother looks like a teething ring?

WHERE DO BIOMEDICAL TREATMENTS FIT IN?

So having a diagnosis, though it can be useful, is not an end in itself but only a beginning. It describes behavior, but not its cause or most appropriate treatment. When it comes to finding the true source and appropriate treatment, you must don your Sherlock Holmes hat. Being the expert on your special child makes you qualified to investigate possible causes and appropriate interventions. You may find your child needs emotional supports, educational efforts, structure, discipline, and more. Biomedical treatments are a very important part of this total treatment plan. Filling a critical void, they delve into potential medical issues that provoke or intensify the behaviors. In fact, for the most part, they do not even address behaviors directly; rather they identify medical problems within the body and address those. As the medical conditions improve, so do the behaviors. It is forever a mystery to me exactly how that works. But I know for a fact it is real. We have lived it.

Take a look at the autism spectrum in Figure 16.1 (you've seen this figure before in Chapter 7, but it's worth a second look). Now think of light shining through a prism and of how the light is scattered along the spectrum into different colors. Each band of color is unique, yet it is all light. Likewise, each child and each diagnosis is unique, yet it is all autism. At the time of Will's AS diagnosis, I considered AS to be quite distinct from autism, but not any more. I have come to believe that autism, no matter which of the spectrum colors is expressed, still sprouts from the same root causes, the same light. The colors are each individual's way of responding to these root causes. Often people get so distracted by the colors they do not see the light. Yet this light (the causes) is virtually the same across the spectrum. The underlying medical conditions that result from these causes are the same as well, though they can vary in severity.

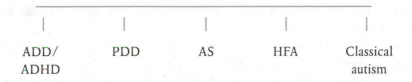

| ADD/ | PDD | AS | HFA | Classical |
| ADHD | | | | autism |

Figure 16.1 The autism spectrum

Furthermore, the treatments for these underlying conditions are the same. Both the underlying conditions and the treatments span the spectrum without regard to the lines drawn by psychiatric diagnoses. So, in terms of biomedical treatment, psychiatric diagnosis is not very relevant because the same interventions apply as readily to a child with ADHD as they do to a child with classical autism. It is the individual's underlying medical conditions that dictate treatment, not the psychiatric diagnosis. The mainstream thinking of the first school tries to treat behaviors without addressing what provoked them. That approach limits progress from the start. Though you can make progress focusing on behaviors alone, launching an attack at the source has much more potential for a higher payback.

THE AUTISM SPECTRUM: A TRAIN WRECK WHERE INDIVIDUALITY IS KEY

For purposes of illustration, imagine an unlucky passenger car that derails from its train track. Each person in the car will experience the wreck in his own unique way. Some will be wrenched from their seats and thrown like popsicle sticks, while others manage to hang on tightly, clutching desperately to the arm rails. Luggage will topple from overhead racks and assail some of the passengers below. One person is pelted in the shoulder by a handbag. Another is cracked across the back by a trunk hurtling with the force of a sledge. Shattered glass flies, striking some but missing others. A can of pepper spray in one hapless lady's purse is crushed and explodes on her. The accident results in a multitude of different aches and pains from broken limbs, internal injuries, and whiplash to concussions, gashes, and bruises. Our poor pepper-spray victim is temporarily blinded. Chances are that no one person will have every type of injury; it is more likely there will be varying combinations of injuries that differ in extent from person to person. An individual's injuries will depend on exactly what he experienced during the wreck, as well as his prior physical condition, age, and who knows what else.

If we did not know better, we might give all these people the same diagnosis based on their shared behavior of being hysterical. We might dub it "derail hysteria" and say it in Latin so it sounds official. Or perhaps we might create a whole spectrum called "derail hysteria disorders" and subdivide it into various categories of diagnoses that parallel the severity of hysteria. The least-hysterical folks might be assigned a diagnosis called "abbreviated derail hysteria disorder" (ADHD, for short). There could be other classifications along the continuum with the most extreme being named "classical" hysteria disorder. We could go on to define each diagnosis explicitly based on the extent of hysterical behaviors. Yet, our classifications would not tell us how to treat victims in the passenger car to make them feel better.

So let's take it a step further. What treatment should we give all these people? Should we put them all on sedatives and psychotherapy to calm them down? If we do, we can suppress their hysterical behavior, but how much have we really helped them? So many are bleeding, broken, disoriented, or blind that we must do more. Yet, we will find that no single treatment can solve all their varied problems. Take a neck brace, for example. Will it help everyone? No. It would benefit some, but, for others, it would have no effect. It may even be detrimental in certain cases. Conflicting treatment responses to the neck brace would not mean that a neck brace was not a good intervention; it would simply indicate that some people had a need for it, while others did not. In the end, we would be forced to evaluate each person individually and tailor a treatment plan to address only the issues relevant to that person. Our unfortunate group may have all shared in a similar disaster and exhibit many common problems, yet treatment must be individualized. One size does not fit all.

And so it is on the autism spectrum. There will be physical issues that are common among many children, but not all. There will even be some very unusual situations analogous to our pepper-spray sufferer. Unfortunately, however, identifying the underlying problems in autism and fixing them are not as easy or straightforward as the treatment of broken bones and whiplash. And though autistic behaviors can result from a single incident, more often multiple insults are at play. Like a passenger who is not only thrown from his seat but is also struck by overhead luggage and even shattered glass, a fetus, infant, or toddler can be assailed by various insults from the environment. These will be discussed in later chapters.[11]

Considerations of individuality are key in autism. Because a one-size treatment does not fit all, I should expect to hear of children being helped by a treatment that does not turn out to help my child. I should also accept that a godsend intervention for my child may not be worth a hoot to the little boy down the street. Children will respond to treatment differently for various reasons. There are differences in their genetic makeups, initial triggers, the timing and intensity of insults, how long the conditions have existed, and the extent of injury done to various systems and organs in the body before treatment begins.[12]

Nevertheless, data from thousands of children reveal subgroups of individuals who have similar biomedical characteristics.[13] Increased understanding of these subgroups has implications for predicting which treatments will be most effective for each group of children. Therefore, we will get better at diagnosing and predicting which children will respond to which treatments.

One problem is that tests are not always available that tell us everything we want to know. And some of the tests we have do not provide definitive answers, but partial information instead. Even when we know what we want to accomplish, knowing the best means of accomplishing it in a particular individual is not always clear. There are other challenges as well. We need advances in technology, knowledge, and experience. We can be thankful for what we have, yet eager to have more. However, a lack of perfect knowledge and tools does not prevent us from helping our children, sometimes significantly, through biomedical treatment. Even with variable responses to different interventions, most children improve.[14]

HOW CAN A HEALTHY BABY BE DERAILED ONTO THE AUTISM SPECTRUM?

That was my question. I had seen this situation unfold before my very eyes, despite my most conscientious efforts. In most cases, the answer of how a healthy baby regresses into autism is not simple. Envision an intricate pattern of dominoes falling one against the other until many or all of them are lying down. The cascade may have started with only one tumbling domino, or perhaps dominoes in different locations began to tumble independently. Whatever the case, once the dominoes have fallen, it is hard to decipher what the exact timing and interplay of factors were. Nonetheless, a mess remains. In some instances, the mess appears suddenly. In others, it evolves slowly over time. Either way, unfortunately, the brain is ensnared in the mess.

At the fall 2005 Defeat Autism Now! conference, Kenneth Bock, MD, presented an excellent visual to illustrate the interaction of genes and environmental influences in autism. I will paraphrase his description here with some variations (since I can never leave well enough alone). Imagine that every child is a lake. Each child's unique set of genes determines the depth of his lake. A child who is genetically more vulnerable to expressing autistic behaviors will have a shallow lake, a more resistant child, a deeper one. Take, for example, two children who have identical sets of genes, except that one is a boy and the other is a girl. The boy's lake will be more shallow than the girl's because being male is a genetic risk factor for autism. In fact, as mentioned before, the risk of autism is four times greater for males than females.[15] In addition to gender, there may be many other genetic factors that influence the likelihood of a child developing autistic behaviors. In each case, those factors will dictate the depth of the child's lake. It follows that the volume of rain water that a lake can hold without over-flowing will be different from one child to the next. Indeed, the same amount of water that one lake can accommodate easily may send another lake into a flood stage.

Now, let's say that any time a cloud passes over a lake, it can drop rains of insult into it. As a lake collects more rain, its water level inches a little closer toward its banks. So what might those clouds of insult be? Allergies and sensi-tivities; infectious agents like viruses, bacteria, yeast, or parasites; nutritional deficiencies; environmental toxins such as chemicals and heavy metals; hormonal imbalances. Even psychosocial factors like stress may rain down into a lake. For some lakes, a cloud may pass by without losing a drop. Over other lakes, the same cloud may sprinkle a few drops of insult. Still other lakes may suffer a deluge of insulting rains. The amount of rain that falls from each cloud will be specific to each child's situation.

Let's say that, at some point, a lake cannot hold all its rain water. A little begins to spill over its banks. In that case, only a few, minor autistic behaviors will appear above the surface. Maybe this child would receive a psychiatric diag-nosis of ADHD or ADD. Now suppose a second lake overflows its banks, only this time the excess water washes all the way out to a nearby street. This child exhibits more autistic behaviors that are more pronounced than the first child. Perhaps the diagnosis this time will be AS. You get the idea. There will be a whole range of flood stages: the more severe the flooding, the more severe the behaviors, and the more severe the autism-spectrum diagnosis. Eventually, a full-blown flood that picks up houses and carries them off will be diagnosed as classical autism. Figure 16.2 shows lakes and rain clouds to illustrate the interac-tion of genes and environmental influences in autism.

So, each child is the culmination of a unique genetic base that is hammered by different insults, different in their nature, their extent, their combination, and goodness knows what else. The timing of insults also has an impact. For instance, an offense sustained en utero has greater potential for injury than the identical offense made at a less vulnerable age. Another example would be an assault that happens on the heels of some other assault. The two will have a more severe, combined impact than if each had occurred in isolation. As in the illus-

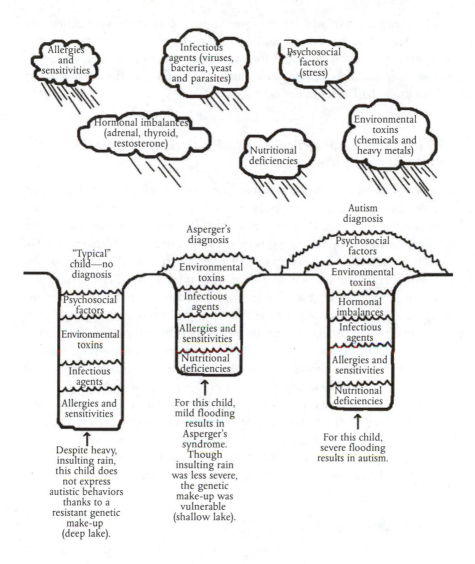

Figure 16.2 The interaction of genes and environmental influences in autism

tration with lakes, two large rains back-to-back can cause flooding that would not have occurred had the rains been a year apart.

So, it is easy to see why autism is such a complicated puzzle. There are so many variables. For any one lake, we cannot know its depth. Often we may not even be aware of some of the clouds raining into a lake or the extent of their rains. All we see is the overflow at the surface, which tells us very little about the underlying factors involved. Yet, these are the factors that must be addressed in order to reduce the flooding. How frustrating! Unfortunately, our biomedical knowledge to date cannot explain everything to the level of detail we want. But it can give us ideas of what to look for, and it also provides some tools we can use to test the waters and decipher their sources. Best of all, it offers some buckets we can use to bail water out of our lakes.

THE RELATIONSHIP BETWEEN SYMPTOMS, TREATMENTS, AND TREATMENT RESPONSES

In a straightforward illness, symptoms give easy-to-follow clues that can be traced back to their cause in the body. A sore throat, for example, may implicate a strep throat infection. However, in chronic illnesses like autism, diagnosing the initial source of dysfunction gets more complicated. A problem may start in one place but not generate symptoms that are apparent on the outside. As the problem worsens and cascades into other areas, symptoms or behaviors eventually surface, but they are distant from the initial starting point. Therefore, the symptoms may not give helpful clues about the origin of the problem, making it harder to determine an effective treatment. Despite this difficulty, symptoms can still serve a useful purpose in treatment. That is, when an intervention alleviates an underlying medical problem that has been intensifying autistic behaviors, an improvement in symptoms tells us we are on the right track.[16]

Sometimes a given biomedical intervention does not improve any symptoms. Such feedback is helpful for modifying the treatment plan. There are even times when an individual may have a negative response to an intervention. Such responses are temporary and reversible. Though they are not pleasant, they can yield valuable information for guiding future treatment.[17]

AN APPROACH OF COMPARISON

As a parent, I am a detective pulling together the clues I see in my child and evaluating them against the line-up of suspects offered by Defeat Autism Now! In other words, I need to compare my child's health issues to descriptions of common medical problems in autism. To perform this comparison effectively, parents must observe their child carefully, as well as educate themselves about the potential problems in autism. If, during my comparison, I find a slipper that fits Cinderella's foot, I may be on to something. Treating along that line may make sense.

But there are no guarantees. That means time, money, and effort could go down the drain. I wish that were not the case, but Will would not be where he is today if I had not taken the risk. I must hasten to add that not all interventions require money. Changing what your child eats, for example, can be of great benefit yet does not have to cost you. If you do spend money, being informed and knowledgeable will empower you to make optimal decisions about how to allocate the money you spend. Sometimes it is tough to decide whether "to do, or not to do." That is the question.

WHAT QUESTIONS DO BIOMEDICAL INTERVENTIONS INVESTIGATE?

When evaluating any health problem, including those of the autism spectrum, there are three key questions to ask:

1. *Does the body lack something it needs?* This could be a deficiency of a nutrient, for example. The treatment may be as simple as supplying the nutrient as a supplement. In other situations, it may involve giving a prerequisite substance that the body can use to produce the needed nutrient on its own.

2. *Is there something the body should avoid?* If an environmental substance is causing the body trouble, avoidance of that substance is a sensible intervention. For example, it may be necessary to minimize exposure to foods that cause allergic reactions or sensitivities. Steering clear of chemical toxins and heavy metals can be important as well.

3. *Does the body have something it should get rid of?* Sometimes substances that harm the body, like chemical toxins and heavy metals, have found hiding places in the body. In such cases, treatments are available to remove the substances or to support the body so it can remove them itself.

During biomedical treatment, each of these three questions is asked. As a result, many issues may come to the surface. A number of substances may be lacking. There may also be several agents to avoid or get rid of. As always, it depends on the individual.

A TYPE OF TREATMENT THAT CAUGHT ME BY SURPRISE

When I first started learning about biomedical intervention, there was one category of treatment that threw me for a loop—vitamins, minerals, and other supplements. They were often the Defeat Autism Now! answer to the question, "Does the body lack something it needs?" At the time, I felt Will ate plenty of healthy foods and already took a multivitamin from the department store. How could he have any deficiencies? Besides, it did not make sense to me that vitamins could be much of an "answer" to the severe problems we faced on the autism spectrum. Vitamins are not *real* medicine—are they? They seemed a little on the wimpy side to tote as an "intervention." Sure, sometimes people take them as extra insurance in case they don't eat right. For health maintenance, that approach is okay, but, when a person gets sick, only a prescription drug can make him well.[18]

As it turns out, that is not the case. According to research, nutrients influence genetic risk, disease, and behavior.[19] And the majority of children with autism-spectrum disorders, especially the younger ones, enjoy noticeable improvement within days to weeks of starting a good basic nutrient program.[20] I, myself, have seen "mere" vitamins, minerals, and supplements work wonders, a surprising and unexpected result. Now even I am a believer—guess you really can teach an old dog new tricks.

Besides, when you stop to think about it, it makes sense that nutrients would be an important part of restoring a body to good health. Consider a brick house with structural damage. To make repairs, it is going to take a few bricks, and, if the brick house is dilapidated, it may take a lot of bricks to restore it. That is how it is with nutrients and the human body, too. Vitamins, minerals, and supplements are the building blocks of the body and a natural part of its optimal functioning. It only makes sense they will be needed in times of trouble. Consider the brain, for instance. It is a chemical factory that produces neurotransmitters, receptors, and other complex biochemicals that are essential for communication between nerve cells. The only raw materials for production of our brain chemicals are vitamins, minerals, and amino acids. Inadequate levels of these raw materials can create problems in mental functioning. The point here is that to fix a body, you often have to use what it is made of.[21]

In addition, those on the spectrum are not physically healthy in the first place, though you may not be able to tell on the surface. Many are deficient in vitamins, minerals, fatty acids, and more due to poor diet or an impaired ability of the digestive tract to obtain nutrients from food.[22] Disruption in body chemistry can also interfere with production of substances that the body normally is able to produce on its own. Thus, many of the common physical problems of autism impair health and leave the body nutritionally deficient. The use of vitamins, minerals, and other supplements addresses these fundamental issues to restore health. They are a way of smuggling in what the body needs most but cannot make for its self. Furthermore, supplements sometimes act like medications to trigger healing. Then later, after there has been progress toward healing, certain supplements that had been necessary earlier may no longer be needed.[23] Supplements are available in numerous forms including pills, chewables, liquids, powders, and creams. Supplement manufacturers who cater to the autism spectrum recognize how difficult it can be to get vitamins into some children, so they offer a wealth of options to make them more palatable or easy to hide in food or drink.

Hypersensitivity to nutrients is rare for most children on the spectrum. If a certain nutrient does not agree with a child, it may indicate that bad gut "bugs" are present. As the gut bugs thrive on the nutrient, they can impair health. In this case, it is not the nutrient itself that is the problem. When such a reaction occurs, the best course of action is to deal with the bad bugs.[24] This will be discussed later in Chapters 23 and 26.

Perhaps, all that is "mere" about vitamins is their level of publicity. Their financial advantage to promoters pales in comparison to that of prescription drugs. Moreover, medical students receive far more training in prescription medications than in nutrients. So, if you go to a doctor with a problem, the doctor's solution will likely be in terms of what he or she knows the most about. Not that Dr. Biomedical has not used her prescription pad for Will at times; she most certainly has. But she does not resort to it nearly so readily as most doctors I have known. The bottom line is that you should not discount the strength of vitamins and other nutrients for improving health and behaviors on the autism spectrum.

ARI PARENT RATINGS OF BIOMEDICAL INTERVENTIONS

Unfortunately in life, we often make treatment decisions for an ailment (be it high blood pressure, heart disease, or a belly ache) without much knowledge of treatment success rates. We tend to rely heavily on advertising or what our particular medical provider recommends. Sometimes, we also seek out people with the same condition and ask about their experience with a proposed treatment.

Autism intervention is no different. But who can we ask? Well, other parents of children on the spectrum, right? Because when it comes down to it, who knows the most about whether a treatment is working? It is the parents who are in the trenches with their child every day and night, who know their child's behaviors better than anyone and are the best suited to judge whether those behaviors are better, worse, or unchanged over the course of an intervention. Also, parents are the central reservoir of knowledge about how their child is doing since they receive input from teachers, therapists, and others who spend time with their child.

The Autism Research Institute (ARI) highly values parent observation in evaluating the effectiveness of various interventions. So, starting in 1967, the year of the first Apollo space mission, ARI began collecting parent ratings of many treatments used in autism, both traditional and biomedical. In the years since, more than 26,000 parents have rated their experiences with various drugs, special diets, and non-drug supplements. For each intervention, parents indicated whether their child's behaviors became better or worse or were unaffected. ARI maintains a list of interventions and their associated counts of "better, worse, and no effect." The number of parents who rated each intervention is also recorded. Furthermore, ARI calculates a helpful ratio that compares the "better" count for each treatment to its "worse" count. The bigger the ratio, the better. Higher ratios indicate that more children improved compared to those whose behaviors got worse. On the other hand, a ratio below the number 1 indicates that more children got worse than got better. Ratio values in the ratings for autism range from 32:1 (the best) down to 0.3:1 (the worst).

So, if you do not know 26,000 parents who have tried treatments for autism, guess what? Now you do. The ARI parent ratings cannot tell you what will work with your individual child, but they offer useful input to aid you in your treatment choices. They certainly give a sense of the potential chance for success of one treatment option versus another. A table of the ratings for autism appears in Appendix B. Also included there is an "Asperger's Only" version of the ratings based on responses of nearly 1,300 parents of children with Asperger's. Better:worse ratio values in this table range from 44:1 (the best) down to 0.2:1 (the worst). Both tables are updated annually by ARI as more parents contribute their experiences. The latest versions are available on the ARI Web site and for free from ARI as publication 34 (go to www.autism.com and type in "publication 34").

As you look over the tables, only a few of the interventions may be familiar. Even so, it is interesting to note that most of the better/worse ratios in the drug category are strikingly low compared to the other two categories: special diets and biomedical (nondrug) supplements. The coming chapters of this book discuss several interventions, so you will come to understand what many of them are. Certain ones in each of the three categories will be covered, and values from the parent ratings for autism (not Asperger's) will be reviewed.

INTERVENTION TRIALS

In a perfect world, we would have in-depth knowledge of all biomedical issues on the spectrum. In addition, completely reliable, inexpensive tests would be available to pinpoint health problems. With such perfect information, we could flawlessly predict who would respond to which treatments and who would not. But, alas, our world is less than perfect, so we have to settle for doing the best we can with incomplete knowledge, imperfect tests, and limited financial resources.

This brings us to a discussion of trials, which will be mentioned frequently in the coming chapters. Trials are a necessity of our imperfect world.

In the absence of a reliable test to drive treatment decisions (or the money to pay for it), a trial is the next best way to learn if an intervention will help. It is like giving everyone from the derailed passenger car a neck brace. For those it helps, they keep it; otherwise, they put it aside. According to *Autism: Effective Biomedical Treatments* (the book of consensus on the Defeat Autism Now! approach) the risks of supplements are low.[25] Even when a negative response does occur, it is temporary. Furthermore, the reason most supplements work is very well understood, even though in some cases, such as vitamin B6, it may be difficult to pinpoint which of its 300 functions in human biochemistry did the trick. At any rate, given the well-understood roles of supplements in the body, their low risk, and high potential for benefits, a trial is an acceptable and effective strategy.

Though you may not realize it, you are probably quite familiar already with the concept of running trials. For example, have you ever caught a cold and taken vitamin C for a few days in the hope of improving your symptoms? If you have, I doubt you ran a vitamin C test first or consulted a doctor. To you, all that was important was knowing you had a cold and that vitamin C might be a good treatment since it supports the immune system, among other things. In essence, you were matching a condition to a reasonable line of treatment. From top to bottom, you applied the intervention on your own, just using a little knowledge. If you have ever done anything like that, it was a biomedical trial of a nondrug supplement. It corresponds to a whole category of nondrug supplement interventions found in the ARI parent ratings.

Moreover, if you have ever tried to lose weight, you have experience with special diet trials, too. Special diets are a second category of interventions in the ARI parent ratings. When dieting, a person is trying to influence a symptom (weight) by changing what he eats (intervention). Similarly, a person who suspects that caffeine is upsetting his stomach might avoid caffeine-containing foods and drinks for a time to see if the stomach situation improves. That is a dietary trial.

Drug interventions are the final category of the ARI parent ratings. Most likely, you have done drug trials, too. Have you ever gone to the doctor for a problem and come home with a prescription drug from the pharmacy? Whether the medication did the trick or not, you were running a trial. A trial is merely trying out an intervention to see if it will improve symptoms.

Many of the trials used in biomedical treatment, like the ones for nondrug supplements and special diets, can be done without the assistance of a medical professional. Of course, choosing not to consult a doctor depends on your comfort level, which only you can access. Still, you need some information, so turn to one of the treatment guides written by doctors associated with Defeat Autism Now! They include:

○ *Healing the New Childhood Epidemics* by Kenneth Bock, MD, and Cameron Stauth

○ *Children with Starving Brains,* 3rd edition, by Jaquelyn McCandless, MD

○ *Autism: Effective Biomedical Treatments* by Jon Pangborn, MD, and Sidney Baker, PhD.

These guides offer dosing information and safety cautions, as well as explanations about supplements and their functions in the body. In addition, other tips are offered to ensure that a trial enjoys its best shot at success with minimal side effects. For example, during a vitamin C trial, it is helpful to know that vitamin C does not last long in the body. Therefore, taking it in small divided doses throughout the day is more beneficial than a single, daily megadose. The guide books also offer ways to prevent or contend with potential side effects. For example, gastrointestinal irritation from vitamin C can be avoided if it is taken in its buffered form. Moreover, if vitamin C causes diarrhea, the guides explain what can be done to alleviate the problem without discontinuing the vitamin C.[26]

The bottom line on trials is that they tell you whether a given intervention will help your child. If the intervention has a positive effect, continue its use, at least for a time. Some interventions are necessary only for healing, while others are for the long run. At some future point, it might make sense to run a trial that removes an intervention that had been helpful earlier. Such a trial tells you if the intervention has served its purpose and can now be discontinued *or* if you need to go back to it for a longer period.[27] Trials are an indispensable tool to guide your decisions as you decipher your child's riddle of what works and what doesn't.

A FEW POINTERS ABOUT BIOMEDICAL INTERVENTION

In case you start thinking you would like to try some biomedical treatments, there are a few things to know up front. One is that it can be overwhelming when a child has several issues and you are just starting out. There is so much to learn, to understand, and to do. Keep in mind that it does not all have to happen at once. Pick and choose which interventions have the most potential benefit for your individual child and are within your ability to manage. Do not push yourself too hard. Anything you do will be better than nothing.

Furthermore, a biomedical treatment plan for autism is more involved than most people expect. This fact takes some getting used to. Typically in life, we follow very simplistic treatment plans. We go to the doctor and come home with a prescription. Maybe we are instructed to drink fluids and get plenty of rest. That's it, short and sweet. However, biomedical treatment for autism is not like that. Think about it. Autism is a pervasive disorder that reaches into the brain, body chemistry, gut, and the immune system. This multiplicity of problems dictates a multiplicity of treatments to target those problems. The treatment plan usually isn't simple, but it can be managed. Only bite off what you can chew, and you will do just fine.

Also recognize that, when doing biomedical treatment, a person has to have some tolerance for uncertainty. No one has all the answers. Perhaps, you will never know everything that is going on with your child, what is causing the problem, and how to resolve it. You just do your best, and that is as good as it gets. This brings us to the question of doctors. Do you have to have one? What are your options? The answers depend heavily on your particular situation and comfort level.

DOES BIOMEDICAL INTERVENTION REQUIRE A DOCTOR?

When I first considered biomedical treatment for my son, the whole idea seemed very mysterious and even risky. Anything going under the name of bio-medical "treatment" was certainly not something I felt comfortable attempting on my own. Fortunately, I could afford a doctor who followed the Defeat Autism Now! approach (www.autism.com). So I went the doctor route. If you have the money to go the doctor route yourself, I highly recommend it. Having a doctor accelerated the process significantly. Dr. Biomedical knew which medical tests were most appropriate for Will and how to interpret the results. She recommended treatments and offered advice, as well as prescriptions if needed. And having her involved certainly made me feel more comfortable. Fur-thermore, if you have an extremely sensitive child whose body tends to overre-act to the smallest of changes, an experienced doctor may indeed be indispens-able. There are also certain treatments that should only be done under a doctor's guidance.

According to Kenneth Bock, MD, a frequent speaker at Defeat Autism Now! conferences, another option is to use the online doctor referral service of the American College for the Advancement of Medicine (www.acam.org). This is one of the largest organizations of doctors who practice integrative medicine. Most of its doctors will be quite familiar with the tests commonly used for bio-medical treatment in autism. Some are even familiar with treatments as well.[28]

It may also be possible that your current pediatrician would be willing to work with you on biomedical intervention, though this is iffy. Most pediatricians, though they may be excellent doctors, are not familiar with the emerging area of biomedical treatment for autism-spectrum disorders. Some may be downright discouraging about it. Even if your doctor is willing to work with you, it is questionable how helpful that person may be if he or she is not familiar with the commonly used tests or their interpretation, let alone treatment.[29] Nevertheless, you may want to give your doctor a copy of *Changing the Course of Autism* by Bryan Jepson, MD, with Jane Johnson. One of the main goals of this book is to show mainstream physicians that a shift in thinking about autism is in order. The shift redefines autism as a medical illness rather than a behavioral disorder. The authors have compiled and organized sound medical research published in mainstream medical journals to form a comprehensive model of the disease. Reading this book may spark your doctor's interest in learning about biomedical treatment.[30] Defeat Autism Now! offers several publications, as well as doctor training twice a year, that a doctor could use to self-educate.

There is also a training center for doctors interested in learning the Defeat Autism Now! approach. It is called the Rimland Center (www.rimlandcenter.com) in honor of ARI's founder, Bernard Rimland. Located in Lynchburg, Virginia, the Rimland Center offers biomedical evaluations, education, and treatment to families. Also committed to educating doctors is the Thoughtful House Center for Children in Austin, Texas (www.thoughtfulhouse.org). This facility strives for recovery of children with autism and related conditions through a combination of medical care, education, and research.[31]

So, in terms of doctors, there are some options to consider. Yet the question remains: do you *have* to have a doctor? In the cases of many children and many of the interventions, I would not think so. There are exceptions, of course. Certainly, in your particular situation, it is something you must decide for yourself based on your individual child and which interventions you are considering. Say you are just plain skeptical that biomedical intervention even works. Why would you want to spend any money on a doctor, let alone tests, when you don't even think it will help? It is a valid question. Yet, perhaps trying a few interventions on your own would help you decide whether biomedical intervention—doctor or no doctor—is for you.

Or say you flat out don't have the money for any kind of doctor. Should that mean your child is completely shut out of all forms of biomedical intervention? I would hope not. While it is true that some treatments such as those requiring a prescription would not be available to you, there are still numerous other interventions within your reach.[32] These include changes in diet and use of over-the-counter nutritional supplements like vitamins and minerals. For many children, these interventions alone improve autistic behaviors significantly.

Besides, diet and vitamins are areas parents typically govern themselves anyway, aren't they (albeit not with such deliberate intent and care as is used in biomedical intervention)? Why would these areas, now that they are termed "biomedical intervention," take on a mystical quality like tarot cards or an Ouija board? With the exception of when my children were very small, their pediatricians never asked about their diet or vitamin intake; that area was always left up to me. In fact, in my experience, doctors are not typically even good resources of information about diet and nutrition. Drugs? Yes. But diet and nutrition? Not really. When it came to these subjects, I was pretty much on my own. Indeed, books or the services of a dietician are the best sources of information in this area.

MONEY MATTERS

Whether you decide to use a doctor depends on your own unique circumstances and comfort level. It is something you must decide for yourself. Often, the deciding factor comes down to money. Unfortunately, in the biomedical treatment of autism, insurance coverage is often lacking. Insurance tends to be part of the mainstream community that contends that autism-spectrum disorders are *mental* disorders, which makes them reluctant to cover *medical* expenses for these disorders. Rather, their coverage generally focuses on psychiatric medications and behavioral therapies. Of course, there is variance on this issue among insurance carriers. You would have to investigate your own personal situation to determine what level of coverage you could expect. So what would it mean to your wallet if you find insurance coverage lacking? For biomedical intervention, you can spend nothing, something, or a lot. It is up to you.

Spending "nothing"

To spend nothing, you will be limited to dietary changes, an area with high-impact benefits. Taking Will off dairy products, for instance, was the single most dramatic event of our entire biomedical experience. His calcium supplement and water substitute cost me less than his milk and cheese did.

Spending "something"

This spending category covers a broad range whose upper limit varies depending on the financial resources available. It allows for more flexibility when making changes in diet, such as purchase of convenience-food substitutes or special ingredients. It also allows for purchase of vitamins, minerals, and other over-the-counter supplements. For the less-expensive ones (like calcium), you can get by on less than $5 a month, though the costs go up from there. Depending on how much money you have available, the spending-something category may allow for some lab testing as well. Most of the tests mentioned in this book range from $100–$300 per test. Though these tests generally come with reference ranges and interpretive comments from the laboratory, they may not be as useful to you if you do not have a doctor who can interpret them and make appropriate treatment recommendations.

Spending "a lot"

By most people's definition, the services of an experienced biomedical doctor, lab testing, and treatment (which can include prescriptions) are considered "a lot." In a perfect world, this level of medical service would be available to every child on the autism spectrum. Unfortunately, our world is less than perfect.

For me, the most stressful decisions I have ever made regarding biomedical intervention have not involved the interventions themselves but, rather, if the intervention would cost me money and, if so, how much. To me, money decisions are hard because they pit my limitations against my child's potential improvement. Talk about a rock and a hard place. All I can say is to stay within your limits, do those things that you think offer the most potential bang for your buck, and do not feel bad about what you cannot spend. You are a fantastic parent who cares deeply about your child and is doing the best you can within your constraints. That child is lucky to have you. Repeat those facts to yourself as often as needed.

Would you like to know what I think is the most frightening expense of all? The expense of supporting a child for his *entire life* because his autistic symptoms have crippled his abilities. *That* expense is staggering. Only a very few years ago, it was a very likely prospect for me. Today, however, I have hope—no guarantees, but hope. Through the money I spend now on biomedical intervention, it may be possible for Will to be independent someday or at least to contribute financially to his support. I do not know yet for sure. I will have to wait and see. But at least the biomedical intervention of these last few years has brought that dream within the realm of possible. The money I have spent has not gone out the window, even when reduced to purely financial terms.

BIOMEDICAL SELF-EDUCATION

There are not enough doctors using the Defeat Autism Now! approach to meet the demand for their services. They tend to be very busy and not have time to explain biomedical intervention to you as much as you (or they) might like. So, whether or not you choose to use a doctor, self-education is important. Furthermore, you understand your child's issues better than anyone else, which makes you a powerful force to help him *if* you are educated about interventions that might match his needs. The whole intent of this book is to help you educate yourself. The more you read and learn, the less mysterious and confusing biomedical intervention becomes. As you will see, it is all very logical, rational, and reasonable. In a nutshell, you learn how to detect problems that may exist and then use interventions to fix them. The interventions are all based on clinical experience, research findings, and the successful experiences of other parents. There is no voodoo, tarot cards, or Ouija boards. The more you understand biomedical intervention, the more comfortable you will become and the more effective you will be at helping your child. That said, don't do anything you are not comfortable with. Consult a doctor if you are in doubt.

A COMMENT ABOUT LABORATORY TESTING

This book will mention several ways to help you figure out what is going on inside the black box that is a child. Laboratory testing is one of those ways. It can be very helpful. Several of the tests described in this book are available from an online laboratory service without you having to involve a medical professional. Most other laboratories require the signature of a licensed health professional, which may include medical doctors, nutritionists/dieticians, nurse practitioners, chiropractors, or naturopaths. Also be aware that urine collection is possible even for those who are not potty-trained, thanks to the use of special tape-on bags. For now, that is enough about laboratory testing. More details will be discussed in Chapter 29.

THE COMING CHAPTERS

Biomedical problems in autism encompass several areas: body chemistry, the gut, and the immune system. Understanding the underlying problems is key to appreciating the appropriateness of various treatments and understanding why they work. Thus, the coming chapters alternate between describing the problems in one of these areas and discussing safe and effective biomedical treatments that target them. Only common problems and treatments will be discussed.

A doctor or research scientist may cringe at my simplified explanations and lack of technical terms. That is okay. The goal here is just to help you understand the concepts. Besides, I am not a doctor, so am not qualified to give medical advice. At times, I will include information about dosing and trial length, as well as where specialty lab work and nutrient products can be purchased. Such information will come directly from a source referenced in the text. So, if you catch yourself thinking, "How can she say that? She is not a doctor," I am not saying it. I am *repeating* it. It comes from an MD associated with Defeat Autism Now! who is identified in the references. Moreover, these references often include additional details that may interest you. So, if you would like more extensive information than this book presents, take note of my references and look them up. Not all references come from Defeat Autism Now! sources; many other sources are included as well. Defeat Autism Now! makes no claim to have all the answers.[33] Take advantage of what they have to offer, but also remain open to input from other sources that seem promising. And, finally, if a reference refers to a research study, you can find additional information about the study on an Internet search engine for medical journals (www.PubMed.com). Okay, enough boring explanations. Let's get on with the show.

WHAT TO COVER FIRST

The problems of autism span the brain, body chemistry, the gut, and the immune system. You are probably most interested in the brain, right? The funny thing is that, in biomedical intervention, the way you influence the brain is through the other three areas. Restoring their health is what brings improvement in brain function. It is intriguing how that works, almost hard to believe, yet I have seen it work many times, sometimes dramatically. Chapter 29 will discuss the treatment approach used by Defeat Autism Now! This approach starts treatment in the gut. After all, 70–80 percent of children with autism have gut symptoms like diarrhea, constipation, abdominal pain, or other symptoms. Plus, there is evidence of a strong link between the gut and the brain in autism.[34] So, the next chapter is about the gut, right? Wrong. Though we begin a child's treatment with gut interventions, I believe it is more helpful to understand first what, for many children, is the *root cause* of their autism-spectrum disorder. To understand cause, we have to look at body chemistry first. Then, with that background of understanding, we can move on to the gut and, finally, to the immune system. As you read through the rest of this book, just try to get a general understanding of the biomedical problems and their interventions. Don't let the details bog you down. As you go, you might want to use a highlighter or pencil to mark information that interests you most. Then, once you finish the book and have the big picture in your mind, you can revisit the text you marked. That way you won't lose track of information that is important to you.

So, if you are ready, onward to body chemistry and what—for many—is the cause of their detour onto the autism spectrum.

NOTES

1. Jepson and Johnson 2007, pp. 11–17.
2. Rimland 2006e, p. 7; McCandless 2007, p. 2.
3. Jepson and Johnson 2007, pp. 20–23.
4. McCandless 2007, pp. 11–12, 17; Rimland 2006e, p. 7; Green 2006a, p. 3.
5. Pangborn 2006c, p. 31; Pangborn and Baker 2005, pp. 3:3–5.
6. Usman 2006, p. 59; El-Dahr 2006a, p. 154; McCandless 2006b, p. 159; Comi *et al.* 1999, pp. 388–94; Sweeten *et al.* 2003, p. e420; Croen *et al.* 2005, pp. 151–57.
7. Cave with Mitchell 2001, pp. 82, 100.
8. Ibid., pp. 74–75; Megson 2000, pp. 979–83.
9. Bock and Stauth 2007, p. 259; Pangborn and Baker 2005, p. 5:32.
10. Jepson and Johnson 2007, p. 254.
11. Pangborn and Baker 2005, p. 1:11. The analogy of autism to a biochemical train wreck is a common reference at Defeat Autism Now! conferences. The term was first coined by researcher Boyd Haley, PhD, of the University of Kentucky.
12. McCandless 2006a, p. 224; McCandless 2007, pp. 46, 104.
13. McCandless 2007, pp. 46, 65.
14. Ibid., p. 46.
15. Ibid., p. 18; Pangborn and Baker 2005, p. 1:11.
16. Pangborn and Baker 2005, p. 2:1.
17. Ibid., p. 2:2.
18. Ibid., pp. 1:8–9; Baker 2004, pp. 26–29.
19. Pangborn and Baker 2005, p. 1:6.
20. McCandless 2007, pp. 95, 106, 111, 115.
21. Lewis 2005, p. 19.
22. McCandless 2007, pp. 106, 111, 142, 144–45.
23. Bock and Stauth 2007, pp. 247–49, 256.
24. Pangborn and Baker 2005, p. 1:44.
25. Ibid., p. 2:7.
26. Ibid., pp. 5:26–29.
27. Pangbourn and Baker 2007, p. 25.
28. Bock and Stauth 2007, p. 192.
29. Ibid., p. 193.
30. Jepson and Johnson 2007, pp. 8–9.
31. Ibid., pp. 186–87, 358.
32. McCandless 2006a, p. 227.
33. Pangborn and Baker 2005, p. 2:50.
34. Jepson and Johnson 2007, p. 210.

Chapter 17

Common Problems of Body Chemistry in Autism

WHAT THIS CHAPTER IS ABOUT

A fundamental piece of the puzzle for healing autism-spectrum disorders lies in the details of ailing body chemistry. Its impairment leads to corruption in three key systems: the brain and nervous system, the digestive tract, and the immune system.[1] Through research and clinical trials, critical processes have been identified that commonly malfunction on the autism spectrum. Unlocking key secrets of these processes has led to practical interventions that have made a profound impact on the lives of many.

One reason that the processes of body chemistry discussed in this chapter are so crucial is that they function in *every* living cell of the body, and they operate billions of times a day throughout the body.[2] Personally, I would rather not have a problem that runs the gamut of every single one of my cells. Any problem that hampers each individual cell amplifies its malfunction to a cataclysmic level in the overall functioning of the body. In autism, we can plainly see the overall dysfunction. But to unravel autism's mysteries so we can rescue our children, we must zoom in to the level of cells and their household duties.

So what are these critical chemical processes that are taking place inside cells? And what do they do for a cell that is so incredibly important? Furthermore, how do these processes get out of whack on the autism spectrum? And what happens to the cells and the body as a result? This chapter will answer these questions, so you can appreciate the appropriateness and value of the interventions discussed in the chapters that follow. Those chapters will discuss interventions to get these chemical processes working better, as well as ways to repair the injury that occurred while they were malfunctioning.

KEEPING CHEMISTRY SIMPLE

Of all the biomedical topics, most people find the chemistry of human metabolism the most difficult to understand. There is a good reason for that: it *is* the most difficult, unless you are a chemist. Therefore, this chapter merely presents a high-level overview. It does not get up close and personal with chemistry since this chemistry gets very complicated very fast. The illustration used here will make the chemistry seem easy, but don't you believe it. A multitude of steps and entities have been left out for the sake of simplicity.

When we think of the body's many systems, a few familiar ones come to mind, like the circulatory system, the digestive tract, and the respiratory system. But have you ever thought of the body as a chemistry set? Well, it is. Your "chemistry system" all boils down to chemicals and chemical reactions strung along an intricate and complex pattern of pathways. All along the way, the body depends on various chemicals in the correct amounts at the right times for numerous important functions. Think of these chemicals as exquisite dancers in a synchronized ballet where timing, flow, and proportion are an art form. They merge and coalesce in just the right amounts at the correct moments. Taken together, they create a complicated choreography of numerous interactions called a chemical pathway. As long as your body is a good chemist, the functions it supports, like attention, for instance, will be of high quality.

However, things can go awry in our pathway if a poor performer trips one of the dancers. The result is a shortage of the dancer's chemical, which can lead to shortages and excesses of other chemicals along the pathway. Worse still, neighboring pathways that rely on chemicals from the disrupted pathway will be affected. The various shortages and excesses created by the original mishap can ripple across a far-reaching web of interconnected, dependent pathways. Numerous chemical wrecks will occur throughout a massive pathway system. Though the initial chemicals danced in a synchronized ballet, now they trip, stumble, and fall in an ever-widening span. Those still upright are hobbling and shuffling out of rhythm and proportion to one another.

How does this impact the body whose performance depends on its chemical system? The body will try to limp along functioning as well as it can with what it has got. But something has to give. Inadequacies will become manifest one way or another. Symptoms falling under the label of autism-spectrum disorders may begin to surface; these symptoms reflect underlying flaws in performance at a basic chemical level. Medications are available that try to offer some relief by suppressing unwanted behaviors. However, even when these medications appear to work, they rarely fix the broken chemistry.[3] They are not a tool of repair, but rather a band-aid. As soon as their effects wear off, autism comes flooding back. Use of such drugs may be necessary, but they are not the best long-term answer. As you will see, there are better options for the long run.

THE AILING BODY CHEMISTRY OF AUTISM

There are four pathways that are commonly malfunctioning on the autism spectrum. They operate inside each of the body's cells. The first pathway is called the methionine (mə-thī-ənēn) cycle, and it sits in the middle of the other pathways. Every living being performs this cycle, even single-celled fungi. So, we are talking about a *basic* function of life here. In all of human chemistry, this is the most important chemical pathway because it is vital to other critical functions throughout the body. Trouble in this pathway not only impacts autism but a wide variety of other health problems including cardiovascular disease, cancer, Alzheimer's, Parkinson's, and other conditions you sincerely do not want. If there is one pathway you need to work well, it is the methionine cycle. Unfortunately, it is impaired in most children on the autism spectrum, and it shows.[4]

In the following paragraphs, I'll provide more details about the methionine cycle but, first, what are the other three interrelated processes that are running amiss in autism? One of them feeds the methionine cycle, thus playing a crucial role in its smooth operation. The other two processes are fed by the methionine cycle—that is, they depend on contributions from it for their own proper functioning. One is an energy pathway that gives a cell its energy. For brain cells, this energy pathway provides cohesive, synchronized signaling. The second pathway dependent on the methionine cycle is the detoxification pathway. Now, if you thought that the liver was the main detoxifier in the body, you are absolutely right. The liver processes most toxins in the bloodstream before they can reach and injure the other organs. Once processed by the liver, toxins are set on a course for safe excretion in urine or stool. But the liver cannot completely detoxify every harmful invader. Thus, each cell of the body has to have its own mini-detoxification system.[5] This mini-system has two weighty responsibilities. For one, it cleans toxins and heavy metals out of the cell. For another, it defends against a beast called oxidative stress, which can injure the cell and disrupt its function. In fact, oxidative stress can even cause a cell to die.[6] For now, oxidative stress will be left undefined; just know that it is damaging and nobody wants it. It will be discussed in more detail later in the chapter. Figure 17.1 shows a simple drawing of the four interrelated chemical processes at center stage in autism-spectrum disorders. In some cases, to help those of us who are not chemists, the names have been changed to make them easier to understand and remember.[7]

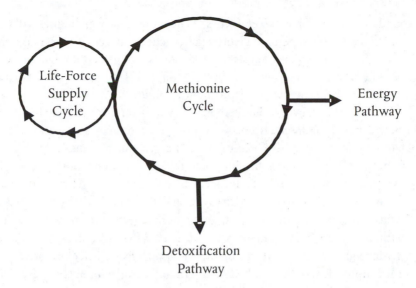

Figure 17.1 The four interdependent chemical pathways ailing in autism-spectrum disorders

THE METHIONINE CYCLE AND THE CYCLE THAT FEEDS IT

First, let us try to understand a few key concepts of the methionine cycle; then the interventions that target its problems will be easy to appreciate. The methionine cycle is similar to a European roundabout. Such a roundabout is a circular roadway where traffic can periodically enter on entrance ramps and leave on exit ramps. In the methionine roundabout, we focus on a particular traveler, methionine, who starts his journey at the top of the round roadway and drives clockwise. As he drives past the first quarter turn, he makes an important delivery before continuing on his merry way. Later, as he reaches the bottom of the roundabout, he encounters an exit ramp that forces a critical decision: he must decide either to take the downward exit or to continue looping around the circle. If he stays in the circle, he will restock delivery supplies at the three-quarter turn. Finally, he will revisit the top of the roundabout where his journey had begun. Once there, he can retrace his steps exactly as before. So, basically, that's all there is to it. Congratulations! You're a chemist.

Well, not so fast. Let's take a closer look at this process by expanding it with a little more information. We'll spice it up a little too, to make it easier to remember. Imagine this methionine delivery boy is actually a famous superhero. We'll call him Captain Delivery. Captain Delivery enters the top of the methionine roundabout on a motorcycle. The side buggy attached to his motorcycle is full of a precious commodity, life force. As Captain Delivery circles the roundabout, he will have several types of encounters. Each encounter will transform him to a new superhero identity (a new chemical, actually). Though there are many encounters and transformed identities along the roundabout, only a few will be mentioned here. So, back to Captain Delivery and his roadway, which, quite conveniently, is mapped out in Figure 17.2.

As Captain Delivery rounds the first quarter-turn, he approaches a ramp where certain prominent citizens are waiting for him. As was the plan, Captain Delivery transfers his life-force cargo to the grateful citizens. Taking an exit ramp, these citizens carry the life force out of the roundabout and begin a journey along a whole new path called the energy pathway. Empowered with life force, these citizens are now up to the task of turning the wheels of progress in this important sector. Notice that the exchange of life force between the methionine cycle and the energy pathway marries the two processes in a state of interdependent reliance. At this point, Captain Delivery is feeling pretty good about himself. He has fulfilled a crucial requirement by dispensing much-needed life force to the citizens.

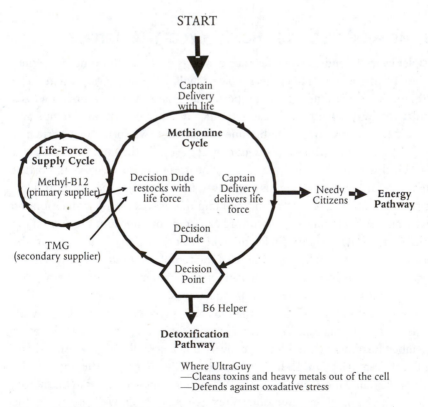

Figure 17.2 The methionine cycle (according to superheroes)

By now, without his life-force cargo, Captain Delivery has transformed into a new superhero identity—Decision Dude. His mission is hardly complete since he must continue along the circle until he reaches an important exit at the bottom of the roundabout. There, Decision Dude has a choice. He can either take the exit ramp or complete the loop restocking his side buggy with new life force along the way. For the moment, let's say Decision Dude opts to complete the loop. As he circles upward past the three-quarter turn, he passes a set of ramps where an adjacent roundabout touches his. For kicks, we'll call it the life-force supply cycle. As Decision Dude drives past it, life force is resupplied to him. The transfer comes primarily from a special agent of the life-force supply cycle known as methyl-B12 (a specific form of vitamin B12). Life force can also be given to Decision Dude by another agent called TMG.[8] Think of the two roundabouts as interlocking gears that turn in synchronous, harmonious motion. One propels Decision Dude along the loop, while the other sends methyl-B12 and TMG to greet Decision Dude with a fresh supply of life force. Though the cycles can work beautifully together, they represent a level of inter-dependent complexity in our roadway system. Once our traveler is fully replen-ished with life force, he is completely restored to his original identity, Captain Delivery. As he rounds the top of the methionine roundabout with his side buggy full, he is poised to repeat the identical orbital path, fulfilling his vital role dispensing life force to the needy citizens. He can repeatedly travel this course of delivery and pick up as many times as he likes.

Let's pause here to find out where Captain Delivery and his side buggy of life force come from in the first place. Captain Delivery is really methionine, an essential amino acid that comes from the food we eat. The key role that methionine plays in the methionine cycle highlights the importance of a healthy diet and a digestive tract that can digest and absorb properly for the sake of methionine production. Since no one eats incessantly, cells need a way to keep life-force deliveries going between meals. That need is fulfilled by recy-cling Decision Dude around the loop. As long as the life-force supply cycle has methyl-B12 or TMG to restock Decision Dude with life force, he is ready for another trip. For those instances when Decision Dude exits at the bottom of the roundabout, he must be replaced by a new Captain Delivery from the diet.

To expand our illustration slightly, there is not just one traveler in the methionine cycle. There are many. Each doles out life force to the needy citizens and then has the option to continue looping or to detour down the exit ramp at the base of the roundabout. The methionine cycle is a very busy roadway crowded with hard-working motorists. So there you have it. You now know the gist of how the methionine cycle is *supposed* to function, and you know the most important feature of the life-force supply cycle—it keeps a steady supply of life force flowing into the methionine cycle. Now let's take a look at a third key chemical process affecting autism, the energy pathway.

THE ENERGY PATHWAY

The energy pathway begins where Captain Delivery transfers life force to the citizens. Think of life force as hot potatoes that activate their owner to energetic pursuits. They can transform a loafer into an accomplished champion. With life force in hand, the citizens get motivated. And what do motivated citizens do in their pathway? Their most important purpose is to give the cell energy. We want cells vigorous and up to the task of doing whatever it is they are designed to do. Otherwise, a cell in energy crisis would suffer impaired awareness and inappropriate response.

For just a moment, consider the energy needs of brain cells. They support the brain, which is the most metabolically active organ in the body. At rest, it uses nine times more energy than any other organ,[9] so the brain's energy supply is important. Also, the brain has virtually no saved-up energy stockpile to draw on if the energy supply were to fall short. It must rely on "just-in-time" delivery from the energy pathway.[10]

But there is more that life-force-energized citizens do besides give a cell energy. They perform several other functions including production of melatonin, a hormone that helps regulate sleep. If deficient, nighttime waking can occur. In addition, citizens control gene activity within the cell. Even though all body cells have the same DNA, an individual cell's genes can be turned on or off to enable the cell to perform the functions specific to its type of cell. Life-force delivery to the citizens is critical so the right adjustments in DNA function are made.[11] Now the time has come to look at the fourth pathway known to be ailing on the autism spectrum.

THE DETOXIFICATION PATHWAY

As was shown in Figure 17.2, the detoxification pathway starts at the bottom of the methionine cycle where Decision Dude has the option to exit. And why might he want to exit? The transfer of life force to the energy pathway is not the only vital delivery that needs to take place. The delivery of an adequate supply of sulfur to the detoxification pathway is also required. And it just so happens that Decision Dude's pockets are crammed full of sulfur. Based on the relative need for sulfur versus life force, Decision Dude will decide whether to stay in the methionine cycle or strike out down the detoxification pathway.

So what happens when Decision Dude chooses to exit and deliver his sulfur to the detoxification pathway? As before, he will have multiple types of encounters, each transforming him to a new identity. One particularly valuable assistant he meets along the way is vitamin B6. With aid from vitamin B6 and other helpers, Decision Dude will eventually transform into his most powerful form, UltraGuy. UltraGuy, whose actual chemical name is glutathione (gloot-ə-thī-ōn), is the central hero of the detoxification pathway. He performs two crucial services for the cell. One is detoxification; the other is anti-oxidant protection. Each service will be described in turn.[12]

Detoxification in the detoxification pathway

One of the key services performed by UltraGuy (glutathione) is detoxification, the elimination of toxins from the cell. Though toxins sneak into the body, effective detoxification will clean them out at the first available opportunity before they cause harm. Each cell does its part by following a two-step process for clean-up. First, the valuable sulfur that Decision Dude brings down the detoxification pathway is used to make the toxin sticky so it is easy to pick up. Second, the sticky toxin is collected and carried out of the cell by the supreme detoxifying agent, UltraGuy (glutathione). Think of him as the garbage collector. He mightily kicks the sticky toxin out of the cell into the body of water that surrounds cells. From there, the toxin is whisked away for eventual excretion in urine, stool, hair, or sweat. The body does not want any delay in disposal of the sticky toxins since they can get stuck on all sorts of bodily workers whose important jobs are impaired when gummed up by harmful, gooey toxins.[13]

And when does the body do most of its clean-up work? As it turns out, nighttime is primetime for detoxification, as well as for growth and repair activities. Though the body may appear to be resting while asleep, it is really hustling and bustling around in there. Without the drain of its energy for daytime wakefulness and physical activity, the body finally gets a chance to get some work done. And as far as toxins and refuse go, the body wants them out of there—pronto. It knows that any source of toxin left to accumulate will cause injury.[14]

Anti-oxidant protection in the detoxification pathway

The second key service performed by UltraGuy (glutathione) in the detoxification pathway is anti-oxidant protection. To understand it, you must first know what oxidative stress is. Think of oxidative stress as a big, tough bully that no one can beat. He goes around looking for a defenseless cell molecule to pick on.

When he finds one, in effect he takes its lunch money. To some degree, oxidative stress lives in each of us as a destructive force that affects nearly all the molecules in the body, causing aging and deterioration. Oxidative stress can come from physical trauma, even from something seemingly minor like a sunburn. It can also result from exposure to chemicals or heavy metals like mercury or lead.[15]

Even though oxidative stress cannot be *fought* off, he can be *bought* off. If a cell molecule is lucky, he will have friends around like anti-oxidants. Vitamin C, for example, is one of the chief anti-oxidant allies. A good, protective friend like him will appease oxidative stress by interceding with his own lunch money. Satisfied, oxidative stress will leave the cell molecule alone. Of course, now the anti-oxidant is out of money. Fortunately, he can get back into the game thanks to a supremely wealthy and generous anti-oxidant friend—UltraGuy (glutathione). When playing the role of an anti-oxidant, UltraGuy (glutathione) gives spent anti-oxidants more lunch money. By resupplying them, he protects the health and normal functioning of cells, thus preventing their poor performance or untimely death.

In reality, oxidative stress is the result of stolen electrons, not lunch money. Even though it is hard for us to get excited about electrons, if you were a cell, you would be intensely upset about the loss of electrons from your molecules. Such losses can spell injury, disease, or death to a cell. Oxidative stress results from a nasty habit oxygen has. Though we usually think of oxygen as good, it is not in this respect because of its greed for electrons. By stealing them, oxygen leaves its victim "oxidized," which is a stressful event: thus, the term *oxidative stress*. Visually, we see victims of oxidative stress in rust on metal, tarnish on silver, and fire on wood. In these examples, the victims (metal, silver, wood) are being robbed of their electrons by oxygen.[16] If you had magical eyes that could see the effects of oxidative stress on a cell, you would be able to appreciate the injury that can be inflicted on cells. It is as though the cells are rusting.

SUMMARY OF THE FOUR CHEMICAL PATHWAYS

So far, you have been introduced to the main functions of the four chemical pathways known to be ailing on the autism spectrum.[17] The various "characters" involved in each pathway were identified along with a description of what each is *supposed* to be doing. A summary of this information is provided in Table 17.1. The key characters in each pathway and their activities are listed. Also noted are the names of the true chemical counterparts of each character in the superhero illustration.

Table 17.1 Summary of the four chemical pathways

Chemical pathway	Key characters and activities	True chemical identities
Methionine Cycle	Captain Delivery delivers life force to needy citizens at the mouth of the energy pathway. Decision Dude can either: • detour onto the detoxification pathway with his sulfur or • restock life force from the life-force supply cycle so the methionine cycle can be repeated.	Captain Delivery (with life force)—methionine (an essential amino acid) Life force—methyl groups (like hot potatoes, they energize their owner) Decision Dude (has no life force)—homocysteine (a chemical)
Life-Force Supply Cycle (actually called the folate cycle)	Methyl-B12 or TMG restock life force to Decision Dude in the methionine cycle.	Methyl-B12—a specific form of vitamin B12 TMG—trimethyl glycine (a methyl group supplement)
Energy Pathway	Needy citizens receive life force from the methionine cycle. Together, citizens and life force influence energy, sleep, and gene changes within cells.	
Detoxification Pathway (actually called the transsulfuration pathway)	Decision Dude delivers sulfur to the detoxification pathway. Vitamin B6 assists in Decision Dude's transformation to UltraGuy. UltraGuy has a dual role: • As leading detoxifier, he acts like a garbage collector to carry toxins and heavy metals out of the cell. • As the ultimate anti-oxidant, he rescues molecules in the cell from injury or death at the hands of oxidative stress.	UltraGuy—glutathione

GENETIC SUSCEPTIBILITY OF BODY CHEMISTRY TO AUTISM-SPECTRUM DISORDERS

Like anything else in the body, the operations of chemical pathways are influenced by genes. Researchers have identified several genetic variations of the methionine cycle and detoxification pathway that are significantly more frequent in autistic children than control children.[18] That tells us that certain combinations of genetic variation in body chemistry are more vulnerable to autism. As long as stressors from the environment remain within the chemistry's ability to cope, no disorders surface. However, if environmental stress is too great, genetically vulnerable chemistry will succumb to impairment, sending powerful waves of impact throughout the body and setting a course for an autism-spectrum disorder.[19] This leads us to the next logical question. Do we find any unusual stressors in body chemistry on the autism spectrum?

AN OVERWHELMING STRESSOR: SEVERE OXIDATIVE STRESS

On the autism spectrum, the tranquil scene of smooth-running body chemistry has been overshadowed by a dark cloud, an extremely high level of oxidative stress. Children with autism, as a group, are found to have substantially more oxidative stress than typical children. In fact, they exhibit signs of severe oxidative stress. This stress is a major force that perpetuates the autistic condition.[20]

Oxidative stress disrupts the methodical clockwork of the methionine and life-force supply cycles, thereby impairing the other pathways in turn. An unfortunate weakness of interdependent pathways is that a problem in one place often leads to problems in other places, like a food fight that starts with the small, careless fling of a single cheese cube. Before you know it, an entire wedding reception is engulfed in a frenzy of air-borne cuisine. In the end, the lovely bride in her regal gown and flowing veil is assailed by the cherished wedding cake. Every guest is horrified and marvels how the situation got so out of hand. Even as the cake top sinks to the bottom of the champagne fountain, they all know the happy couple's future lies in jeopardy. Yes, one thing leads to another in interdependent chemical pathways. Each "thing" is actually an attempt by the pathways to regain balance, but the immense flood of oxidative stress found on the autism spectrum is too great. The pathways are overwhelmed, and their attempts to regain a foothold are in vain. The rest of this chapter will explore the disruption caused by oxidative stress, as well as its impact. Along the way we will discover *why* oxidative stress is so severe on the autism spectrum.

Points of disruption in body chemistry due to oxidative stress

The flood of oxidative stress seen on the autism spectrum upsets normal cell chemistry at the three key points where the methionine cycle interacts with the other pathways.[21] Figure 17.3 shows these points of disruption.

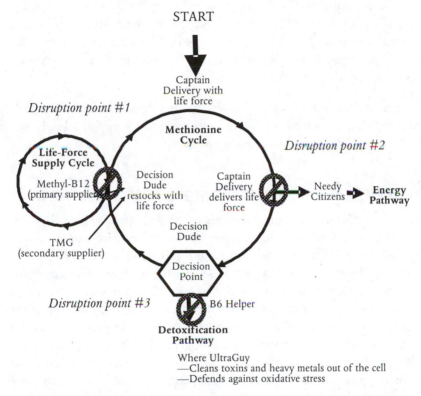

Figure 17.3 Three points of disruption caused by oxidative stress

Disruption Point #1: Life-force supply cycle. Oxidative stress inhibits restocking of life force (methyl groups) to Decision Dude (homocysteine). As a result, Decision Dudes (homocysteine) stop in the roadway to wait for the arrival of life force (methyl groups) from the life-force supply cycle (folate cycle). The waiting Decision Dudes (homocysteine) create a traffic jam along the methionine roundabout.[22]

Disruption Point #2: Energy pathway. Oxidative stress inhibits delivery of life force (methyl groups) to needy citizens. This problem results from the long back-up of Decision Dudes (homocysteine) who are waiting for the life-force supply cycle.

As they wait, they form a traffic jam that wraps all the way to the opposite side of the methionine roundabout and blocks the entrance to the energy pathway. The Captain Deliveries (methionine) who want to deliver life force (methyl groups) find themselves stuck in traffic unable to reach the citizens.[23]

Disruption Point #3: Detoxification pathway. Oxidative stress prevents Decision Dudes (homocysteine) from exiting onto the detoxification pathway. The Decision Dudes (homocysteine) sense that the citizens are in dire need of life-force (methyl groups) deliveries. As a result, they decide to pass up the opportunity to deliver their sulfur. Rather, they stay in the methionine cycle in the hope of helping the citizens. Unfortunately, they get stuck in the paralyzed traffic like everybody else and are of no help to anyone.[24]

The impact of missed deliveries to the energy and detoxification pathways is severe. We'll first take a look at the consequences in the energy pathway before moving on to those in the detoxification pathway.

CONSEQUENCES OF DISRUPTION IN THE ENERGY PATHWAY

When oxidative stress interrupts the supply of life force (methyl groups) to the energy pathway, the cell does not get enough energy. As a result, its awareness and ability will be impaired, thus hindering its job performance. Furthermore, the energy pathway may not be able to produce adequate levels of melatonin to regulate normal sleep patterns. In addition, severe and sustained oxidative stress can induce the energy pathway to turn off certain genes within the cell. Such gene changes are the result of a metabolic cause rather than a genetic cause. The affected genes include ones that promote production of UltraGuy (glutathione). Turning them off is the exact opposite of what is needed to cope with the flood of oxidative stress and to promote detoxification. Unfortunately, such gene changes can have significant, long-term effects on cell function. The good news is that, when genetic abnormalities are acquired in this way, oxidative stress can, at least to some extent, be reversed. However, reversal may not be complete due to the long-term nature of altered genes.[25]

THE ENERGY PATHWAY AND BRAIN CELLS

So far, we have been discussing cells in general. But there are many different kinds of cells, and some are more important than others. For example, take the cells that grow hair on your legs—maybe not all that important. If they rust a little, so what? But what about cells in our organs? We care about them. And what about brain cells in particular? There the stakes are supremely high.

Let's focus on brain cells for a moment. With their high energy requirement, they are particularly sensitive to oxidative stress, making the brain a high-risk organ.[26] What exactly do brain cells do with the energy they receive from the energy pathway? Most of the energy is spent on various forms of communication, synchronized communication, that is.[27] In fact, synchronized communication is the meaning of life to a brain cell. Whether the cells are perceiving their world, responding to it, thinking, or learning, they are communicating. And their communication *should* be a chorus of unified voices all singing the same song. Each cell needs to do his part at a precisely timed moment so that together the cells create a masterpiece of unity. Think of a choir. The sopranos, altos, tenors, and basses all sing different parts, but their harmonious music is carefully integrated so the result is a glorious, unified composition. The listener hears *one* song, not a multitude of songs. Likewise, thanks to synchronized communication, the brain can behave as *one* mind, not the many individual minds (or cells) that it actually is.

AN EXAMPLE OF SYNCHRONIZED COMMUNICATION

Take vision, for example. When light enters the eye, it activates millions of individual sensory cells in the retina. Some cells detect color, others depth, texture, or movement. All these scattered bits of perception are useless unless they can be combined in a meaningful way to form an image. That is the brain's job.[28] It not only unites diverse fragments of visual information but goes a step further to fuse the resulting image with additional sensory collections like smells, sounds, tastes, and touches. It integrates these perceptions with knowledge from memory to form recognition, understanding, and response, all in an instant. What a fascinating, incredible ability. So, say I go to a picnic at a campground. Thirsty, I flip open a cooler of drinks and jut my hand inside for refreshment. Unexpectedly, my fingers seize hold of a bewildered, trapped skunk. Boom! My brain cells blaze in rapid fire and pelt the brain with a full gamut of perception—sight, smell, sound, and touch. Each tidbit coalesces in the brain to form the essence of "skunk," complete with recognition and a revelation of potential consequences. In a nanosecond, on legs that are a blur, I have cleared the picnic area and am half-way down the turnpike. What an incredible, instantaneous leap from initial stimulus to response! But that is what brains do; they are masters of communication through synchronized firing of cells.

AN ESPECIALLY IMPORTANT FUNCTION: THE D4 DOPAMINE RECEPTOR

Within the brain, dopamine receptors specialize in conducting impulses. These receptors play key roles in many processes including attention, motivation, learning, and fine motor development. Abnormal signaling from dopamine receptors is implicated in several neuropsychiatric disorders. Therefore, these receptors are common targets for neurologic drugs.

In a perfect world, we would have complete knowledge of how malfunctions in the methionine cycle affect every type of cell in the body, including the brain's dopamine receptors. However, in the real world, we have to settle for less than complete knowledge. Nevertheless, some intriguing research has been done that sheds considerable light on one type of dopamine receptor: the D4 dopamine receptor. This receptor affects synchrony in the brain during attention.[29] It is of keen interest since every autism-spectrum disorder, from ADD (attention deficit disorder) to autism, displays a significant attention problem. So let's take a look at this important receptor.

Everything presented earlier about the operations of the methionine cycle holds true for D4 dopamine receptors with one important exception. The exception lies in the available ways that the receptor can get or create Captain Delivery (methionine), the all-important delivery boy of both life force (methyl groups) and sulfur. As discussed earlier in the chapter, the methionine cycle obtained or created Captain Delivery (methionine) in three ways:

○ methyl-B12 restocking of life force (methyl groups)

○ TMG restocking of life force (methyl groups)

○ the diet.

D4 dopamine receptors, however, are a little different. They only have one of these sources at their disposal: methyl-B12 restocking. By relying on a single source, all the eggs are in one basket. So, if there is no methyl-B12 to restock life force (methyl groups), you can just forget it—no other backup options exist for creation of Captain Delivery (methionine). This makes the D4 dopamine receptor especially vulnerable to disruption by oxidative stress. When oxidative stress interferes with methyl-B12 restocking, the impact on attention is severe. Genetic differences in the D4 receptor have already been linked to risk of ADHD and also the personality trait of novelty seeking. These same genetic differences affect synchrony in the brain during attention. It seems likely that the impaired brain synchrony we see in autism is caused by impaired performance of D4 receptors due to oxidative stress.[30]

On the autism spectrum, brain cells suffer energy deficiency, as well as loss of coordination with each other. The two go hand in hand. When some cells have to wait for energy to arrive, they will chime out of sync with their comrades, so that the brain is no longer a chorus of unified voices all singing the same song to create an integrated masterpiece of unity and precision.[31] Instead, it has deteriorated into a jumble of individual voices sounding off as they are able. Synchrony of cell firing is impaired and, with it, appropriate response and behavior.

A PORTRAIT OF AUTISM: OUT-OF-SYNC PROCESSING

Can you possibly imagine what it is like to live in a body whose perceptions of reality are jumbled and distorted, a body where internal signaling is so clumsy and haphazard that we are of many minds, not just one? Perhaps it is like watching a video when the sound track is slightly out of sync from the motion picture. Or maybe it is like viewing a foreign film in which voices in your language have been dubbed over the original ones. In both these examples, the movement of people's lips is out of time to the words being heard. Facial expression and body language briefly—but constantly—contradict the tone of voice, inflection, and spoken meaning. Such out-of-step messages grate our nerves and detract from our comprehension. In self-defense, we move our focus away from the sources of conflicting signals—certainly the lips, maybe even the faces. They are much too annoying to watch.

Now try to envision adding another layer of complexity in our video. This time, let's say the voices are no longer distinct and clear, but are stretched out and distorted as if running on slow speed. The depth of concentration required to decipher the words would grow quite taxing. We might even give up trying to visually match the voices to the lips or facial expressions. Perhaps we would have to ignore completely tone of voice and inflection in the hope of gaining comprehension. To do so, we would focus on the words alone. If we could just decipher them, we might understand enough to get by. However, when we do this, some nuances of communication escape us. Take sarcasm, for instance. Its requirement for integration of the words with other communication clues would be much too difficult. Figurative language would elude us as well since we would be riveted on simply decoding the words as we try to grasp their literal meaning. It would be unrealistic for us to be able to translate the words further from the literal to the figurative. But so what? Who cares? We are doing the best we can, right?

It may give you a headache, but now try to compound this mismatched experience with even more complexity. Factor in sensory inputs like smells and tastes and include sensations like touching, being touched, and awareness of body position and of room temperature. Imagine that this time, again, perception of each input is out of sync with all the other perceptions. It would be enough to drive us mad. The world would become a confusing, demanding, and agitating place. We would have to withdraw from such an annoying world, don't you think? Its chaos would force our retreat. We would be compelled to tune it all out as best we could. Only within our limits for tolerance could we occasionally sample its offerings. Even then, we would sometimes feel violated. At times, in self-defense, we would be forced to lash out or run away from such a maddening world. It wouldn't be our fault, of course, because we are feeling so cornered and harassed. Fight or flight would be our only choices. Such a world leaves no in-between.

This description paints a bleak, though perhaps realistic, picture of what it might be like to live within a disordered body. For our lifetimes, we would be assailed by stampedes of conflicting, mismatched messages. In a body like that, how could we be expected to respond appropriately or to function at all? The more out of sync our world, the less able we would be to respond to it and abide by its unreasonable expectations for behavior and conduct.

CONSEQUENCES OF DISRUPTION IN THE DETOXIFICATION PATHWAY

Now that we have explored the consequences of oxidative stress in the energy pathway, we can move on to its impact in the detoxification pathway. Along the way, we will discover the cause of the flood of destructive oxidative stress that is so common on the autism spectrum.

As already discussed, the high level of oxidative stress found on the autism spectrum prevents Decision Dude (homocysteine) from exiting onto the detoxi-fication pathway with his precious sulfur.[32] What impact does this have? Research has found that autistic children have some severely abnormal levels of substances involved in the methionine cycle and detoxification pathway. For one, they have low levels of methionine (Captain Delivery), the central figure of importance in the methionine cycle. Other key substances are also significantly low, including the critical player glutathione (UltraGuy).[33] These are clear signs that body chemistry is ailing.

Right in the pinch of the game, when glutathione (UltraGuy) is needed the most for protection of cells from oxidative stress, he is not around. But where could he be at a time like this? Without his fulfilling the role of the supreme anti-oxidant, there is no one to replenish other anti-oxidants as they try to protect the cell. So, once they are spent, they stay that way. As a result, the cell takes a beating from the merciless bully, oxidative stress. Like an old car body being eaten away by rust, the cell can slip into decline or suffer an untimely death. When oxidative stress is persistent, a cell will often try to protect itself by becoming inflamed. This helps limit oxidation and its harmful effects. Inflammation is a common finding on the autism spectrum. We often see it in the digestive tract and other body tissues, even the brain itself.[34]

And what about the role of glutathione (UltraGuy) as the indispensable garbage collector? When glutathione is lacking, clean-up work gets neglected. As a result, everyday toxins and heavy metals do not merely pass through the body for a visit. With no one to boot them out, many will be left to loiter in the cell, where they settle down and make a home. By forming bonds with molecules in cells, they become a harmful part of the cell impairing its health and ability.[35] The thought of toxins accumulating in the bodies of our children on the autism spectrum is alarming. What proof do we have that it is really happening?

BABY HAIR TELLS A TALE IN AUTISM

No matter who we are, some level of heavy metals will manage to sneak into our bodies. But as long as our bodies' detoxification processes are in working order, the heavy metals will be purged out. Hair is one means of flushing out heavy metals. So we expect to find some level excreted in our hair. Now you know how some of us put clips of baby hair into baby books? What would we find if we analyzed that hair for heavy metals? The results might be interesting since they would tell us something about the quality of a child's detoxification chemistry.

Amy Holmes, MD, and her colleagues were curious about this, especially about mercury levels in baby hair. So, baby hair cut at 15–24 months of age was collected from baby books of both typical children and autistic children. The hair was tested for mercury. The findings sent a message that was loud and clear. The baby hair of children who developed autism had mercury levels that were seven times *less* than the children who developed normally.[36] That means they were holding on to incoming mercury, rather than purging it out through their hair. And the more severe the autism, the lower the level of mercury in the hair.

Let's pause for a minute to consider what it means to find a seven-times difference. That is an unheard of magnitude for a research study. Such a finding leaves no room for doubt. For comparison, take drug research. If a drug being studied works 15 *percent* better than a placebo, we consider that proof that the drug really works.[37] Yet 15 percent is peanuts compared to the seven-times difference found by Dr. Holmes. Later, James Adams, PhD, at the University of Arizona repeated this baby-hair study with a similar result. Again, the difference was huge, only this time it was five times rather than seven.[38] Another confirmation came from a study at Massachusetts Institute of Technology (MIT) where nuclear scientists used neutron activation analysis to analyze the hair.[39] The findings of these studies reveal that the quality of the autistic children's detoxification chemistry is exceedingly poor. The flow of heavy metals entering their bodies is staying, not leaving.

After learning of these studies, I decided to have Will's baby hair tested. I used hair that had been lovingly put away in his baby book when he was 7 months old—long before any inkling of autism spectrum disorders loomed on the horizon. Of the 15 toxic elements evaluated, only six—including mercury—were low enough to fall within the expected range. Six others rocketed to the extreme high end of the scale on the very edge of the chart; they included aluminum, lead, uranium, tin, cadmium, and antimony. Something had to have been seriously out of place for such a seemingly protected and nurtured baby to have such shockingly high levels of numerous toxic elements.

HIGH BODY BURDEN OF HEAVY METALS ON THE AUTISM SPECTRUM AND ITS EFFECT

Various research has shown that many children on the autism spectrum carry a high burden of heavy metals in their bodies, particularly mercury, but also lead, arsenic, antimony, tin, and aluminum. PCBs (polychlorinated biphenyls) and volatile organic solvents have been found as well.[40]

Researcher Richard Deth, PhD, at Northeastern University in Boston found that even low levels of heavy metals are capable of impairing detoxification chemistry and triggering high levels of oxidative stress. It is likely that other toxins like pesticides have a similar effect.[41] Thus, a person exposed to heavy metals will suffer an explosion of oxidative stress that can injure tissues throughout the body including the brain.[42]

Think of the body's detoxification chemistry as if it were a dam that protects a town from flooding. As long as the dam holds, the town is safe. But if it breaks, flood water will overwhelm the town causing extensive damage. Oxidative stress is the flood water; it does the bulk of actual damage. Yet, the breaking of the detoxification chemistry is what allowed the destructive flood of oxidative stress.

The tragedy of heavy metals or other toxins is that they impair the very chemistry that is indispensable for their removal.[43] Over time, the continuing tide of toxins can further enfeeble the weak detoxification chemistry. Picture a mudslide swallowing up an expressway. That is what is happening to detoxification on the autism spectrum.[44] Though a single heavy metal may have caused the initial impairment, it will not be the only heavy metal to accumulate because, once detoxification is weakened, any heavy metal or toxin that comes in the door will stay if it doesn't get booted out. Thus, multiple heavy metals and toxins may begin to accumulate.

Unfortunately, when it comes to heavy metals exposure, the detoxification chemistry is not the only bodily treasure in torment. It is well known that heavy metals and toxins also suppress the immune system.[45] As a result, a weakened immune system will succumb to infection, often followed by antibiotic use. Together, they compound and intensify the body's problems.[46] As Chapter 23 will explain, streams of tumbling dominoes in the digestive tract may begin to cascade along new and expanded trails. Disruption makes its way not only into the immune system and digestive tract but the brain and nervous system as well.[47] Along the way, many of the body's treasured abilities can ebb away. They are replaced by:

- impaired attention and cognition
- out-of-sync brain signaling
- intensified fight-or-flight response
- inflammation in the brain, gut, and immune system
- autoimmunity (immune system attacks tissues of the body)
- skewing of immune system balance (which results in increased vulnerability to infection, as well as hypersensitivity to harmless substances like pollen and food)
- leaky gut and poor absorption of nutrients in food
- undesirable changes in gene expression.[48]

Many of these problems will be described in detail in later chapters. See Figure 17.4 for the flow of key events in body chemistry and their main consequences which can ultimately lead to an autism-spectrum diagnosis.[49]

A MAJOR CULPRIT BEHIND THE AUTISM EPIDEMIC

Many who suffer from autism-spectrum disorders have acquired this condition through malfunctions in detoxification, oxidative stress, and inflammation.[50] The epidemic we are witnessing has emerged in children with a vulnerable genetic makeup in basic cell chemistry. Heavy metals or toxins from the environment have overwhelmed that chemistry and crippled it to varying degrees in different children.[51] Without the insults, a vulnerable child could have escaped a diagnosis on the autism spectrum. In fact, his predecessors had done so for generations. However, with the insults in play, it is another story. The insults cause a derailment that spawns an altogether different journey.

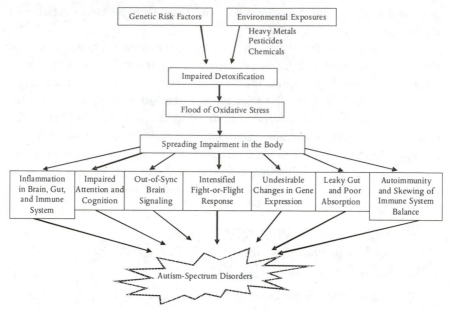

Figure 17.4 Flow of key events in body chemistry and their main consequences

As you have seen in this chapter, several research discoveries have illuminated key pieces of the autism puzzle. These pieces involve the crucial pathways of body chemistry that encompass the methionine cycle and its neighbors. Through research, many children on the autism spectrum have been found to have:

- O   genetic vulnerability in these critical pathways
- O   clear signs of impaired health in these pathways (low glutathione, low methionine, etc.)
- O   extremely high levels of damaging oxidative stress
- O   high body burden of accumulated heavy metals.

In addition, research has demonstrated the extreme effectiveness of heavy metals to impair this body chemistry and trigger high levels of oxidative stress. As a result, cells are injured and their performance impaired. Even cell death is a possibility. As more and more cells succumb to the effects of oxidative stress, their cumulative malfunction amplifies to a cataclysmic level in the overall functioning of the body. Outward symptoms and behaviors eventually surface. As a society, we have grown skilled at describing and classifying these behaviors under many labels: ADD, ADHD, PDD, AS, HFA, and autism. Yet, what has thrown us for a loop is figuring out what *causes* these behaviors. The good news is that Defeat Autism Now! is rapidly gaining knowledge in this area. Research has unlocked some of the secrets in body chemistry that enable us to help the ailing chemistry and remove accumulated heavy metals. Through such treatments, many on the autism spectrum have improved dramatically.[52]

I WAS SKEPTICAL THAT HEAVY METALS COULD CAUSE AUTISM

When I first heard Defeat Autism Now! talk about toxin-induced autism, I was skeptical. First of all, it was not a message I had ever heard from any of my mainstream "experts." How could it possibly be true? Second, Will had never been exposed to heavy metals—or so I thought.

Nevertheless, it was quite unsettling to discover that heavy metals like mercury and lead cause some of the same symptoms and behaviors I saw in Will. Mercury, for example, can cause poor memory and concentration, agitation, and staring spells, as well as cognitive and social deficits. Lead poisoning is linked to attention deficit, as well as impaired intelligence and lower school performance. In addition, heavy metals can impair the immune system and injure something called gut flora, thus serving as a trigger for a downward spiral of decline in the digestive tract.[53]

It was cause to make me wonder. Besides, Defeat Autism Now! had been right several times before about interventions that really made a difference in Will. Perhaps there was something to their notion about heavy metals. It would cost dearly if I discounted the idea and later discovered Will really had needed treatment. So, to me, it seemed sensible at least to have Will tested. Testing would either lay to rest my concerns over heavy metals or make me aware of something critically important that I needed to treat. So, I ran tests. And you know what? The tests revealed heavy-metal overload. It was a traumatic but pivotal discovery. What had been mere speculation became a known fact. My son's body was home-sweet-home to damaging heavy metals that were inflicting harm wherever they festered. It was hard for me to believe, but my protected, nurtured child had heavy-metal poisoning. No wonder he faced so many problems. At least now I knew.

This knowledge put me in a powerful position to do something about the problem. There are effective interventions to salvage the body chemistry and also treatments to remove heavy metals that accumulated while the chemistry was under-performing. According to the ARI parent ratings of interventions, treatment for removal of heavy metals (labeled Detox. Chelation) made 74 percent of children better. That is the highest "got-better" rating of any intervention in the entire chart across all drugs, diets, and supplements. Only 3 percent of children got worse. So, to me, it made sense to treat. I did not feel I could leave accumulated heavy metals in my son that would continue to perpetuate his problems. I treated, and you know what happened? Heavy metals have poured out of him month after month. Excessively high levels of mercury, tin, nickel, and arsenic have raised their ugly heads on his periodic test results. The good news is that, through treatment of Will's ailing body chemistry and heavy-metal overload, his autistic behaviors loosened their grip. He kept getting better, a lot better.

INTERVENTIONS IN THE COMING CHAPTERS

I encourage you to read the coming chapters that discuss biomedical interventions for body chemistry and heavy-metal overload.[54] There are interventions to:

1. *Get the ailing body chemistry working better.* Chapter 18 covers common interventions to improve the operation of the methionine cycle and its neighbors.

2. *Remove accumulated heavy metals and toxins.* Chapter 19 describes lab testing for heavy-metal overload, as well as treatment options to remove heavy metals if an overload is found to exist.

3. *Minimize ongoing exposures to heavy metals and toxins.* Chapters 20 through 22 explore various ways children get exposed to heavy metals, particularly mercury, the most common offender on the autism spectrum.

NOTES

1.   James 2007, p. 172.
2.   McCandless 2007, p. 220; McCandless 2005, p. 3; Kirby 2005, p. 293.
3.   Pangborn and Baker 2005, p. 2:7.
4.   Ibid., p. 1:14; Pangborn and Baker 2007, p. 14; Lewis 2005, pp. 19–20.
5.   Jepson and Johnson 2007, pp. 100–101.
6.   Deth 2006, p. 108.
7.   James 2007, p. 167.
8.   Pangborn and Baker 2005, p. 3:23.
9.   Cordain and Friel 2005, p. 149.
10. Pangborn and Baker 2005, p. 3:11.
11. Kirby 2005, pp. 293, 321; Jepson and Johnson 2007, p. 102.
12. Pangborn and Baker 2005, p. 3:12.

13. Baker 2006a, p. 203; Pangborn and Baker 2007, p. 6.

14. Pangborn and Baker 2007, p. 17.

15. Ibid., p. 5.

16. Baker 2004, pp. 176–80.

17. For in-depth information about the chemical pathways discussed in this chapter, see Pangborn and Baker (2005), *Autism: Effective Biomedical Treatments*, pages 1:12–16 and 3:9–27. Additional information is provided in the *2007 Supplement of Autism: Effective Biomedical Treatments*, pages 37–46.

18. Kirby 2005, pp. 294–95, 407; Jepson and Johnson 2007, pp. 110–11.

19. Kirby 2005, p. 407.

20. Pangborn and Baker 2007, pp. 5, 37; Deth 2007b, p. 174; James *et al.* 2006, pp. 947–56; James *et al.* 2004, pp. 1611–17.

21. Deth 2007a, pp. 41–44.

22. Kirby 2005, p. 347.

23. Pangborn and Baker 2005, pp. 3:13–14; James 2007, pp. 167–68.

24. James 2006b, p. 176; McCandless 2007, p. 223.

25. Deth 2007a, pp. 41–44.

26. Jepson and Johnson 2007, p. 221.

27. Pangborn and Baker 2005, pp. 3:21–22.

28. Ibid., p. 3:26.

29. Ibid., pp. 3:23, 26.

30. Pangborn and Baker 2007, p. 43; Deth 2006, p. 108; James 2006a, p. 114.

31. Pangborn and Baker 2005, pp. 3:11, 25.

32. James 2006b, p. 176; McCandless 2007, p. 223.

33. Kirby 2005, pp. 294–95, 337, 347; Jepson and Johnson 2007, pp. 108–10; Pangborn and Baker 2007, p. 5.

34. Pangborn and Baker 2007, p. 37; Baker 2004, pp. 176–80; El-Dahr 2006b, p. 158; Lewis 2005, pp. 19–20.

35. Pangborn and Baker 2005, p. 3:17; McCandless 2007, p. 49.

36. Holmes, Blaxill, and Haley 2003, pp. 277–85; Kirby 2005, pp. 200–201, 322.

37. Pangborn and Baker 2007, p. 4; Baker 2006a, p. 204.

38. Adams, Levine, and Lin-Wen 2006; McCandless 2007, p. 51; Kirby 2005, p. 319.

39. Kirby 2005, p. 354.

40. McCandless 2007, pp. 49, 51; Green 2006a, p. 3; Bradstreet 2006, p. 270; Nataf *et al.* 2006, pp. 99–108; Bradstreet *et al.* 2003, pp. 76–79; Bock and Stauth 2007, p. 293.

41. Waly, *et al.* 2004, p.358; Pangborn and Baker 2005, pp. 1:11, 3:16; Pangborn and Baker 2007, p. 20.

42. McCandless 2007, p. 52; Pangborn and Baker 2005, p. 1:11.

43. Pangborn and Baker 2007, p. 18; Baker, James, and Milivojevich 2006, pp. 115–16; Bock and Stauth 2007, p. 56.

44. Green 2006a, p. 3.

45. McCandless 2007, p. 177.

46. Pangborn and Baker 2007, p. 18; Pangborn and Baker 2005, p. 1:11.

47. James 2007, p. 172; McCandless 2007, p. 52.

48. Deth 2006, p. 108; Mumper 2005, webcast; Deth 2007b, p. 181; Deth 2006, p. 108; Mumper 2005; Bock and Stauth 2007, p. 294; James 2007, p. 170; James 2006b, p. 179; Deth 2007a, pp. 41–44.

49. Deth 2007b, p. 181.
50. Pangborn and Baker 2007, pp. 20, 25, 28.
51. Ibid., p. 43; Bock and Stauth 2007, p. 293; Deth 2007b, p. 174; James *et al.* 2006, pp. 947–56; McCandless 2007, p. 134; Rimland 2006a, pp. 406–407; Green 2006c, p. 11; Kirby 2005, pp. 294–95, 347.
52. Kirby 2005, pp. 294–95; Edelson and Cantor 1998, pp. 553–63; Bock and Stauth 2007, p. 294; McCandless 2007, pp. 49–50, 59.
53. McCandless 2007, pp. 28, 53, 54, 82, 97; Bernard *et al.* 2001, pp. 462–71.
54. Pangborn and Baker 2007, p. 43.

Chapter 18

Common Interventions for Ailing Body Chemistry

WHAT THIS CHAPTER IS ABOUT

The previous chapter described the problems commonly found in fundamental body chemistry on the autism spectrum. This chapter reviews the interventions most frequently recommended by Defeat Autism Now! to get the chemistry working better. It also introduces the Pfeiffer Treatment Center, a clinic that researches biochemical imbalances and individualizes treatment programs to correct imbalances in children and adults.

Although it is best to start interventions for autism-spectrum disorders in the digestive tract rather than body chemistry, I chose to discuss body chemistry first because it is important for you to understand what, for many children, is the *root cause* of their autism-spectrum disorder. You should recognize that, until problems in the digestive tract are addressed, other interventions will be less effective and more complicated.[1] Nevertheless, since we started in body chemistry, we will stick with it before going on to the digestive tract in later chapters.

BODY CHEMISTRY IS NOT SIMPLE, SO NEITHER IS ITS INTERVENTION

For simplicity, the superhero illustration of the previous chapter left out a multitude of intermediate players and processes. Body chemistry is actually quite complex, so do not be surprised if interventions for body chemistry can get a little involved. There is not just one magical intervention that can fix all the varied problems of faltering chemistry; rather, there are several different points in the chemistry where we can lend a helping hand. At these points, it helps if we provide a substance that is deficient or at least the raw materials that the chemistry needs to produce the deficient substance on its own. Therefore, many substances (be they vitamin, mineral, or supplement) will be recommended in this chapter. Try not to be overwhelmed by their number. Instead, think of each one as an *opportunity*, a secret weapon, to help your child. Then the various options will seem more like friends that help rather than foes that overwhelm. Besides, they are not a to-do list so much as they are a list of options to try. Pick and choose those interventions you think might be of most benefit to your individual child. To assist, the ARI parent ratings are presented for those interventions that have been rated. Like any good detective, try out an intervention to see what effect (if any) it has on your child. When you find something that works, pat yourself on the back. Congratulations are in order. For those interventions that do not seem to help, retire them. And, as always, stay within your limits of comfort level, time, finances, or whatever other constraints you face.

CATEGORIES OF INTERVENTIONS TO GET BODY CHEMISTRY WORKING BETTER

Various vitamins, minerals, and supplements can be used to improve the performance of body chemistry. The three areas targeted by these interventions are:

- restocking of life force (methyl groups) to Decision Dude (homocysteine)
- detoxification
- oxidative stress.

The following pages explore each of these areas in turn. Some of the nutrients that are named will be familiar from the superhero illustration in the last chapter, while others will be new. Think of the new ones as supporting actors. They are part of the details left out of the superhero illustration, yet they are important just the same. The interventions identified in this chapter are the ones most often recommended by Defeat Autism Now! to help body chemistry. However, they are not the only ones. If you like, you can investigate additional ones by looking up the references mentioned in these pages. All interventions identified in this chapter are available over-the-counter unless otherwise noted.

This chapter names several nutrients. A few will be discussed in some detail. Additional information about nutrient supplementation appears in Appendix C, which includes recommended dosages from Defeat Autism Now! sources. The appendix also points you to additional sources of excellent information about various nutrients.

Supplements to restock life force (methyl groups) to Decision Dude (homocysteine)

As pointed out in the last chapter, there are several trouble spots in body chemistry on the autism spectrum. If we can tweak that chemistry in the right ways, we might be able to get those cycles humming again. But what are the "right ways"? One obvious trouble spot is the impaired ability to restock life force (methyl groups) to Decision Dude (homocysteine). Trouble at this point sends problems rippling throughout the chemical pathways.

Jill James, PhD, of the Arkansas Children's Hospital Research Institute led a team of researchers and medical doctors to investigate how to improve life-force (methyl groups) restocking. She found a three-way tweak that restored UltraGuy (glutathione) to near-normal levels and reversed oxidative stress. The tweak involved the following supplements:[2]

1. *Methyl-B12* is the primary supplier of life force (methyl groups) to Decision Dude (homocysteine). It will be discussed in more detail momentarily.

2. *TMG* (trimethyl glycine) is a secondary supplier of life force (methyl groups) to Decision Dude (homocysteine). Dr. James' study used 1000mg per day of TMG. For some individuals, a similar supplement, DMG (dimethyl glycine), is used in place of TMG to do the same job.[3]

3. *Folinic acid* plays a vital supporting role by helping to produce methyl-B12. Many children cannot get body chemistry working right without taking it. Folinic acid is a specific form of the B-vitamin folic acid. It is important for autistic children to take it in this exact form since the body metabolizes it differently than ordinary folic acid. Dr. James' study used 800mcg per day of folinic acid.[4]

Though each of these supplements can be beneficial alone, when used together as a team, they create a synergy whose benefit is greater than the sum of their individual contributions.[5] Here is what the ARI parent ratings have to say about use of some of these supplements. Though the ratings evaluate folic acid, it is not listed here since folic acid is not the same as the folinic acid used in Dr. James' study.

	Got Worse	No Effect	Got Better	Better: Worse Ratio	No. of Cases
Methyl-B12 (subcut.)	7 percent	26 percent	67 percent	9.5:1	170
Methyl-B12 (nasal)	15 percent	29 percent	56 percent	3.9:1	48
Vitamin B12 (oral)	7 percent	32 percent	61 percent	8.6:1	98
TMG	15 percent	43 percent	42 percent	2.8:1	803
DMG	8 percent	51 percent	42 percent	5.4:1	5,807

Source: This and other ARI parent ratings found throughout the book are reproduced with permission of the Autism Research Institute. The complete rating tables can be found in Appendix B.

METHYL-B12 (ALSO CALLED METHYLCOBALAMIN)

Methyl-B12 merits special attention because it generates a remarkable response in a high percentage of children when given "the right way," according to pioneering researcher James Neubrander, MD.[6] Dr. Neubrander was the first to use methyl-B12 in autism and study various ways of administering it. His Web site, www.DrNeubrander.com/page1.html, offers detailed information from his research and experience. He reports that methyl-B12 affects all regions of the brain. The most obvious improvements for autistic children relate to:[7]

- o speech and language
- o emotion and socialization
- o spatial orientation and gross and fine motor skills
- o executive function (which includes numerous mental operations such as planning, inhibition of inappropriate action, initiation of appropriate action, time perception, working memory, and abstract thinking).

Yet these are not the only areas that may show benefit. Dr. Neubrander's Web site includes a comprehensive "Parent Designed Report Form." Parents can use this checklist of over 140 items to determine if and how their child is responding to methyl-B12 treatment. Dr. Neubrander is concerned that, if parents don't consider all the possible signs of improvement, they may not recognize improvement, even though it is taking place. This may be a possible explanation for why the ARI parent ratings don't necessarily reflect the findings of Dr. Neubrander's research.[8]

Methyl-B12 treatment is exceedingly safe, though, in some children, it can cause hyperactivity, irritability, or insomnia.[9] As long as these unwanted behaviors are tolerable, parents are encouraged to stay the course. Often times, the children with the most side effects make the most recovery. Within 2–6 months, most side effects diminish or disappear, while the child continues to improve. If treatment must stop due to intolerable side effects, the side effects will go away, though it may take several days to a few weeks for them to disappear completely.[10]

One might think that only those who have methyl-B12 deficiency will benefit from methyl-B12 treatment. However, for reasons that are not understood, that is not the case. Many children who benefit from treatment actually have high or high-normal levels of methyl-B12 in their blood before treatment begins. Thus, the only way to find out if a given person will respond to methyl-B12 is to run a trial.[11]

Vitamin B12 is not a single vitamin, but rather a family of five different B12 vitamins. Each member is distinctly different from the others. There is methyl-B12, hydroxy-B12, adenosyl-B12, and others. Though they are all members of the same family, they are *not* interchangeable. Methyl-B12 is the only one that makes a big splash on the autism spectrum.[12]

According to Dr. Neubrander's research, the most highly effective method of giving methyl-B12 is by injection (i.e., subcutaneously). Sorry, I know that is not what you wanted to hear. Yet several methods have been tested, and injection is the one that benefits the highest percentage of children. A positive response usually surfaces within the first few days.[13] Thus, thousands of parents throughout the U.S. and around the world have learned to give their children methyl-B12 shots. Some get a lesson at the doctor's office, while others read the detailed instruction sheet provided by the pharmacy. Instructions are also available on Dr. Neubrander's Web site along with videos of parents offering advice and demonstrations. Shots are given at home, usually one shot every three days. Some parents use a numbing cream at the injection site, which is on the child's bottom. Other parents forego the numbing cream because it is slow to take effect. Methyl-B12 shots are available only by prescription. They come in small syringes with short needles, only about ¼-inch long. Often, parents receive the pre-filled syringes by mail from a compounding pharmacy that is skilled in proper preparation of methyl-B12 injections for autism.[14]

The advantage of an injection over other methods is that the methyl-B12 is deposited into fatty tissue where it is slowly released to the body over a period of days.[15] This continuous feed stimulates a greater response than the temporary bursts supplied by other methods such as:

o   oral (swallowed by mouth)

- o sublingual (held under the tongue until dissolved)
- o nasal spray
- o cream (rubbed into the skin)
- o injection into muscle.

Injection into the fat of the bottom offers the slowest rate of release compared to injection in the arm, abdomen, or thigh. The benefit of a slower rate of release is that injections can be given less often.[16]

If shots are out of the question for you or your child, there are other methods of providing methyl-B12, though these methods have a lower rate of success. According to Dr. Neubrander, the second-best method of giving methyl-B12 is by nasal spray. This form requires a prescription and use of a compounding pharmacy.[17] You might be wondering why oral forms of methyl-B12 are not considered as effective as injections or nasal spray. The reason has to do with the complexity of B12 absorption from the digestive tract, especially when gut problems are present.[18]

Interventions that target detoxification chemistry

Rescue of detoxification chemistry is a high priority since many and probably most children on the autism spectrum have an impaired ability to detoxify.[19] The supplements already mentioned to improve the restocking of life force (methyl groups) to the methionine cycle also help detoxification since it lies in a depend-ent pathway. A couple of additional interventions are frequently promoted at Defeat Autism Now! conferences to help the detoxification chemistry. One is vitamin B6 with magnesium; the other is Epsom salt baths. Both are discussed next.

B6 AND MAGNESIUM HELP DETOXIFICATION

In the superhero illustration, B6 was an important player in the detoxification pathway. It assisted Decision Dude's transformation into UltraGuy (glutathione). Through its impact on body chemistry, B6 helps minimize autistic behaviors in many children on the spectrum.[20] Of all the biomedical interventions for autism-spectrum children, high-dose vitamin B6 has the longest history of safe and effective use. If a person's body needs B6, benefits will often show within a few days. However, if three-to-four weeks go by without improvement, B6 supplementation can be stopped. Since B6 can lower magnesium in the body, magnesium is always supplemented when B6 is given.[21] Here is what the ARI parent ratings have to say about the team of vitamin B6 and magnesium:

	Got Worse	No Effect	Got Better	Better: Worse Ratio	No. of Cases
Vitamin B6/ Magnesium	4 percent	48 percent	48 percent	11:1	6,634

EPSOM SALT BATHS HELP DETOXIFICATION

In a healthy body, Decision Dude (homocysteine) brings his precious sulfur down the detoxification pathway to help rid the body of heavy metals and toxins. Unfortunately, sulfur is deficient in many children on the autism spectrum.[22] Not only is it important for detoxification, but it also helps the lining of the gut and production of hormones.[23] One of the most effective ways to bring up sulfur levels is with Epsom salt (magnesium sulfate) baths. The magnesium and sulfate absorbed through the skin help detoxification.[24] So, two-to-three times a week, get out the rubber ducky for a 20-minute soak in a tub of warm water and two cups of Epsom salt.[25]

Anti-oxidants defend against oxidative stress

Children on the autism spectrum are often under significant oxidative stress.[26] To help protect cells from this stress, high doses of anti-oxidants are often needed. Of the many supplements available to combat oxidative stress, the ones cited most often are vitamin C, vitamin A, vitamin E, CoQ10, selenium, zinc, and melatonin.[27] The ARI parent ratings shed light on the helpfulness of some of these. Keep in mind that these supplements perform additional services for the body besides oxidative stress protection. For example, melatonin helps regulate sleep. Thus, the ratings reflect more than just the supplement's virtues as an anti-oxidant.

	Got Worse	No Effect	Got Better	Better: Worse Ratio	No. of Cases
Vitamin C	2 percent	55 percent	43 percent	19:1	2,397
Vitamin A	2 percent	57 percent	41 percent	18:1	1,127
Melatonin	8 percent	27 percent	65 percent	7.8:1	1,105
Zinc	2 percent	47 percent	51 percent	22:1	1,989

PFEIFFER TREATMENT CENTER

Defeat Autism Now! is not the only group able to alleviate autistic symptoms through nutrients that target body chemistry. There is also the Pfeiffer Treatment Center, a nonprofit, outpatient clinic. This clinic researches biochemical imbalances and treats both children and adults.

Pfeiffer's roots began in the 1970s with research into the causes of violent behavior in adults. Some of the prisoners and ex-offenders studied were found to have distinctive imbalances in body chemistry. Nutrient therapies were developed to correct these imbalances. Over time, Pfeiffer Treatment Center began treating imbalances in other disorders including depression, anxiety, bipolar disorder, schizophrenia, Alzheimer's, developmental delay, and learning and attention problems.

Treatment of autism-spectrum disorders began in 1994. Since that time, over 4,000 autism-spectrum patients have been evaluated and treated. These patients come from all over the U.S. and numerous other countries. They meet Pfeiffer physicians at the clinic's primary location in Illinois or at periodic outreach clinics in Minnesota, Maryland, California, and Arizona.[28]

Pfeiffer Treatment Clinic performs laboratory tests that its physicians use to diagnose biochemical imbalances. The physicians then design individualized nutrient programs of vitamins, minerals, fatty acids, and/or amino acids to correct the imbalances identified. Additional interventions such as special diets, digestive aids, and probiotics may also be recommended.[29] Over time, a patient's program is modified depending on subsequent changes in patient behavior and the results of follow-up laboratory tests.

The experience of the Pfeiffer Treatment Center is that the biochemistry of autism-spectrum disorders is very different from the rest of the population. Autism-spectrum patients often show increased heavy metals, low UltraGuy (glutathione), delivery problems with life force (methyl groups), zinc deficiency, copper excess, and decreased metallothionein (a sulfur-based protein that performs many key functions in the body). These abnormalities all point to significant problems with oxidative stress. According to the Pfeiffer Treatment Center, the primary cause of autism is an impaired metallothionein system. Autism is believed to result from genetic weakness in metals chemistry followed by an environmental insult such as heavy-metal exposure in the first two-to-three years of life.[30] More information about Pfeiffer Treatment Center and its autism research is available in a 30+-page booklet entitled *Metallothionein and Autism*. The booklet can be purchased from Pfeiffer at (630) 505 0300 or www.hriptc.org.

RESEARCH THAT MAKES A DIFFERENCE

The majority of research funds spent on autism in the past 20-to-30 years have focused on genetics.[31] Yet, as a parent of a child on the autism spectrum, I don't know how any of it has helped us. ARI, on the other hand, has been skilled at identifying and funding research that makes a difference *today* to those of us living on the front lines with autism-spectrum disorders. Consider the work of people like Jill James, PhD; Richard Deth, PhD; James Adams, PhD; and a host of other researchers and medical doctors. These pioneers are cracking the codes in body chemistry and solving the mysteries related to heavy metals. In so doing, they move our afflicted children along the road toward recovery. They help us in the here and now. From their discoveries, we have begun to learn which children may be at risk for autism-spectrum disorders, as well as how to prevent these disorders in the first place. Prevention is key; for, truly, when it comes to autism, an ounce of prevention is worth 300 pounds of cure.

Yet, there is still much more about body chemistry that we need to under-stand, harness, and refine. With the crux of autism lying in the hands of faltering chemistry, it is vital that our research efforts are aimed at unlocking its secrets and gaining mastery of the best ways to restore these critical chains of chemical reactions. In the restocking of life force (methyl groups) alone, there are numerous avenues to explore.[32] Both as individuals and as a society, we need to redirect more funds to research in body chemistry, as well as in finding better ways to remove accumulated heavy metals. We must also learn to identify children who are genetically vulnerable and to pinpoint harmful sources of heavy metals and toxins. In these areas lie the most significant opportunities to improve the lives of people on the autism spectrum *today* and to prevent others from joining their ranks.[33]

NOTES

1. Pangborn and Baker 2005, p. 1:35.
2. James *et al.* 2004, pp. 1611–17; Pangborn and Baker 2007, p. 38; Jepson and Johnson 2007, p. 110; Kirby 2005, pp. 337–38.
3. Bock and Stauth 2007, p. 274.
4. Ibid., pp. 271–72.
5. Ibid., pp. 271, 274.
6. Kirby 2005, p. 347; Pangborn and Baker 2005, pp. 1:15, 2:5.
7. Pangborn and Baker 2005, p. 3:17; Neubrander 2006, pp. 110–11; McCandless 2007, p. 227; Kirby 2005, p. 415; McCandless 2005, p. 3.
8. McCandless 2005, p. 3.
9. Pangborn and Baker 2005, p. 2:4.
10. Bock and Stauth 2007, p. 270; McCandless 2007, p. 228.

11. McCandless 2007, pp. 228–29; Pangborn and Baker 2005, p. 2:4; Jepson and Johnson 2007, p. 194; Kirby 2005, p. 183.
12. Kirby 2005, p. 415; Bock and Stauth 2007, p. 271.
13. McCandless 2007, pp. 125–26.
14. McCandless 2007, pp. 226–27; Bock and Stauth 2007, pp. 270–71; Pangborn and Baker 2005, p. 2:4; Neubrander 2002, pp. 2–3.
15. McCandless 2005, p. 3.
16. Neubrander 2002, p.4; McCandless 2007, p. 227.
17. McCandless 2007, pp. 228–29; Neubrander 2006, p. 110.
18. Pangborn and Baker 2005, pp. 1:15, 2:4; Bock and Stauth 2007, pp. 270–71.
19. McCandless 2007, p. 134.
20. Kartzinel 2006, p. 98.
21. Edelson and Rimland 2006, pp. 323, 335, 341–42; Pangborn 2006a, p. 42.
22. Waring and Klovrza 2000, pp. 25–32.
23. Adams 2007, p. 22.
24. Cave with Mitchell 2001, p. 80.
25. Adams 2007, p. 22.
26. Autism Research Institute 2005, p. 18; James *et al.* 2006, pp. 947–56; James *et al.* 2004, pp. 1611–17.
27. McCandless 2007, p. 52; Baker 2004, p. 184; Bradstreet 2006, p. 274; Jepson and Johnson 2007, p. 221.
28. Lewis 2005, pp. 19–20; Walsh *et al.* 2002, pp. 2–4, 17; Kirby 2005, pp. 143–44.
29. McCandless 2007, p. 77.
30. Lewis 2005, pp. 19–20; Walsh *et al.* 2002, pp. 2–4, 17; Kirby 2005, pp. 143–44, 296.
31. Jepson and Johnson 2007, p. 23.
32. Deth 2007a, pp. 41–44.
33. Kirby 2005, pp. 373, 407.

Chapter 19

Common Interventions for Heavy-Metal Overload

WHAT THIS CHAPTER IS ABOUT

For many, the autism-spectrum epidemic has emerged in children with a vulnerable genetic makeup in fundamental cell chemistry. Heavy metals or toxins from the environment have overwhelmed that chemistry and crippled it to varying degrees in different children.[1] One of the results is that many (though not all) children carry a high body burden of heavy metals. Such an overload deserves serious consideration given:

- its widespread presence on the autism spectrum
- its severe impact on the individual
- the significant improvement many children enjoy through detoxification treatment that reduces the toxic load
- the poor hope of recovery if a high level of heavy metals is present but not removed.[2]

Therefore, this chapter discusses:

- clues that raise suspicion of heavy-metal overload
- potential benefits of detoxification treatment
- lab testing for heavy-metal overload
- detoxification treatment.

CLUES THAT RAISE SUSPICION OF HEAVY-METAL OVERLOAD

Having an autism-spectrum diagnosis is reason enough to suspect heavy-metal overload. However, there are also other clues found to be common in the early histories of children with excessive heavy metals.[3] They include:

1. *Family history of autoimmune disorder* such as rheumatoid arthritis, insulin-dependent diabetes (Type I), psoriasis, hypothyroid disease, lupus, and rheumatic fever.[4]

2. *Heavy metal exposures to the child's mother during pregnancy.*[5] Mercury exposures to an unborn baby include his mother's:

    (a) *fish consumption*

    (b) *amalgam fillings.* Amalgams, a mix of silver and mercury, are about 50 percent mercury.[6]

    (c) *dental work involving dental amalgams during pregnancy*

    (d) *rhogam injections.* If a pregnant woman has an RH-negative blood type while her unborn baby's blood type is RH-positive, she receives rhogam injections to ensure she will not develop antibodies that would attack her RH-positive babies in future pregnancies. Until 2001, these injections contained a mercury preservative called Thimerosal.[7]

3. *Newborn Hepatitis B vaccination.* From 1991, when this vaccine was first mandated in the U.S., until late 2001, it contained a mercury preservative, Thimerosal.[8]

4. *Reaction to vaccination.*[9]

5. *Persistent colic as an infant.*[10]

6. *Frequent ear infections and antibiotic use.*[11]

7. *Persistent diarrhea, constipation, reflux, and self-restricted diet.*[12]

8. *Unavailability of breast feeding.*

POTENTIAL BENEFITS OF DETOXIFICATION TREATMENT

It is encouraging to know that, for those autism-spectrum children who have heavy-metal overload, many show dramatic improvement when the overload is removed through detoxification treatment.[13] Though many children regress to some degree at the outset of this treatment, they may make significant gains later.[14] And what might those gains be? Benefits have included rapid progress in language, increased eye contact, improved social interaction, and decreased self-stimulatory behaviors ("stimming"). In addition, some children with motor problems have enjoyed significant improvement in both strength and coordination.[15] There are children who have even gained enough ground to be mainstreamed in school or to leave their autistic diagnosis behind.[16]

As mentioned earlier, parents in the ARI parent ratings voiced a resounding "yes" to the success of detoxification treatment (labeled "Detox. Chelation" on the rating chart in Appendix B). Of the children who tried it, 74 percent got better, according to the parents. That is higher than any other treatment in the entire chart, be it drug, special diet, or biomedical (nondrug) supplement. Only 3 percent got worse. The reason detoxification treatment helps is that it can break the cycle of decline and set the stage for repair and recovery.[17]

Amy Holmes, MD, conducted a study of 85 autistic children ages 1 to 18+. Each had been in treatment to remove heavy metals for at least four months. Dr. Holmes measured their progress in several areas including memory, cognitive function, and social interaction. She categorized each child's progress into either marked progress (little or no autistic symptoms remained), moderate progress, slight progress, or no progress. The youngest children (ages 1–5) showed the greatest improvement, with 35 percent achieving marked progress and nearly 40 percent achieving moderate progress. Though lower percentages of older children responded this well, many benefited, some significantly.[18]

TESTING FOR HEAVY-METAL OVERLOAD

Testing can reveal whether a heavy-metal burden is present and, if so, which particular villain(s) is at work. Knowing the villain(s) is especially helpful when there is a current, ongoing source of exposure. Identifying that exposure is much easier when you know which heavy metal to look for. Consider lead poisoning, for example, which can mimic autism. There have been children whose autistic symptoms improved when previously unrecognized sources of lead were identified and eliminated. Until a test revealed lead poisoning, no one knew to search for a source of lead.[19]

There are several ways to test for heavy metals. However, according to Defeat Autism Now!, the special circumstances of autism make two particular kinds of urine tests most relevant. One is a newer test called the urinary porphyrins (pōr-fə-rəns) test. Parents may be interested to know that it is possible to have this test performed without the signature of a health professional. Thus, parents, on their own, can investigate the possibility of heavy-metal overload in their child. The other test for heavy-metal overload is called the pre-/post-challenge urine toxic elements test; for short, we'll call it the pre-/post-challenge test. Since this test has been around longer than the urinary porphyrins test and more doctors have experience with it, it will be discussed first.

Pre-/post-challenge urine toxic elements test

The pre-/post-challenge test used to diagnose heavy-metal overload is actually a *procedure*, involving testing two different urine samples and comparing their heavy-metal content in order to make a diagnosis.

Here is how it works. At home, a parent follows instructions using kits provided by a laboratory. First, a "pre-challenge" urine sample is collected. Then, a single dose of a prescription detoxification drug is given. The drug causes the body to purge heavy metals, primarily into the urine.[20] For the next six hours, urine is collected and placed in a jug provided by the lab. A small sample of this total "post-challenge" urine is sent to the laboratory for analysis; the pre-challenge urine sample is also sent. Both samples are analyzed using a test called the urine toxic-metals test.[21] This test measures the individual levels of several different heavy metals, including mercury, lead, arsenic, aluminum, antimony, tin, and cadmium. If there is a large increase in heavy-metal excretion between the two samples, it means excess heavy metals are present, and the particular drug used in the test is effective for removing them from this individual.[22]

A medical doctor experienced in detoxification in autism is needed for comparing the pre- and post-challenge results because interpretation can be tricky for a couple of reasons. One relates to the reference ranges provided for comparison by the laboratory. For each heavy metal, the reference range defines the limits of what is considered "normal," "elevated," and "very elevated." However, these limits are based on people who did *not* take a detoxification drug. Therefore, a trained eye is needed to interpret the results correctly. In addition, for some individuals the single dose of medication used for the test is too low to purge a lot of heavy metals, creating a borderline result that may be difficult to interpret. In such a case, a heavy-metal overload could exist without the test making it obvious. An experienced doctor is necessary to make the call.[23]

Be aware that, if the post-challenge test shows a high level of at least one heavy metal, there could still be other metals in the body that did not show up on the test. Take mercury, for example. It makes an especially strong chemical bond to molecules in the body and is not going to let go at the drop of a hat. The single dose of medication used for the test might only remove less-tightly bonded metals, and those will appear elevated on the test. Though the test may not reveal it, mercury is in the body hanging on tight. Detoxification treatment may have to remove significant amounts of these other easier-to-get metals before mercury will begin to appear elevated on follow-up tests. That could take some time.[24]

In other words, the pre-/post-challenge procedure does not necessarily give you a complete picture of the heavy-metal status in the body. It simply measures how much of each heavy metal is coming out in the urine. Think of an ice cream machine at a buffet restaurant. From looking at it, you have no idea how much ice cream is in it. For all you know, it could be empty. Say that you pull the lever and ice cream comes out. That tells you there *had been* ice cream in the machine, but you still don't know how much remains inside. Only when nothing comes out any more do you know how much is inside. Nothing—it's finally empty. The pre-/post-challenge test is like pulling the lever. It shows you what is coming out. But as long as heavy metals continue to be excreted, you have no idea how much is still in the body. The amount is hidden from you. Only when no more comes out do you know the body is "empty" of heavy metals.

Urinary porphyrins test

The urinary porphyrins test is a newer test that is still in the process of being explored and clarified. Many doctors associated with Defeat Autism Now! have been using it to diagnose heavy-metal overload and monitor its treatment. Some feel it is a better way to confirm mercury overload. This test's approach and the nature of the information it provides are quite different from the pre-/post-challenge test.[25]

To understand the porphyrins test, start by thinking about the body chemistry of the methionine cycle and its neighbors. When this chemistry becomes impaired, it offers no clues about *who* the guilty vandal(s) was that disrupted it. Was it mercury? Or maybe lead? Perhaps both of them or neither. Who knows? It could have been another culprit altogether. The chemistry's lips are sealed. However, there is an entirely different chemical pathway in the body that is willing to point some fingers. This pathway is also disrupted by heavy metals and chemical toxins. The difference is that, when it gets disrupted, it produces some unique "eyewitnesses" to the crime. The eyewitnesses are compounds called porphyrins, and each has a story to tell. We just have to ask.

The way we ask is with the urinary porphyrins test. This test measures levels of different porphyrins that get produced during the making of hemoglobin (the oxygen carrier in blood). Think of the pathway that constructs porphyrins as though it were an assembly line. If a heavy metal or toxin comes along, it sabotages the assembly line at certain steps in production that are somewhat unique to that heavy metal or toxin. As a result, some porphyrins will be incompletely assembled. The degree of incompleteness depends on which heavy metal or toxin is disrupting the assembly line. In such a state, the porphyrins are useless to the body so get dumped into the urine for disposal. When we measure levels of various discarded porphyrins, identifiable patterns emerge. Like a fingerprint, each pattern tells us "who done it." For example, consider mercury, a common culprit on the autism spectrum. It dramatically affects porphyrin production making porphyrin testing one of the most sensitive ways to measure mercury exposure. Mercury leaves a unique and easily recognizable fingerprint. Normally, its associated porphyrin (precoproporphyrin) is relatively low in urine unless mercury is inhibiting the pathway. Besides mercury's pattern, distinct porphyrin patterns emerge in the presence of excess lead, arsenic, aluminum, or toxic chemicals like PCBs and pesticides. Though this is not a long list of heavy metals and toxins, it covers the most common offenders on the autism spectrum. Be aware that, in some instances, a porphyrins test will indicate that heavy metals are excessive, yet leave doubt about who the specific vandal(s) is. In such cases, the pre-/post-challenge test may also be necessary to refine the picture.[26]

Use of the urinary porphyrins test in autism began with publication of a 2006 study at the Laboratoire Philippe Auguste in Paris, France. This study compared porphyrin levels of control children to those of 269 French children with neurodevelopmental and related disorders including autism, AS, PDD-NOS, and attention deficit. Researchers found that at least 53 percent, and possibly more, of the 106 children with autism showed elevated porphyrins that indicated heavy-metal exposure. Nine other children with both autism and epilepsy showed some even higher levels. These elevations were statistically significant. Also statistically significant were small elevations in porphyrins in two children with epilepsy and two others with mental retardation and epilepsy. The only children on medication during the study were those taking anticonvulsants for epilepsy. The researchers suggested that anti-epileptic medications might contribute to elevated porphyrins. They also noted that seizures can be a symptom of heavy-metal toxicity. Furthermore, the researchers felt it was unlikely that medication contributed to the elevated porphyrins in those subjects with autism who had no evidence of seizures since these children were not on medication. It is interesting that statistically significant porphyrin elevations in other disorders such as AS, PDD-NOS, and attention deficit were *not* found. Another feature of the study was to treat a parent-selected subgroup of autistic children with a detoxification medication called DMSA. As a result of this treatment, there was a statistically significant reduction towards normal in these children's porphyrin levels.[27]

This 2006 French study stimulated interest among doctors associated with Defeat Autism Now! Many began using the French lab's porphyrins test to access heavy-metal status in their patients.[28] In addition, news of the test was presented to parents at Defeat Autism Now! conferences.

A valuable article explaining porphyrin testing and how to interpret results was recommended in the 2007 Supplement to *Autism: Effective Biomedical Treatments* (the book of consensus on the Defeat Autism Now! approach).[29] The article, "The Use of Urinary Porphyrins Analysis in Autism," was written by Dan Rossignol, MD. It appeared in the April 2007 edition of *Medical Veritas* and is available from www.medicalveritas.com. In the article, Dr. Rossignol favors the French lab (Laboratoire Philippe Auguste at www.labbio.net) for the porphyrins test. According to Dr. Rossignol's article, the comparison ranges that define "normal" on this lab's test are based on their research findings in children. If you are testing a child, this provides a more appropriate comparison than ranges based on healthy adults, which is the standard used by most other labs. In addition, Dr. Rossignol says the French lab has machinery that is calibrated to detect small variations in porphyrin levels. That can make a difference when evaluating children on the autism spectrum.

Parents may also be interested to know that a porphyrins test done by the Laboratoire Philippe Auguste does not require the signature of a health professional. Thus, it gives parents a chance to investigate on their own whether their child has heavy-metal overload. At the time of this writing, the cost of the test is $120, plus shipping to France. To initiate testing, a parent can email the lab (www.labbio.net) and request a lab kit to be sent in the mail The kit contains instructions and supplies for collection of the urine sample. The parent collects the sample at home and mails it back to the lab with payment. Depending on the results of the test, parents can decide whether to consult with a doctor who is familiar with porphyrin testing.

It needs to be made clear that interpretation of this test is not a piece of cake, by any stretch. Depending on the specific lab result, interpretation can be straightforward, quite confusing, or somewhere in between. To help, the laboratory does provide some printed interpretative comments along with the test results. In addition, Dr. Rossignol's article is very valuable. Appendix D of this book contains a paraphrase of the test-interpretation portion of Dr. Rossignol's article. If there is any doubt as to the meaning of a child's test result, parents can seek the opinion of a doctor experienced in detoxification on the autism spectrum (www.autism.com). Not all those listed have detoxification experience, particularly with the porphyrins test which is relatively new at the time of this writing, so ask before scheduling an appointment.

I do not know about you, but I find it very hard to be worried about something I cannot see, such as body chemistry and accumulated heavy metals. Problems in the gut and immune system are different because they can be observed. I can see diarrhea, constipation, fevers, and ear infections. They tell me something is not right. But body chemistry? Heavy-metal overload? Come on—give me a break! Though, for many children, heavy metals are at the crux of autism's miseries, I cannot see them directly. How can I appreciate what I cannot see? The turning point for me was to get test results because, if test results (whether a porphyrins test or pre-/post-challenge test) show that your child has heavy-metal overload, it speaks for itself. You no longer have to speculate about *if* or *how* or *why*. You simply know that it *is*. There is a vast difference between hearing that your child *might* have heavy-metal poisoning as opposed to *knowing* that he actually does. It changes your whole view of the world. But at least there is a bright side, even to an unhappy test result: the bright side is that there is something you can do about it. Facing the bad news puts you in a powerful position to help your child. What I like about the French lab's porphyrins test is that it makes it easy for a parent at least to try to investigate the possibility that their child may have a problem with body chemistry and heavy metals before investing time and money to locate and pay for an experienced biomedical doctor.

To help clarify the differences between the pre-/post-challenge test and the porphyrins test, Table 19.1 shows a comparison.

In 2007 when Dr. Biomedical suggested testing Will with the urinary porphyrins test, Will had already been monitored several times during detoxification treatment with the urine toxic-metals test. Since the results of these tests had commonly shown mercury excretion, I was not surprised when the comment line at the bottom of Will's porphyrins test result read "moderate mercury toxic effect." The disturbing finding for me was a different comment. This one referred to his level of chemical toxins and stated, "slightly increased rate." That was news to me since chemical toxins are not measured on the urine toxic-metals test.

Now a truth in the world of science is that the findings of a study done by one research group need to be confirmed by other research groups. That's how we know that the original findings are truly accurate. As of the time of this writing, the French lab's study regarding porphyrin testing has not been confirmed. In fact, in 2008, William Shaw, PhD, director of the Great Plains Laboratory, posted an article on his laboratory's Web site. The article (not published in a scientific journal) raises several objections to the French study's methodology. It also presents urinary porphyrin results that vary substantially between those of the French lab and those of the Great Plains Laboratory

Table 19.1 Features of porphyrin and pre-/post-challenge tests for heavy metals

	Porphyrin	Pre-/Post-Challenge
Measures heavy metals exiting the body	no	yes
Requires use of detoxification medication	no	yes
Evaluates toxic chemicals (e.g., PCBs, pesticides)	yes	no
Evaluates mercury, lead, arsenic, and aluminum	yes	yes
Evaluates many heavy metals	no	yes
Requires involvement of a medical professional	no*	yes

*Though some laboratories require the signature of a medical professional, Laboratoire Philippe Auguste at www.labbio.net does not.

though they were performed on a shared urine sample.[30] So who is right? Obviously, further research is needed. Nevertheless, it is important that you are aware of this state of uncertainty if you are making decisions regarding testing for heavy-metal overload for your child.

Testing for heavy metals using hair or blood

Urine is not the only way to test for heavy metals. Hair, blood, and stool can also be used. However, for children on the autism spectrum, such tests are not as helpful for detecting accumulated heavy metals, so they are not the best choice when trying to decide whether detoxification treatment is needed. Here's why.

Take hair for starters. To the body, excreting heavy metals into hair is like tossing out the garbage. We can test the hair to see what got tossed out, but children on the autism spectrum often have *lower* levels of heavy metals in their hair than siblings, parents, and typical children.[31] It is what you might expect from a body whose detoxification system is not up to snuff. Rather than being booted out into the hair, heavy metals are staying in the body and accumulating. Thus, low levels of heavy metals in the hair do not necessarily mean there are low levels in the body.

Blood can also be tested for the presence of heavy metals. For instance, consider a test called the red blood cell elements test. In biomedical treatment, it is primarily used to assess the status of important minerals in the body like calcium, magnesium, and zinc. But the test also checks for a few heavy metals like mercury and lead. However, blood testing shows only recent large exposures, not past exposures that may have since settled into body tissues.[32] Thus, blood is not helpful for deciding whether detoxification treatment is needed. However, that is not to say it has no value. If testing the blood indicated a recent mercury exposure, for example, you would know to identify and eliminate current sources of mercury exposure such as high fish consumption or use of low-quality fish oil supplements.

HOW DETOXIFICATION MEDICATIONS WORK IN THE BODY

If either the porphyrins or pre-/post-challenge test indicates heavy-metal overload, various detoxification medications can be used to remove heavy metals. Such medications contain sulfur and work like the body's own natural detoxification system.[33] Recall that sulfur was the key ingredient that Decision Dude (homocysteine) brought down the detoxification pathway. Its stickiness for heavy metals and toxins is what makes it useful for detoxifying. Think of the sticky sulfur in a detoxification medication as you would a bouncer in a bar. It apprehends toxic metals so they can be escorted out of the body. However, it is not quite that simple. Heavy metals are not just sitting around loose for easy extraction like marbles in a sandbox. They are chemically bonded to other molecules and are actually part of the body's cells. From the bouncer's point of view, he has to break up a fight, so he must get a good, solid grip on the offending party and yank him off the innocent person who is getting clobbered. Once the bouncer has accomplished that, he is ready to drag the offender out the door with the help of UltraGuy (glutathione). Together, they pitch the offender out into the street. Removal of accumulated heavy metals is a cooperative effort between the detoxification drug and the body's natural detoxification system. They work together as a team.[34]

And what happens to the innocent party left battered after the bar brawl? Once free of the heavy metal, he slumps back onto his bar stool, a bit dazed. He needs time to recover. Similarly, cells in the body need time (and energy) to repair after heavy-metal molecules have been torn loose and hauled away. We can lend them a healing hand to ensure a rapid recovery. In fact, we don't even wait until after the fight is over to help. We can start ahead of time—before the separation—to build them up and get them ready.

DETOXIFICATION TREATMENT IS NOT A FIRST STEP

A body undergoing detoxification treatment will have a high-energy require-ment for repair of cells. This energy requirement in children is second only to that of growth.[35] Therefore, detoxification treatment is something we need to get a body ready for in advance. After all, treatment often lasts six months to two years or longer.[36] Think of it as a marathon. No couch potato hops off his couch and runs the 26.2 miles to the finish line. He has to train first and get in shape. He also needs to address existing problems, as well as plan for potential future problems that may arise during the race. If he tries to run the marathon before he is ready, the results will probably be disappointing. That is how it is with detoxi-fication treatment, too. We need to bolster the body and address its issues. We also anticipate potential problems that detoxification treatment may bring so that we are ready for them, too. By stacking the deck in the body's favor, we maximize its chances for success.[37]

PREPARING THE BODY FOR DETOXIFICATION TREATMENT

A few key areas need to be addressed when preparing for detoxification treat-ment. Almost all children improve on the preparations alone. Dosing and other information for those preparations that involve supplements appear in Appendix C on nutrient supplemention. Preparations include:[38]

1. *Bolstering with vitamin and mineral supplements.* Most children with autism-spectrum disorders need increased amounts of vitamins and minerals. Zinc especially tends to be low. Therefore, a strong nutrient program needs to be in place before and during detoxification treatment. In addition to a comprehensive multivitamin/mineral supplement, certain other supplements are emphasized because they either fight oxidative stress or help with detoxification. They include vitamins C, E, and B6, as well as the minerals zinc and selenium. It is especially important that minerals be well-supplied since detoxification drugs can remove minerals. We would rather they did not, but that's the way it is. A red blood cell elements test is commonly used to measure a person's levels of various minerals like zinc, calcium, magnesium, and selenium. Any minerals found to be deficient can be supplemented during the preparation phase of detoxification treatment.[39]

2. *Restoring healthy gut flora (if needed).* Some medications and supplements used during detoxification treatment can create or aggravate problems with "bad gut flora." This will make more sense after you read about gut flora and its problems in Chapter 23, as well as interventions to improve

it in Chapter 26. For now, just know that gut flora needs to be in good
shape before detoxification treatment begins.[40]

3. *Increasing glutathione* (UltraGuy). Detoxification medication and the
body's own natural detoxification system work together to drive out
heavy metals. So we want the body's natural detoxification system as
robust as possible before treatment begins. The main player of interest
is glutathione (UltraGuy). He is the leading detoxifier, the garbage
collector. Unfortunately, his level is typically 50 percent lower in
children with autism. However, there are multiple ways to use
supplements to increase glutathione levels.[41]

   (a) *Glutathione* as a cream, injection, or IV. It is unclear if giving it
   by mouth is effective.

   (b) *Combination of methyl-B12 injections, TMG, and folinic acid* (and
   potentially vitamin B6).

   (c) *Vitamin C.*

4. *Minimizing exposures to toxins and heavy metals.* This will be discussed in
Chapters 20–22.

To the degree possible, the above preparations should be well in place before
detoxification treatment begins. Otherwise, the success of treatment will likely
be disappointing due to gut problems and nutritional deficiencies.[42] Detoxification treatment will be described in the following pages. However, there is one
important point to address first—the use of a doctor experienced in
heavy-metal removal.

AN EXPERIENCED MEDICAL DOCTOR IS NECESSARY FOR DETOXIFICATION TREATMENT

When using the detoxification medications about to be discussed, you need the
expertise of a medical doctor.[43] And not just any ol' doctor will do. Find one
with experience in detoxification on the autism spectrum. A good place to start
is the list of doctors who use the Defeat Autism Now! approach
(www.autism.com). Contact any doctors you are considering to ask how much
detoxification experience they have.

And *why* do you need a doctor? The most important reason is your child's
safety. The liver and kidneys play special roles in our body's natural system of
detoxification. Since detoxification medications drum up extra business for
these important organs, it is possible for them to get stressed. Thus, periodic lab
tests are necessary to monitor the liver and kidneys. You want a trained eye

reviewing such tests. Sometimes treatment needs to be suspended temporarily so the detoxification organs get a break.[44] An experienced doctor can make the call when a break is needed and, if so, decide how long the break should last. In addition, a doctor's knowledge is valuable for deciding which medication is most effective for the heavy metal(s) your child has in overload, as well as which form of the medication best suits your child's needs. Experience is also important for evaluating a child's response to treatment and making appropriate changes. Finally, having a good doctor makes the entire process much easier for you. They know which laboratory tests need to be repeated and how often. They can also write prescriptions for medications and supplements that are suitable to your child's detoxification needs.

LAB TESTING PRIOR TO DETOXIFICATION TREATMENT

Before treatment begins, some blood tests are needed. They serve as a "before" picture that can be used for comparison later when the same tests are repeated during treatment. The tests include:[45]

1. *Red blood cell elements test.* This test, mentioned earlier, reports the levels of various minerals like zinc, calcium, magnesium, and selenium.

2. *Blood tests* (from a single blood draw):
   (a) complete blood count with platelet count
   (b) kidney function check
   (c) liver function check.

SUPPORTING THE BODY DURING DETOXIFICATION TREATMENT

Many of the same supports that were used to prepare the body for detoxification treatment need to continue during treatment. They are an important part of the treatment plan. Furthermore, since treatment increases the demands placed on the body, additional supports may be appropriate once treatment begins.[46]

DETOXIFICATION MEDICATIONS

Treatment officially begins when a detoxification medication is used. The four most common medications are DMSA, DMPS, calcium EDTA, and TTFD. Which one(s) is appropriate depends, in part, on which heavy metal(s) the child needs to offload. DMSA is effective against a wide range of toxic metals including mercury, lead, arsenic, tin, nickel, and antimony. DMPS is especially effective for mercury and also works for lead, arsenic, tin, cadmium, and silver. Calcium EDTA removes lead and cadmium and is somewhat effective for aluminum. Lastly, TTFD has been shown to remove arsenic in particular, but also cadmium, nickel, lead, and mercury.[47]

Each medication is available in various forms. There are oral, rectal, and intravenous forms, as well as intramuscular injection and creams that are rubbed into the skin. The particular medication used and its form depend on the needs of the individual child.[48] How often a particular medication is given depends on which form is in use. While one form of a medication is administered every other day, another form may only be given once every two weeks. Another common schedule involves repeating a two-week cycle in which three daily doses are given on three consecutive days followed by an 11-day break.[49] The doctor will specify the schedule that is appropriate for the medication and form being used.

The FDA approval status of these medications varies. The oral form of DMSA is FDA approved for lead poisoning in children. Like any approved medication, it can be prescribed by a doctor "off-label" for other types of heavy-metal poisoning. DMSA is also available over-the-counter, as is calcium EDTA. DMPS, however, is not FDA approved; nevertheless, a doctor can still have it compounded for a patient at a pharmacy. Though DMPS is considered experimental in the U.S., it is widely available in Europe by prescription. In Germany, it is available over-the-counter.[50]

TTFD as an "add-on" to another detoxification medication

TTFD is a unique form of vitamin B1 (thiamine) that acts as a mild remover of heavy metals. It enjoys an exceptional safety record and can be given indefinitely as a good source of vitamin B1. TTFD is most effective in its cream form, which is rubbed into the skin. This form is available over-the-counter under the brand name of "Authia Cream" from Ecological Formulas. When TTFD is used simultaneously with the cream form of glutathione (reduced), it becomes even more effective against heavy metals. Many doctors use TTFD as an "add-on" to another detoxification medication. Combined, the two detoxifiers purge higher levels of heavy metals into the urine than either could do alone. The biggest drawback of TTFD cream is that, in some patients, it causes them to give off a bad smell—possibly as bad as the odor of a skunk. No kidding, really. For those who valiantly continue treatment anyway, the smell gradually lessens. Giving 10mg of biotin, a B vitamin, by mouth often removes the odor rapidly. Another strategy is to apply the TTFD cream on the lower legs or feet at bedtime. These areas can easily be washed the next morning. The good news is that the odor problem never occurs when the oral form of TTFD is used.[51]

EVALUATING TREATMENT PROGRESS WITH LAB TESTS

To find out if detoxification treatment is removing heavy metals effectively, lab work is repeated periodically.[52] For instance, say a urinary porphyrins test had been done prior to the start of treatment. Then, the same test will be repeated occasionally during treatment, perhaps every 3–4 months. If the current treatment plan is working, the total body burden of heavy metals will keep dropping from one test to the next.[53]

Another test option for evaluating treatment progress is the urine toxic-metals test. When a repeat test shows that excessive levels of heavy metals are being purged from the body, that means your treatment plan is working well. Stick with it.

However, if a repeat test shows unsatisfactory progress, something needs to change. Perhaps the individual would do better with a different detoxification medication. Or maybe switching to a different form of the current medication is the answer. Sometimes the appropriate change does not involve the detoxification medication or its form. Instead, an adjustment in the supporting cast of nutrients or other agents will do the trick to get heavy metals on the run. This is an area where the knowledge of an experienced doctor makes an important difference.

MONITORING THE BODY TO ENSURE SAFETY

During the course of detoxification treatment, certain lab tests need to be repeated periodically to monitor body function and ensure safety.[54] They are the same tests that were performed before treatment began, but are repeated here to stress the importance of continued maintenance:

1. *Red blood cell elements test.* This test should be repeated every 3–6 months to check mineral levels.[55]

2. *Blood tests* (from a single blood draw). The following tests should be repeated every 2–3 months:[56]

   (a) complete blood count with platelet count

   (b) kidney function check

   (c) liver function check.

POSSIBLE SIDE EFFECTS OF DETOXIFICATION TREATMENT

Some side effects can occur during treatment. The two most common are bad gut flora and depletion of minerals, particularly zinc, selenium, magnesium, and copper.[57] These side effects can cause behavioral issues, but they are often preventable using mineral supplementation and intestinal supports (described in Chapters 24–27). If necessary, treatment can be temporarily suspended until gut flora is restored or minerals are restocked. Serious allergic reactions to detoxification medications are quite rare; however, rashes may indicate a need to change either the medication used or its form. Concerns have been raised about the impact on the liver, kidney, and bone marrow; however, there has been no evidence of irreversible problems. To be on the safe side, lab tests are repeated regularly to monitor complete blood count, liver function, and mineral levels.[58]

SAFETY OF DETOXIFICATION TREATMENT

Detoxification medications have been used for decades to treat heavy-metal poisoning in cases of both single high-dose exposures and repeated low-dose exposures over time. To date, no controlled studies of detoxification treatment in autistic children have been published, though quality research in this area is needed. Nevertheless, detoxification treatment has been used widely in thousands of autistic children and has received positive reports from parents and treating physicians.[59]

Yet, two notable exceptions need to be mentioned. First, know that intravenous calcium EDTA has been used safely for decades in thousands of elderly people and in lead-poisoned children. However, in 2005, mistakes by inexperienced doctors using the *wrong* drug for detoxification resulted in the tragic deaths of two children. The correct drug known to be safe for detoxification is *calcium* EDTA. What was disastrously given to these two children was *disodium* EDTA. The mix-up came from the similarity in the drug names. These tragedies send a loud and clear message that underscores the importance of having an *experienced* doctor.[60] In the past 50 years, no death has ever resulted from correctly performed detoxification using the medications discussed in this chapter.[61]

Nevertheless, there are strong voices both in favor and in opposition to detoxification treatment in autism. In ARI's quarterly newsletter, *Autism Research Review International*, John Green, MD, offered an explanation for the differences of opinion.[62] Dr. Green is a clinical specialist in ecology and nutritional medicine who has treated autistic children exclusively since 1999. He is experienced using all the detoxification medications discussed in this chapter. Dr. Green describes those in favor of detoxification treatment as professionals who use it regularly and have seen excellent results with very few side effects. The opposition, on the other hand, are individuals who have not used detoxification therapy in practice and raise theoretical reasons against its use.

So what is a parent to think? Take a look at the ARI parent ratings below. It shows that only 3 percent of parents thought detoxification treatment made their child worse. That is an extremely low figure when you look at the "got-worse" percentages in the drug category. Compare it, for instance, to medications like Adderall, Amphetamine, and Ritalin, which are readily prescribed by mainstream physicians. Yet, these drugs have exceptionally high "got-worse" ratings according to parents. Roughly half of the children who tried them got worse. For another 25 percent of the children, these drugs had no effect. In the end, only 25–32 percent were helped. That's only about one out of four children. What kind of odds are those? Chances are that, with these drugs, your child will get worse or stay the same. Does mainstream medicine consider drugs with a track record like that to be safe for use in children? If so, then how can the safety of detoxification treatment be challenged when it helps 74 percent of children while making only 3 percent worse? As more food for thought, consider that 160 Ritalin-related deaths (mostly cardiovascular) were reported to the FDA between 1990 and 1997. It would seem that detoxification treatment (for those with heavy-metal overload) is safer than certain mainstream-endorsed treatments.[63]

	Got Worse	No Effect	Got Better	Better: Worse Ratio	No. of Cases
Detox. (Chelation)	3 percent	23 percent	74 percent	24:1	803
Ritalin	45 percent	26 percent	29 percent	0.7:1	4,127
Amphetamine	47 percent	28 percent	25 percent	0.5:1	1,312
Adderall	43 percent	25 percent	32 percent	0.8:1	775

TAKING BREAKS DURING TREATMENT

As already mentioned, there are times it makes sense to take a temporary break during detoxification treatment. In fact, some children improve while taking time off. The reasons to take a break include:[64]

○ to restore gut flora

○ to replenish minerals

○ to wait for redistribution of heavy metals to body tissues where they can be reached by detoxification medication. The medications cannot

retrieve heavy metals from deep tissues, the bones, or the brain. However, heavy metals in these locations can redistribute to other tissues where they become accessible. Taking a break in treatment can allow time for redistribution. Then treatment can resume later to purge the newly accessible heavy metals.

○ to rest the liver or kidneys, which play special roles in detoxification.

HOW DO YOU KNOW WHEN TREATMENT IS COMPLETE?

Every child is unique, so length of treatment can vary considerably from one child to the next. While some children respond very quickly, others move much more slowly. Often, younger children will take six months to two years. Older children seem to excrete heavy metals more slowly and may take longer.[65] Two factors weigh in deciding when treatment is complete.[66] They are:

1. *Test results that evaluate progress.* For people using the porphyrins test to evaluate progress, the total body burden should, at some point, drop low enough to discontinue treatment. For those who use the urine toxic-metals test to monitor progress, treatment is stopped when heavy metals being discharged into the urine have dropped sufficiently. Since low levels of heavy metals in the urine can also mean that the treatment plan is not working, you must rely on the judgment of your experienced doctor to draw the correct conclusion from test results and to take appropriate action.

2. *Improvement in the child's autistic behaviors.* An indicator more important than lab tests is the rate of improvement seen in the child's behaviors. When progress plateaus, detoxification treatment can end. Sometimes treatment continues for a few months after a plateau in the hope of seeing a little more progress. Other times, treatment may be put on hold for several months and then restarted on a trial basis.

THE BEST SOURCE OF INFORMATION ABOUT DETOXIFICATION TREATMENT

This chapter has presented a high-level overview. More detailed information is available in a document published by ARI. This document is the premier, authoritative source of information for the safest and most effective methods of detoxification in autistic children. It embodies a consensus of over 30 carefully selected physicians, chemists, toxicologists, and other scientists knowledgeable on the subject. Its title is *Treatment Options for Mercury/Metal Toxicity in Autism*

and Related Developmental Disabilities: Consensus Position Paper. Its 30+ pages offer specific guidance on detoxification issues like testing and preparation, as well as details about medications and their various forms. The document is updated periodically.[67] It can be viewed, printed, or downloaded for free from the ARI Web site (www.autism.com). It can also be ordered from ARI for about $4, a bargain. The book *Children with Starving Brains,* by Jaquelyn McCandless, MD, also contains a helpful chapter of practical information about removing heavy metals (Chapter 7: Removing the Heavy Metals), as does *Healing the New Childhood Epidemics* by Kenneth Bock, MD, and Cameron Stauth (Chapter 19: Detoxification). Different people come to different conclusions about preferred testing methods and whether to pursue use of detoxification medications. This is an area about which you need to be particularly well informed so that you and your doctor make decisions that are right for *your* child. You also need to be comfortable with whatever decisions you make.

SO, WHAT DO WE TALK ABOUT NEXT?

This chapter has focused on treatment to remove accumulated heavy metals, yet it is also important to minimize ongoing exposures to heavy metals and toxins. The less a body's detoxification system has to deal with, the better. So where do toxic exposures come from and what can we do to avoid them? That is the topic of the next few chapters (20–22). Had I read these chapters before I started a family, I doubt my path would have detoured onto the autism spectrum.

NOTES

1. Bock and Stauth 2007, p. 293; Deth 2007c, p. 174; Pangborn and Baker 2007, p. 43; James *et al.* 2006, pp. 947–56; McCandless 2007, p. 134; Rimland 2006a, pp. 406–407; Kirby 2005, pp. 294–95, 347; Binstock 2007b, p. 309.
2. Bock and Stauth 2007, p. 270.
3. McCandless 2006c, pp. 249–50.
4. Usman 2006, p. 59; El-Dahr 2006a, p. 154; McCandless 2006b, p. 159; Comi *et al.* 1999, pp. 388–94; Sweeten *et al.* 2003, p. e420; Croen *et al.* 2005, pp. 151–57.
5. McCandless 2007, p. 65.
6. Shaw 2004, p. 11.
7. www.rhogamfyi.com/thimerosal.html.
8. McCandless 2007, p. 65.
9. Ibid., p. 51.
10. McCandless 2006c, pp. 249–50.
11. McCandless 2007, p. 51.
12. Information on (7) and (8) can be found in McCandless 2006c, pp. 249–50.

13. McCandless 2007, pp. 49–50, 59; Edelson and Cantor 1998, pp. 553–63; Bock and Stauth 2007, p. 294.
14. Autism Research Institute 2005, p. 18.
15. Ibid., pp. 10, 11, 13.
16. McCandless 2007, p. 150.
17. Green 2006a, p. 3; Kirby 2005, p. 411.
18. Kirby 2005, p. 202; Holmes 2001, www.healing-arts.org/children/holmes.htm#results.
19. Rossignol 2007, p.1281
20. McCandless 2007, p. 135.
21. Ibid., pp. 141–42.
22. Adams 2007, p. 24.
23. Autism Research Institute 2005, p. 6.
24. Ibid.
25. Rossignol 2007, p. 1277; Shaw 2008, p. 1; McCandless 2007, pp. 140–41.
26. McCandless 2007, pp. 140–41; Rossignol 2007, pp. 1276–77; Haley and Small 2006, pp. 921–22.
27. Nataf *et al.* 2006, pp. 99–108.
28. Shaw 2008, p. 1; McCandless 2007, pp. 140–41.
29. Pangborn and Baker 2007, p. 21.
30. Shaw 2008, pp. 1–16.
31. Holmes *et al.* 2003, pp. 277–85; Hu, Bernard, and Che 2003, pp. 681–82; Levinson 2006b, pp. 153–55; Bernard *et al.* 2000, p. 52; McCandless 2007, pp. 51, 139.
32. Haley and Small 2006, p. 929; Rossignol 2007, p. 1276
33. Green 2006a, p. 3; Pangborn and Baker 2005, pp. 2:51–52.
34. Baker 2006a, p. 204; Pangborn and Baker 2007, p. 22.
35. Pangborn and Baker 2007, p. 16.
36. McCandless 2007, pp. 150–51.
37. Ibid., p. 176.
38. Ibid., pp. 135, 138, 145; Adams 2007, p. 24; Autism Research Institute 2005, pp. 7–8.
39. McCandless 2007, p. 142; Autism Research Institute 2005, pp. 8, 14–15.
40. Autism Research Institute 2005, p. 8.
41. Ibid.
42. Ibid., p. 9; McCandless 2007, p. 143.
43. McCandless 2007, p. 97.
44. Ibid., pp. 69–70; Baker 2006a, p. 201.
45. Autism Research Institute 2005, p. 8.
46. McCandless 2007, p. 118.
47. Ibid., pp. 152–53; Autism Research Institute 2005, pp. 9, 11; Green 2006a, p. 3.
48. Green 2006a, p. 3.
49. Autism Research Institute 2005, pp. 10, 12–13.
50. Ibid., pp. 9, 11.
51. Ibid., pp. 13–14; Pangborn and Baker 2005, pp. 2:51, 54–55; Levinson 2006b, p. 154; McCandless 2007, pp. 154–56, 158.
52. McCandless 2007, p. 160.
53. Rossignol 2007, p. 1281
54. McCandless 2007, p. 160.
55. Ibid., pp. 136, 142.

56. Autism Research Institute 2005, pp. 8–9, 12.
57. Ibid., pp. 14–15; Mumper 2008a, personal communication.
58. Green 2006a, p. 3.
59. Jepson and Johnson 2007, pp. 229, 231.
60. Green 2006a, p. 3; Rimland 2005, pp. 1, 3; Bradstreet 2006, p. 274; McCandless 2007, p. 141.
61. Rimland 2006b, p. 3.
62. Green 2006a, p. 3.
63. Rimland 2006b, p. 3.
64. Green 2005, webcast; Freedenfeld 2005, webcast; McCandless 2007, pp. 69–70.
65. McCandless 2007, pp. 136, 150–51; Autism Research Institute 2005, p. 19.
66. Autism Research Institute 2005, p. 18; Freedenfeld 2005, webcast; McCandless 2007, pp. 150–51.
67. McCandless 2007, p. 137.

Chapter 20

High Mercury on the Autism Spectrum: Its Sources and Symptoms

WHAT THIS CHAPTER HAS IN STORE

This is the first of three chapters that explore issues of heavy metals and toxins. The focus of this first one is the heavy metal mercury, one of the most neurotoxic compounds known to man. It is toxic to both the immune system and the nervous system, which includes the brain.[1] Mercury is believed to play a role not only in autism-spectrum disorders but also a host of other disorders including learning disabilities, obsessive-compulsive disorder, anxiety, depression, chronic fatigue syndrome, dementia, Alzheimer's, Parkinson's, multiple sclerosis, rheumatoid arthritis, schizophrenia, Tourette's, and ALS (Lou Gehrig's disease).[2] In this chapter, the high frequency of mercury overload in children on the autism spectrum will be discussed, as well as potential sources of mercury. Being aware of these sources helps us to avoid mercury no matter which disguise it takes. This chapter also discusses the symptoms of mercury poisoning, so you can compare them to the symptoms you see in your special child. Its intent is to help you decide if you should test your child for mercury overload.

INFANTS AREN'T REALLY EXPOSED TO TOXINS AND HEAVY METALS, ARE THEY?

At the outset of my biomedical awakening, I could not think of any ways Will could have been exposed to toxins, particularly the nasty heavy metals. He was a little kid, for crying out loud! It was not like he worked in a chemical plant. His time had been spent at home, in day care, on playgrounds, and in schools. He had not handled household toxins like pesticides, herbicides, or fertilizers. And besides, the toxic dangers of the past had been removed, right? Mercury thermometers had long since disappeared from store shelves, and lead was gone from gasoline and paint. Even asbestos insulation in buildings was going the way of the dinosaurs. Yet if all that were true, then why do the majority of autistic children have heavy-metal overload? Somehow, somewhere, they had been exposed to heavy metals in their environment.[3]

I have since learned there are surprisingly many ways infants and children get exposed to heavy metals and toxins. Unless we make an effort to educate ourselves about potential sources of exposure, serious threats can easily go unrecognized or be downplayed as harmless.

HIGH LEVELS OF MERCURY IN CHILDREN ON THE AUTISM SPECTRUM

A study published in the *Journal of American Physicians and Surgeons* compared the heavy-metal excretion of autism-spectrum children to typical children. For three days, all the children in the study received a medication to remove heavy metals (DMSA). The levels of mercury, lead, and cadmium excreted by each child were measured. Mercury levels were *four times* higher in the children with autism-spectrum disorders. Neither lead nor cadmium was statistically different between the two groups.[4] Where on earth would our kids on the spectrum be getting so much mercury?

Mercury in air, water, and food

Mercury is a heavy metal that exists in nature. It can be released as minerals in the earth's surface breakdown or as volcanoes spew forth their contents. However, a whopping 70 percent of atmospheric mercury comes from coal-burning power-plant emissions and refining waste. Over the course of the last century, atmospheric mercury has increased three-fold from industrial pollution. Once mercury is released, it remains in the environment indefinitely.[5] To some extent, your degree of exposure depends on where you live since some locations are more polluted than others. Though the EPA says the amount of mercury in drinking water is not harmful, some experts worry about the cumulative effects of daily consumption of mercury from municipal water supplies. They recommend drinking filtered water or purified bottled water. Mercury is also used in fertilizers, pesticides, and fungicides. Use of these products deposits residues on food, especially grains, a fact that highlights the health value of organic and unprocessed foods.[6] Though many pages of this book will focus on mercury exposure through childhood vaccines, vaccines are by no means the only source of toxins afflicting the autism spectrum. Widespread exposure to environmental toxins in air, water, and food are also a huge source of problems.[7]

Mercury in childhood vaccines

Before discussing mercury in vaccines, it is important to make the point that vaccines are one of the greatest public health achievements of the past century. They have played a crucial role in the prevention of outbreaks of devastating diseases like smallpox, polio, diphtheria, and whooping cough (pertussis).[8] Not many of us are old enough to remember the tragic epidemics that once terrorized entire populations before vaccines were invented. Thanks to the widespread use of vaccines, those once-fearsome diseases have been reduced to unthreatening theoretical notions, at least in the U.S. Yet, these particular diseases, each one preventable, can kill our children.[9] We need the protection that vaccines provide. For safety, it is imperative they are free of heavy metals and are given on a prudent schedule to abundantly healthy children who have no extra risk factors.[10] Nevertheless, mercury exposure through vaccines began in a very small way in the 1930s. It mounted increasingly in volume as more childhood vaccines became mandatory and peaked at a level above federal safety standards from 1991 to roughly 2001.[11] This will be discussed in more detail in the next chapter. At the time of this writing, the mercury threat in vaccines has been greatly reduced but unfortunately not eliminated (more about that later).[12]

Mercury in fish

Fish can be a sizable source of mercury exposure depending on the type of fish and how much is eaten. Four government agencies have set safety limits on mercury consumption from fish or whale meat, despite efforts by the food industry to minimize the risk.[13] But how did mercury get in fish anyway, and not, oh, say, parakeets? Coal-burning power plants put significant amounts of mercury into the air, which rainfall washes down and carries into lakes, rivers, and oceans. There the mercury enters the food chain starting with aquatic organisms. The higher up the food chain you go, the more mercury stockpiles into the bodies of bigger predators (or scavengers) as they eat the less-contaminated little guys. Among saltwater fish concern focuses on tuna, swordfish, shark, snapper, halibut, shrimp, and shellfish; among freshwater fish, on bass, pike, and trout.[14] Pregnant women can easily pass mercury from the fish they eat to their unborn child. The unborn are especially vulnerable to mercury since their brains are developing rapidly. Thus, avoidance of seafood, especially top predators, is recommended for women when they are pregnant or breast-feeding.[15]

Mercury in dental fillings (amalgams)

Amalgams are a mix of mercury and silver that is about 50 percent mercury. They can be a significant source of mercury depending on the number of amalgams in the mouth and their condition. To an unborn child, maternal amalgams can be a substantial source of mercury. Pregnant women should avoid having dental work done or request mercury-free materials. Nonetheless, the danger of mercury from amalgam fillings is staunchly denied by a strong lobby of the American Dental Association.[16]

Mercury in personal care products

Mercury has a long history of medicinal use. A preservative that contains mercury (Thimerosal) is often present in contact-lens solutions, nasal sprays, ear and eye drops, and hemorrhoid medications. The brand names of these products can be viewed on an FDA Web site (www.fda.gov/cder/fdama/mercury300.htm).[17] There are other sources of mercury besides those mentioned in this chapter, but you now know some of the main culprits.

OUR STORY: DID SOMEBODY SAY SOMETHING ABOUT MERCURY IN VACCINES?

When my children were very small, I once heard someone say there was mercury in vaccines. I was incredulous that someone could be so gullible as to believe something that absurd. Who on earth would put a known neurotoxin in vaccines for infants and children? Nobody, of course. Some people will believe anything, I mused to myself.

Memory of that incident would come back to haunt me years later. By that time, my investigations into biomedical intervention in autism had just begun. I learned that vaccines, particularly at the time Will was an infant and toddler, really did contain mercury. Now why would that be? As it turned out, the mercury was part of a vaccine preservative used to kill bacteria and fungi that might spoil the vaccine. This knowledge made me uneasy, yet I assured myself that the level of mercury must be extremely minute. It could not possibly be enough to harm anyone. Surely it could not cause autism, as some parent groups and Defeat Autism Now! claimed. Besides, I reassured myself, rigorous safety testing had undoubtedly been done before mercury-containing vaccines were given to babies. To believe otherwise was unthinkable. Besides, all the pharmaceutical companies and governmental health agencies were insisting the mercury in vaccines was safe. As far as I could tell, there was no way to verify which side of the mercury-autism debate was right. I decided the governmental agencies must surely know what they were talking about. They had all the data about vaccines and autism cases in their files. If there were a link, they would know it, right? What's more, autistic symptoms did not match my idea of those I would expect from toxic effect.

I remembered back to a time in my dad's garden when Dad had poured liquid pesticide on the ground around a plant. Fleeing the pesticide, two big juicy worms immediately surfaced at Dad's feet. Pleased with his find, Dad scooped up the worms and offered them to my ever-hungry pet robin. The robin merrily gulped them down—and then promptly keeled over, dead as a doornail within 15 minutes. My poor little bird! But that is the way it is with toxins—they act quickly. In lower doses, the reaction might be less severe, but it would still be immediate, or so I thought. Therefore, I concluded that, if mercury in Will's vaccines had affected him, I should have seen an immediate reaction, yet that was not the case. He had completed the full vaccination schedule without ever having any noticeable response. Instead, his autistic symptoms surfaced gradually over time, little by little, not suddenly as I would have expected with a toxic exposure.

In addition, it seemed to me that a toxin would have the same effect on everyone. Dad could have fed those poisoned worms to ten different robins and every one would have keeled over. Perhaps some would take longer than others, but the end result would be the same. Even at a lower dose that only caused illness, all the robins would have the same symptoms, right? Again, that was not what I saw on the autism spectrum. Symptoms there were numerous and diverse, varying widely from one child to the next. To me, autistic symptoms simply did not seem to behave like what I expected from toxic exposure. But just to be on the safe side, I began avoiding the flu shot since I heard most brands of it still contained mercury. In a way, I felt lucky that my kids were not due for any vaccines. I had time to wait for a final verdict on the mercury-autism issue. So, I decided to sit on the fence as the winds of controversy blew.

A FRIGHTENING DISCOVERY: A RESEARCH STUDY ABOUT RESEARCH STUDIES

Then one day I was viewing a free Defeat Autism Now! conference on my home computer. Speaker James Adams, PhD, of the University of Arizona described a study, and his talk aroused an unsettling apprehension in my chest. The study's researchers had examined a multitude of different scientific studies. Some of the studies they examined were about the symptoms of autism; others, about the symptoms of mercury poisoning. In the end, the researchers had produced a long list of symptoms. For each one, they named studies that identified it as a symptom of autism. They also named studies that identified this same symptom as a symptom of mercury poisoning. On the list, there were no autistic symptoms that were not also symptoms of mercury poisoning and vice versa. The researchers proposed that many autism cases were simply undiagnosed cases of mercury poisoning.

A chill swept across my heart. What I had heard about the mercury-autism controversy to that point seemed to be a matter of different people's opinions, opinions I could not verify for myself. But this study of scientific literature was different: I would be able to verify whether Will's symptoms were accurately described by mercury poisoning. My fingers drummed nervously on my knee. Could it really be true that every symptom of mercury poisoning matched the behavioral disorder we called autism? I winced. It was inconceivable to me that my son could have been outright poisoned and then left to endure years of suffering without accurate medical diagnosis or appropriate treatment. Well, at least there was one thing I was sure of: I was going to find that study. I went on the Internet and did a Google search on the study's title, *Autism: A Unique Type of Mercury Poisoning*. It was easy to find. It also appears on the Web sites for ARI (www.autism.com) and Safe Minds (www.safeminds.org). And what did the study say?

Symptoms of mercury poisoning are usually delayed, though not always

The study's descriptions of the characteristics of mercury poisoning described Will's decline in agonizing parallel. For starters, symptoms of mercury poisoning usually do not appear immediately unless the exposure is very high or the individual is especially sensitive. Instead, there is a period of delay between exposure and the onset of observable symptoms. The delay can last weeks, months, or even years. During this time, subtle changes are taking place in the brain and nervous system.[18]

Mercury poisoning symptoms vary considerably among individuals

Symptoms of mercury poisoning vary considerably from one person to the next; there are no "typical" symptoms. The wide variation is due to a combination of driving forces which include:[19]

1. *Dose amount.*

2. *Individual sensitivity.* There is great variability in the effect of mercury on different individuals. At the same level of exposure, one person may be severely impacted, while another person shows no symptoms or only mild ones.[20] An individual's sensitivity depends on:

    (a) *Age.* Children are far more susceptible than adults to the same dose of mercury.[21] Exposure is especially hazardous to fetuses and small infants because mercury accumulates in their bodies; infants under 4–6 months of age do not produce bile that normally helps clear toxins from the body. In addition, during the first few months of an infant's life, the blood–brain barrier that normally would keep mercury out of the brain is not fully developed.[22] Though mercury is extremely damaging to the cells in both the brain and the rest of the nervous system, it is selective, targeting certain areas of the brain—the same areas we see affected in autism, namely,[23]

        (i)   the cerebellum, which plays an important role in perception of senses, motor control, and position of body in space

        (ii) the amygdala, which controls emotional processing

        (iii) the hippocampus, which plays a part in memory.

    (b) *Gender.* At very high doses, males and females are affected equally. Otherwise, mercury has a greater effect on males than females, except in cases of kidney damage. In autism, three out of four afflicted children are boys rather than girls.[24]

    (c) *Genetic susceptibility.*

    (d) *State of health at time of exposure.*

3. *Route of entry into the body.* How the mercury gains access to the body will influence a person's symptoms. Was the mercury eaten, injected, or inhaled? Did it pass through the skin by means of creams, ointments, or ear drops? Another possible route is by IV during medical treatment. Mercury injected into the bloodstream is especially harmful.[25] Unlike mercury that is eaten, injected mercury bypasses the digestive tract that

would otherwise absorb it and route it through the portal vein into the liver for possible disposal before entry into the bloodstream.[26]

4.   *Frequency and amount of exposure.* Is the total exposure delivered in a single dose or repeated doses? If repeated, are the doses frequent, small doses or intermittent, large doses over a short period? The pattern of exposure can make a big difference in symptoms. For instance, there may be a bottle of 30 pills in your medicine cabinet that will not cause any ill effects when taken one a day for a month. However, if you took those same pills, 15 on Monday and 15 on Wednesday, you might end up like my poor robin. Intermittent, large doses delivered in a short time are potentially more harmful than the same total dose delivered in more frequent but smaller amounts.[27] The pattern of exposure during the peak use of vaccine mercury (from 1991 to roughly 2001) was intermittent, large doses over a short time.

5.   *Simultaneous antibiotic use.* Antibiotics greatly reduce the body's ability to excrete mercury.[28]

6.   *Form of mercury.* There are different forms of mercury, such as methyl mercury (found in fish), ethyl mercury (used in some vaccines), metallic mercury, liquid mercury, and ionic mercury.[29] Some forms are more toxic than others. Take methyl and ethyl mercury, for instance. Methyl is more toxic, but that does not mean by any stretch that ethyl is benign.[30] For example, you and a friend are hiking on a remote trail in the wilderness when you are bitten by a snake. How much comfort would you take in your friend's reassurance that, "You're lucky that snake wasn't the Inland Taipan of Australia. Those snakes can inject enough venom in one bite to kill 100 people. Yup, you are really lucky. You only got bit by a rattlesnake." Make no mistake. Mercury is toxic. Period. However, the form of mercury can influence the symptoms that develop in an exposed individual, so expect some variation in symptoms depending on which form of mercury is at work.

Symptoms of mercury poisoning

The researchers made a long list of the possible symptoms of mercury poisoning. For each one, they identified research studies and true-life poisoning accidents that linked the symptom to mercury poisoning. The clincher for me was that, side-by-side, they listed the autism research studies that assigned that same symptom to autism. Autistic symptoms were already quite familiar to me: it was seeing those same symptoms attributed to mercury poisoning that was so disturbing. Here are some of the most common symptoms of mercury poisoning:

1. *Senses.* Sensory distortion arises in nearly all cases of mercury poisoning:[31]

    (a) numbness and tingling around the mouth and in the hands and feet. These are the most common sensory problems, usually the first sign of mercury poisoning. Victims have reported numbness in the face and tongue as well.

    (b) loss of the sense of position in space

    (c) excessive pain when bumping arms and legs

    (d) extreme sensitivity to sudden noise or being touched.

2. *Mental function.* Anyone who shows signs of mercury poisoning will suffer some aspect of mental impairment. However, mercury poisoning is selective about which mental functions it targets; it does not affect them all. Its pattern of selection is remarkably similar to that seen in autism.[32] The primary areas targeted by mercury include:

    (a) short-term memory

    (b) attention and concentration

    (c) visual motor skills such as hand–eye coordination

    (d) spoken expression and comprehension.

    Victims of mercury poisoning may seem forgetful or confused. They may have trouble with abstract thinking and complex commands. Mercury's effect on intelligence varies from person to person. Intelligence testing performed on victims of mercury poisoning may show some have normal IQ or borderline intelligence, while others have mental retardation or are so impaired they cannot be tested. It is encouraging to know that, when the source of mercury exposure is removed, many patients recover their normal IQ.[33]

3. *Movement.* Victims of mercury poisoning will almost always develop some sort of movement disorder. Problems may include:[34]

    (a) gross motor impairment ranging from mild clumsiness or an abnormal posture or stride (including toe-walking) to a complete inability to walk, stand, or sit

    (b) fine motor impairment including unsteady handwriting or inability to hold a pen, as well as poor hand–eye coordination and motor-planning difficulty

(c) spasmodic jerks or twitches in the limbs, fingers, or facial muscles; arm-flapping; rocking.

4. *Emotional instability.* Anxiety, aggression, or irritability will usually surface in cases of mercury poisoning. Potential symptoms that are commonly observed include:[35]

   (a) anxiety and fearfulness. In addition, obsessive-compulsive tendencies and schizophrenic traits have been reported

   (b) irritability in adults and tantrums in children

   (c) indifference to others, avoidance of others, or a desire to be alone

   (d) depression including lack of interest and mental confusion

   (e) crying, laughter, or smiling without cause.

5. *Speech and hearing.* Impairments induced by mercury may include:[36]

   (a) obvious speech difficulties, especially in children. Prenatal exposure can cause severe language deficits or prevent language from developing altogether

   (b) inability to comprehend speech, despite the ability to hear

   (c) inability to generate meaningful speech

   (d) poor articulation such as slow, slurred formation of words

   (e) impaired hearing or, at very high doses, deafness

   (f) noise sensitivity.

6. *Behaviors.* Babies and children with mercury poisoning have been known to be agitated, cry for no apparent reason, cry continuously, or perhaps hit or bang their heads. They might slip into staring spells, wear a "mask face," or have trouble sleeping. Some refuse to eat or only eat a few foods.[37]

7. *Vision.* Mercury poisoning can lead to a variety of vision problems, especially in children. Lack of eye contact, sensitivity to light, and other visual impairments, even blindness, have been reported.[38]

8. *Muscles and skin.* Mercury poisoning can cause both high or low muscle tone. When muscle tone is low, muscle weakness is most apparent in the upper body. Arm strength in particular is weak. Drooling and difficulty in chewing and swallowing are common. Rashes and itches can also result from mercury poisoning.[39]

9. *Gut.* Mercury poisoning is known to cause inflammation in the stomach and intestines. It also inhibits the digestive enzyme, DPP4,

which is used to digest casein (a protein in milk) and gluten (a protein in wheat and certain other grains). Victims may suffer from diarrhea, constipation, abdominal pain, or rectal itching. They may have a poor appetite and lose weight.[40]

Though the study included descriptions of mercury-poisoning symptoms found in research with animals, its coverage of poisoning accidents in humans offered the most striking parallels to autism.

HISTORICAL REVIEW
What's gotten into the hat makers?

In the 1700s, a certain percentage of hat makers were acting strangely, in particular hat makers who worked with felt. They grew nervous and timid. Becoming uncomfortable in social situations, they began to avoid people. Developing acute anxiety, irrational fears, and depression, they were easily upset and prone to irritability and aggression. Their movement and coordination became impaired as well. The famous Mad Hatter in *Alice in Wonderland* was inspired by their example. A diagnosis, called Mad Hatter's disease, was created to describe their behaviors.

But what actually *caused* their decline and stole away their emotional stability? As it turned out, they were victims of prolonged exposure to inhaled mercury vapor. The vapor came from a mercury solution that was commonly used in the process of turning fur into felt.[41] If only they had known of the danger, Mad Hatter's disease could have been prevented.

What's up with the people at Minamata Bay, Japan?

In the early 1950s, hundreds of people near Minamata Bay, Japan, fell ill with an unknown disease. They complained of numbness in their arms, legs, and mouth. Motor skills and coordination deteriorated; for some, it was even difficult to walk. Victims suffered fatigue, sensory distortion, tremors, and seizures. Speech was reduced or became slurred; vision and hearing declined. In severe cases, people developed partial paralysis, jerking movements, difficulty swallowing, and brain damage; some even died. Children born to affected mothers were the most vulnerable. By the time the crisis subsided, some 1,400 people had died, and perhaps 20,000 had suffered. A name was devised for the illness: Minamata disease. But what actually *caused* this large-scale misery? As it turned out, these poor people had eaten fish from Minamata Bay that were heavily contaminated with mercury. The culprit was a factory that was discharging mercury-containing waste into the sea. It took a long time to make the connection. Not until 1957 was fishing banned in the area.[42]

A tragedy in Iraq in 1971

In 1971 and 1972, a large-scale outbreak of illness in Iraq sent 6,000 people to the hospital and 450 to premature deaths. Many times that number suffered without medical attention. Most victims were children. Symptoms began as burning or prickling of the skin and blurred vision. Then they advanced to loss of muscle coordination, hearing loss, blindness, coma, and sometimes death. Older children experienced delayed development and seizures. Infants born to affected mothers suffered weakness, delayed development, seizures, visual impairment, mental retardation, and cerebral palsy. Other such infants appeared fairly normal at birth, with only minor abnormalities in muscle tone and reflexes. However, they later fell prey to seizures and long delays in learning to walk and talk, as well as severe clumsiness. The cause of the outbreak was traced to consumption of wheat seeds treated with a fungicide containing mercury. The seeds had been intended for planting, not eating. About 178,000 tons of this seed had been imported from Mexico. However, in many parts of Iraq, the seed arrived after planting time, so villagers ground the seed into flour to make bread which was eaten by thousands. They did not know the pink dye on the seed itself was a warning, as was the skull-and-crossbones on the seed bags.[43]

A baffling affliction of infants and children in the early 1900s

Perhaps the most striking parallel to today's epidemic of regressive autism occurred in the first half of the 1900s. This large-scale nightmare of undetected mercury poisoning targeted infants and toddlers. From the 1930s through the mid-1950s, tens of thousands of children succumbed to a new and baffling disorder. One symptom, a weepy red rash, earned this disorder the name Pink's disease (or acrodynia). The playing and laughter of afflicted children was replaced with sadness. Some cried constantly. Periods of depression and excitation often alternated. Most were cranky and at times hostile. Some children stopped talking, while others would repeat the same words for hours. A number quit responding to their parents, seemingly unaware of them. A child might avoid human contact, hit, or bite. Some even hit themselves, banged their heads, flopped on the floor, or pulled their hair. Other symptoms included general ill-health, tiredness, sensitivity to light, anemia, peeling skin, and respiratory distress. Fatalities usually ran around 7 percent. For the survivors, Pink's disease was often a life-long disorder.[44]

The popular theories of the day ascribed the devastation of Pink's disease to either infectious or nutritional causes. Not until 1948 did anyone publish findings that associated Pink's disease with mercury. The publication came from a doctor at Cincinnati Children's Hospital who noticed large amounts of mercury in the urine of an afflicted child. The suggestion that Pink's disease was actually mercury poisoning was a radical idea, quite contrary to popular opinion. Most doctors associated mercury poisoning with adults, not infants. Nevertheless, it was true that infants and toddlers did have some exposure to mercury. By far, the largest source of exposure was from powders used to soothe the pain of teething. Mercury was included in them as an antiseptic. This anti-septic function of mercury was also employed in diaper-rash powders, ear oint-ments, calamine lotion, and topical treatments for minor cuts and scrapes. While parents *thought* they were taking care of their babies and toddlers with such products, they were actually harming them to some degree. The notion that Pink's disease was mercury poisoning was stiffly opposed by industry. Compa-nies stood too much to lose if their products truly had devastated the lives of tens of thousands of infants and children. Nevertheless, acceptance grew, slowly. The Cincinnati doctor's publication was six years old before most companies had removed the source of Pink's disease from their products. Though removal was voluntary, the companies had eventually relinquished for fear of potential lawsuits and bad publicity.[45]

However, not everyone who was exposed to frequent, low doses of mercury in teething powders actually developed Pink's disease. Quite the contrary: only 1 in 500 to 1 in 1,000 were noticeably affected. The likelihood of falling ill appeared more dependent on individual susceptibility and possibly age than on the dose of mercury.[46] Pink's disease is an example of a severe disorder that selec-tively affected a small but significant percentage of children. It was induced by doses of mercury that were seemingly benign to some individuals yet damaging or lethal to others.[47]

IS IT POSSIBLE SOME CASES OF AUTISM ARE REALLY MERCURY POISONING?

I could not help but wonder if the current epidemic of regressive autism was simply history repeating itself, only this time the mercury came from vaccines rather than teething powders. The symptoms of autism and Pink's disease were strikingly similar though not identical. Of course, some variation would be expected. The dose amount, pattern of exposure, and the infant's age at time of exposure were different. The nature of exposure in other mercury-poisoning accidents such as Mad Hatter's, Minamata disease, and Iraq's tragedy was different as well. For one, the route of entry into the body was not injected as is vaccine mercury. And these other situations mostly involved methyl mercury, rather than ethyl mercury that is used in vaccines.[48] Injecting infants at birth and intermittent periods thereafter with large doses of ethyl mercury that exceeded safety standards had never been tried before. There was no way to know exactly what form the symptoms might take in susceptible individuals.[49] Is it possible that a unique expression of mercury poisoning has been labeled "autism" just as other forms had been labeled "Mad Hatter's disease," "Minamata disease," or "Pink's disease"? Could it be that "regressive" autism is actually "acquired" autism?

WILL'S SYMPTOMS FIT MERCURY POISONING

As I read the study detailing symptoms of mercury poisoning, light bulbs of recognition flashed in rapid fire. Both the progression of mercury poisoning and its symptoms fit Will to a tee. None of his "autistic" symptoms were left off the list. Sure, there were symptoms listed that Will did not have, like seizures, for instance. However, I knew that even those symptoms were commonplace on the autism spectrum. It especially hurt to see so many of the identical terms I had been hearing for years from Will's therapists for speech, physical therapy, and occupational therapy, terms like motor planning, sensory perception, loss of position in space, low muscle tone—they went on and on. Each one hurled off the page like an icy snowball in my face. Moreover, no category of symptoms offered reprieve. Each one screamed out Will's world in painful detail. They addressed all his issues, every single one. There may be many roads that lead to the behaviors we label autism. However, it was quite convincing to me that Will had taken this one. Mercury poisoning.

My sense of alarm had grown and spiked as I read the study. Trying to force a deep breath, I found a brick wedged in my throat. Like a pebble being swept away in a flash flood, I could feel myself engulfed in a swelling surge of panic. It was *inconceivable* to me that Will had suffered from bold-faced mercury poisoning all these years, and nobody guessed it. He had been to every specialist under the sun, yet no one even suspected. He was never treated. He simply suffered. *We* suffered. And to think it could all have been prevented in the first place. A terrorizing video reel whizzed in my brain. A million painful episodes of my life with Will flashed past at dizzying speed. Life did not have to be that way. It was not our destiny. We had been ambushed—ambushed by mercury.

The raging flood of thoughts had to be dammed. It was carrying me away when all I had were suspicions, no proof. Will's test results for heavy-metal overload had not come back yet from Dr. Biomedical, so there was no sense in emotionally hurling myself over a cliff like some crazed lemming when I did not know for sure. All I knew for certain was that:

1. Will had been exposed to injected mercury that exceeded federal safety standards. Those standards will be discussed in the next chapter.

2. None of Will's "autistic" symptoms fell outside known symptoms of mercury poisoning.

3. The timing of the appearance of Will's symptoms was consistent with the mercury exposure he received in infant vaccines. I was unaware of any other excessive mercury exposures he may have had.

Thus, there was a known exposure and incriminating symptoms. The deciding factor for me would be Will's test results. They would hand down the verdict. I decided to sit tight, take some deep breaths, and wait to see. Yes, the possibility was real, but it was not certainty.

WILL'S TEST RESULTS ARRIVE

At last the results arrived in the mail. As I had feared, they revealed excessively high levels of mercury. It brought a wretch to my gut I had not known was possible. What had been inconceivable was a reality. At first, I could not accept it. The pain was too great. It had been one thing to believe that Will's troubles stemmed from an unlucky draw from the gene pool, a freak of nature; it was quite another to believe they were rooted in an *avoidable* cause. Will truly had been the healthy baby he had appeared to be. Right now, he should be living the happy, healthy life nature intended. But an unseen poison had derailed him and set us both sprawling into a nightmare on the autism spectrum.

What's more, I was appalled that I had played an unwitting role in my own son's undoing. Conscientiously, I had taken my baby to the doctor for each well-baby checkup. There I had signed the papers for his *protective* immunizations. The papers had said there was a very small chance of an allergic reaction—nothing about chances of autism-spectrum disorders to the tune of 1 in 150 with a heavy bias against boys. Per the nurse's request, I had even held his knees for injections. Oh, my God! No! It could not be true. I could not bear it. It hurt too much. I could hear the resounding condemnation of Mother Perfect and was afraid I always would. But I had not known. My God, there was no way for me to have known. If only it were possible to go back in time and relive those few moments, I would make it different this time.

Yet that wish is one I will never get. Instead, I must endure the ache for a chance to do it over again. Will's test results launched me into a mourning that lasted for many weeks. Have you ever been so profoundly traumatized by something that you could not tell a soul? That's where I was. I wept over the loss of my perfect baby. Over the suffering he had endured, suffering that could have been prevented. And I wept over the passing of nine-plus years without appropriate diagnosis or treatment. Each year was a missed opportunity to regain our footing. Those painful weeks of realization were a devastating period that still seeps back into my life from time to time.

But at least now I know what I am dealing with. Finally, I stand a chance to make a difference because I know who the real enemy is. I no longer grope about in the dark searching for solutions blamed on some nameless, changeless gene. At long last, I am in a position of power to intervene and reverse the course of decline. Indeed, there have been many successes. I have to take comfort in that.

HINDSIGHT IS 20–20

My son, Will, was the perfectly healthy baby he had appeared to be. However, he did have a family history of autoimmune disorder, rheumatoid arthritis to be specific. Perhaps that played a role in making him one of those infants who was more vulnerable to mercury's snare.

On the day Will was born and at various short intervals thereafter, he was exposed to large doses of injected mercury through the mandatory pediatric vaccine schedule. Apparently, it took its toll. Its effects were first noticed as pervasive motor delay and low muscle tone, as well as sensory distortion, especially to loud noises. We treated these problems with lots of early-intervention therapy, such as physical, occupational and speech. We hoped that would take care of it, but it didn't. The extremely low muscle tone eventually enabled medium-sized tonsils and adenoids to block Will's airway to the point of sleep apnea and its harmful effects. So the tonsils and adenoids were removed. Yet, we did not remove the mercury. In fact, we did not even discontinue its use. Instead, we injected more mercury-containing vaccines per the all-important—and supposedly safe—pediatric schedule.

As symptoms of mercury poisoning swelled from motor delay into intellectual delay, our treatment efforts expanded to include early education and later special education. In the meantime, Will's weakened immune system succumbed to numerous ear infections, as well as sinus infections and bouts of strep throat. Round after round of oral antibiotics ensured annihilation of good gut flora and gave rise to overgrowths of destructive gut yeast and bad bacteria. The resulting inflammation, chronic diarrhea, and leaky gut impaired digestive capability and harassed an already weakened immune system.

But life went on. By age 5, Will was diagnosed with a "mild" psychiatric disorder, ADHD, which was treated with a drug to mask inattention and lack of focus. In 1999, when Will was 6 years old, a government health agency noticed that, for many years, the mandatory schedule had been exposing infants and children to levels of mercury that exceeded federal safety standards, so they issued a press release. Somehow I missed it, and nobody brought it to my attention. In the past, whenever Will was due for a vaccine, I was unfailingly notified by the pediatrician, day-care center, or school system. Even for my unvaccinated, school-aged foster children, Social Services instructed me that a first order of business was to take them for their vaccines. Yet when there was news of a known overexposure to my children of a potentially dangerous neurotoxin in vaccines, I did not get word. Had I known, I would definitely have had Will tested since he had so many unusual problems. Medical treatment and other rescue efforts could have launched immediately to cut short Will's downward spiral. But no, we did not get word in those days. Rather, we just kept doing more of what wasn't working. We could only watch and worry as the relentless symptoms persisted and cascaded along new and expanded trails.

They further impaired Will's brain function and behaviors. As his social skills languished and out-of-control anxiety surfaced, we tried to suppress the anxiety with an anti-anxiety drug. In vain, we stepped up treatment efforts with training in relaxation techniques and social skills. Nevertheless, Will continued to decline and his diagnosis was revised to a more severe psychiatric disorder, AS. Everybody said it was his genes—nothing we could influence. They said it was all in his head. Nothing else going on in his body had anything to do with his brain. How could they be so wrong? How is it possible Will and our family have paid such a price when we followed all the rules and did everything right?

With biomedical intervention, we are finally treating Will's real problems. We are cleaning up his gut, supplementing heavily with nutrients, and removing heavy metals. As a result, he has made tremendous strides. His smile is back, and he is enjoying life with greater freedom from his bonds than he has since infancy. Indeed, we are making progress toward recovery. Who knows how far we will get. Will's future is much brighter than it had been for a very long time. I am grateful for that. Yet I wish I were as resilient as he. I don't know if I can ever recover from what happened to my child. But at least, over time, I have found that, as Will heals and gets better, so do I.

My experience sparked an interest in learning more about the story behind mercury in vaccines. Over recent years, I had caught bits and pieces of news about it but was not paying much attention. Now, I was really listening. The next chapter relays some highlights of the U.S. history of mercury in vaccines, as well as evidence of its harm.

NOTES

1.   McCandless 2007, p. 55; Kirby 2005, p. 359.
2.   Bernard *et al.* 2000, p. 57; Cave with Mitchell 2001, pp. 47–48.
3.   Green 2006c, p. 11.
4.   Bradstreet *et al.* 2003, pp. 76–79; Kirby 2005, p. 176; McCandless 2007, p. 51.
5.   Baker 2006a, p. 201; Jepson and Johnson 2007, p. 113.
6.   Cave with Mitchell 2001, pp. 42–43, 58; McCandless 2007, p. 54.
7.   Bock and Stauth 2007, p. 21.
8.   Cave with Mitchell 2001, p. xvi; Pangborn and Baker 2005, p. 2:61.
9.   Kirby 2005, p. xiv.
10. Bock and Stauth 2007, p. 58.
11. Cave with Mitchell 2001, p. 43.
12. Ibid., p. 42.
13. Bernard *et al.* 2000, p. 39; Pangborn and Baker 2005, pp. 1:6–7.
14. McCandless 2007, p. 54.
15. Kirby 2005, pp. 119–20; Cave with Mitchell 2001, p. 58.
16. Cave with Mitchell 2001, pp. 42–43, 58; Kirby 2005, pp. 119–20, 141; Eggleston and Nylander 1987, pp. 704–707; McCandless 2007, pp. 54–55; Pangborn and Baker 2005, pp. 1:6–7.
17. Pangborn and Baker 2005, p. 1:6; Levinson 2006b, p. 152; Kirby 2005, p. xii.
18. Bernard *et al.* 2000, pp. 2, 42–44.
19. Ibid., pp. 2, 40–41; Kirby 2005, p. 52; Binstock 2007a, p. 292.
20. Bernard *et al.* 2000, p. 40.
21. Kirby 2005, p. 52.
22. Ibid., p. 48; Bernard *et al.* 2000, p. 39; Binstock 2007a, pp. 291–92; Cave with Mitchell 2001, pp. 66, 78.
23. Cave with Mitchell 2001, pp. 45–47, 67.
24. Bernard *et al.* 2000, p. 40.
25. Binstock 2007a, p. 291.
26. Cave with Mitchell 2001, p. 45; Bernard *et al.* 2000, p. 39.
27. Kirby 2005, pp. 55–56.
28. McCandless 2007, p. 51; Pangborn and Baker 2005, p. 1:11.
29. Bernard *et al.* 2000, p. 2.
30. Kirby 2005, pp. 334, 406.
31. Bernard *et al.* 2000, p. 13.
32. Ibid., p. 30.
33. Ibid., pp. 15–17.
34. Ibid., pp. 14–15.
35. Ibid., pp. 2, 5–6.
36. Ibid., p. 11.
37. Ibid., pp. 6, 18–19.
38. Ibid., pp. 19–20.
39. Ibid., pp. 20–22.
40. Ibid., pp. 22–23; Adams 2007, p. 16; Pangborn 2006b, pp. 62–63.
41. Cave with Mitchell 2001, p. 45; Bernard *et al.* 2000, p. 8; Kirby 2005, p. 51.
42. Kirby 2005, p. 61.
43. Ibid., pp. 49, 61.

44. Bernard *et al.* 2000, pp. 8, 55; Kirby 2005, pp. 62–64.
45. Kirby 2005, pp. 62–64; Bernard *et al.* 2000, p. 55.
46. Bernard *et al.* 2000, p. 40.
47. Kirby 2005, p. 135.
48. Ibid., p. 61.
49. Bernard *et al.* 2000, pp. 4, 39, 54, 58.

Chapter 21

Mercury in Vaccines

WHAT THIS CHAPTER HAS IN STORE

This chapter reviews some of the basic history about mercury in childhood vaccines. It will give you an idea of what your child's level of exposure may have been. Also presented are the key influences that have shaped mercury-in-vaccine policy, as well as some of the evidence against mercury's use. Such knowledge will help you make decisions about vaccine mercury for your child. At the time of this writing, mercury in childhood vaccines is much less than it was during its 1991-to-2001 peak. However, its use has not been eliminated. This chapter identifies some of the best sources of information for keeping current on the changing situation of mercury in vaccines.

THE U.S. HISTORY OF MERCURY IN VACCINES

Mercury has a long history of use in the field of medicine and, for many years, was considered relatively safe.[1] Its use in vaccines began in the 1930s in the form of a preservative called Thimerosal developed by Eli Lilly. The company conducted a single safety study in 1930 that was toted for decades as proof that Thimerosal was safe for use in humans. In the study, doctors injected 22 human patients with high levels of Thimerosal; then, they waited to see if the patients showed signs of toxic effect. All the patients were known to be dying of meningococcal meningitis, a serious bacterial infection. Most died from this disease within days of their Thimerosal injection. No negative effects from the Thimerosal were said to be observed, so the conclusion was made that Thimerosal was safe. Later, when the Food and Drug Administration (FDA) was created, Thimerosal was "grandfathered" onto its list of fully approved medical additives. The preservative never underwent any of the rigorous safety trials currently required for FDA approval. The study of dying patients was the only safety data on Thimerosal ever submitted by any drug company to the FDA.[2]

Throughout the 1900s, most vaccines came in multi-dose vials whose seals were repeatedly punctured by needles. A preservative was needed to kill bacteria and fungi that might be introduced into the vials and cause spoilage. In the beginning, the level of mercury from Thimerosal that babies and children received in their vaccine schedule met federal safety standards. Throughout the 1900s, Thimerosal was the preservative of choice among vaccine makers.[3]

Over time, new vaccines were developed and added to the mandatory schedule. As the number of vaccines increased, so did the level of mercury being injected into American babies. The peak level of exposure through vaccines began in 1991 with the addition of the hepatitis B vaccine to the mandatory schedule. With this new schedule, injected mercury began the day a baby was born and continued in intermittent, large doses at ages 2 months, 4 months, 6 months, and roughly 15 months. This pattern of exposure and dosing contin-ued through late 2001 and possibly beyond.[4]

Though Thimerosal had become a major source of mercury exposure for babies and children, it went unnoticed. No one thought to do the math to calcu-late the increasing levels of mercury. Had someone done so, this is what he would have discovered: in a single day, a 2-month-old baby weighing 11 pounds could have been exposed to a mercury level (62.5 mcg) that was 125 times more than the EPA limit for that child's weight. Other federal agencies had different limits for safe mercury exposure. Though that seems odd, it was the case nevertheless. Using the limit set by the Center for Disease Control (CDC), the 11-pound baby's exposure was 42 times the limit. Using the FDA's limit, 31 times.[5] Moreover, the safety violation would be even greater for a 2-month-old weighing less than 11 pounds.

By act of Congress, the FDA was required to review and evaluate the risk of all food and drugs containing mercury, including Thimerosal. As a result, an announcement was made in July 1999 titled, "Thimerosal in Vaccines: A Joint Statement of the American Academy of Pediatrics and the Public Health Service." The announcement received little coverage in the mainstream press. Downplaying the severity of exposure, it stated, "Some children could be exposed to a cumulative level of mercury over the first 6 months of life that exceeds one of the federal guidelines on methyl mercury." The document went on to say that the acceptable limits provided a significant safety margin and that there had been no evidence of harm. Furthermore, there was no need for children to be tested for mercury exposure. However, the announcement did recommend that Thimerosal-containing vaccines be removed "as soon as possible." Doctors and parents were told not to waver from the vaccine schedule. However, for newborns whose mothers did not have hepatitis B antibodies, the birth dose of hepatitis B could be postponed until 2–6 months of age "when the infant is considerably larger."[6]

The announcement was very reassuring considering the severity of the exposure. It did not mention that the federal safety limit in violation was based on the average *adult*, not infant.[7] Nor did it recall Thimerosal-containing vaccines from doctors' offices and clinics. Instead, the plan was to use them. Furthermore, Thimerosal's removal from vaccines was not *mandated* to vaccine makers, but only *recommended*. And the pediatric schedule remained intact, with the possible exception of the birth dose of hepatitis B. No mention was made that alternative Thimerosal-free brands were available for those who might be interested. Finally, the typical means of communicating vaccine information to parents via pediatricians, school systems, day-care centers, and other means was not invoked. Parents did not receive notification directly that their children may have been overexposed to mercury, not even parents of children with disabilities like autism-spectrum disorders. As far as most parents knew, there was nothing to be concerned about. And the nation's babies and children continued to receive Thimerosal-containing vaccines.

Over two years passed. By late 2001, an unknown quantity of Thimerosal-containing children's vaccines still lingered in doctors' offices and clinics. Though it had taken a couple of years, Thimerosal had been phased out of newly made vaccines for the pediatric schedule (except for trace amounts). However, it was still used for tetanus, diphtheria-tetanus, and meningitis vaccines, which are sometimes given to children. In addition, Thimerosal was used in the majority of brands of flu shot. Despite having 25 mcg of mercury, the flu shot was recommended for use in pregnant women. A pediatric version (two shots with 12.5 mcg each) was recommended for children 6–23 months old. As for the rest of the world, especially developing nations, multi-dose vials of vaccines containing Thimerosal were featured for their cost-cutting advantages.[8]

Despite tenacious efforts by various parent groups and others, Thimerosal, even today, is still not treated as a serious health risk.[9] It remains in use in some vaccines intended for infants, children, and adults, including pregnant women.

UNDERSTANDING THE HISTORY OF MERCURY IN VACCINES

When I first learned the history of mercury in vaccines, I could not understand why it unfolded as it did. It seemed common sense to me that babies should not be given *any* toxins, right? So, why would we knowingly inject babies and children with mercury, a toxin that is considered one of the most brain- and nerve-damaging compounds on earth?[10] I didn't get it. But I have since figured it out. The trick was to read a book that explained both sides of the tug-of-war about the mercury-in-vaccine question.

A book of intrigue about Thimerosal in vaccines

An investigative reporter for the *New York Times* took an interest in the controversy over mercury in vaccines. His name is David Kirby. As he delved into the unfolding story of Thimerosal, Kirby unearthed a drama, with a dynamic cast of players that encompassed parent activists, government health agencies, politicians, vaccine makers, the courts, and more. With an objective eye, David Kirby reviewed the evidence put forth by both sides of the mushrooming controversy. In 2005, he published a book that skillfully tells the tale of mysteries and secrets, cross-purposes and showdowns. It is a story of passion, determination, and struggle on both sides of the fence. Arguments and evidence from both sides are presented along with their strengths and weaknesses. No wonder moviemakers have plans for the book on the silver screen. If you don't want to wait for the movie, the title of the book is *Evidence of Harm*.

A look at vaccine safety from some other people's views

Something I realized as I read *Evidence of Harm* is that I have tunnel vision. As a parent, I can only see one issue—safety. In my mind, it is the single, overriding factor that dictates whether toxins belong in vaccines. From where I sit, safety has no rivals. But thinking that everyone feels that way just goes to show you how naive I am. The book's in-depth look at the controversy enlightened me to the fact that safety is just one of many factors people hold dear. The fact a controversy even exists over whether to put an optional toxin in vaccines is proof of that. You would have to read *Evidence of Harm* to appreciate the powerful impact of these other forces in the Thimerosal struggle. I will merely suggest what some of the other viewpoints are. Try on some other people's shoes, and see if any considerations besides safety come to mind:

1. You are a vaccine maker who potentially faces billions of dollars in legal claims for injured children.[11]

2. You are a politician grateful for large campaign contributions from vaccine makers. Would you propose legislation to protect your benefactors from vaccine-injury liability? Even if you do not propose the legislation yourself, how would you vote if it came to the floor of Congress? Could you bite the hand that feeds you?

3. You are a government health agency with responsibility to build trust in vaccines and to promote compliance nationwide; therefore, you have vigorously promoted vaccines for as long as the public can remember. Though you are also responsible to evaluate safety of the vaccines, you are paid far more to promote than to evaluate. Now, after the fact, it has come to light that your vaccines contain potentially damaging levels of mercury. You are asked to investigate whether this practice is safe. Could you be objective? Could you convict yourself by saying it is not safe? To do so would cause severe public embarrassment and perhaps end some people's careers.[12]

4. You are again a government health agency. For untold years, you have done your utmost to ensure all children are vaccinated. Through doctors, the school system, day cares, and other means, you enforce compliance. What will you think of *any* issue that might frighten some parents away from vaccines and undermine the success of your program? In fact, in your zeal to guard the program, some will charge that you care more about the program itself than the children it was designed to protect.[13]

5. As an "independent expert," you have a seat on an advisory committee to a government health agency. As such, you are involved in decision making about national vaccine policy, including deciding whether new vaccines should be added to the mandatory pediatric schedule. At the same time, you are also involved in one or more of the following:

    (a) You own stock in vaccine makers whose vaccines are affected by your vote.

    (b) You or your academic institution receive research grants from vaccine makers.

    (c) You serve on the advisory board of a vaccine maker.

    (d) You hold a patent to vaccines impacted by your vote.Of course, you recognize new vaccine mandates will benefit you personally since they guarantee vaccine sales growth. In the 1990s, annual sales of vaccines grew at 14 percent, while drug sales grew at just 8 percent. And the global vaccine market reached $6.5 billion, with the expectation of topping $10 billion by the year 2010. Despite your various conflicts of interest, you are still allowed to vote on government vaccine policy.[14] Could you be objective?

Each of the positions has a degree of power and influence. Many people found themselves in exactly these positions and had to decide for themselves how they would respond to the Thimerosal-in-vaccine issue. *Evidence of Harm* gave me a chance to examine the words and actions of some of these people. Their eagerness to discredit and ignore evidence against Thimerosal's safety was often unexpected and disturbing. I could not help but question whether they are as riveted to safety as I am. Thus, their statistics, "scientific" research, and assurances of Thimerosal's safety began to ring hollow for me. Many of them, in both government and industry, sounded too much like tobacco companies investigating a cancer link to smoking or teething-powder makers evaluating a connection between their products and Pink's disease.

A blessing of Evidence of Harm

I found it liberating to read *Evidence of Harm*. Up to that point, I had been carrying a tremendous burden of guilt for having taken Will for his many mercury-containing vaccines. Perpetually surfacing in my thoughts was the rebuke that somehow I should have detected the danger and protected him. Reading David Kirby's book made it unmistakably clear that it would have been humanly impossible for me to have protected Will. When my children were receiving infant vaccines in the early- and mid-1990s, the whole country was years away from discovering the mercury risk that would not be announced until July 1999. And even once the news was announced, there were huge forces at play—both of ignorance and intent—to suppress a connection between autism and vaccine mercury. These forces were much bigger than I. They continue to be at work even today. So, for me, *Evidence of Harm* was a book of great healing. It lifted a painful burden of guilt.

A SAFETY ATTITUDE TOWARD VACCINES

So what position should parents take when it comes to Thimerosal's use in their child's vaccines? Perhaps it all boils down to your willingness to take risks. After all, in life we take many risks. We might change jobs, ask someone out on a date, or order a spicy dish in a restaurant. These are all *acceptable* risks because we can afford to lose what is at stake. However, as a parent of a child receiving vaccines, inclusion of a neurotoxin is *not* an acceptable risk, for I cannot bare to lose what I am risking—my child's health. The stakes are too high and the price too dear. Nowadays, I wonder why I ever sat on the fence of the mercury-autism controversy. Why had I thought that solid, undeniable proof of harm was necessary before I could choose sides? I can't figure that out.

Think about it. The vaccine program is mandated in a one-size-fits-all fashion for our nation's children—regardless of genetic vulnerability, immune status, or other individual differences. To safely meet the needs of every child, that program should be rigorously tested and continuously scrutinized and evaluated. We cannot afford a "mistake" in a program of such massive consequence. Any reasonable cause for concern should be taken seriously.

A known toxin in the mix seems like a reasonable cause for concern, don't you think? Why would we argue over its removal and demand proof of its harm beyond a shadow of a doubt? Where is the sense in that? If we err, shouldn't it be on the side of safety? Especially when the commodity at risk is a national treasure like our children. They are the nation's future—literally. Shouldn't we be zealous about vaccine safety rather than lax? Why would we "grandfather" any product as safe when we inject it into the bloodstreams of babies? And if we wake up one day and realize we have been injecting a neurotoxin far in excess of our safety limit, why would we keep doing it? If safety is of prime importance, wouldn't we recall mercury-containing vaccines and mandate immediate removal of mercury from production lines? At a minimum, shouldn't we at least recommend Thimerosal-free brands to parents? If safety is of utmost importance, wouldn't we want to be sure parents of overexposed children were notified? Given we already had in place a very reliable means of communication to parents, wouldn't we use it? An obscure press release would never do, at least not if safety was our top concern.

As you read the history of Thimerosal's use, did you sense a rigorous attitude toward safety? Or did our national attitude seem rather laid back? Since past performance is a likely predictor of future performance, I worry that safety rigor is not on the horizon either. It appears to me that vaccines are not an area I can relinquish to the "experts." I must take the time to become informed, not only about Thimerosal but other vaccine issues as well. Being knowledgeable improves my chances that the vaccines critical to my children's health will only help them and not harm.

THE CURRENT STATUS OF MERCURY IN VACCINES

An FDA Web site that shows the Thimerosal content of today's vaccines is www.fda.gov/cber/vaccine/Thimerosal.htm. This site includes two very helpful tables for vaccine consumers. They serve as a good starting point for parents in a vaccine discussion with health-care providers. One table shows the Thimerosal content of only those vaccines routinely recommended for children from birth to 6 years old. For each vaccine, the various brand names from different manufacturers are listed. The Thimerosal concentration and dose of mercury for each one is also listed. At the time of this writing, each vaccine brand will either:

- contain Thimerosal, such as some brands of flu shot
- be Thimerosal-free
- contain "trace" amounts of Thimerosal that are introduced into vaccines through use of Thimerosal as a sanitizer in the manufacturing process.[15]

In a few states such as California and Iowa, state law does not allow Thimerosal in vaccines given to babies and pregnant women.[16] In addition, most childhood vaccines in the U.S. are offered in single-dose vials. Since these are only used once, they do not need a preservative like Thimerosal.[17]

The Web site's second table of interest shows an expanded list of vaccines and their Thimerosal content. This more-comprehensive table includes all the vaccines from the first table plus those for older children and adults. According to it, Thimerosal exists to some extent in certain brands of tetanus, diphtheria-tetanus, and flu shot, which are sometimes given to children and pregnant women.[18]

Parents can request Thimerosal-free vaccine brands from their medical provider.[19] Sometimes compounding pharmacies are useful to obtain desired brands, if necessary. If a vaccine contains Thimerosal, Thimerosal will be named in the ingredient list on the vaccine package or paper insert. Parents can ask their medical provider to help them locate this information.

AUTISM GROUPS AS SOURCES OF INFORMATION

Several autism groups exist that oppose use of Thimerosal in vaccines. Their Web sites can be helpful sources of information to stay current about the changing vaccine landscape. They also offer ways to add your voice to the forces of change. These groups include:[20]

- SafeMinds.org
- NationalAutismAssociation.org
- GenerationRescue.org
- NoMercury.org
- MomsAgainstMercury.org
- PutChildrenFirst.org.

YOU BE THE JUDGE

So what is some of the research and information about vaccine Thimerosal and developmental disorders? Is there anything to it? Does it seem flimsy or con-

trived? You be the judge. For your examination, the following pages delve into the most prominent evidence related to use of Thimerosal in vaccines. First come observations that arouse suspicion of Thimerosal's safety and provoke interest in conducting research. They are followed by descriptions of formal population studies, as well as research in laboratories and clinics. For more details, David Kirby's *Evidence of Harm* is an excellent resource because it pulls from numerous sources to provide one-stop-shopping for the story of vaccine mercury and developmental disorders like autism. So, let's get started with a few observations.

The rate of autism increased as use of Thimerosal-containing vaccines increased

Thimerosal was first added to vaccines in the 1930s. It is a curious coincidence that autism was first described among children born in the 1930s.[21] Subsequently, as each new series of Thimerosal-containing vaccines was added to the mandatory infant schedule, the rate of autism increased. Over time, the rate of regressive autism especially skyrocketed.[22]

Autism spread to low-income families after vaccines became free

In the 1940s and 1950s, autism primarily occurred in families of the upper and upper-middle classes who could afford to pay for health care like vaccines. However, after U.S. federal grants made vaccines free to low-income families, autism spread across class lines. Today, autism is widespread in all socioeconomic groups.[23]

Large unvaccinated groups of children have no autism

There are two large populations who do not vaccinate their children for religious reasons. One is the Pennsylvania Amish who, over the course of many years, have had virtually no cases of autism. The other population is a home-schooling organization in the Chicago area, comprised of people who share no common genetics. Of their 35,000 children, none has autism. Based on the U.S. rate (1 in 150), a population that size should have 233 children with autism-spectrum disorders.[24] That's nearly four loaded school buses. Though these two examples are not a direct comparison to Thimerosal in vaccines, they incriminate *something* related to vaccine use.[25]

Autism spread outside industrialized nations after export of Thimerosal-containing vaccines

Until recently, autism had rarely been reported in countries outside industrialized nations. But that has been changing. One possible explanation is the U.S. exportation of Thimerosal-containing vaccines. Shortly after the July 1999 announcement recommending Thimerosal's removal, the Clinton administration bought some $50 million worth of Thimerosal-containing vaccines and donated them to third-world countries. Since that time, Thimerosal-containing vaccines have been exported to nations throughout the developing world. Since manufacture, distribution, storage, and refrigeration of single-dose (preservative-free) vials are not considered practical, multi-dose vials requiring a preservative are used. The low cost of Thimerosal makes these vaccines affordable to poor nations. In 2004, the official Chinese news agency, Xinhua, reported that the country's autism rate had suddenly and unexpectedly skyrocketed. The number of children with autism had leaped from nearly nothing to some 1.8 million in only a few years. That's about 30,000 school buses loaded with children, if you can picture it. Other countries, such as Indonesia, Argentina, India, and Nigeria, are also reporting increased rates of autism. However, improved medical services, and, consequently, more monitoring and reporting, may explain part of the increase.[26]

Vaccine-autism court cases spiked dramatically in the early 1990s as use of Thimerosal-containing vaccines increased

Vaccine-autism cases in U.S. courts began to rise slowly in the 1970s and continued upward throughout the 1980s. But the number of cases spiked dramatically in the early 1990s after Thimerosal exposure reached its pinnacle.[27] To appreciate the drama played out in the courts, it helps to understand the unique situation that surrounds vaccine litigation.

Back in 1986, Congress created Vaccine Court to prevent vaccine shortages. Such shortages had been occurring when some vaccine makers pulled out of the market in fear of lawsuits. The new Vaccine Court was a no-fault alternative in which the federal government assumed liability for vaccine-related injuries and death. The money paid to injured parties or their families does not come from vaccine makers, but rather from a 75-cent-per-vaccine tax. Anyone with a vaccine injury case must first file in Vaccine Court. Only if plaintiffs are denied or dissatisfied with their results can they file a lawsuit in civil court. Awards in Vaccine Court cover medical expenses and cap payment for death or injury at $250,000. Of the 8,075 petitions filed between 1988 and 2003, only

1,790 (22 percent) had won compensation by 2004. However, when payment for medical expenses and other damages are awarded, they are fairly generous. In 2002, they averaged $772,675. Even so, the awards are a far cry from the near millions of dollars sometimes awarded in medical cases by juries in civil court, especially for cases involving children.[28]

A significant issue in Vaccine Court is the statute of limitation. It is just three years, and the clock starts ticking for autism on the day of diagnosis.[29] Many families swept up in the autism epidemic of the 1990s were past the three-year window because they had not suspected Thimerosal as the source of their child's autism at the time of diagnosis. It was much later, after the FDA's July 1999 announcement, that some parents began to test for mercury overload and made a connection to Thimerosal. By that time, these families were ineligible for Vaccine Court, so they took their cases to civil court.

By 2002, the burgeoning number of vaccine-autism lawsuits brought turmoil both to Vaccine Court and Capitol Hill. Vaccine Court had been designed to handle *rare* cases of injury or death, not an overwhelming flood of autism cases. So, in July 2002, Vaccine Court judges issued a ruling to cope with what they called an "unusual situation." They lumped together more than 400 autism cases into one massive proceeding called the "Omnibus Autism Proceeding." Of these cases, over 300 had been filed in the prior six months alone. The plan was to make a combined ruling in July 2004 that would then be applied to each individual case.[30] The timeline, however, has slipped considerably and the number of cases has grown. A May 2007 update published by the Vaccine Court judges states, "At this time, just over 4,800 petitions in autism cases remain pending, stayed until the conclusion of the Omnibus Autism Proceeding. Additional petitions continue to be filed, but at a very reduced rate."[31] At the time of this writing, only the first of several test cases has received a ruling. It came in March 2008. In this case regarding Hannah Poling, the court sided in favor of the family.

Back in 2002, battle lines over conflicting plans for reform were drawn on Capitol Hill. Vaccine makers were pushing Congress to redirect all civil cases into Vaccine Court. Parent groups like Safe Minds were fighting back hard through their own supporters in Congress. They knew that a funneling of all cases to Vaccine Court would mean a dead-end for most families due to the three-year statute of limitations. Such families would be left without any recourse whatsoever through the court system. Thus, the year 2002 was filled with haggling and jousting, each side trying to out-maneuver or block the other.

The tide finally turned when, unknown to most members of Congress, a last-minute rider was anonymously attached to a mammoth bill, the historic Homeland Security Act of 2002. The rider dismissed all Thimerosal lawsuits, present and future, from civil court. The vast majority of families, a figure in the thousands, who were ineligible for Vaccine Court were completely shut out of the court system. When news of the rider became known to Congress after passage of the Homeland Security Act, many were enraged. Yet the search for who to blame for the mysterious appearance of the last-minute rider came up empty-handed. Anyone accused denied having anything to do with it. Though it seems hard to believe that a rider could be attached to a bill in the halls of Congress without any conclusive means of knowing its origin, that is exactly what happened. A subsequent attempt to repeal the rider was defeated by a narrow margin.[32]

So can Thimerosal cause autism? A mushrooming number of court cases means a lot of parents think so. And what about the brazen, midnight rider that created scandal on Capitol Hill? Does its desperate bid for immunity expose a deep-seated fear that Thimerosal's use cannot be defended? After passage of the rider, vaccine makers now enjoy immunity from product liability, on top of mandatory use of their products.

POPULATION STUDIES

Presented so far are observations that make a compelling case for research such as population studies. Such studies can be extremely useful because their large numbers and high statistical power are able to distinguish even subtle differences between groups. However, such analysis is notoriously vulnerable to misinterpretation and even manipulation. Two different researchers can analyze the same data and come up with completely opposite results.[33] As you will see, the Thimerosal-autism question is a perfect example of just such an instance. Thus, a web of controversy surrounds the studies conducted in the U.S. between 1999 and 2003 following the government's discovery that safety standards had been exceeded. These studies used an existing government database called the Vaccine Safety Datalink (VSD). It contained records of many thousands of U.S. children who received varying amounts of vaccine Thimerosal during the 1990s. In total, federal taxpayers paid select health maintenance organizations (HMOs) some $25 million to take part. In addition to the VSD, records from another HMO, Harvard Pilgrim, were purchased by the Center for Disease Control (CDC) researchers investigating Thimerosal.[34]

A note on statistical power

When it comes to population studies, a statistician will tell you that the more data you have, the better because a larger sample size always produces more accurate results by reducing the possibility of error. A result that is "statistically significant" tells you the finding is probably accurate and did not occur by chance. So, say you were running for president and wanted to know where you stood with the voters. A poll of 1,000 voters would be much more valuable to you than a poll of only 100 because the larger sample size has more statistical "power," making it a better predictor of election outcome. In fact, a poll of only 100 voters may be so small that its result, whatever it is, might merely be due to chance.[35]

U.S. population studies investigating Thimerosal

The CDC analyzed the VSD and the Harvard Pilgrim HMO over a four-year period. Four versions of research findings were presented to the public. The ultimate conclusions were very reassuring. Thimerosal does not cause autism or any other developmental disorder for that matter. However, the public announcements tell a very different story from the one revealed—years after the fact—by internal documents plucked from the CDC through Freedom of Information Act (FOIA) requests. Such requests provide a means of public access to unreleased government documents such as internal reports and emails.[36] For the tenacious pursuers of such documents, the process of unveiling them was long, arduous, and costly.[37] Yet in the end, the FOIA documents give those of us sitting on the outside who are trying to make personal decisions regarding Thimerosal a much more complete picture of reality.

Behind closed doors at the CDC

The earliest analysis of data known to circulate among CDC officials showed that, as Thimerosal exposure increased, there were some very large, statistically significant increases in the risk of developmental disorders such as autism, ADD, ADHD, developmental speech or language delay, sleep disorders, night terrors, and "unspecified delay in development."[38] Internal emails among researchers at the time reveal an atmosphere of anxiety and displeasure regarding the research findings.[39] A second internal study incriminating Thimerosal appeared within the CDC in February 2000.[40] Nevertheless, three months later when the public got its first glimpse at research findings, they learned that Thimerosal exposure was *not* associated with any developmental disorder.[41] Surprisingly, only a month after that, there was a change of heart. New findings from a second round of analysis were made public, and they showed several statistically significant associations. Though it seemed a complete reversal to many, apparently the

CDC did not seem to think so. Rather, their advisors had suggested that the new findings made a weak case against Thimerosal.[42]

The CDC's advisors at Simpsonwood

A week before these most-recent findings were made public, a two-day, invitation-only conference was held at a retreat site in Georgia called Simpsonwood. Attendees included 12 consultants and 49 "resource specialists and observers" from vaccine makers, health agencies, universities, and medical academies. Parent activists who had been in communication with the CDC regarding the Thimerosal-autism issue were not invited. The group in attendance was asked to examine the VSD findings and decide if a "signal" existed between Thimerosal and developmental disorders. In addition, the group was asked for recommendations to guide future VSD research. The conference would remain unknown to the public until much later when its minutes eventually surfaced amid a pile of other documents pried from the CDC through FOIA requests.

The Simpsonwood minutes reveal that lead VSD researcher, Thomas Verstraeten, PhD, believed the findings made a clear case against Thimerosal. "You can look at this data and turn it around," he argued, "and look at this, and add this stratum, and I can come up with very high risks. And I can come up with very low risks, depending on how you turn everything around. You can make it go away for some and then it comes back for others." Verstraeten's "bottom line" was that "our signal will simply not just go away." In addition, the Simpsonwood minutes illuminated obvious conflicts of interest and concern about lawsuits. "What if the lawyers get hold of this?" one attendee queried. "There's not a scientist in the world who can refute these findings." Another contended, "We are in a bad position from the standpoint of defending any lawsuits. I am concerned." There was widespread interest in holding back the results, as well as suppressing a relationship in future studies. Nevertheless, the advice of most of the 12 consultants was that the signal was weak and not significant. Thus, the public presentation was made. A year would pass before the next public announcement of research findings.[43]

Public announcement no. 3

In July 2001, a presentation of new VSD research showed that risk levels overall had dropped. Some had even gone away. This time the two VSD HMOs had been analyzed separately rather than combined as before. Though some findings in the large HMO of 70,000 children showed high statistical significance, the smaller HMO of 16,000 children did not provide confirmation.

Critics questioned why CDC statisticians would reduce the statistical power of their data by splitting its large population into two smaller ones for separate analysis. They asserted the smaller HMO lacked sufficient power to achieve statistical significance. Critics also objected to a side analysis in which the researchers used not only very strict, but unusual, definitions of various neurological disorders. This caused about half of diagnosed cases to be excluded. Even without knowledge of Simpsonwood, critics alleged that the CDC had tailored the analysis to hide relationships.

The CDC's presentation of findings included an announcement that lead researcher, Dr. Verstraeten, had been hired by vaccine maker GlaxoSmith-KlineBeecham, effective immediately. In the years to come, this would be a point of serious contention for those demanding an objective evaluation of the VSD. For despite Dr. Verstraeten's employment with a vaccine maker under Thimerosal litigation, he would remain on the VSD team for more than two years.[44]

Wrestling over access to the VSD

By this point, what the critics really wanted was to get their hands on the raw VSD data so they could perform their own analysis. In fact, they had wanted those data for a long time. They felt the VSD, purchased and maintained at taxpayer expense, should be available outside the CDC.[45] However, FOIA requests and other efforts to gain access to the VSD data failed. Throughout the life of the VSD, the CDC would steadfastly refuse open access on the grounds of protecting patient privacy. And removal of children's names and a change of birth dates to only reflect month and year would not suffice.[46] Eventually, however, under repeated pressure, the CDC relented, after a fashion. In February 2002, the VSD became available for outside research if would-be researchers could overcome an extensive list of qualifications and hurdles.[47]

Outside researchers: The Geiers

Only one research team would ever overcome these sizable barriers to VSD access. In so doing, they would find themselves embroiled in a controversy in which the public-health establishment would zero in on them with a full frontal assault. These researchers were Dr. Mark Geier and David Geier, a father–son team. The father, Mark Geier, is an MD with a PhD in genetics. He is also an authority on the biological effects of vaccine-induced infant death. To his credit, he was one of the first to criticize the whole-cell pertussis vaccine that was replaced in 1996 by a safer version less likely to cause severe or fatal reactions in infants.[48] In over 30 different peer-reviewed journals, Dr. Geier has published over 50 papers on safety issues relating to numerous vaccines. At the time, his son, David, was a graduate student at the National Institutes of Health and had founded a medical-legal consultancy. In addition, both father and son had testified in Vaccine Court on behalf of families.[49]

For months the Geiers had heard pleas from parents to investigate a possible relationship between Thimerosal and neurological disorders. Though they believed the requests were merely the grasping of straws by overwrought parents, they finally gave in. At the time, they were conducting vaccine research of their own using a government database called VAERS. They decided to use VAERS to test the Thimerosal question by comparing children whose DTaP vaccines contained Thimerosal to those whose DTaP vaccines were Thimerosal-free. What they found startled them: the relative risk of developing both autism and mental retardation was *six times higher* for children who received Thimerosal-containing DTaP vaccines compared to those whose DTaP vaccines were mercury-free. For speech disorders, the relative risk was 2.2 times higher. The Geiers published these findings in the peer-reviewed journal *Experimental Biology and Medicine* in 2003.[50]

The findings spiked the Geiers' interest in performing the same analysis on the VSD, which is considered more reliable than VAERS. They spent over a year tenaciously trying to meet the CDC's many requirements, including a 150-page research proposal and a $3,200 processing fee. Even so, as each obstacle was overcome, new ones were erected. In the end, with significant intercession from Congressman Dave Weldon's office, the Geiers satisfied all the requirements. For their pains, they earned a once-in-a-blue-moon glimpse at the highly guarded VSD. In October 2003, they collected their two-day prize.[51]

Despite being officially granted access, the Geiers were quite nearly shut out during their days of access because their assigned terminal did not have the software necessary for VSD access. After hours of delay, a CDC staff member secretly offered assistance citing an "affected child" in the family as the reason. The Geiers' analysis found that children who received three Thimerosal-containing DTaP vaccines had an increased risk of autism nearly 27 times that of children who received three Thimerosal-free DTaP vaccines. The Geiers were stunned.[52] Their analysis, however, came under harsh criticism from the CDC. The Geiers would defend their conclusions resolutely.[53]

With more help from Congressman Weldon's office, the Geiers overcame new barriers to VSD access and spent two more days with the VSD in January 2004. Yet the time they spent was in vain. Their results printed to a printer in a locked room, and the person with the keys was nowhere to be found. When the Geiers eventually received their printouts, they believed most of the findings had been whited out. In the end their window of opportunity closed when their assigned computer terminal crashed.[54]

I don't know about you, but I marvel at the Geiers' account of their adventures at the CDC. Either the Geiers are crazy to invent such stories, or the CDC was flagrantly determined to deny them access. It has to be one or the other, but which is it?

Public announcement no. 4

Meanwhile, in 2003, the CDC's research team published their final analysis. They had used the large (70,000 children) and small (16,000 children) VSD HMOs from before, as well as the more recently acquired Harvard Pilgrim HMO (15,000 children). Each was analyzed separately. In addition, the large HMO was subdivided into its individual clinics for separate analysis. The only significant risks found by the analysis were for tics and language delay. However, since these existed only in one subgroup, not in any others, the findings were inconsistent. The researchers, including Dr. Verstraeten who had been employed by a vaccine maker for over two years, concluded that "no consistent significant associations were found between Thimerosal-containing vaccines and neurodevelopment outcomes."[55] It was the CDC's final word on population studies.

CDC research under fire

Critics contended that the CDC study breached sound research practices and drastically reduced the likelihood of finding statistically significant relationships between Thimerosal and developmental disorders. Some of the chief objections follow.[56]

1. *Objections to the method of analysis.*
    (a) *Division of the large population into several small populations.* By analyzing the HMOs and clinics of the large HMO separately, statistical power of the data was undermined, and margin of error was increased.
    (b) *Elimination of the combined category "neurological developmental disorders."* This category, which had been used in earlier studies to evaluate the risk of disorders as a whole, was not used in the final study. Given the wide variety of developmental delays in children and the many different ways mercury can disrupt

neurological development, critics considered its use important. By only evaluating individual diagnoses, the chance of finding statistically significant relationships was reduced.

(c) *Inclusion of a vaccine maker (Dr. Verstraeten) on the research team.*

2. *Objections to the data that was included or excluded.*

(a) *Inclusion of many children too young to be diagnosed with autism.* At the time of the study, the average age to receive an autism diagnosis was 4.4 years.[57] The researchers included numerous children younger than that age in the study population, which reduced the risk of autism. To make this clear, say you wanted to determine the risk of baldness. If you include men in their twenties in your study population, the risk of baldness will be lower. It will drop even more if you add teenagers to the population.

(b) *Removal of about 45 percent of older children.* The researchers excluded many children aged 4 or older from the study population reportedly due to incomplete records. Like eliminating older men from a study on baldness, this would reduce risk.

(c) *Use of Harvard Pilgrim HMO.* Analysis of Harvard Pilgrim found no risk for any disorder at all. This created "inconsistency" with risks found in other slices of data and was used to discredit them. Critics objected to use of Harvard Pilgrim altogether, saying it:[58]

(i) was too small to show relationships

(ii) used diagnostic codes so different from the other HMOs that comparisons were impractical

(iii) had such little variation in Thimerosal-exposure levels that comparisons among its children were meaningless

(iv) had questionable data accuracy. The HMO was under state receivership partly due to problems with information systems and record keeping.

Critics questioned why the CDC would go outside its own massive VSD database to purchase another HMO. They believed that, if the CDC really wanted to confirm VSD findings, it would not have chosen an HMO that was as small and unfit for the task as Harvard Pilgrim.

The death of the VSD

In 2004, the public learned that the CDC had stopped monitoring the VSD for adverse Thimerosal effects after the year 2000. Critics were outraged that, just as mercury had begun to be removed from vaccines, data collection had stopped. Thus, the effect of Thimerosal's removal could not be evaluated. Furthermore, the original data files used by Dr. Verstraeten and his team had been deleted to "protect privacy." Now they could never be used by other researchers wishing to confirm or refute the CDC's findings. The VSD case was closed.[59]

Drawing conclusions about U.S. population studies

So here we sit on the outside of all this turmoil trying to draw conclusions on which to base Thimerosal decisions for our children. What can we say? There was a paper trail of internal CDC emails and documents. The CDC public announcements. The opinions of the critics. And, finally, the tale of the Geiers and their research. What do you make of it all? For me, the sharp contrast of the CDC's private words to their public ones sends a disturbing message. It leaves me with the sense that the CDC has too many conflicting interests to satisfy the likes of a safety-riveted parent like me. And what of the methods and data used by the CDC studies themselves? Were they the work of objective-minded scientists in search of truth, or are they a reflection of those disturbing private words that were never intended for the light of day? Also consider the CDC's resolute stance against VSD access to outsiders. Was its sole motivation an intense desire to protect patient privacy as was said? And what do you make of the discontinuance of the VSD near the crucial time of Thimerosal's withdrawl from vaccines? Lastly, what of the CDC's decision to destroy the original VSD data on which its research was based? How many ways are there to interpret this collection of actions and documentation? Furthermore, what can we conclude about the Geiers' research? It was vehemently criticized and ridiculed by the public health establishment. Either the Geiers knew absolutely nothing about how to conduct valid research or they had stepped on some very big toes. How can those of us on the outside know which it is?

A digression, brought to you by my sister Laura

I don't know how Mark Geier's track record of publishing over 50 articles in more than 30 different peer-reviewed journals strikes you, but it got my attention. To explain why requires a brief digression. Here goes.

My younger sister Laura has always had an insatiable sense of curiosity and adventure that has gotten her into a great deal of trouble on many occasions. Nevertheless, she eventually channeled her curiosity into three college degrees in chemistry and engineering before landing a job at NASA. For many years, from a console in Guidance and Navigation, she guided space shuttles among the stars and returned them safely home. It was as close as she ever got to her treasured bridge of the Starship Enterprise.

However, NASA would not let Laura be an astronaut, so, after 12 years, she changed course and set her sights on Duke University and a PhD in genetics. Hmm. Genetics. Now there is a curious field. Goodness only knows what trouble one can get into there. Among the many hoops Laura had to jump through to earn the three little letters of "PhD" was the publication of two papers in scientific journals. She spent years of arduous effort focused on the genetics of fungi—no kidding, really—fungi. She designed and conducted numerous experiments until she could draw meaningful conclusions and formally document her findings. Each paper was a true masterpiece of terminology, complexity, and dizzying tables and charts. However, even as each paper was completed, Laura faced yet another hurdle. She had to submit the paper to a scientific journal in the hope it would be deemed worthy of publication. In case you didn't know, publication is not a given in the world of science. These journals, in a class by themselves, are very selective, especially the higher up you go on the pecking order. Never make the ghastly blunder I did of calling a scientific journal a "magazine." Journals are far more distinguished, scientific, and sacred. Or so I concluded from the emphatic flare in Laura's eyes when she denounced my error, and the vein popping from the side of her neck like an exclamation point. In the end, Laura overcame all the obstacles of publication, and now basks in delight of her accomplishments.[60] She has truly earned the three little letters of PhD that now dangle at the end of her name.

This tangent brings us back to the point I set out to make about Mark Geier, PhD, MD. He had published over 50 articles in more than 30 different peer-reviewed journals, including the impressive likes of *Annals of Internal Medicine* and *Rheumatology*.[61] Could there be any doubt that a researcher laying claim to such a legacy has some talent? Could such a person truly conduct research that was worthy of the harsh criticism he received from the CDC? I hardly think so. If the Geiers say they found a relationship between Thimerosal and autism to the tune of nearly 27 times, we should not disregard it.

THE U.S. GOVERNMENT MAKES ITS THIMEROSAL-AUTISM DECISION

In 2004, at the CDC's request, the Institute of Medicine (IOM) held a one-day meeting to decide if there was a link between Thimerosal and autism. Relevant population studies and laboratory research were presented. On one hand, the laboratory research built a case against Thimerosal's safety. On the other hand, the population studies, excepting the Geiers', insisted there was no link. Three months after the meeting, the IOM issued a report of conclusions for the CDC. The report dismissed all the laboratory research as "theoretical," and the Geiers' research was deemed "uninterpretable" due to an incomplete description of methods. The IOM favored the CDC's analysis of the VSD, as well as population studies done in the UK and Denmark. The foreign studies were valued despite the fact the exposures involved were a fraction of those incurred in the U.S. Nor was it taken into account that the rate of autism in Denmark (a country that removed Thimerosal from vaccines in 1992) was only 3–6 in 10,000 compared to the U.S. rate of 66 in 10,000 (i.e., 1 in 150). The IOM report concluded that Thimerosal-containing vaccines did not cause autism.[62] It was intended to be the U.S. government's final word on Thimerosal. As a result, Thimerosal is not treated as a serious health risk in the U.S.[63] It remains in use in some vaccines intended for infants, children, and adults, including pregnant women.

LABORATORY AND CLINICAL RESEARCH

Given that population studies are notoriously vulnerable to misinterpretation, and even manipulation, they do not normally stand alone. To determine if one event actually *causes* another, population studies must be supported by biological evidence produced in laboratories and clinics. Immunology, toxicology, pathology, virology, and other disciplines can each contribute a piece of understanding to paint a more reliable and complete picture of reality.[64] So what was some of the laboratory and clinical research presented to the IOM or available at the time of their 2004 meeting? A sampling of the most prominent research follows. See if you agree that it should be dismissed as "theoretical."

The effect of Thimerosal on nerve cells of the brain and nervous system

A study at the University of Kentucky exposed mouse nerve cells in culture to the same 0.01 percent solution of Thimerosal used in vaccines. After 24 hours, nearly all the cells in the unexposed control group were still alive. However, among the cells exposed to Thimerosal, only 30 percent were still living.[65]

A study at Baylor College of Medicine in Houston found that even miniscule amounts of Thimerosal triggered brain-cell death. In the study, cultured brain cells incubated with Thimerosal were evaluated after 6 and 24 hours of exposure. At 6 hours, researchers found that the lowest toxic concentration was just two micromolars (two-billionths of a gram) of mercury. At 24 hours, the lowest toxic dose was only one micromolar, which showed that brain-cell sensitivity to Thimerosal increased with longer exposure.[66]

Research done in Canada at the University of Calgary's Faculty of Medicine found that even miniscule amounts of mercury can cause direct injury to the branchlike structures of nerve cells that relay impulses in the brain. The researchers captured in vivid, time-lapse video the shriveling of these nerve-cell structures as they came in contact with tiny amounts of mercury (one micromolar or one-billionth of a gram).[67]

The effect of Thimerosal on body chemistry

In the first years of life, proper function of the methionine cycle is critical to normal development of nerve cells in the brain and nervous system. Research at Northeastern University in Boston found that Thimerosal doses 100 times *lower* than a single Thimerosal-containing vaccine could drastically affect the methionine cycle. It was hypothesized that, by impairing body chemistry, Thimerosal interferes with memory and attention, as well as the body's ability to remove heavy metals.[68]

The effect of Thimerosal on boys and girls

Three out of four children with autism are boys. Similar boy–girl ratios are found in ADD and other developmental disorders. What might explain this?[69] Research at the University of Kentucky exposed mouse nerve cells in culture to Thimerosal using the same 0.01 percent solution used in vaccines. Some cells had been pretreated with estrogen, some with testosterone, and others with nothing. After 12 hours of exposure, most of the estrogen-pretreated cells were still alive. The estrogen had protected them from dying, compared to the untreated cells. However, the nerve cells pretreated with testosterone died 100 times *faster* than the untreated cells. Thus, while estrogen was protective against Thimerosal's toxicity, testosterone dramatically increased Thimerosal's ability to kill cells.[70]

A mouse-version of the pediatric vaccine schedule

Researchers at Columbia University translated the mercury exposure of the pediatric vaccine schedule into its mouse counterpart, making adjustments for weight, rate of aging, and timing of developmental milestones. The study used different strains of mice whose genetic sensitivity to mercury varied substantially. After exposure, mice from the most sensitive strain were significantly slow to gain weight; they suffered substantial "behavioral impoverishment" as well. After reaching 6 months of age, some 40 percent of them began frantically grooming themselves or biting their own tails compulsively. One mouse who self-groomed wildly also groomed its cage mate so severely as to groom through its skull, eventually killing it. In addition, the sensitive mice also had enlarged brains, a characteristic some researchers have identified in autistic children as well. The peer-reviewed journal *Molecular Psychiatry*, which published this study, also issued a press release at the time of publication, asserting that the study was "the first to show that the administration of low-dose ethyl mercury can lead to behavioral and neurological changes in the developing brain." It emphasized that this research reinforced earlier studies "showing that a genetic predisposition affects risk in combination with certain environmental triggers."[71]

Clinical findings of mercury overload in children with developmental problems

Also presented to the IOM committee was a study by Jeff Bradstreet, MD, which showed that autistic children treated with a medication to remove heavy metals excreted nearly six times more mercury than vaccinated control children.[72] This was consistent with the experience of Stephanie Cave, MD, who had testified before a U.S. Government Reform Committee in 2000. At her Louisiana clinic whose patients included over 300 autistic children, every child with a developmental delay was tested for heavy metals. In these children, she found elevated mercury not only in those with autism but also in those with learning disabilities, ADHD, and AS. It was rare for her to find a child with developmental problems who did not have elevated mercury. When mercury was removed, these children improved, with some making miraculous recoveries. Moreover, Dr. Cave's experience is not unusual. Many doctors following the Defeat Autism Now! approach relay similar experiences.[73]

MOVING ON

I hope this chapter has given you a better understanding of the Thimerosal-autism issue so you can make informed decisions. Though many doctors within Defeat Autism Now! believe vaccine mercury played a damaging role in many cases of autism, they do not believe it is the only source of heavy metals and toxins afflicting the autism spectrum.[74] Widespread exposure to environmental toxins in air, water, and food are also a huge source of problems.[75] There can be others as well. The next chapter about minimizing exposures to heavy metals and toxins will explore this topic further.

NOTES

1.   Pangborn and Baker 2005, p. 1:6.
2.   Kirby 2005, p. 207.
3.   Ibid., p. xv; Cave with Mitchell 2001, pp. 29–30.
4.   Bernard *et al.* 2000, pp. 38, 42; McCandless 2007, pp. 56–57.
5.   Kirby 2005, p. 49, 82; Bock and Stauth 2007, pp. 52–53; Halsey 1999.
6.   Kirby 2005, pp. 44–47; Bernard *et al.* 2000, p. 38.
7.   Kirby 2005, pp. xii, 119.
8.   Ibid., p. 333; McCandless 2007, p. 57.
9.   Cave with Mitchell 2001, p. 49; Bock and Stauth 2007, p. 57.
10. McCandless 2007, p. 55.
·11. Kirby 2005, p. xvi.
12. Binstock 2007a, p. 282; Kirby 2005, pp. 289, 305.
13. Kirby 2005, p. 72.
14. Ibid., pp. 123–4, 264; Cave with Mitchell 2001, pp. 37–38.
15. Bernard *et al.* 2000, p. 38; Kirby 2005, p. 417.
16. Kirby 2005, pp. 397–98.
17. Cave with Mitchell 2001, pp. 30, 288.
18. Kirby 2005, p. 333.
19. Ibid., p. 362.
20. Binstock 2007a, p. 281.
21. Kanner 1943, pp. 217–50.
22. Bernard *et al.* 2000, p. 40; Cave with Mitchell 2001, pp. 64–65; Grandin *et al.* 2006, p. 88; Bock and Stauth 2007, p. 53; McCandless 2007, pp. 56–57.
23. Cave with Mitchell 2001, pp. 65–66.
24. Center for Disease Control and Prevention 2008a, Web site.
25. Bock and Stauth 2007, pp. 56–57.
26. Kirby 2005, pp. 417–18.
27. Ibid., p. 81.
28. Ibid., p. 156.
29. Ibid., p. 157.
30. Ibid., p. 223.
31. U.S. Court of Federal Claims, Docket of Omnibus Autism Proceeding (2008).

32. Kirby 2005, pp. 198, 202–203, 235–37, 239–42.

33. Ibid., p. 309.

34. Ibid., pp. 115, 148.

35. Ibid., p. 166.

36. Ibid., p. 118.

37. Ibid., pp. 140, 148, 160, 167, 190, 349.

38. Ibid., pp. 115–16, 379–82, 407.

39. Ibid., pp. 192–93.

40. Ibid., pp. 190–92.

41. Ibid., pp. 115–16.

42. Ibid., pp. 126–30, 148, 166–67.

43. Ibid., pp. 168–73.

44. Ibid., pp. 176–77, 283–85, 288, 395.

45. Ibid., pp. 204, 332, 396.

46. Ibid., pp. 184–85, 213–14.

47. Ibid., pp. 204–205.

48. Cave with Mitchell 2001, pp. 148–50.

49. Kirby 2005, pp. 228–31, 317.

50. Ibid., pp. 229–30.

51. Ibid., pp. 230–31, 279–80, 287.

52. Ibid., pp. 280–82.

53. Ibid., pp. 301, 315–16, 332, 336, 352.

54. Ibid., pp. 305–306.

55. Ibid., pp. 283–84.

56. Ibid., pp. 193, 283–88, 291–92, 300–301, 315, 395.

57. Ibid., pp. 147, 315.

58. Ibid., pp. 148, 166–67, 193–94, 285–88.

59. Ibid., pp. 396–97, 403.

60. Kavanaugh, Fraser, and Dietrich 2006, pp. 1879–90.

61. Kirby 2005, pp. 229, 332.

62. Ibid., pp. xiv, 292, 308–25, 350–55; Bock and Stauth 2007, p. 57.

63. Cave with Mitchell 2001, p. 49; Bock and Stauth 2007, p. 57.

64. Kirby 2005, p. 309.

65. Ibid., p. 199.

66. Ibid., pp. 320–21; Rimland 2006d, p. 5.

67. Kirby 2005, p. 161.

68. Ibid., pp. 293–94, 337, 353.

69. Pangborn and Baker 2005, p. 1:11.

70. Kirby 2005, pp. 199, 322; Haley and Small 2006, p. 930.

71. Kirby 2005, pp. 310–12, 347, 352, 365.

72. Ibid., pp. 322–23.

73. Kirby 2005, pp. 133, 135–36, 142, 411; Autism Research Institute 2005, pp. 10, 11, 13; McCandless 2007, pp. 11–12, 49–50, 59, 150; Bock and Stauth 2007, p. 294; Green 2006a, p. 3.

74. McCandless 2007, pp. 19–23, 54, 56; Autism Research Institute 2005, pp. 21–23; Baker 2004, pp. 105–18; Rea 2007, pp. 221–26.

75. Bock and Stauth 2007, p. 21.

Chapter 22

Minimizing Exposures to Heavy Metals and Toxins

WHAT THIS CHAPTER HAS IN STORE

Unless we make the time to become self-educated about potential sources of toxic exposure, hazards can easily go unrecognized or downplayed as harmless. This chapter discusses sources of toxins, related safety concerns, and steps you can take to avoid toxins when possible.

WHERE DO TOXINS COME FROM?

Unlike an allergen, such as a peanut, that is harmful to some people but not others, a toxin is harmful to everyone, even in small quantities. It poses a hazard that our bodies recognize and strive to eliminate through specially designed collection and disposal activities. Unfortunately, there are surprisingly many ways babies and children get exposed to heavy metals and toxins. Some come from outside the body, while others originate within the body itself. Sources of toxins include:[1]

1. *Air pollution.* Pollutants and heavy metals are sucked into our bodies when we inhale.

2. *Food, drink, and medications.* Eating and drinking are common ways for toxins to slip inside. Many foods, for example, are treated with pesticides in the fields and orchards. Meats often contain hormones, antibiotics, and steroids that the body must expel. In addition, manufactured foods regularly contain food dyes, additives, and preservatives. Alcohol and drugs, both prescription and over-the-counter, also

require clean up by the body. Though these substances may not be toxic in proper dosages, they can build up over long-term use if not adequately processed and expelled.

3. *Vaccines.* Some vaccines contain heavy metals or toxins such as mercury, aluminum, and formaldehyde.[2]

4. *Micro-organisms.* Yeast and other fungi, bacteria, viruses, and parasites living inside the body generate toxins. Though some level of toxins from bad flora in the digestive tract is unavoidable, the level needs to be kept within tolerable limits. Bad gut flora will be discussed in the next chapter.

5. *Bodily functions.* Even the necessary operations of our organs and other natural processes inside the body produce unwanted "exhaust."[3] Though we cannot stop production of these unwanted metabolic leftovers, it is still worthwhile to recognize that they exist and add more items to the body's to-do list for detoxification.

6. *Skin-permeable toxins.* Toxins even pass into our bodies through our skin. True, skin is a barrier of sorts, but it is hardly as impenetrable as we might think.

As you can see, the body's to-do list for detoxification is quite long, making detoxification a constant, daily chore. A body's work is never done. We help the body when we lighten its work load through avoidance of heavy metals and toxins.[4]

OUR RAPIDLY CHANGING ENVIRONMENT

The human body evolved over millions of years, adapting to a *slowly* changing environment. Yet, in the last hundred years, a mere blink of evolutionary time, we have introduced into our environment more than 80,000 man-made chemicals. These are alien molecules never before seen on this planet. Is there any conceivable way to test adequately such a huge number of substances for safety? And even if it could be done for individual chemicals, what about combination testing to detect additive or synergistic effects of different chemicals? Just to test those 80,000 chemicals in *pairs* would require an additional 6,320,000,000 tests. The task is as mind-boggling as it is impossible. Even when testing is performed, say, on rats or chimps, we cannot evaluate the effects on uniquely human abilities such as language and high-order brain function. For these reasons and several others, assurances of safety have to be taken with a grain of salt, especially when it comes to susceptible individuals.

Industry tends to consider new substances harmless until proven otherwise. The burden of proof to show harm falls on academic and independent researchers, but they rely on industry for much of their funding. Of course, there are government agencies that are charged to investigate the safety of chemicals and to regulate or restrict their use. However, these agencies have been accused of many shortcomings. A significant one is that they are strongly influenced by industry, as seen in the case of vaccine mercury, for instance. Thus, these agencies are slow to acknowledge safety concerns and even slower to restrict use of substances found to be unsafe. As a society, our attitude is one of "use it first, and then if it hurts somebody, we'll reconsider." Over the last 100 years, this philosophy has caused harm through many avenues such as lead, DDT, asbestos, mercury, and chlordane, to mention only a few. We find out the hard way when a product is not safe.[5]

So how do we know if the chemicals we use are safe for us and the other living things we depend on? We don't really. And studies in recent years have found large numbers of toxins within the human body. For example, toxic molecules have been found in amniotic fluid, the placenta, blood of the umbilical cord, and breast milk.[6]

WE HAVE GOT TO STOP PEEING IN THE POOL

I once had a friend who never wanted to swim in the shallow end of a swimming pool because he felt sure all the little kids on that end were peeing in the water. And though he may well have been right, I found it funny that he seemed to think the other end of the pool was okay. I figured that, if those little kids really were peeing their hearts out as he supposed, the pee was getting around. It wouldn't stay in one place, at least not when there are water jets and movement of people from one end of the pool to the other.

A parallel scene is playing out on the planet Earth. We use pesticides, chemical fertilizers, and herbicides around our crops and lawns, but they don't stay where we put them. As the four winds blow and the rains pour down, these toxins are scattered into our air, soil, and water. To make matters worse, many of these man-made chemicals don't break down quickly. Rather they remain intact for years, harming whatever living things they encounter. As they accumulate in unintended places, we are back in our fields, orchards, and yards dumping new supplies of freshly manufactured toxins. In addition, industrial sources like coal-burning power plants discharge mercury and other pollutants into our environment. We have landfills and smog. And we keep inventing new toxins in different forms. We act as if any idea we come up with is a good one as long as it meets our goal in some way and we can sell it. We figure that's good enough.

But "good enough" can harm us. We reap what we sow. That is what our autism-spectrum children are telling us with their rocking and flapping, their stolen voices, and their blown-away anxiety and aggression. Like canaries in a coal mine, their sacrifice warns us of danger. They are telling us something is wrong, terribly wrong. And we must put our ingenuity to the task of fixing our mess. We have to stop peeing in the pool and figure out how to clean it up. What other choice do we have when this is the only pool we've got?

MEANWHILE, ON THE HOME FRONT

Will's test results had showed mercury and other heavy metals, as well as pesticides and chemicals. Finding this out really shook me up and totally changed how I look at products that contain toxic substances, even in small amounts. These days I avoid vaccine mercury like the plague. I have made other changes over time as well, such as switching from tap water to filtered water for drinking and cooking. When I can, I buy organic produce and natural meats. Seafood and processed-food consumption is minimal. And dental amalgams are out of the question, despite reassurances at the dentist office. The way I look at it, toxins may have fooled me once. Shame on them. But to fool me twice—that would be shame on me.

DRAGGING MY FEET

At the spring 2006 Defeat Autism Now! conference, John Green, MD, led a session on minimizing toxic exposures around the house. Among many points made during the session, he highly recommended a book called *Less Toxic Alternatives* by Carolyn Gorman with Marie Hyde. Though the book was out of print, it was still easy for me to order on the Internet. When it arrived in the mail, I promptly stuck it on a bookshelf because—in truth—I really did not want to crack open that book. I was sure it would create a big hassle for me. It would send me searching hither and yon for all sorts of bizarre products that were nowhere to be found. Even if I did find them, they would be ridiculously expensive. Worse yet, the book might contain exotic recipes calling on me to concoct the products myself. No doubt each ingredient would be hard-to-find or expensive. I could see the ingredient lists already…one cup of homemade beeswax; two handfuls of moss collected from the *south* side of ginko trees; and three eyes of newt. The clincher was that I felt sure none of the less toxic stuff would work anyway. If they worked, people would already be using them instead of the toxic stuff, right? In that case, all my effort would be in vain. No, that book was definitely not for me. Besides, heavy metals and toxins seemed so, well, invisible. It is hard to be motivated to defend against things I cannot see. Then one day...

ANTS ARE CARRYING AWAY MY KITCHEN

Like no place I have ever lived, my neighborhood is built on an ant hill. In the summer time, tiny ants show up in droves in people's mailboxes and flower beds. They march in long, wide trails that encircle the house like a noose. This past summer, like most, ants were making their way onto my kitchen counters. And, of course, it was just as my house guests arrived. How lovely. In the past, I would reach for an arsenal of commercial traps, sprays, and powders—in other words, toxins. It was the only option I knew. But this summer was different. After seeing Will's test results, I could not stand the thought of setting out toxin baits or spraying with toxins. If I did, ants would be tracking their toxic little feet all over my food-preparation surfaces. Surely there was another way.

So with a heavy sigh I went to the bookshelf and dusted off *Less-Toxic Alternatives*. Maybe it said something about ants. I flipped to the index. Well, what do you know? It directed me to a long list of recommendations for ants. Not one was an exotic recipe. Hmm. Promising. I scanned down the list looking for something recognizable and easy-to-do. I spied "honey and boric acid mixture." Sounded simple enough. The pharmacy section at the Walmart had boric acid, a fine white powder. It was even inexpensive. Imagine that. I mixed a bit of it in a little honey and set it out on a piece of cardboard. At least I would be able to tell my guests I was doing something about the ants, right? Even so, I didn't expect my bait to work. The performance of commercial baits I had used in the past had never been very impressive. They were good at attracting ants, yes. But the fantasy they proposed about the ants carrying toxins back to the nest and wiping out the whole colony never seemed to materialize. The ants always kept coming to varying degrees. Yet to my surprise, this time, with the boric acid and honey, it was different. By the third day there wasn't an ant in sight. Huh? That was pretty good for stuff that didn't work. We had several days' reprieve before new ants showed up. I repeated my new prize-winning trick with the same triumphant result.

However, as the summer wore on, renewed waves of ant invasions took place. Even though my boric acid trick worked, it got tiresome. Perhaps there was some wisdom to another of the book's suggestions, "caulk all entry points." Besides, *less* toxic is not the same as *non*-toxic. So I flipped to the book's index in the hope of finding guidance about less-toxic caulk. Lo and behold, I was led to yet another list. Again, no exotic recipes. Hmm. Not bad. The local home center carried a couple of the book's suggestions. I purchased "100 percent clear silicon caulk". Then I baited the ants with a dab of plain honey or ice cream. Within an hour, they had formed a convenient dotted line that pointed the way to their rebel base. They were sneaking into the enemy territory of my kitchen through a tiny crevice at the window frame. Feeling smug, I caulked their entryway.

However, the ants were back the next day, showing complete disregard of my prowess. They had some nerve, the little monsters. So, again, I baited with plain honey or ice cream. And, again, they divulged their secret path, a new spot around the window frame. I sealed it shut. There were a few iterations of this game of hide-and-seek as I battled the ants at various points around the window. But in the end, I shut them down. The me of 20 future summers cheered wildly at my success. I had been spared many a would-be ant invasion from the secret passageways at the window frame. This time my fortress stood for several weeks.

Before the summer was out, the ants reappeared from an altogether new location. I beat them back again. Ants can be very persistent. But then so can I. I have a new empowering perspective now, one of determination. Now I care more about pesticides and less about ants. After seeing my son stare into space with no response to his name, ants don't seem all that important any more. But pesticides do. I don't care so much now about weeds in my lawn after my son lost his smile and lived in terror of his own anxiety. Instead, I care more about what is in chemical fertilizers and herbicides. And I think about what is in our food and drinks. I am not so impressed with food and drinks that are colorful or can last forever in my cabinets when my son loses eye contact and cannot hold a conversation. Some things in life are important. Others are not. Moreover, toxins and heavy metals are not only an issue for autism-spectrum disorders. They can play a role in many other conditions as well such as learning disabilities, obsessive-compulsive disorder, anxiety, depression, chronic fatigue syndrome, dementia, Alzheimer's, Parkinson's, multiple sclerosis, rheumatoid arthritis, schizophrenia, Tourette's, and ALS (Lou Gehrig's disease).[7] Does anyone in my family need any of these? Hardly. It seems that anyone who lives in a human body would be wise to minimize exposures to toxins and heavy metals in every form.

WHAT ARE WE EATING?

When I was a kid, my girlfriend and I used to make some truly exquisite mud pies in the dirt pile behind her house. A multitude of imaginary customers went delirious with delight over our enchanting creations. They flocked to us from all over the country to rave in aristocratic accents about our spell-binding pies. So thrilled for a taste, they were happy to pay exorbitantly high prices for even a single slice. Yet, no matter how rampant our imaginations carried us, we never lost sight of the fact that our pies were made of mud. It never occurred to us to actually *eat* one.

Today, however, we seem to have lost sight of this fundamental recognition of what is food and what is not. I hear of hormones, antibiotics, and steroids in our meat and petroleum-based dyes in our food and drink. Nowadays, many of our manufactured foods contain a glut of preservatives and other additives for various purposes. Some seem okay, while other inventions like trans fats and MSG get some pretty bad press. Furthermore, we spray pesticides on our produce and grains; then, we eat it. Does that seem like a healthy idea? What effect might it have especially on our autism-spectrum children with impaired detoxification?[8]

'LESS-TOXIC ALTERNATIVES' BY CAROLYN GORMAN WITH MARIE HYDE

As it turned out, that book wasn't so bad after all; it has actually been a great help. I turn to it increasingly as issues arise or as I feel ready to take on a new step toward toxin reduction. More than a third of the book is devoted to list after list of less-toxic alternatives, covering numerous topics from food, water, and air to pesticides, herbicides, and fertilizers. There are lists for household cleaners, laundry and dish detergents, paints and carpets, as well as personal-care products like toothpaste, deodorant, and soaps. On and on they go. I have found many of these products at local stores. For those that are not available locally the book includes an extensive directory that is a gold mine of mail order and Internet sources.

You may wonder how I know that minimizing exposures around the house and in our food really makes a difference for Will and the rest of the family. I don't really, but I would rather be safe than sorry. I am willing to take other people's word for it that the effort is worthwhile.

TAKING OTHER PEOPLE'S WORD

Consider again my younger sister Laura, who always liked to find things out for herself. She wasn't big on taking other people's word. Once when she was about 10 years old, she became intrigued with a very interesting question. Was gasoline really as explosive as everyone said? Of course, she could have taken their word for it, but, then, would she ever really know for sure? It was something she simply had to find out for herself.

After enlisting the aid of a gullible playmate, she made ready. It was a cold day, so she bundled up in a heavy coat, pulling the strings of her hood tightly to bring a ring of fake fur snug against her face. Together, she and her friend slipped off into a wintry field of high weeds, the perfect hiding place to conduct an important scientific investigation. Little did anyone suspect that the innocent-looking pair had a cup of gasoline and a matchbook concealed under their coats. Once safely hidden behind a curtain of tall weeds, the scientists set up their experiment. Laura did the honors since, after all, it was her idea. She lit a match and tossed it into the intriguing cup of noxious clear liquid. *Woof!* The hot blast was instantaneous and astounding. Riveted in shock, Laura stood dumbfounded, her eyes as big as the moon. "Why, yes," her mind sputtered, "everyone is right. Gasoline is *indeed* highly explosive. It does not just burn; it…it *woofs!*" She blinked repeatedly trying to grasp the significance of what she had just witnessed. "Such an amazing discovery," she marveled. "My experiment is an indisputable success for the field of scientific inquiry." Nevertheless, it had been a very close call. Laura's eyelashes had been singed off in the blast. And her ring of fake fur was now pitted with black flecks of melted plastic. She knew she had come within an ace of becoming a human torch.

We can only hope that Laura learned something significant that day, as did her bewildered accomplice. Maybe there are times it is worth taking other people's word for it, at least when the stakes are high. After all, they might be right. It may not be worth it to doubt them. I have no definitive way to know if minimizing toxins around my house helps, but I definitely do it anyway. It just makes sense when so many doctors at Defeat Autism Now! find heavy metals and toxins in children on the autism spectrum. I'll take their word for it that household toxins should be avoided. It is not worth the risk to find out the hard way.

The most vulnerable among us are the very young, the old, and the sick. When caring for these special groups, we take extra precautions that we might not otherwise. I never used to think of Will as being sick since his "autistic" symptoms did not match my image of traditional illness. There were no fevers, hacking coughs, or flu symptoms. However, the presence of his heavy metal and toxin overload tells me that he is vulnerable, so I take extra precautions. If I err, I want it to be on the side of safety. Thus, it seems prudent not to wait for a definitive study to prove beyond a shadow of a doubt that something is harmful. If there is a reasonable doubt of a product's safety, I don't want it around my sick child. If I hear suspicion cast on public drinking water, food raised with pesticides (i.e., not organic), home-use of pesticides and herbicides, and meats with hormones, steroids, and antibiotics, I think it wise to avoid them when possible. My child is sick. I want to be extra careful about what he is exposed to.

ADVICE FROM JOHN GREEN, MD

From the fall 2006 Defeat Autism Now! conference, Dr. John Green gave the following advice:[9]

o   switch to natural (i.e., "green"), environmentally friendly alternatives for many products, including those for lawn and garden use, household cleaning, and personal care

o   find a source of clean water not stored in polycarbonate bottles

o   eat organically grown produce and healthy meats

o   eat "whole" foods like an apple rather than processed foods containing apples that often contain questionable ingredients

o   don't microwave in plastic

o   store food in glass, avoiding plastics and Styrofoam

o   switch to organically grown natural fabrics like cotton for clothes and to bedding material that is free of flame retardants; they contain antimony

o   avoid contact with arsenic-treated wood.

MOVING ON

These last several chapters have taken a look at problems of body chemistry and heavy-metal overload, as well as related interventions to restore health. Now it is time to change gears and move into the digestive tract. So, onward to the gut!

NOTES

1.   Bock and Stauth 2007, pp. 294–95.
2.   Cave with Mitchell 2001, pp. 28–30.
3.   Baker 2006a, pp. 201–202.
4.   Ibid., p. 201; Baker 2004, p. 184; Bock and Stauth 2007, p. 296; Green 2006c, p. 19; Binstock 2007b, p. 309.
5.   Green 2006c, pp. 12–13.
6.   Binstock 2007b, pp. 307–10.
7.   Bernard *et al.* 2000, p. 57; Cave with Mitchell 2001, pp. 47–48.
8.   Bock and Stauth 2007, p. 202.
9.   Green 2006c, pp. 18–19.

Chapter 23

Common Gut Problems in Autism

WHAT THIS CHAPTER HAS IN STORE

This chapter begins by discussing the existence of gut problems on the autism spectrum and the connection between the gut, the brain, and spectrum behaviors. Then follows a brief description of how the gut is *supposed* to work, before turning to environmental triggers that can spawn a downward spiral of problems in the gut and beyond. These problems and their impact on the body are described. If your child has gut trouble, this chapter will help you recognize the tell-tale clues that can be pieced together to understand his riddle. Behind-the-scenes gut troubles might be exposed, placing you in a position of power to intervene. Understanding the problems enables you to appreciate the appropriateness and importance of the gut treatments presented in the next four chapters, for, when you understand the problems targeted by a treatment, it is easier to decide if that treatment might help *your* child.

GUT PROBLEMS

At the beginning of my biomedical journey, I was surprised to learn that the majority of autistic children have digestive tract problems.[1] In fact, they have significantly more of these problems than both typical children and children with other developmental disorders.[2] Now, isn't that odd? Using endoscopy, colonoscopy, and biopsy, numerous research studies have revealed that woes in the digestive tracts of children on the spectrum are very real and, unfortunately, quite common. Problems can be found anywhere from the esophagus to the colon. Many of the names of these unfortunate conditions are a challenge to pronounce or to know what they mean. However, translated into plain English, they indicate inflammation, reflux, small ulcers, abnormal tissue, low levels of digestive enzymes, impaired absorption of nutrients, constipation, diarrhea, and abnormal gut flora. It is indeed a disturbing picture of the unseen world of the gut.[3]

At the beginning of my biomedical education, I did not suspect that Will had any major gut issues. However, once I learned what to look for and ran some medical tests to get a peek behind the scenes, I was dismayed by what I discovered. It was bad news. However, by treating Will's gut problems, we were rewarded with substantial improvements in many of his spectrum behaviors. Even so, continuing struggles in the gut over time convinced me of the need for an in-depth evaluation by a gastroenterologist. A colonoscopy and endoscopy revealed inflammation in both Will's esophagus and colon. Also evaluated during the procedure were his levels of digestive enzymes, so I could better understand which ones were adequate for digestion of certain foods and which were not. It seems so strange to me now that this was a kid I did not think had major gut problems in the beginning. So, even if you do not suspect your child has gut issues, I encourage you to read the next few chapters anyway. You may spot some red flags. But take heart, though red flags indicate trouble, they equate to opportunities for improvement as well.

Gut–brain connection

Defeat Autism Now! conferences repeat an intriguing phrase: "Heal the gut and the mind will follow." Since when is there a connection between the gut and the brain? I had never heard of such a thing. Other than Defeat Autism Now!, all my medical advisors gave me the impression that the brain was like an isolated ruler who lived far away from his kingdom, the body. Malfunctions in the kingdom had little effect on the ruler himself; he could continue to perform his duties as usual without taking notice. But such a viewpoint hardly seems realistic. We are talking about the brain, the most metabolically active organ in the body. At rest, it uses nine times more energy than any other organ.[4] The brain lives in the body and relies on bodily functions for its sustenance. It requires vital nutrients and depends heavily on complex interactions between the digestive tract, immune system, and hormonal system. Isn't it reasonable to believe that any disorder affecting one or all of these systems will have an impact on the brain? Unfortunately, the gut–brain connection is not clearly understood. Yet, it is quite convincing that connections exist when we see children's brain function improve as a result of better gut health. It turns out that gut health is key to enhancing brain function and healing the immune system in children on the spectrum.[5]

A high-level description of common gut problems and their impact

Usually when we eat spinach or an apple, we pat ourselves on the back for doing our bodies a favor. We assume the digestive tract will do a good job of breaking down the food and absorbing it into our bloodstream for nourishment. But what if a person's ability to do these functions is impaired? If digestion and absorption become inefficient, then eating spinach or an apple may be in vain. Just because food goes inside the tunnel of the digestive tract does not necessarily mean it will ultimately nourish the body. When there are gut problems, all that good nutrition can pass right out the other end. If you do not digest and absorb, you can eat like an elephant and still be starving. Starving bodies, starving brains—not a good situation any way you look at it.

Furthermore, gut woes do more than simply rob the body of its nutrition. There are also negative consequences to having undigested food left to ferment as it passes through the tract. And to make matters worse, harmful effects can also result when undigested food slips out of the digestive tract into the bloodstream, where it does not belong. There, it can stir up trouble when the immune system recognizes it as a foreign invader and launches offensives against it. Food sensitivities can result that spawn unwanted symptoms and behaviors of their own. In addition, offensives launched by the immune system can have unintended, adverse effects on the body itself. To further complicate matters, certain types of undigested food closely resemble some of the body's own agents. In a case of mistaken identity, the food is accepted to play a role in bodily functions, a role it cannot perform. The unfortunate result is a mind-numbing effect that resembles the effects of drugs like opium, morphine, and codeine.

Behaviors resulting from gut problems

So what kinds of behaviors might be expected from a person with an undernourished body and brain? Then add on the complications of immune reactions gone awry. Also factor in mistaken-identity issues that may create brain-numbing effects. Finally, top it all off with the pain or discomfort that often accompanies distress in the gut. Many spectrum behaviors would fit this profile of impaired gut health all too well.

For starters, gastrointestinal problems, like reflux and gas, can keep a person awake at night. They can also make him lose his appetite; since only his favorite foods would tempt him, he gets labeled a picky eater. Distress in the digestive tract can also make a person impatient, cranky, short-tempered, or aggressive. He may even scream sometimes for no apparent reason. But, hey, it hurts. Sometimes you have to scream. Constipation, diarrhea, and a tendency to throw up may also be present. In addition, a person who is used to pain or discomfort may develop a high tolerance for pain in general. Even if verbal, he may not complain because he does not realize the discomfort is out of place. Doesn't everybody feel like this? Furthermore, he may be distracted from the world around him by the discomfort of the world within him. And what if certain undigested foods have escaped the gut and are mistakenly allowed to participate in brain function? It might cause a person to stare into space and have trouble paying attention or concentrating, as a drug user does. In such a case, social skills go out the window. They are complicated and take way too much effort to understand and apply. Moreover, when attention and concentration are in short supply, a person may be able to focus on only his favorite subjects or activities. These favorites might be called obsessions, but he doesn't care. He just knows he likes them and only they can hold his fleeting interest.

Is it coincidence that so many spectrum behaviors fit the profile of a troubled gut? Not likely. We have to quit dismissing symptoms as irrelevant just because the person displaying them is on the spectrum. We have to realize that the symptoms may have a legitimate physical basis, just as they do for anybody else. Harvard gastroenterologist Timothy Buie, MD, raises a valid point when he says that children on the spectrum are more than just mentally and neurologically dysfunctional—they are ill and in distress and pain.[6] Recognition of this reality puts parents and medical professionals in a powerful position to help these children. The physical pain or discomfort can be relieved, and the poor health of body and mind, as well as behaviors, can indeed improve.

Signs that arouse suspicion of gut trouble

There are several signs that justify suspicion of gut health. One is a family history of digestive tract issues (including those of siblings) because such a history implies vulnerability in the gut. Signs of a weak immune system also raise concern about gut welfare. They include frequent ear infections in infancy, chronic viral or yeast infections, eczema, inhalant allergies, and food allergies including intolerance to wheat or milk. These bode ill for the gut since normal gut function relies firmly on a healthy immune system.[7] Specific physical symptoms such as diarrhea, constipation, and abnormal stools are other signs of gut distress and build an even stronger case for concern.[8] Strangely enough, some children with gut issues have few or no symptoms. In these cases, medical testing or response to intervention is the only way to tell that gut problems exist.[9]

Gut symptoms have shared causes

Even when multiple symptoms of gut trouble are present, parents and professionals may not recognize that they all stem from a central underlying source. As a result, each symptom is dealt with independently without addressing the root problem. When this happens, the root problem persists, worsens, and spreads. In Will's case, many gut symptoms were prominent in his very early years, albeit unrecognized for what they were—the tip of an iceberg. Each symptom was medically treated as an isolated incident unrelated to the whole, so the root cause and its spiraling ramifications in the gut were not recognized or addressed. By the time biomedical treatment began at age 11, Will's gut-related symptoms either seemed minor or were not recognized as emanating from the gut. Nonetheless, these underlying gut woes and their legacies had been making a profound impact on his well-being—not only within the gut, but beyond.

DIGESTIVE TRACT REFRESHER

Before addressing what commonly goes wrong in the digestive tracts of children on the spectrum, it is helpful to pause for a brief review of how a healthy system is *supposed* to work. The process of breaking food down into progressively smaller parts starts in the mouth when we chew our food. Next, the food goes down the hatch (esophagus) and is dumped into the acid bath of the stomach. Once food has been reduced to soup by stomach acid, it is dribbled in manageable quantities into the small intestine. Digestion here is primarily accomplished by digestive enzymes with some help from bile salts (courtesy of the liver) to contend with fats. The digestive enzymes are supplied by the pancreas, and each is specially designed to break down a certain component in food. It is a big job, but the food is gradually reduced into successively tinier bits called peptides. Only when the peptides are reduced to amino acids, the most minute form, will they be able to nourish the body. Yet, even in the form of amino acids, this nourishment is still *outside* the body.

A tunnel on the outside

The contents of the small intestine, and the entire digestive tract for that matter, are inside you without *really* being inside you. In truth, the digestive tract is like a tunnel that runs through us. Anything inside that tunnel—be it food, waste products, or otherwise—is *outside* the body proper, as outside of you as is a tree in your front yard. So, if a stomach ulcer allows blood to escape from the body into the tunnel, that blood is as lost as if it had spilled onto the ground. Furthermore, anything in the tunnel stays outside the body unless it is allowed to pass through the tunnel wall.

The beauty of absorption

In addition to being a mixing bowl for digestion, the small intestine is perfectly designed as the queen of absorption as well. Absorption comes into play after the complicated task of digestion has produced amino acids. Now the body finally gets to have dinner. You can almost hear the sucking sound. Through the wall of the small intestine, amino acids are transported out of the tunnel and into the body. The body finally got what it had been working so hard to achieve—nourishment. Think of the wall of the small intestine like a border-control cop. It serves both as a gateway into the body for amino acids, as well as a barrier that prevents others from illegal access to the body. The gut's ability to digest and absorb nutrients effectively is the cornerstone of optimal performance of every other bodily system.[10]

Yeast in the intestinal tract

There is more in the digestive tract than most of us suspect. Our bodies also play host to many species of single-celled organisms called yeast that live in the tunnel all the way from the mouth to the exit end at the anus.[11] These creatures prefer warm, moist mucous membranes in the body like those of the digestive tract, sinuses, and vagina.[12] Their numbers are typically kept in check, which keeps the chemical byproducts they produce at very low concentrations that are not harmful.[13] Fortunately, many of us can get through life without giving much thought to the distasteful idea of alien freeloaders onboard. However, yeast can be hard to ignore if it overpopulates in the vagina as a yeast infection or in the mouth as thrush. In such cases, treatment is usually required for relief of the resulting discomfort.

The colon and its inhabitants: Bacteria

To continue the tale of the digestive tract, the runny liquid that remains at the end of the small intestine is passed to the colon. I hate to break it to you, but the colon is infested by vast numbers of bacteria. These stowaways moved in immediately after you were born. You have carried them, their descendants, and newly arriving immigrants around with you ever since. More than 500 different types of these organisms have been identified, though their quantity and species in any given person can vary over time.

Many of these bacteria are downright hostile and stay under control only as long as the body's immune system is strong. If any of them try to break out of the colon, the immune system will open fire; it is prepared for life with the treacherous bacteria. However, not all bacteria are bad. Many types of bacteria are our friends because of the good deeds they perform. One important service they perform is that they wage battle against bad bacteria and yeast as each struggles for dominance in the gut. Their constant competition prevents any one kind of germ from taking over and escaping the colon to invade the body. Good bacteria also fight pathogens that sneak in on food. They can unlock vitamins from food for us and can even make certain vitamins on their own like biotin and vitamin K. Digestion, absorption, metabolism, and the immune system all get a helping hand from good bacteria.[14]

The digestive tract and the immune system: An intimate relationship

The digestive tract is on the frontlines with a potentially hostile environment. It must be on guard and wary for the treachery of any Trojan horse. Viruses, bacteria, fungi, parasites, and toxins (such as pesticides and herbicides) can all gain access to the tunnel as stowaways on anything we swallow. Believe it or not, it is a jungle in there. The body must arm itself, and that is where the immune system comes in. It recognizes that the gut is a critical point of environmental exposure, so it devotes an enormous amount of its defense budget to it. In fact, 60–70 percent of the immune cells of the entire body are centered in the gut. They have the bad guys surrounded. They trust no one and take no chances; one false move, and they open fire. The immune system's message to the gut is clear: "I'll cover your back, while you digest this stuff." Isn't it nice to have such a tough guy on your side—or inside, that is? A strong, capable immune system is every gut's dream. They share an intimate relationship, for they are together in the trenches on the frontlines of the environment, day after day, working to nourish and protect.[15]

If you are interested, there are plenty more details about the digestive tract in Part II of *The Second Brain* by Michael D. Gershon, MD. The majority of what was just presented about how the digestive tract is *supposed* to work was based on Dr. Gershon's expert descriptions in that book.

INTRODUCING THE DOWNWARD SPIRAL

The chain of events about to be described shows what *can* happen in the gut. However, what actually does happen for any given individual will vary in scope and severity. It depends on several factors, including the person's underlying genetic makeup, the extent and timing of environmental insults, and other factors, such as what the person eats. Furthermore, this presentation shows a sequence to the events, but there is also a great deal of simultaneous cross-interaction among the factors involved.[16] These interactions are complex and may feed off each other in some cases. Recall the intricate pattern of tumbling dominoes. Even if only a single domino initiated the cascade, there may be junctions where multiple streams of dominoes are triggered to fall. These streams may even loop back across each other at various points. Amid the confusion of simultaneous and crisscrossing movement, it can be difficult to determine the original sequence of downfall or precise interaction among various dominoes. All that is seen in the end is a big mess.

The discussion here centers on antibiotic use as an initial trigger of gut disruption. However, other triggers are also possible, such as mercury in childhood vaccines, persistent infant colic, unavailability of breast feeding, and the body's inability to rid itself of toxins and heavy metals. These factors can also stress the gut and contribute to impaired gut function.[17]

Gut wars

An important part of gut health involves the vast number of organisms that live and battle for supremacy in the gut. They include yeast, good bacteria, and bad bacteria and are collectively known as gut flora. Bacteria primarily strive for domination by reproducing like crazy; they can multiply in minutes (ironically, by dividing). Their offensive strategy is to overwhelm foes by their sheer numbers. Yeast, on the other hand, are much more complex organisms; they employ a sophisticated tactic—they produce toxins to kill their enemies. In fact, even some of the bad bacteria like Clostridia employ this technique as well. But never fear. In a fair-and-square game of gut wars, the three challengers maintain a healthy system of checks and balances. In such a setting, digestion and absorption of food can roll merrily along.

Antibiotics and gut wars

But what happens when the game of gut wars is not fair and square? If some of the unsavory contestants gain an unfair advantage, balance in the gut is upset

and detrimental effects to the body can result. Unfortunately, gut flora is susceptible to damage and can be very difficult to restore.[18] It can go from good to bad
to ugly. Ugly flora can be dominoes that start a downward cascading chain
reaction that eventually reaches the brain.

Suppose that one day oral antibiotics arrive in the gut. They were intended
to kill bacteria that caused an ear infection, but antibiotics are not smart enough
to be selective. They randomly go about slaughtering bacteria wherever they
find them, including large numbers of bacteria they meet as they flow through
the digestive tract. What a terrific ally for the yeast who are unaffected by antibiotics! With the number of bacteria reduced, yeast can enjoy a population
explosion and usurp a stronghold. The many women who suffer vaginal yeast
infections following antibiotics can attest to the obvious cause-and-effect relationship between antibiotics and yeast overgrowth in the vagina.[19] A similar
phenomenon takes place in the gut, as hundreds of scientific and medical
articles have attested.[20]

Yeast overgrowth in the gut

Yeast overgrowth is the most common problem resulting from a disruption in
normal gut flora.[21] For some individuals, even a short course of antibiotics can
cause a long-lasting imbalance that stubbornly defies repair.[22] Those with weak
immune systems are particularly susceptible.[23] Unfortunately, antibiotic use in
newborns and recurring antibiotic use in the early years of life increase the
chances of future problems with yeast.[24] When it comes to people on the autism
spectrum, we find that bad flora is quite common.[25] Their impaired immune
systems and inflamed intestines make them easy targets for yeast, especially to a
species known as *Candida*.[26]

But how do you know if yeast has taken over? Usually, outward physical
signs are present. However, people often do not recognize that these symptoms
are caused by an underlying yeast overgrowth that requires treatment. Conse-
quently, they treat the symptoms only, but not the yeast. So, the yeast problem
persists and, in time, triggers secondary problems, each a tumbling domino of its
own.

Outward signs of yeast overgrowth

Yeast overgrowth has the potential to create a huge laundry list of physical and
behavioral symptoms that vary from one person to the next. A short list of the
physical symptoms includes constipation, diarrhea, particularly foul-smelling
stool, diaper rash, a red ring around the anus, reflux, thrush (white patches of

yeast overgrowth in the mouth), a white coating on the tongue, gas, abdominal bloating or discomfort, fatigue, and poor coordination. Sometimes, however, there are no physical symptoms, and abnormal behavior is the only clue. Behavioral symptoms may include poor attention, hyperactivity, irritability, aggression, sugar or starch cravings, drunken behavior, or inappropriate "drunken" laughter.[27] Surprisingly, symptoms can seem unrelated to each other, such as thrush in the mouth and diaper rash, for example. However, they both stem from the same underlying problem—yeast overgrowth.

Yeast is not only a problem in autism. It can play a major role in many diseases such as psoriasis, lupus, multiple sclerosis, Crohn's disease, and inflammatory bowel disease. It can also cause symptoms in people who do not have any identifiable disease. These symptoms can vary greatly from person to person. A few include fatigue, headache, depression, and problems with the skin and digestive tract.[28] William Crook, MD, spent a successful career becoming an expert on yeast overgrowth and educating people about it worldwide. His mini-book, *Dr. Crook Discusses Yeasts and How They Can Make You Sick*, is very easy-to-understand, concise, and brief. It describes yeast overgrowth and its resulting symptoms and treatment. Dr. Crook wrote several other books as well that offer greater detail, including *The Yeast Connection Handbook*.

The gut wall under attack

Destruction of good bacteria and the overgrowth of yeast are worrisome developments, especially when you recall what yeast and some bad bacteria like Clostridia do for a living: they produce toxins to kill their enemies. A lot of yeast or bad bacteria means a lot of toxins, so much, in fact, that they begin to irritate the wall of the small intestine.[29] In addition, the originally tame, round yeast cells begin to transform into a more aggressive and invasive form. The cell sprouts a branch that grows limbs ending in pointed little barbs.[30] Once in this armed-and-dangerous form, yeast are able to grip into the tissue of the gut lining; there, they cling like ivy to a brick wall, a posture that keeps them from being swept away by passing food. Where yeast dig in, they secrete digestive enzymes to digest the gut wall for a better grip.[31] These enzymes can destroy tissue and digest antibodies that the immune system sends to attack the yeast.

Now, come on, immune system! You better have a Plan B. You are supposed to be looking out for the gut, remember? Quick, do something.[32] Figure 23.1 illustrates the beginning of the downward spiral.

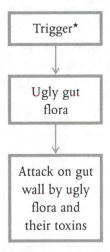

*Triggers may include antibiotics, vaccine mercury, persistent infant colic, unavailability of breast feeding, and body's inability to rid itself of toxins and heavy metals.

Figure 23.1 The downward spiral has begun

Inflammation and a hyperactive immune system

As the wall of the digestive tract becomes inflamed, its swelling and redness are cries for help. The immune system responds and tries to heal the injury. However, repair mechanisms were designed for quick fixes like healing cuts, burns, and infections. How can they heal something that is under perpetual attack and repeated injury? They can't, so the inflammation persists. The constant nagging of inflammation goads the hard-working immune system. It knows it is supposed to come to the rescue, yet all its efforts are foiled. In effect, it grows increasingly desperate and frantic. In fact, the immune system can get stuck in an inappropriate state of hypervigilance. Meanwhile, the chronic inflammation continues and can even worsen long after the initial trigger of bad gut flora is gone.[33]

Researchers who have examined the intestinal tracts of children on the autism spectrum have found that the majority are inflamed.[34] This inflammation goes by many different names depending on its location. In the esophagus, it is called esophagitis; the stomach, gastritis; the duodenum region of the small intestine, duodenitis; and in the colon, colitis.[35] Different names, different places. But it all boils down to chronic inflammation.[36]

To make matters worse, continuous inflammation can reduce the immune system's ability to fight off viruses, bacteria, parasites, and yeast. This welcomes further overgrowth of bad flora, as well as repeated infections that may invite more rounds of antibiotics. Thus, a vicious cycle is created. Figure 23.2 shows the downward spiral with its most recent additions.

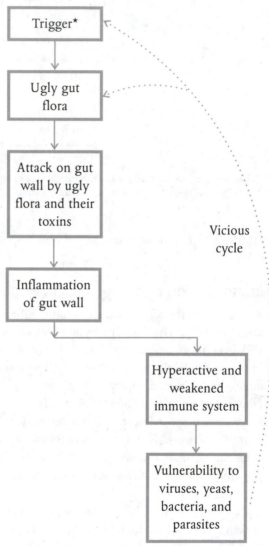

*Triggers may include antibiotics, vaccine mercury, persistent infant colic, unavailability of breast feeding, and body's inability to rid itself of toxins and heavy metals.

Figure 23.2 The downward spiral continues

Injury to digestive enzymes and the cells of the gut wall

The physical and toxic attacks of bad flora injure the cells of the gut wall. This is bad for a couple of reasons. For one, amino acids need to be able to pass through these cells to nourish the body. For another, the final stages of digestion for certain components in food take place on the surface of these cells. Thus, when the cells and their specialized digestive enzymes are injured, problems can arise in digestion of:[37]

1. *Complex sugars.* Complex sugars exist in milk sugar (lactose), table sugar, corn syrup, and a host of manufactured foods that contain them. They also appear in starchy foods such as grains, corn, and potatoes. Unlike the simple sugars in fruit, honey, and some vegetables, complex sugars are not in their simplest form ready to be absorbed; rather, they must first be broken down into simple sugars by specialized digestive enzymes. Take the enzyme called lactase, for example. It breaks down the complex sugar in milk (lactose). No other enzyme can do the job; it is lactase or bust. This is unfortunate since at least 60 percent of those tested on the autism spectrum are deficient in lactase.[38] Though lactase deficiency is the most common, many with autism are also deficient in other enzymes necessary for digestion of complex sugars and starches (maltase, isomaltase, and palatinase).[39]

2. *Proteins in milk and certain grains.* There are also deficiencies of enzymes that digest certain proteins too. These merit special attention since they can create future problems as the downward spiral continues. The proteins involved come from milk (casein) and certain grains (gluten) like wheat, oats, barley, rye, and triticale. For digestion, casein and gluten share a special protein-splitting enzyme called DPP4. DPP4 is the only enzyme that can fulfill this role; it has no substitute. If there is a shortage of DPP4, digestion of both casein and gluten is hampered. As a result, these proteins are stuck in their useless peptide states and hang around the gut looking for trouble. Unfortunately, on the autism spectrum, there appears to be a shortage of DPP4. This may be due to exposure to mercury, pesticides, lead acetate, or other substances or possibly an autoimmune reaction.[40]

3. *Fats.* Frequently on the autism spectrum, there is a lack of the enzyme lipase that breaks down fats.[41]

In the end, lack of these enzymes leads to a mounting number of useless peptides accumulating in the tunnel. They are too large to be absorbed into the body; even if they could be, they would still not nourish. Only our friends the amino acids can do that. Yet, the amino acids remain locked up in the peptides like Rapunzel in the tower.

Poor fat processing

The body's strategies for both digestion and absorption of fats are relatively complex, so it follows that, if the small intestine is ailing, fat handling may be the first to suffer. Fat in the stool is one of the earliest and most enduring signs of woes in digestion and absorption. Unfortunately, bacteria in the colon are quite happy about this turn of events because they enjoy feasting on undigested, unabsorbed fat now left to ferment and stink in the tunnel. Their increased numbers wash out in the stool, making the stool larger. The color of the stool may be gray or tan rather than the reassuring brown we typically expect. Stool with excess fats and a bumper crop of bacteria may also be oily, particularly foul-smelling, and lighter than water, which makes it float. Clogging toilets is its specialty.[42]

Mucus

As conditions in the gut deteriorate, the body may use mucus to shield the intestinal lining, just as it shields nasal passageways during a cold. However, mucus coating the gut wall can interfere with digestion and absorption. Even so, it is better than the alternative. If mucus-production becomes exhausted at some point, the gut wall must face physical and toxic attack without protective cover. At this stage, ulceration of the intestinal lining can occur, as seen in ulcerative colitis.[43] Figure 23.3 shows the downward spiral with its latest additions.

A body robbed of nourishment

When digestion is impaired, the body is less able to break down food into amino acids. Even amino acids that are produced have trouble being absorbed through a gut wall that is injured, inflamed, and coated in mucus. Yet the body really *needs* those amino acids; they are necessary to build numerous structures like brain neurotransmitters, hormones, and muscle. In addition, amino acids make enzymes that control every chemical reaction in the body. Our energy, blood sugar stabilization, and the purging of toxins are dependent on them.[44] Poor digestion and absorption, therefore, can be a serious impairment to a host of bodily functions. The disturbing image of a starving brain and body comes to mind.

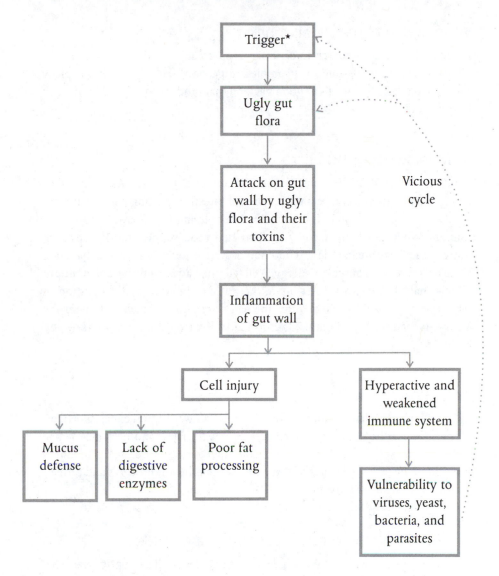

*Triggers may include antibiotics, vaccine mercury, persistent infant colic, unavailability of breast feeding, and body's inability to rid itself of toxins and heavy metals.

Figure 23.3 The downward spiral continues

Vitamin and mineral deficiencies

Indeed, the majority of children on the spectrum are deficient in several vitamins and minerals due to incomplete digestion, faulty absorption, picky eating habits, and low levels of good bacteria that produce vitamins like vitamin K and biotin.[45]

A buffet table for bad flora

Food that is undigested or unabsorbed lingers in the tunnel. As it meanders along, it ferments and can become a source of intestinal gas and pain.[46] Unfortunately, it is also a welcome sight to the bad flora living in the lower small intestine and colon. Such flora enjoy an increased food supply from the passing buffet table. They are happiest to find starches and especially sugars in the refuse since these are rich sources of energy. Well fed, the bad flora thrive and multiply, which enables them to further injure the gut and interfere with digestion. A vicious cycle is established in which the bad flora's interference with digestion boosts its food supply.[47] Figure 23.4 shows the downward spiral with its newest additions.

Introducing leaky gut

Spurred on by escalating woes in the gut, the downward spiral expands. Microscopic cracks or holes begin to open in the gut wall. This condition, nicknamed leaky gut, makes the wall more permeable than it should be.[48] This tumbling domino in the cascade creates a legacy that reaches beyond the gut and propels the downward spiral outward.

The tunnel on the outside just got on the inside

The fall of the gut wall is a serious development. The wall's integrity was what kept the contents of the digestive tract isolated from the rest of the body, as it should be. That important isolation is lost once a leaky gut allows unwanted refuse to seep into the bloodstream. Think of the bloodstream as a superhighway that links every part of the body to every other part. Gut refuse is foreign in the superhighway and has no business with such powerful admittance. The opening of illegal entrances to the superhighway allows access to the brain that does our thinking, the liver that cleans out toxins and heavy metals, and the endocrine organs that carefully regulate hormone levels—you name it, our bloodstream connects it all.

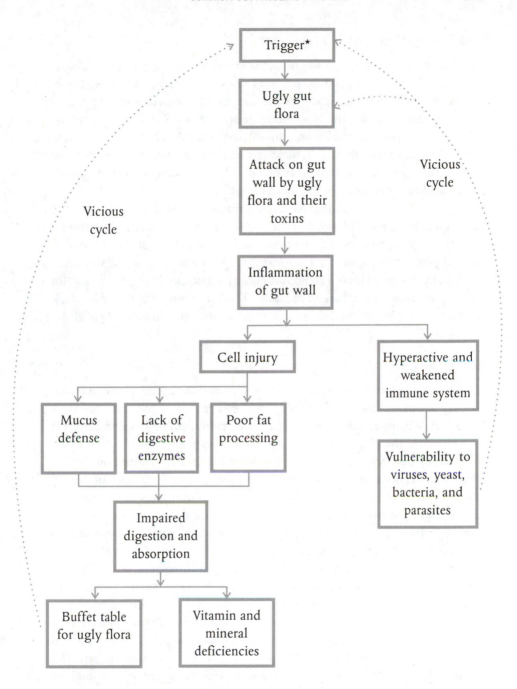

*Triggers may include antibiotics, vaccine mercury, persistent infant colic, unavailability of breast feeding, and body's inability to rid itself of toxins and heavy metals.

Figure 23.4 The downward spiral continues

The misfortunes of a leaky gut

With leaky gut, anything in the tunnel is at risk of escaping into the blood-stream, including toxins and by-products from yeast and bad bacteria. There, they can encounter something called the blood–brain barrier, a physical blockade that separates the bloodstream from the brain and the rest of the central nervous system. Ideally, only authorized molecules should be allowed to pass. If irritating toxins and by-products inflame or cross the blood–brain barrier, they can interfere with the brain's supply of nutrients, as well as hamper consciousness, cognition, speech, or behavior.[49]

What else is in the gut that we don't want in the body? What about those incompletely digested particles of food called peptides? Ideally, they should stay in the gut to be broken down to amino acids. If that is not possible due to poor digestion, they should at least pass through the tunnel into the stool. But with leaky gut, peptides can escape into the bloodstream. Though they cannot provide nourishment, is there any harm in them? As it turns out, they can wreak havoc in multiple ways and thus extend and amplify the downward spiral.[50]

Escapees and the immune system

The immune system is like a watchman who patrols the border of the gut wall. He expects that a few sneaky peptides will escape from time to time, so he is prepared. Whenever there is a break out, he deploys antibodies that handcuff themselves to the illegal escapee-peptides. Now they are marked for clean up. The twosomes circulate in the bloodstream until they are cleared out by the body. It is important that twosomes are removed in a timely manner since they are potentially inflammatory and can cause injury. Unfortunately, this method of dealing with escaped peptides was not designed for the heavy onslaught that comes with leaky gut. If the body is overwhelmed, circulating twosomes take extended tours traveling throughout the body on the superhighway. They eventually settle out in any number of places creating inflammation wherever they land. They may choose a spot where damage already exists or where genetic vulnerability dictates. In the joints, they cause arthritis; in the kidneys, hypertension. Any organ can be their destination including the brain, heart, and lungs. A wide variety of symptoms is possible, which varies from person to person.[51] In the end, the immune system's efforts to protect have been inadequate and resulted in injury to the body. It is no wonder that this overwhelmed immune system gets exasperated, edgy, and hyperactive.

Delayed food sensitivities

A common result of leaky gut is delayed food sensitivities.[52] To understand how these sensitivities occur, it is helpful to know a little about the various types of antibodies commanded by the immune system. Just as the government has several branches of military service, the immune system has several branches of antibody service. Though all branches aim to protect, each is designed for a special purpose and uses different tactics. When it comes to food reactions, the immune system directs two types of antibody forces: the IgE forces and the IgG forces. Though their names are similar, they are as different as the army and the navy.

Let's talk about IgE first since it is the one most people are familiar with. The "E" in "IgE" stands for "Everyone knows about them." Well, maybe not, but it can help us keep the two types straight. Anyway, IgE antibodies are the ones that cause *immediate* and *severe* reactions to food such as breathing emergencies, gut distress, or hives.[53] Here some unlucky person, minding his own business, eats an innocent-looking peanut or shellfish. Then, boom!—his immune system completely freaks out. The next thing he knows he is watching his life flash before his eyes. The effect is quite dramatic, which is why everyone knows about IgE reactions despite the fact only 1 to 2 percent of American adults have this type of food allergy.[54] Come to think of it, maybe the "E" is for "Exciting."

IgE, however, is not the branch of the antibody service most relevant to the autism spectrum. No, the autism spectrum is afflicted more often by IgG food sensitivities, something entirely different. So forget all you know about food allergy and start over. With IgG sensitivity, the length of time between eating the offending food and the appearance of symptoms is different. So are the types of symptoms themselves and the possible number of symptoms. How long the immune system holds a grudge against a food can vary as well. Often children crave the food that causes them problems, which is rarely the case with IgE.[55] Even the medical testing for IgG food sensitivity is different; no scratch test on the skin will do. As you are about to see, all these differences make it much harder to recognize the connection between a food and the symptoms it causes. Maybe the "G" in "IgG" is for "goofy."

With IgG, the reaction to a food is not immediate; instead, it is delayed. Symptoms often do not appear for several hours or days after the offending food is eaten.[56] When they do appear, the variety of possible symptoms is huge. They can include seizures, diarrhea and other gut problems, asthma, frequent ear and sinus infections, joint pain, and headaches. Be particularly suspect of food sensitivity if there have been problems with rashes, sleep trouble, bowel symptoms, colic during infancy, known food reactions, or allergies to dust, mold, animals, pollens, or chemicals.[57] Other observable clues of delayed food reaction include red ears, dark circles under the eyes, a red or flushed face, easy bruising, eczema, or itchy skin.[58] Symptoms can also involve behaviors.[59] So what foods are problematic on the autism spectrum? It is common for reactions to be caused by frequently eaten foods like wheat, milk, corn, and eggs.[60] That should not be surprising since whatever is eaten the most will probably leak the most and arouse the immune system. Fortunately, the delayed food sensitivities of IgG do have one likable quality. They do not necessarily last forever. If the offending food is avoided for a time while steps are taken to heal the leaky gut, the immune system can forgive its grudge.[61] At that point, the person can go back to enjoying the food again, at least occasionally.

Casein and gluten escapees in the brain: Opioid effect

Have you ever noticed how, in a moment of emergency or exertion, you can be injured and barely feel it? Later you might notice you are bleeding and wonder what happened. That happens because, during an emergency, our bodies release substances called endorphins that inhibit pain. They block out sensations we normally feel, so we are free to focus on the emergency at hand. No doubt, it was a handy survival technique for our Stone Age ancestors escaping danger.

It just so happens that drugs derived from opium have a similar molecular structure to our own natural endorphins. This similarity enables these drugs, called opioids, to have a comparable effect on the body. Famous members of the opioid family include morphine, heroin, and codeine. They have a tremendous ability to alleviate pain, though sometimes with side effects of altered perception and hallucinations.[62]

This brings us to two peptides that can be particularly disruptive to people on the autism spectrum. They are the incompletely digested peptides of casein protein from milk and gluten protein from certain grains (wheat, oats, barley, rye, and triticale). On the autism spectrum, there may be an abundance of these peptides due to a shortage of the DPP4 enzyme required to digest them. Along with other food peptides, casein and gluten escape the leaky gut and circulate in the bloodstream. It is an ill-fated coincidence that these two peptides also have a similar molecular structure to our natural endorphins.[63] Those peptides that make their way to the brain can interact with the brain's opiate receptors, causing an effect similar to that of drugs like morphine, heroin, and codeine. Known as opioid effect, perception, cognition, emotions, mood, and behavior can be affected.[64]

Numerous studies have found high levels of casein and gluten peptides in the urine of children with autism and adults with schizophrenia.[65] It is not surprising that high levels of opioid peptides are found in those autistic children who are insensitive to pain or who intentionally injure themselves.[66] Professor Paul Shattock is one of the published autism researchers who has studied opioid peptides in the urine of children with autism. His studies show a rough association between a child's level of opioid peptides and the severity of his impairments.[67]

So what would you do if you got a little high whenever you ate dairy or wheat products? You might eat a little more, right? And if dairy and wheat were actually addictive to the body you live in, you might even eliminate everything from your diet except them. Who could help it? As it turns out, a majority of children on the spectrum reject all but a few favorite foods that are rich in casein and gluten. Typically, these favorites include pizza, chicken nuggets, cakes, cookies, and ice cream.[68] In addition, there are children who do not recognize which particular foods make them feel good, so they respond by eating unusually large amounts of all foods.[69]

A SUMMARY OF THE DOWNWARD SPIRAL

Figure 23.5 shows a summary of the downward spiral. It starts with a trigger that disrupts gut flora and leads to overgrowth of yeast and possibly resistant bad bacteria. The resulting abundance of bad flora toxins and physical attacks on the gut wall destroy certain digestive enzymes and cause inflammation and injury to the cells that line the gut. Mucus secreted to shield the gut wall, coupled with inflammation, cell injury, and lack of digestive enzymes, impairs digestion and absorption. Hardest hit is digestion of complex sugars, starches, and fats, as well as proteins from milk (casein) and certain grains (gluten). Deficiencies in vitamins and minerals surface as the body and brain are robbed of nourishment. As the bad flora thrive on unabsorbed food refuse, they establish a vicious cycle in which their interference with digestion boosts their food supply. Eventually, the assaulted and weakened gut wall begins to leak. Undigested food peptides and toxins from bad flora seep into the bloodstream through the leaky gut. As the immune system's forces are overwhelmed by the flood of escaping peptides, inflammation occurs in parts of the body outside the gut. Additionally, a novel situation is created by the leaked proteins of casein (milk) and gluten (certain grains). Like morphine, heroine, and codeine, these particular proteins can impersonate the body's own natural endorphins. Perception, cognition, emotions, mood, and behavior are altered. Meanwhile, gut inflammation has weakened the immune system, making it less able to fight off viruses, bacteria, parasites, and yeast in the gut. A weak immune system invites further overgrowth of bad flora, as well as repeated infections that may be treated with antibiotics. A vicious cycle is created in which bad flora and antibiotics further weaken the ailing immune system. Aroused to inappropriate hypervigilance and aggression, the immune system overreacts to the peptides escaping the leaky gut. The results are delayed food sensitivities that can provoke a wide variety of symptoms. It is a picture of what often happens on the autism spectrum though the extent, severity, and specific outcomes vary from one individual to the next.

Somewhere along the way, behavioral and/or physical symptoms of this sprawling chain of events begins to surface. It becomes obvious that something is wrong, very wrong. The trick is recognizing that a downward spiral in the gut is the source. That critical realization is key to combating the symptoms.

HINDSIGHT IS 20-20

Will received vaccine mercury through the mandatory pediatric schedule during its years of peak exposure (1991–roughly 2001). He also received nine rounds of antibiotics before age one. There were seven more rounds by age two. Six followed the next year before he was placed on a maintenance antibiotic dose to prevent ear infections. Knowing what I know now, I cannot fathom why my pediatrician dished out oral antibiotics so freely and without a counter strategy for repair of gut flora. I can only conclude that he did not know the danger. Nor did he recognize that the pattern of recurring ear infections, sinus infections, thrush mouth, diaper rash, and chronic diarrhea was a flashing neon sign of gut distress. Each symptom was treated as a separate, unrelated incident. The two instances of chronic diarrhea were not treated at all. They would "go away"; and after several weeks, they did.

Tragically, we were in a downward spiral of injury and never even knew it. But that kind of injury cannot keep itself a secret. As we slipped deeper onto the autism spectrum, we addressed these symptoms with early education and special education; drugs to suppress inattention and anxiety; physical and occupational therapies; speech therapy, social skills training, and more. We did it all, but we were missing the boat. Not that these aren't valuable interventions; they are. Yet the root causes of our woes were going unrecognized and untreated—for years. That was why we continued to lose ground against peers, despite all our striving.

MOVING FORWARD

I don't know about you, but this chapter leaves me somewhere between anxious and depressed. Perhaps it is because many of the problems described here have clouded Will's life and mine. Even so, the most appropriate emotional response to this chapter should be hope because, when there are problems, there are opportunities.

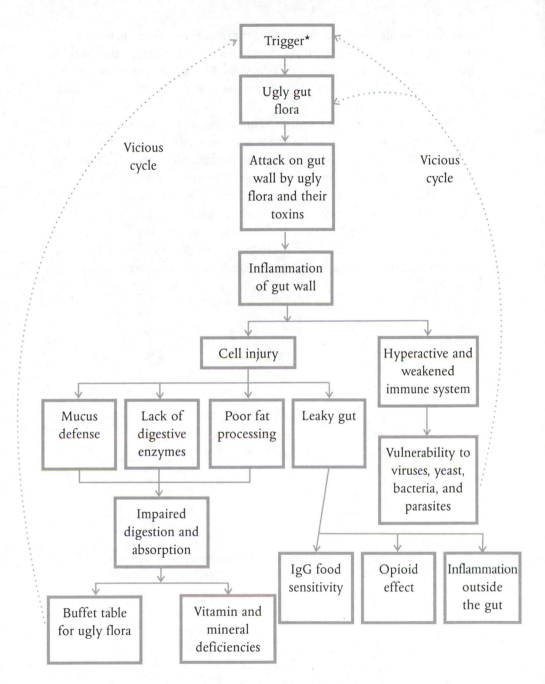

*Triggers may include antibiotics, vaccine mercury, persistent infant colic, unavailability of breast feeding, and body's inability to rid itself of toxins and heavy metals.

Figure 23.5 Summary of the downward spiral

Seize the opportunities. Take advantage of the treatments offered in the following chapters on gut-related interventions. They hold some of the keys to improved health, brain function, and behaviors. Though they do not work for everyone, they work for many. They offer hope. It is within our grasp to transform that hope into reality.

On the autism spectrum, we start treatment in the gut. Success here is a top priority.[70] Starting any place else if the gut is a mess will be less effective and more complicated. First steps include removing troublesome foods from the diet, restoring healthy gut flora, and starting basic nutritional supplements. Diet and gut flora are covered in the next few chapters. The starting of basic nutritional supplements will be discussed in Chapter 29. Following on the heels of these initial interventions comes methyl-B12 shots and repair of detoxification chemistry with its links to inflammation. In some cases, infections such as viral infections need to be addressed as well.[71] But for now, let's focus on rescuing the gut.

NOTES

1. McCandless 2007, p. 81.
2. Rimland 2006f, p. 2.
3. El-Dahr 2006a, pp. 154–55; www.AutismNDI.com/news (reprinted abstracts of many studies).
4. Cordain and Friel 2005, p. 149.
5. McCandless 2007, pp. 36, 105–106.
6. Rimland 2006c, p. 4.
7. McCandless 2007, p. 82; Mumper 2008a, personal communication.
8. Pangborn and Baker 2005, p. 1:12.
9. McCandless 2007, pp. 67, 81.
10. McDonnell 2006b, p. 85.
11. Crook 1999, p. 120; Pangborn and Baker 2005, p. 2:11.
12. Lewis and Fink 2005, pp. 7–8.
13. Shaw 1998, p. 17.
14. Ibid., p. 82; Furlong and Hanaway 2006, p. 18; Pangborn and Baker 2005, p. 5:52.
15. Hanaway 2006, p. 51; Herbert 2006, p. 39; Baker 2004, p. 96; McCandless 2007, pp. 83, 177.
16. McCandless 2007, p. 45.
17. Ibid., pp. 28, 82, 97.
18. Pangborn and Baker 2005, p. 2:11; Baker 2004, p. 71.
19. Lewis and Fink 2005, p. 7.
20. Lewis 1998a, pp. 33–34; Shaw 1998, p. 16.
21. Shaw 1998, p. 16; Pangborn and Baker 2005, p. 2:13.
22. Pangborn and Baker 2005, p. 2:11; Baker 2004, pp. 10, 71.
23. Pangborn and Baker 2005, p. 2:11.
24. Ibid.
25. Ibid., p. 1:44; Shaw 2004, p. 9.
26. McCandless 2007, p. 28.

27. Pangborn and Baker 2005, p. 1:22; McCandless 2007, pp. 28, 74, 100–101; Lewis and Fink 2005, p. 4.

28. Lewis and Fink 2005, p. 4; Crook 2001, pp. 16–19.

29. Shaw 1998, p. 17.

30. Lewis and Fink 2005, p. 8; Lewis 1998a, p. 34.

31. Shaw 2004, pp. 9–10.

32. Shaw 1998, p. 17; McCandless 2007, pp. 42, 83–84.

33. McCandless 2007, p. 42; Baker 2006b, pp. 70–71; Baker 2004, pp. 92, 95.

34. Rimland 2006c, p. 4; McCandless 2007, p. 27.

35. McCandless 2007, p. 112.

36. Ashwood *et al.* 2004, pp. 664–67; Wakefield *et al.* 1998, pp. 637–41; Wakefield *et al.* 2000, pp. 2285–95; Buie 2003, pp. 163–69; Krigsman 2004, pp. 253–58; Horvath *et al.* 1999, pp. 559–63; Rimland 2006c, p. 4.

37. Bock and Stauth 2007, p. 266.

38. Rimland 2006c, p. 4; Pangborn 2006b, p. 63.

39. Pangborn 2006b, p. 63; Gottschall 2004, pp. 22–30; Rimland 2006c, p. 4; Horvath *et al.* 1999, pp. 559–63; Kushak *et al.* 2005, p. 508; McCandless 2007, pp. 91–92.

40. McCandless 2007, p. 27; Pangborn and Baker 2005, pp. 2:36–37; Bock and Stauth 2007, p. 266; Pangborn 2006b, pp. 62–63.

41. Pangborn 2006b, p. 64.

42. Gershon 2003, pp. 122, 143.

43. Gottschall 2004, pp. 19, 24, 26.

44. Ibid., p. 21; McCandless 2007, p. 75.

45. McCandless 2007, p. 46; Shaw 1998, p. 82; Kartzinel 2006, p. 98.

46. Gottschall 2004, p. 17.

47. Ibid., pp. 9–10, 16–18, 47; Pangborn 2006b, pp. 62–63; Pangborn and Baker 2005, p. 5:50; McCandless 2007, p. 91.

48. McCandless 2007, pp. 42–44, 83–84; Shaw 1998, pp. 17–18.

49. Shaw 1998, p. 296; Pangborn 2006b, p. 63; Crook 1999, p. 11; McCandless 2007, pp. 28, 42, 94.

50. D'Eufemia *et al.* 1996, pp. 1076–79; White 2003, pp. 639–49; Shaw 1998, p. 142.

51. Torrente *et al.* 2002, pp. 375–82; Baker 2004, pp. 96–97.

52. Shaw 1998, p. 18.

53. Lewis 1998a, pp. 37–38.

54. Baker 2004, p. 95.

55. Lewis 1998a, p. 41.

56. McCandless 2007, p. 74.

57. Pangborn and Baker 2005, p. 2:43.

58. Ibid., p. 1:24.

59. Baker 2004, pp. 18, 95.

60. McCandless 2007, pp. 74–75.

61. Shaw 1998, p. 18.

62. Pangborn and Baker 2005, p. 2:38.

63. Ibid., p. 2:37.

64. Shattock and Whiteley 2002, pp. 175–83; White 2003, pp. 639–49; Shattock and Savery 1997, pp. 204–205; Shaw 1998, p. 127.

65. Shaw 1998, p. 124; Pangborn and Baker 2005, p. 2:38; McCandless 2007, pp. 42–43; Lewis 1998b, pp. 201–202; Seroussi 2002, p. 115.

66. Lewis 1998a, p. 24.
67. McCandless 2007, p. 43.
68. Ibid., p. 85.
69. Seroussi 2002, pp. 206, 214.
70. McCandless 2007, p. 90.
71. Pangborn and Baker 2005, pp. 1:35–36, 2:1–3; Baker 2006c, p. 4.

Chapter 24

Common Gut Interventions: Food Issues

WHAT TO EXPECT IN THE GUT-INTERVENTION CHAPTERS (24–27)

Many opportunities to improve autistic behaviors significantly lie in the gut. These opportunities relate to food sensitivity, gut flora, and a few odds and ends. When these issues are addressed, the gut wall heals, and digestion and absorption improve. In many cases, physical symptoms and autistic behaviors that were intensified by gut problems are reduced.

This chapter is the first of four chapters that explain various biomedical interventions in the gut. It covers those that relate to food. Using food to influence ailments is not a new idea. For example, the progression of diabetes can be slowed when carbohydrate intake is limited. The same goes for heart disease through reduction of saturated fats. Childhood epilepsy can be greatly controlled or even cured through the elimination of carbohydrates. There are also people who can significantly control multiple sclerosis by reducing fats to an ultralow level.[1] When it comes to being influenced by foods, autism is no different. In fact, a powerful impact can be made by eating only foods that help and not harm.

This chapter will familiarize you with the reality of food sensitivity and the potential benefits of avoiding foods that cause negative reactions. It also suggests an attitude that makes it easier to adjust to dietary change. A way to experiment with changes in diet—the elimination/binge food trial—is explained as well. Finally, optional lab tests that are available to guide dietary decisions are discussed. The next chapter will review the various diets that have been beneficial to people on the autism spectrum. Following chapters will address interventions that target gut flora, as well as other areas of concern in the digestive tract. No matter what form gut intervention takes, its aim is always to repair, avoid, or compensate.

ARE FOOD SENSITIVITIES REAL?

The bottom line on food sensitivity is individuality. A food that is healthy for one person can be downright offensive and injurious to another. We find it easy to accept food allergy when we see an immediate, dramatic reaction like a flaming rash or breathing emergency. In such a case, the connection between the food and the reaction is obvious. It is still weird, but there is no denying its existence.

On the other hand, when a food causes a delayed response whose symptoms are not so easily recognized, we are understandably skeptical. The link between cause and effect is harder to recognize and to accept. Nevertheless, it too is real. For instance, if this body I live in eats an ear of corn or a bowl of popcorn, a migraine is guaranteed within the next several hours. Now, what sense is there in that? There is nothing wrong with corn, and besides I love it, popcorn especially. I have tried to ignore this bizarre phenomenon and eat popcorn anyway. But, alas, I always end up sorry, migraine and all. *Why* this happens is immaterial and academic. It is a fact of my existence, maybe nobody else's but definitely mine. For whatever reason, this body stubbornly insists on pitching a fit over a measly bag of popcorn. I have no choice but to accept it (grudgingly) and sit on my hands when the popcorn bag passes by. The same goes for individuals on the spectrum and their peculiar responses to food. Even though we may think a body's response to a food is inappropriate, that is a mute point. The food is a problem nevertheless.

Now, migraines as a reaction to food are one thing. But autistic behaviors? Come on! How could a seemingly wholesome and harmless food cause a person to lose his mind? The idea is very hard for a sensible person to accept. I never would have believed it myself if it had not happened before my eyes. I hit the jackpot when I removed milk products from Will's diet. There really was some-thing to the mumbo-jumbo about delayed food sensitivity after all. As it turns out, food sensitivities play a huge role in the health and behaviors of many children on the spectrum. I guess it makes sense. The immune systems of these children are in overdrive. Agitating such a system with foods it objects to will incite and intensify autistic behaviors. Soothing the system through avoidance of objectionable foods, on the other hand, calms its rattled nerves and allows the autistic behaviors to relax as well.

In working to recover my son, I have learned a thing or three. One is that it pays to focus on results. Explanations are secondary. The medical profession is not far enough along in its quest to conquer autism to have all the answers. Though perfect understanding of why something works is desirable, it is not a necessity. It is enough for me to know that it has helped many others on the spectrum and has a good safety record. I want my child better *now.* All the scientific vindication can catch up to me later. In the meantime, I am not willing to wait around. The price paid for delay is too dear.

WHAT ARE THE PAYOFFS OF FOOD RESTRICTION?

The most effective initial step parents can take to help their child is to remove foods that are stressing his body in some way.[2] Many children make phenomenal progress when they stop eating foods that harm them. Improvements in sleep, behavior, and attention can make it well worth the effort.[3] Take a look at the ARI parent ratings in Appendix B. The special diets' category enjoys many of the highest success ratings. Its better/worse ratios put the category of highly promoted drugs to shame. Though a handful of nondrug supplements have high ratios, diets still reign supreme overall. In addition, until food issues have been addressed, other interventions often cannot reach their full potential.

There are also other benefits to dietary change. Though these benefits pale in comparison to reductions in autistic symptoms, they are worthwhile bonuses nevertheless. In the beginning of our journey with special diets, I thought diets were all about limitations. Oddly enough, I discovered that special diets both limit and expand the diet at the same time. As some foods were taken away, I sought out allowable foods that we had never tried before. And what do you know? Some of them turned out to be pretty good. Imagine that. Had I never been pushed out of my comfort zone, I would have missed several tasty discoveries.

Furthermore, through learning about dietary change to alleviate symptoms of autism, I have found ways to resolve other health problems in the family. Take, for instance, my migraines. I would never have caught on to the corn connection if I hadn't been learning about delayed food sensitivity on Will's behalf. Now I spare myself all those miserable corn migraines that were once frequent and seemingly mysterious. I have also found I can control my annoying problem with restless legs syndrome (RLS) through the low oxalate diet that will be discussed in the next chapter. So, do you or members of your family have any health issues you could do without? Maybe you will find some solutions through food as you learn about biomedical intervention.

In addition, what I learned about food and nutrition on Will's behalf has benefited the healthy-eating habits of the whole family. Over time, Rich and I were surprised to find that our tastes have actually changed, really. How unexpected. We always thought our ideas of what tasted good or bad was fixed—funny that it is not. Who would have thought one might actually *like* eating healthier? Originally, we thought we ate what we liked. What we have come to find is that we like what we eat. Don't get me wrong: there are still old foods we enjoy. Yet there are other old foods that have lost their appeal, and we avoid them without feeling deprived.

IS THERE SOME WAY AROUND FOOD RESTRICTION?

Food is a wonderful source of pleasure in life. We often view eating more like a hobby than a source of nourishment. From such a vantage point, food restriction is a rude affront, flying in the face of our desires. Surely, there must be some way around it. Perhaps a magic pill could solve the full gamut of food-related woes. Digestive enzyme capsules, maybe? Unfortunately, this notion is too simplistic for the complicated issues that encompass food, the immune system, bodily functions, and behaviors. Digestive enzymes are, in fact, a helpful intervention that will be discussed in a later chapter. Yet, their benefits are nowhere near those of dietary restriction.[4] Unfortunately, there is no magic pill today that can enable a food-sensitive person to eat an offending food without suffering the consequences. Whatever genius cracks that code will make a fortune. In the meantime, the only way to avoid the problems that come from eating offensive foods is not to eat them in the first place.

HOW LONG DO DIETS LAST?

Many children on the spectrum have self-restricted their diets so severely that parents panic at the thought of taking away any food their child will actually eat.[5] Such alarm is understandable. But take heart. Many picky eaters become much better eaters after they stop eating the foods that cause them problems. The transition phase can be difficult, but there is light at the end of the tunnel.[6] Also consider supplementing zinc; it helps improve appetite and the sense of taste in some children.[7]

Before starting any diet, most people want to know how long they will have to do it. It is a valid question, but only your child's body knows the answer. Experimentation is the only conclusive way to find out. It may be encouraging to know that a diet that was important during a child's healing phase may not be the best diet long term.[8] Only dietary experimentation with your individual child will reveal what is best over time. The important thing is not to torture yourself at the outset with dramatics about *forever*. You will defeat yourself before you even begin. Instead, strive to maintain an attitude that this is merely an experiment.[9] Give it an honest effort for a reasonable length of time. If it doesn't pay off, you can always go back. It is at least worth trying when you stand so much to gain. And who knows? If it does pay off, then it was not a curse at all, but a blessing.

In 3½ years of perpetual dietary experimentation with Will, I have found that some foods are still on the "avoid" list, while others have been able to return after a period of time, maybe 6–12 months. And though 6–12 months may sound like a life sentence for a food you really love, the time does pass. No change has ever killed us despite prior certainty that it would. Our whole family does not go on Will's diet. However, for convenience of meal preparation and out of courtesy to Will, meals that we all eat together follow Will's diet. After using diets, some parents find that they do not even want to go back to their old eating habits. They have learned so much about foods and the impact of good nutrition on the whole family that those once-loved foods have lost their glow. These parents are not willing to risk a setback in their child's hard-earned success.[10]

THE HARDEST PART IS ADJUSTING TO CHANGE

Of all the biomedical interventions, adjusting to dietary change is by far the hardest challenge. It is for me anyway. Diets can be overwhelming, like trying to take a drink from a fire hose. Though they can be rewarding, they are not easy, which explains my love–hate relationship with them. Without even realizing it, we are so set in our ways and our ideas of what we think tastes good. Creatures of habit—entrenched habit—we want to shop at the same stores in the same ways we always have. We want to buy the same food and spend the same amount of time preparing it using the same methods we are used to. It is our comfort zone. We hold it dearer than we realize, until we try to change it. Dietary change is hard on the person being denied a food, the person(s) managing the change, and the rest of the family, too. I have read that it is easier for people to change their religion than their diet.[11] I am not sure about that, but I agree that changing diet is tough. It is no place for sissies like me. Yet, with the right incentive, even I can stick with it.

Though I would love for my son to eat anything he wants, I recognize how important it is to his health and behaviors that he does not. If he were a child with diabetes, I would not let him eat harmful foods. Similarly, because he is a child on the spectrum, harmful foods cannot be allowed. I do require proof that a food is harmful; that is where the food trials come in. But once I have proof, the food is out of his diet for as long as necessary. Illness is the body's plea for change, and I must answer its call. And though living with change is hard, it is not nearly as hard as living with autism.

Over time, I have found that making changes gets easier. I can make a transition better now than I did early on. The trick for us has been getting through the transition. After that, it gets easier. At some point, we accept and adjust. The new habits, foods, style of shopping, and preparation become the new normal. Then it does not seem so bad. So do not envision that the initial stress of a change in diet will last for the life of the diet. It is mostly for the short term. Just focus on getting through that.

I was amazed one day to overhear Will tell his brother that giving up milk products was not so bad. Huh? This I had to hear. He went on to explain that he had forgotten what milk products taste like. He said he really did not care about them anymore. I was shocked. Indeed, I had noticed that for some time that he had not seemed bothered when people ate milk products in front of him, even ice cream, yet I never suspected he no longer cared. I had always felt bad that he could not eat foods he saw others eat. I had been carrying a pain for him that he did not even carry for himself. He had adjusted, so it was time I did the same. Will is quite content even at special events like birthday parties as long as he can celebrate with some allowable treat of his own. It does not have to be the same as whatever his brothers or friends are eating. Who'd a thot it?

MANAGING CHANGE

Some parents can start their child on a dietary change cold turkey, just like that. That is great if it works for them. Others need to ease their way into a diet. They transition into the diet over time. First, they learn the rules of the diet. While some diets are simple, others are more involved. Some changes require planning and preparation; others do not. For diets that require a lot of change, parents can start with the small changes and work their way up to the bigger ones. The child may need some transition time too as he adjusts to old foods going away and new ones being introduced.[12] The best approach is whatever works for you and your child. Here are a few ideas that may smooth the adjustment.[13]

○ Remove one "hard" food at a time.
○ Allow time to adjust before removing the next "hard" food.
○ Focus on what *can* be eaten.
○ Keep on hand best-liked, allowable foods so the child can treat himself.
○ Try substitute foods before dismissing them.

It is important to manage change within your limits. If you stretch yourself too far or put too much pressure on yourself, the whole thing will collapse. Rather than throwing in the towel, back off. Something may have to give, but it can't be your sanity. Sometimes I do not feel up to making a change when I first learn of it. That's okay. I give myself some time to make the emotional adjustment, knowing that, at some point, I will actually make the change. Then somewhere along the line I do it…and it is not so bad. By letting it sit on the back burner a little while, I get used to the idea. Sometimes I let Will know the change is coming so he has time to adjust as well. As time goes by, he and I make progress. We solve problems. With each experiment, we learn a little more. Together, we are unraveling his mystery.

WHICH DIET IS BEST?

There is no *best* diet. Sorry, I know that would make things less confusing, yet, when it comes to food, individuality is center stage. It all goes back to the derailed-passenger-car analogy employed a few chapters back. Each body is different to start with, and its experiences during the derailment are unique. Similarly, there is no one right diet that can apply to everyone. Even so, there is one diet that is generally recommended as a starting point. Try that one to see how it goes. From there, you feel your way. I hope you like playing detective; it is not as much fun as playing doctor, but it will have to do.

To help you understand the issues, the next few sections offer some background information about the relationship between the human body and food. Tools of the detective trade follow, including information on the food-experiment process and lab tests that can be helpful. In the next chapter, some of the most common diets that have helped children on the spectrum will be introduced and described.

WHAT WAS A BODY DESIGNED TO EAT?

Once when I was a kid, my dad could not get his riding lawn mower to start, try as he might. Finally, he gave up and hauled it in for repair. Word came back that the mower had a severe case of garden fertilizer in the gas tank. "Laura Anne!" My little sister had been at it again, this time inspired by an open bag of fertilizer in the garage. "Hmm," her inquisitive mind had wondered, "do you suppose these interesting little pebbles will fit in that opening on the lawn mower?" They did—by the handful. Alas, lawn mower engines don't eat fertilizer; to run well, they need gasoline. Likewise, for a body to give its *best* performance, it needs the kind of food it was designed to eat.

And what is that exactly? The human body evolved over millions of years eating certain kinds of foods. If we start our timeline at the beginning of the

Stone Age when the first crude stone tools were made, we are talking roughly 2.6 million years ago. Over that time, the human body naturally developed to run optimally on the foods our ancient ancestors hunted and gathered. And though the specific foods varied from one geographic region to another, the staples were essentially fruits, vegetables, lean meats, and seafood. A mere 13,000 years ago, the Stone Age ended with the fossil find of crude stone-grinding tools in the Middle East. Aha! Our innovative ancestors were up to something. They had developed tools to grind grains. Apparently, they had started cultivating grains and adding them to their diet. However, though many people were able to digest and utilize these new foods, eating grain was not what our millions of years of evolution had designed us for.[14] As time went on, agriculture spread from its humble beginnings in the Middle East to Europe and Asia about 5,000 to 8,000 years ago.[15] Grains are one of the foods of particular interest to the autism spectrum because some of them contain this stuff called *gluten*.

WHAT IS GLUTEN?

I had never even heard of gluten before my first Defeat Autism Now! conference. At the time, I figured I must not eat much of it, right? Wrong. Gluten is everywhere in the typical American diet, or so it seems. It is a protein component of wheat, oats, barley, rye, and triticale (if you know what that is). We like gluten because it is sticky like glue. It bonds pasta together in all those wonderful shapes like curly cues and hollow tubes. Being sticky and stretchy, gluten can also trap air bubbles, a neat trick that enables bread to rise. It is so handy that we manufacture it into a multitude of foods, medicines, and even the glue on the envelopes we lick.[16]

As already mentioned, gluten consumption began in the Middle East a few thousand years earlier than in other parts of the globe. Therefore, people of Middle Eastern descent are better adapted to gluten than are other populations. Those whose ancestors originated in Northern Europe, the Americas, Africa, and the Far East got a relatively late start with gluten, so they typically do not do as well with it. The rate of gluten intolerance in those of European stock is around 1 in 100.[17]

Celiac disease

Unfortunately, some people cannot handle gluten at all and suffer from what is called celiac disease (or celiac sprue). It affects at least 1 in 250 people. For celiac disease sufferers, gluten has a toxic effect on the gut wall. If this hereditary condition goes undiagnosed, continued consumption of gluten will damage the wall resulting in impaired absorption and severe nutritional deficiencies. Symptoms, which, again, vary significantly from person to person, may develop in children or adults. Amid a long list of possibilities, symptoms include abdominal pain, bloating, nausea, vomiting, diarrhea, constipation, failure to thrive or gain weight, stunted growth, seizures, and fatigue. It is a pretty nasty list that provides ample incentive for sufferers to pursue diagnosis and treatment. And the treatment? Don't eat gluten. Zip, zero, nil.

Interestingly, a few women with celiac disease once spoke at an Autism Society meeting I attended. They came to offer tips and advice for gluten-free living. Though some of their children had celiac disease, their husbands did not. So their families lived both gluten-laden and gluten-free lives. These women handled gluten in their kitchens like one might handle arsenic. Masters of gluten avoidance, they had separate counters for gluten-food preparation and gluten-free. They had separate toasters for gluten bread and gluten-free bread. They even labeled separate mayonnaise jars for use with gluten and gluten-free breads. That seemed amazing to me. What miniscule amount of gluten bread crumbs can make it back into a mayonnaise jar on a knife? Not much. However, though their family members varied in their sensitivity to gluten, some could actually get sick from a shared jar of mayonnaise. Now *that* is sensitive. Also amazing to me was how something harmless to so many people could wreak such havoc in anyone. It is certainly a case where individuality is key.

Celiac disease and autism

It is common to have a far less severe form of celiac disease than the full-blown form just described. However, even milder forms can cause damage to the gut wall if years go by without a diagnosis or treatment. Oddly enough, it is also possible to have no symptoms in childhood yet still suffer damage from gluten. Fortunately, there are blood tests that can be used to rule out or implicate celiac disease including its milder forms. If these tests leave room for doubt, intestinal biopsy can make a determination. It is a good idea to have children with autism tested for celiac disease since both disorders have some similar symptoms and can coexist in the same individual. Just be aware that the tests may not be reliable for people who are already on a gluten-free diet.[18]

WHAT OTHER FOODS ARE NEW TO OUR ANCIENT DESIGN?

When our bodies of ancient design have trouble with food, it is reasonable to be suspicious of the relatively new-fangled foods. The human body has had less time to adapt to these, and such foods are more likely to tax the capabilities of our machinery than the long-standing foods of evolutionary days. So, besides grains maybe, what else is new?

Milk is another relatively new arrival; it came with the domestication of animals. Somewhere between 4000 and 3000 B.C., animals were first milked in northern Africa and southwest Asia. There are those among us who have trouble digesting milk, too. For some, the problem is milk sugar (lactose). For others, the issue is milk protein. Cow's milk has about 20 different proteins that require a complex system for complete digestion. The milk proteins that cause the most trouble are casein and whey.[19]

Newer still to our bodies of ancient design are refined sugars and hydrogenated fats. Hydrogenated fats are the result of a technological process developed in the early 1900s to prolong the shelf life of fats and foods that contain them. In this process, vegetable oils are solidified into margarine or shortening. Hydrogenation can introduce transfatty acids into foods; these acids are credited with raising blood cholesterol and may increase the risk of heart disease.[20] Maybe not all our technological innovations are true advances, particularly when they are for use in ancient machinery like the human body.

Most of today's food colorings are made from petroleum, a fact I found quite surprising. Why would we ever think eating petroleum is a good idea, pretty colors or not? It is great for making cars go, but can it benefit a living thing like the human body? Of all the chemicals added to foods, colors are the most notorious for receiving bad press.

Following the technology boom after World War II, numerous non-natural, chemical additives were developed to preserve food and to improve flavor, texture, and smell. Today, thousands exist and more are constantly under development. There are chemicals to control acidity and alkalinity, foaming, moisture, and caking. There are emulsifiers, stabilizers, binders, texturizers, and more. You name it, we've got it. In addition, we spray our fruits and vegetables with pesticides, ripening agents, and chemicals to preserve freshness.[21]

How well do you suppose all these newer foods and substances are received by this human body of ancient design? As long as our food tastes good and we suffer no immediate ill effects, we figure it *is* good. But is it really? How can we be sure, especially for our growing numbers of vulnerable children on the autism spectrum?

Figure 24.1 shows a breakdown of the typical American diet by food group. It indicates that over 70 percent of our daily calories come from newer foods, such as grains, dairy, refined sugars, and refined vegetable oils.[22] Is it really possible that 70 percent of what we feed our children is foreign to their evolved design of millions of years? And even if those foods do not hurt us, they take the place of the staples of our Stone Age blueprint—the fruits and vegetables, lean meats, and seafood. After all, who wants to eat a pear when he just polished off a bag of chips and a cupcake?

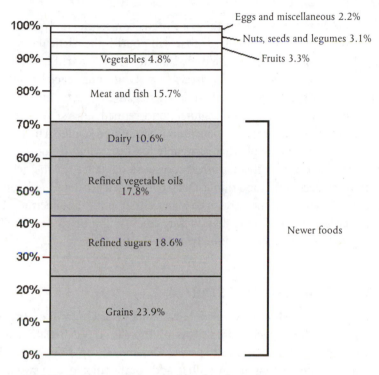

Figure 24.1 Typical American diet by food group

OUR FINEST ATHLETES KNOW A SECRET

Now, let's step back and take a look at diet from another angle. While training for a marathon, my husband Rich asked his family doctor for advice. The doctor, who quite conveniently was a marathon runner himself, recommended a book called *The Paleo Diet for Athletes* by Loren Cordain, PhD, and Joe Friel, MS. It was written to give athletes a competitive advantage through a diet that maximizes performance. It turns out that diet is in essence the ancient diet of the Paleolithic Age or Stone Age. The book repeatedly emphasizes the importance of the intimate relationship between human development and the foods that fostered that development. Its bottom line is that, if you are going to push a body to its ultimate capacity, you must operate it on the premium fuel the body was designed to use. So, in either case, whether the ill-health we see in autism or the extreme physical challenge required of athletes, it pays to consider what goes in the fuel tank.

THE BOTTOM LINE

Though foods do not cause autism, they can intensify it considerably. We should be careful to provide only those foods that will nourish the particular body in question. Foods that are beyond the body's ability to utilize will harm it.[23]

There are several questions to start asking about your special child. Are there any foods or food ingredients that have a negative effect on him? Can his body utilize newer foods like milk, gluten, and refined sugars? Any food or ingredient can come under scrutiny, including Stone Age staples. The individual's body is the sole judge of what is suitable food and what is not.

The remainder of this chapter offers tools and guidance for the detective who is trying to decipher a food riddle. Detective work takes time and effort but has been well worth it to the parents of many children on the spectrum. Ultimately, the choice of what our child eats is up to us. Will it be garden fertilizer, premium gasoline, or something in between?

WHERE DOES A DETECTIVE START?

There are so many foods in this world. How can a person zero in on the ones that are a problem for a specific child? Though there is no *best* diet, there is one that is recommended as a starting point. Depending on how your child responds to that one, you might stay with it, add another diet to it, or switch to a different diet altogether (special diets will be discussed in the next chapter). In addition, you may have some hunches of your own that should be investigated. For example, is your child's body sending signals like food cravings, a red face, or other telltale clues that suggest something is afoot? A book called *Is This Your Child?* by Doris Rapp, MD, is excellent for helping you recognize symptoms that are linked to foods. Lab testing, though optional, can also be helpful for identifying potential troublemakers. Do what you can on a timeframe that works for you. Manage the changes. Stay within your limits. Anything you do will be better than nothing. Coming up is a description of how to run a food trial to evaluate the effect (if any) that a food has on your child. A discussion about lab tests will follow next. Using these various tools of the detective trade, you can feel your way through the maze of your child's relationship to food.

ELIMINATION/BINGE FOOD TRIALS

An elimination/binge food trial is merely an experiment with food. The general idea is to remove a food or food group from the diet for a period of time to see what happens. It is the only way to know for sure if a food or group of foods has a negative effect on your child. Though lab tests can be helpful, they are not decisive; thus, they can only play a supporting role in decision making.[24]

A trial involves strict elimination of a food for about five days while no other interventions are in flux. Wait to see what happens. If physical symptoms or behaviors improve, congratulations—you have found one of the tacks your child has been sitting on. Keep the offending food out of his diet. However, if there is no improvement or results are unclear, the next step is to binge eat the food for a period of time. Watch for a response. If there is a negative one, remove the food from the diet. Otherwise, the food is probably okay. At those times when an initial elimination/binge trial leaves room for doubt, simply repeat the scenario as many times as necessary until it becomes clear whether or not the food causes a problem. In some cases, like for casein and gluten, for example, a five-day elimination of a food is not long enough to show improvement.[25] The next chapter will detail the varying trial lengths necessary for different diets.

If desired, a trial can be modified to determine the degree of sensitivity to a food. This might be worth exploring if an initial food trial reveals a negative response to a food your child loves. It can also be helpful if a food added back into the diet appears to be tolerated at first but then starts causing symptoms. You might find that the food can be tolerated but only infrequently or in moderation. Repeated variations of a trial can determine what the level of tolerance is.[26]

Some diets require elimination of several foods at once. However, if a child has a great response to such a diet, you won't know which particular foods made the difference. Some parents are happy to continue following the diet just as it is. Others, however, want to experiment with reintroducing some of the foods. To do this, add a single food back into the diet for three days. If no symptoms return, the food can stay; otherwise, remove it from the diet. Wait until the symptoms have subsided before trying another food. By reintroducing foods systematically one at a time, you can separate the good guys from the bad guys.[27] If you want more details about how to do your detective work using elimination/binge trials, *Is This Your Child?* by Doris Rapp, MD, also offers help on this topic.

IF YOU ARE GOING TO DO IT, DO IT RIGHT

Consider the story of some friends of mine, a married couple, that stopped at a gas station to refuel. After the husband had pumped the gas and gone inside to pay, his wife noticed a line forming at the pumps. Being a considerate sort, she decided to move the car. And move it she did, though with a catch. She attempted the maneuver from her spot in the passenger seat. She ploughed the car straight into the side of the station building. As the huge, store-front window shattered with a thunderous crash, her husband and the cashier inside leaped backward. There they froze, gaping in shocked amazement.

Sometimes you have a good idea, but you need to go about it the right way. An elimination/binge food trial is like that. It is a good idea, but only if done right. Otherwise, you might draw the wrong conclusions and miss an opportunity for your child to improve. Here are some steps that can be taken to ensure a trial is valid:

1. *Self-education.* The person implementing the change needs to self-educate about the food(s) to be avoided. For example, when eliminating milk, you can guess that ice cream and cheese will need to be eliminated since they contain milk. But would you know to inspect ingredient lists on packaging for casein and whey? These are components in milk that need to be avoided as well. To learn about such details, diet books and Web sites abound. Some of the best ones will be mentioned in the next chapter.

2. *Read ingredient lists.* Reading ingredient lists on manufactured foods is very important for ensuring a valid trial. Otherwise, there is a high risk that the food on trial will be eaten in some form without realizing it. It is amazing how often foods like corn, soy, wheat, and milk pop up in the most unexpected places. Even products like vitamins that we do not think of as "food" often use corn, soy, or other foods as fillers. For me, reading ingredient lists seemed odd and time-consuming at first, but, once I got used to it (adjusted to the change), it became second nature.

3. *Get compliance from others who provide food to your child.* Granted, this can be extremely difficult in some situations, yet cooperation of ex-spouses, extended-family members, day-care providers, or school staff is critical for a successful trial. For help with others, see a book by Lisa Lewis, *Special Diets for Special Kids,* pages 91–93.[28] The ace in the hole is if you can persuade your child to avoid banned foods on his own, though obviously that is not possible in many situations. I am blessed: Will truly believes that off-limit foods really do harm him. He is careful not to eat anything if he is in doubt. He certainly could take advantage of many opportunities if he wanted. Instead, he turns the food down or brings it home to ask me. Sometimes if it is something he cannot have, I trade with him for another treat; at other times, I buy the item from him.

He loves Halloween, a real moneymaker, and even enjoys trading with other kids for my favorites that bring top dollar.

4. *Compensate for lost nutrition.* Also consider vitamins or minerals that may be lost due to a food restriction. Calcium in milk is an excellent example. If a cornerstone food leaves the diet, compensate for the nutritional loss with other foods or supplements.

It takes some effort to ensure that a trial is valid so that it yields accurate results and maximum benefit for your child. But it is worth it. After all, if you intend to move a car, you need to do it from the driver's seat.

LAB TESTING

Most lab tests are specialty tests that are only available from mail-order laboratories. Chapter 29 will offer practical information about how to get this type of lab work done. Until then, I will merely describe a test so you know it is available, what its purpose is, and the type of specimen collected. Specimens may be stool, blood, hair, saliva, or urine (taped-on collection bags are available for those not potty-trained). The three tests covered in the next few pages are helpful for assessing IgG food sensitivities, leaky gut, and the level of casein and gluten peptides escaping the tunnel.

Testing for IgG food sensitivities

The IgG ELISA test for delayed food sensitivity is a blood test that measures the level of IgG antibodies to various foods. Do not confuse it with skin-scratch tests or IgE blood tests. Those tests look for an IgE reaction, which is a different type of immune response.[29] They may be helpful for some, but it is IgG food sensitivity that is most relevant to children on the spectrum. The IgG ELISA test identifies foods that might be causing delayed food reactions. It can be extremely useful when facing a world of foods without knowing which ones may be intensifying autistic behaviors or physical symptoms.[30]

Depending on the laboratory, antibody levels of roughly 90 foods are evaluated. For each food, the results show the intensity of the reaction. Not all foods showing sensitivity necessarily cause symptoms, however. Think of the test as one that identifies suspects rather than condemns the guilty. Nevertheless, there is a good chance that at least one or more of the suspects are provoking symptoms; so elimination/binge trials can be done to determine which foods actually cause symptoms. Only confirmed offenders need to be eliminated from the diet. Test all foods that show a reaction, regardless of the intensity assigned to them by the test.[31]

So how many foods might be regarded as suspects? Many children on the spectrum will have from one to several.[32] More than a dozen is evidence of an overly sensitive immune system, while more than two dozen is even stronger evidence.[33] In addition, let's say you are suspicious of a particular food, maybe due to food craving, for instance. Even if your test result does not point the finger at that food, run an elimination/binge trial on it anyway. There are other ways besides IgG sensitivity that a food can bother a person and generate symptoms. Furthermore, it may be helpful to be aware of a common misconception among doctors about the IgG ELISA test. They often think that the test simply shows what the person has been eating. If that were true, people with the same diet would get the same test results. However, that is not what happens.[34] That said, it can be true that IgG test results merely reflect what a person eats if leaky gut is severe.[35]

Even if you are not able to do the IgG ELISA test, you can still get some valuable insights from those who have. On the spectrum, the most notorious offenders are milk and wheat, which are identified in about 90 percent of those tested. Also quite common are cheese, yogurt, soy, barley, rye, and spelt. Put these foods at the top of your list for elimination/binge trials. Other common troublemakers are peanuts, eggs, corn, sugar, citrus fruits, and baking yeast. Put them to the test next. And though it is tough, definitely test any food your child seems to crave.[36]

And here is the big question: how long will a food that provokes symptoms need to stay out of the diet? Fortunately, the immune system can be forgiving when it comes to IgG sensitivity. If the immune system is not repeatedly provoked by a certain food for a long-enough period, it can give up its grudge and forget about it. At that point, the food can come back into the diet without provoking symptoms. But how long is "long enough"? It varies tremendously from person to person and food to food, but probably at least six months.[37]

I have found the IgG food sensitivity test to be one of the most useful of all biomedical tests. It helps take out so much of the guesswork. For me, it has been worth the money to repeat the test about once a year—at least for now. Will's first IgG ELISA test showed six reactive foods in addition to a slew of dairy products. I find it interesting that the profile of offending foods keeps changing from one test to the next—with the glaring exception of dairy. The dairy section continues to go ballistic, though Will has not had any dairy in over three years. That's okay. We are happy to live without milk foods because of the immense payoff. But back to the other reactive foods. Eliminating them from the diet for several months usually seems to soothe the immune system. For the most part, they are off the reactive list by the next test. Unfortunately, other foods pop up as offenders, often ones Will consumes in large quantities despite consumption on a rotating basis. But we can deal with that. Since the attitude of Will's immune system is a moving target, repeating the test occasionally helps us see where we stand. Again, you can get by without the test, but if you have the money to do it, it is helpful.

Oh, and remember the other type of immune system antibody? The IgE antibody response? It was the one that involves an immediate food reaction in the skin, respiratory system, or gut. At one point, I was concerned about its potential influence on Will, so I had an IgE blood test run. And you know what? He did not have a single IgE reaction to any food, not even milk. That test made milk look like Mr. Friendly. So, it really is true: IgE is an entirely different antibody that plays ball by its own rules in another universe. It certainly can coexist with IgG sensitivity but not necessarily. My conclusion: the immune system is one wacky dude, fascinating but definitely wacky. A discussion of food allergy testing, as well as recommended laboratories and contact information, appears in the book by Jon Pangborn and Sidney Baker, *Autism: Effective Biomedical Treatments*, pages 4:4–5.

Testing for leaky gut and the ability to absorb properly

The official name of the leaky gut test is the intestinal permeability test. It determines if the gut is leaky and, if so, by how much. It also indicates whether the gut wall can absorb properly. For this test, the person drinks a liquid containing two types of sugars, one big and one small. If the gut wall is healthy, the big sugars will be too large to pass through it into the bloodstream, while the small sugars will be readily absorbed. As the kidneys filter the blood to produce urine, sugars of both types will be collected if they are present. What you hope to find is a very low level of big sugars (meaning the gut is not leaky) and a high level of small sugars (indicating proper absorption). The leakier your test result, the higher your risk of both IgG food sensitivities and opioid effect from escaped casein and gluten. Furthermore, a low level of small sugars indicates poor absorption, perhaps from injury to the cells of the gut wall. The lab report also includes text to help you interpret the findings. The test can be repeated again later to see if efforts to improve gut health have been successful. This test and recommended laboratories with their contact information is discussed in the previously mentioned *Autism: Effective Biomedical Treatments*, page 4:3.[38]

Another way besides testing to know if a child has leaky gut is to try the gluten-free/casein-free (GF/CF) diet or the specific carbohydrate diet. These diets will be discussed in the next chapter. If the child improves on these diets, it is highly likely he has leaky gut. The diets are a way to keep undigested peptides from leaking because what is not eaten cannot leak.[39]

Testing for opioid peptides of gluten and casein

If opioid peptides of gluten or casein escape the gut and enter the bloodstream, they can reach the brain, causing an effect similar to drugs like heroin and morphine. This "opioid effect" is a completely different phenomenon from food allergy. It involves food, yes, but the similarity ends there since opioid effect is not an immune reaction as an allergy is.[40]

Fortunately, there is a sure-fire way to stop opioid effect: keep gluten and casein foods out of the diet. Unfortunately, this is a major dietary change for anyone accustomed to the average American diet. Sometimes parents want evidence that opioid peptides are escaping their child's gut before they are willing to take the plunge to this diet. That is where the gluten and casein peptide test comes in. It measures both the gluten and casein peptide levels in the urine. And how did peptides get there? Like everything else in the bloodstream, they pass through the kidneys where some are filtered out into the urine.[41]

When people with autism take this test, at least 50 percent will have abnormally high levels. A high level is a fairly reliable predictor that the person will benefit from a GF/CF diet. However, if the test shows normal levels, the diet may still help, particularly if the person is a picky eater or has any bowel problems. Many with normal test results have improved on the diet. Now why would that be? We want tests to be infallibly decisive, yet, in the real world, we sometimes have to settle for something less. The bottom-line recommendation from Defeat Autism Now! is to run a trial of the GF/CF diet regardless of the outcome of the test. Despite the test's shortcomings, some people still find it helpful. A result showing high levels of peptides gives them the extra incentive they need to try the diet. *Autism: Effective Biomedical Treatments* discusses the urinary peptide test and a lab that performs it (pages 4:6–7).[42]

Be aware that if a child is already on a GF/CF diet, the source of opioid peptides is gone. Doing the test at this point would not yield anything meaningful. Even if discontinuing the diet, it takes a long time for the peptides to build back up to pre-diet levels.[43]

WHERE WE'VE BEEN AND WHERE WE'RE GOING

So let's collect our thoughts. Where are we? In the last chapter, you read about gut problems that commonly arise in autism. Then this chapter introduced concepts related to the use of foods to address those problems. It began by discussing the reality of food sensitivity and the powerful impact that can be achieved from avoiding foods that intensify autistic behaviors and physical symptoms. Suggestions were made to help ease the adjustment of dietary changes. Next, the intimate relationship between early human development and the foods that fostered that development was reviewed. Then came a discussion of the foods that are relatively new to this body of ancient design, as well as the potential problems these foods pose to some individuals. Finally, tools for the detective, including the elimination/binge trial and optional lab tests, were presented. The coming chapter explores various diets shown to be beneficial to people on the autism spectrum. Later chapters will describe interventions that target gut flora, as well as other areas of concern in the digestive tract.

NOTES

1. VP Foundation 2005, p. 3.
2. McCandless 2007, pp. 84–85.
3. Pangborn and Baker 2005, p. 2:45.
4. McCandless 2007, pp. 43, 92.
5. Lewis 1998b, p. 210.
6. Seroussi 2002, pp. 206–207, 214; Semon 1998, p. 173; Bock and Stauth 2007, p. 201.
7. Bock and Stauth 2007, p. 259; Pangborn and Baker 2005, p. 5:32.
8. Pangborn and Baker 2007, p. 14.
9. Pangborn and Baker 2005, p. 2:46.
10. McCandless 2003, pp. 113–14.
11. Pangborn and Baker 2005, p. 1:36.
12. McCandless 2007, pp. 86–87.
13. VP Foundation 2005, pp. 53–54.
14. Shaw 1998, pp. 124–25.
15. Cordain and Friel 2005, pp. xviii–xix, 83, 147.
16. Lewis 1998a, pp. 23–28; Pangborn and Baker 2005, p. 2:36.
17. Pangborn and Baker 2005, pp. 2:36–37; Shaw 1998, pp. 124–25.
18. Information on celiac disease is taken from Bock and Stauth 2007, pp. 207–208; Lewis 1998b, pp. 211–14.
19. Pangborn and Baker 2005, p. 2:40; Shaw 1998, pp. 124–25; Zukin 1996, pp. 8, 25.
20. Zukin 1996, p. 190; Cordain and Friel 2005, pp. xviii–xix, 97; McCandless 2007, p. 76.
21. Hersey 1999, pp. 57, 64; Feingold 1975, pp. 109–11, 122–23, 127; Lewis 1998a, pp. 43–44.
22. Cordain and Friel 2005, pp. xix, 178.
23. Gottschall 2004, p. 6.
24. Pangborn and Baker 2005, p. 2:58.
25. Ibid., pp. 1:41, 2:15, 48–49; Lewis 1998b, p. 284.
26. Lewis 1998a, p. 40; Pangborn and Baker 2005, pp. 2:22–23.
27. Pangborn and Baker 2005, p. 2:49.
28. Ibid., pp. 2:33–34, 38–39.

29. Bock and Stauth 2007, p. 223.
30. Shaw 2004, p. 8; McCandless 2007, pp. 74–75; Pangborn and Baker 2005, p. 2:47.
31. Pangborn and Baker 2005, pp. 1:41, 2:45–48; Baker 2004, pp. 97–104.
32. McCandless 2007, p. 27.
33. Pangborn and Baker 2005, pp. 2:46, 58.
34. Ibid., pp. 2:47–48; Lewis 1998b, p. 198.
35. Mumper 2008a, personal communication.
36. Shaw 2004, p. 8; Lewis 1998a, p. 41; Lewis 1998b, p. 198.
37. Pangborn and Baker 2005, p. 2:48; Baker 2004, p. 104.
38. Hanaway 2006, p. 50; Lewis 1998b, pp. 214–15; Pangborn and Baker 2005, p. 4:3.
39. Pangborn and Baker 2005, p. 4:3.
40. Shaw 1998, p. 143.
41. Pangborn and Baker 2005, p. 2:41.
42. Ibid., pp. 2:35, 39, 41; McCandless 2007, pp. 73–74, 89.
43. Lewis 1998b, pp. 210–11.

Chapter 25

Common Gut Interventions: Diets

WHAT THIS CHAPTER HAS IN STORE

The previous chapter discussed the use of foods to address problems in the gut. It also offered some tools and guidance for exploring a child's relationships with foods. Now we move on to the many different diets that have helped children on the spectrum. It is difficult to raise research funds to investigate such diets since most studies in the U.S. are funded by pharmaceutical companies motivated by potential profits. Diets don't generally generate profits.[1] Yet each diet has a devoted following, which is proof of its success in relieving autistic behaviors and physical symptoms for a segment of children. This chapter explains the purpose of each diet and the situations where it might be useful. A general description of the kinds of foods eliminated by each diet is also included. While some diets are easy to understand and implement, others are more involved. For the more involved diets, books or Web sites are recommended that give details and advice. From the information in this chapter, you will be able to gauge which diet or combination of diets may be most helpful to your individual child.

GLUTEN-FREE/CASEIN-FREE DIET (GF/CF DIET)

Though you can gradually work your way up to being on the gluten-free/casein-free diet, in the end it means the total elimination of casein from milk and gluten from specific grains. Those grains are wheat, oats, barley, rye, and triticale. Many doctors of Defeat Autism Now! believe this diet is the single most effective step parents can take on their own to help their child.[2] It is so effective because it ends the harassment of multiple autism-spectrum problems. These include opioid effect, IgG food sensitivity to casein or gluten foods, and lactose intolerance. Think of the diet as a bowling ball that knocks down several troublesome pins at once.

Will's dramatic response to a ban on milk products was very exciting. Apparently, he is not alone. The ARI parent ratings show over 80 different interventions using drugs, supplements, and special diets. The reigning champion according to better/worse ratios is the removal of milk products.

	Got Worse	No Effect	Got Better	Better: Worse Ratio	No. of Cases
Removed Milk Products/ Dairy	2 percent	46 percent	52 percent	32:1	6,360
Gluten-/ Casein-Free Diet	3 percent	31 percent	66 percent	19:1	2,561

Of more than 6,000 children who quit eating dairy products, 32 got better for every 1 that got worse. Another way to look at the numbers is that over half of the children who removed dairy from the diet got better. When it comes to intervention on the autism spectrum, that is as good as it gets.

For some children, casein is the bigger culprit that intensifies autistic behaviors and physical symptoms. For others, it is gluten.[3] The ARI parent ratings for the combined GF/CF diet show that 19 children got better for every 1 that got worse. And 66 percent of those who ran a trial of the diet got better. Regardless of whether you choose to focus on the better/worse ratios or another statistic in the ratings, it is obvious that casein and gluten make a big impact. It is within our grasp to stop that impact dead in its tracks.

That brings us to a burning question for every parent. What impact are gluten and casein having on *my* child? Only your child's body knows the answer, and it's not telling, at least not in advance of trying the diet. Nevertheless, the body may be dropping some hints. The people most likely to improve on the GF/CF diet are those with:

○ a self-limited diet, especially to milk and wheat foods. These children are our picky eaters[4]

○ regressive autism, as opposed to autism from birth[5]

○ constipation, diarrhea, or other digestive tract symptoms[6]

○ insensitivity to pain[7]

- o sleep problems[8]
- o extremely dry skin or dermatitis, migraines, bouts of screaming, red cheeks, red ears, or seizures[9]
- o a tendency to eat unusually large amounts of food. Perhaps these children get an opioid effect from food but do not recognize *which* foods are making them feel good, so they just eat a lot of everything[10]
- o a tendency to eat an unusually small amount of food. Perhaps food makes these children feel ill, so they try to avoid it as much as possible.[11]

Though some bodies are generous and drop hints, others are stingy and don't. There are those who have had none of the above symptoms yet still improved on the GF/CF diet.[12] Beats me why, but they do. And though lab tests offer some guidance, they are not decisive. Some children have made remarkable progress on the diet despite test results for IgG antibodies and opioid peptides that predicted otherwise.[13] Perhaps there are more factors at work than we understand at present. Whatever the explanation, the conclusion is the same. There is only one way to find out for sure if—and to what extent—gluten and casein affect your child, and that is to eliminate them from the diet for a period of time and then wait to see what happens. If you get good results, stick with it. The diet seems like a lot of work when there are no guarantees. Yet it could be the most important step you ever take to help your child.[14]

That brings us to burning question no. 2. What benefits might result from use of the GF/CF diet? Though they vary from person to person, gains have been seen in sleep, behavior, mood and emotions, speech, eye contact, awareness of surroundings, attention span, and concentration, not to mention improved stools and physical health. There is also less sensory scrambling and stimming (repetitive self-stimulating actions). Though younger children are more likely to benefit dramatically from this diet, even adults have enjoyed rewards.[15]

Now let's move along to burning question no. 3. How long does a GF/CF trial have to last? The trial length is different for casein as opposed to gluten. Many parents strongly recommend beginning with a casein-free trial before adding gluten-free on top of it. One reason is that the trial length for the casein-free (CF) diet is shorter; it needs to last three weeks.[16] Another reason is that it does not require as much self-education or preparation as the gluten-free diet. Take advantage of the time during the casein-free trial to learn and prepare for going gluten-free.[17] In addition, it pays to stagger the start times of the two trials to reduce the withdrawal reaction that sometimes occurs. Withdrawal reactions will be discussed shortly. For now, the point is that, if you are going to go through withdrawal, you want to take it in smaller increments, not all at once.

So how long does a gluten-free trial need to last? That gets tricky. Though urine tests for opioid peptides show casein can leave the body within three days of starting a GF/CF diet, gluten can linger for months, possibly up to eight months.[18] The recommended length for a GF trial varies depending on whom you ask. Here is the advice of several experts. Pangborn and Baker in *Autism: Effective Biomedical Treatments* (the book of consensus on the Defeat Autism Now! approach) suggest a trial last somewhere between three weeks and three months. Then there are a couple of parent-champions of the GF/CF diet: Lisa Lewis, PhD, and Karyn Seroussi. Both have labored extensively with other parents, assisting them with the GF/CF diet. Their counsel is to go gluten-free religiously for at least three months—no cheating or you will never know if it helped or not. Then we have Jaquelyn McCandless, MD, a central figure in Defeat Autism Now! with a great deal of treatment experience; she recommends a trial period of at least 4–6 months.[19] It may also help you to know that, for people with full-blown celiac disease, it can take over a month on a GF diet to see improvement.[20] Perhaps the variability in recommendations reflects the wide variation of responses that individuals experience during a GF trial. No doubt you are tired of reading that it depends on the individual. Yet there is no helping it; so many things really do differ from one person to the next, sometimes by a lot.

So where does that leave you? At the outset of the diet, you do not have to pre-declare how long your trial will last. For all you know, it could be a great success within a few weeks, and you'll be so happy that you won't even give a hoot about what a hassle the diet is. There is no point in stressing yourself out now when you don't even know what is going to happen. Something I have learned—the hard way—is that it does not help to fret over the length of a trial in the beginning. Efforts are best focused on managing the change. After some time has passed and I am more accustomed to the changes, I will have a much clearer head for evaluating whether I should continue. Granted, it can be a tough call. On the one hand, you do not want to cut the trial short at the threshold of a breakthrough. By the same token, why prolong a trial that is not paying off? Hang in there—you will figure it out. And remember that there is plenty of support available if you want to tap into it (more about that in a minute). But right now, what is this about withdrawal?

A temporary bad reaction is possible when gluten or casein are removed from the diet. This response is most common in children who seem addicted to eating large amounts of gluten or casein foods. They may do fine for the first few days, but then take a down turn. Symptoms, lasting up to two weeks, can include increased agitation, aggression, frustration, loss of appetite, diarrhea, and tiredness.[21] Although withdrawal can be severe in some cases, there is an up side to it.

It almost certainly means that the diet will bring rewards. So hang in there; it will be worth it.[22]

A withdrawal reaction can be minimized by removing casein and gluten in stages. Take away dairy first. Then wait a few weeks before taking out wheat products. A few weeks later, the rest of the gluten foods can go. This approach may be particularly helpful for children under age 4 since they sometimes have more severe withdrawal reactions.[23]

People approach the GF/CF diet in different ways. Some go for GF/CF convenience foods that are available in health-food stores or the health-food aisles at the grocery. Others prefer to make recipes from scratch using GF/CF ingredients. Still others shy from recipes and do without breads altogether. To save time, they prefer to eat plain cooking. Perhaps their dinner is a pork chop, a couple of steamed vegetable sides, and a cut-up cantaloupe. Recognize that there are numerous variations of GF/CF living and choose whatever style suits you best.[24]

Finally, one last burning question: if a child benefits from the GF/CF diet, will he have to stay on it forever? Again, only the child's body knows the answer. In some simple cases, a child can go off the diet after his leaky gut heals. There are also some parents who have found that the diet was not necessary after their child was treated for immune problems. In addition, some children have been able to eat previously offending foods following successful treatment for heavy-metal overload. Unfortunately, for many children who have been taken off the diet, the gut injury and behaviors returned within weeks, sometimes more severely.[25]

So where do you go for help with the GF/CF diet? There are many good GF/CF resources and cookbooks in this world. Only a couple will be mentioned here, along with a brief description to help you choose what suits you.

A good resource to zero in on dairy-free living is *Raising Your Child Without Milk* by Jane Zukin. The author describes the various problems an individual can have with milk such as lactose intolerance and milk-protein sensitivity. Both are seen in excess on the autism spectrum:[26]

1. *To avoid lactose* (milk sugar), the author advises not to consume milk or any foods containing it, such as cheese, ice cream, and yogurt. In addition, read ingredient lists of manufactured foods, even "non-dairy" products. Reject any that contain whey as an ingredient since it contains both lactose and milk protein.

2. *To avoid milk proteins like casein*, avoid all foods that contain milk. Also avoid manufactured foods whose ingredient lists include whey, casein, lactalbumin, lactoglobulin, sodium caseinate, and calcium caseinate.

In addition, the book explains how to ensure that your child gets sufficient calcium in the absence of milk. It is not nearly so treacherous as we have been led to believe by dairy marketers. Think about it. Generation upon generation of our ancient ancestors lived out their entire lives without a drop of nonhuman milk. How indispensable could it be? Calcium is vital, yes; but there are many sources of that, including supplements. The book also shares the ins and outs of grocery shopping and dairy-free living at school, day care, and restaurants. Dairy-free recipes are included as well.

An excellent resource for both the gluten-free and casein-free diets is *The Kid-Friendly ADHD & Autism Cookbook* by Pamela Compart, MD, and Dana Laake, RDH, MS, LDN. This book not only educates about food reactions and their sources but also offers extremely practical advice for parents' greatest concerns—coping with the picky eater, sensory issues with foods, withdrawal reactions, and more. It teaches ways to disguise healthy food while getting away from junk food. Finally, it offers a wealth of GF/CF substitutes and recipes. Quick and easy recipes are included for those under a time crunch, as well as more complex recipes for those with more time and a flare for cooking.

An excellent Internet resource for the GF/CF diet is the Autism Network for Dietary Intervention (ANDI) at www.AutismNDI.com. Its purpose is to help parents around the world who want to start and continue the GF/CF diet. In addition to GF/CF information, the Web site offers a "parent support system" that can be used to email volunteers worldwide for advice. Another Web site, www.gfcfdiet.com, also offers GF/CF information and an Internet support group.

ELIMINATE ANY OTHER FOODS THAT CAUSE SYMPTOMS

In addition to the GF/CF diet, eliminate any other foods that are causing symptoms. To identify these, first consider those that seem suspicious for some reason. Be wary of a food if:

○ your child craves it[27]

○ it brings on physical symptoms like digestive problems, red ears, dark circles under the eyes, a red or flushed face, easy bruising, eczema, or itchy skin[28]

○ it brings on behavioral symptoms[29]

○ it was identified as a potential trouble maker on the IgG ELISA sensitivity test

○ it is a common offender on the autism spectrum, such as soy, peanuts, eggs, corn, sugar, citrus fruits, baking yeast, and spelt.[30]

Run an elimination/binge trial for each questionable food. If the food is found guilty of causing symptoms, eliminate it from the diet, at least for a time.

WHAT ARE THE OTHER DIETS IN THIS CHAPTER FOR?

So far, you have only been introduced to the GF/CF diet. As a starting point, it is the gold standard because it has made such a significant difference for many children on the spectrum. Though this diet can be a godsend for those who have problems with gluten and casein, what about those whose primary dietary problem is something else? Or what if the GF/CF diet helps but doesn't seem to go far enough? In these situations, other diets may be the answer. They each have a purpose and value. The trick is figuring out the one or combination of ones that address the needs of your particular child. The only way to find out if they help is to try them. Your child's body and behaviors will let you know its verdict.

For some people, gut issues persist even while on the GF/CF diet. Such people may want to consider a trial of the yeast-free/mold-free diet, the specific carbohydrate diet, or the low oxalate diet. Sometimes a combination of diets works best. For instance, a person having success with the GF/CF diet may still struggle with yeast overgrowth in the gut. For that person, it makes sense to "add on" the low sugar diet to target the yeast issue. Still other people on the GF/CF diet find that hyperactivity or stimming continues. In their case, the Feingold diet might fit the bill.[31] Figure 25.1 organizes the diets to help guide you. It starts with the GF/CF diet and adds elimination of other foods known to cause symptoms. Together, these two powerful interventions will generally take care of many food-related symptoms.[32] After that, you have to play it by ear.

As this chapter discusses each of these diets, some may strike you as a good fit for the symptoms you see in your special child. If so, you might consider running a trial of that diet at some point. There is no doubt it can be tricky to solve the riddle of your child's relationships with foods, but rest assured that, with some persistence, you can crack the case.

Rotation diet

A rotation diet is not even really a diet at all. Rather it is a pattern of how often a certain food can be eaten. This pattern can be applied to any diet, GF/CF or otherwise. Its goal is to keep any one food from being eaten often enough to attract the unwanted attention of the immune system. It comes in particularly handy with leaky gut. Say your child loves oranges and snacks on them constantly, every day. Like everything else inside the leaky gut, orange peptides will

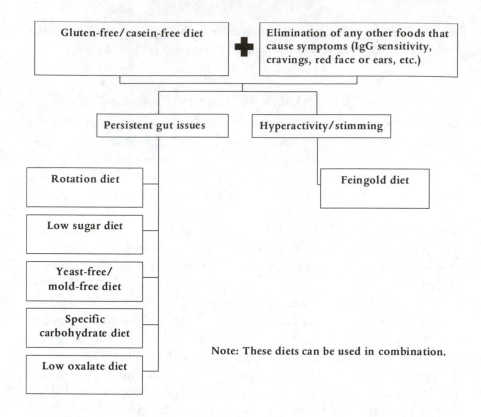

Figure 25.1 Dietary options

escape into the bloodstream. And what is any self-respecting immune system going to do about this flood of orange peptides in its bloodstream? It will deploy waves of antibodies to apprehend them. Oh, that's great, just great. The last thing we need is a new food sensitivity and its associated behaviors or physical symptoms. Eating oranges or anything else every day can be asking for trouble with a leaky gut. That is where a rotation diet comes in. It does not care *what* you eat so much as *how often* you eat it.

Food can rotate on a four-day-to-eight-day cycle. Usually four days is adequate to ensure that a particular food has time to clear the body before being eaten again. However, people with chronic constipation may need a longer cycle to allow extra time for foods to exit.[33] If using a seven-day cycle, for example, you could eat pears every Monday, while, on a four-day cycle, you could eat pears one day but not on the next three days until the cycle repeats.

That is the basic gist of a rotation diet, except for one wrinkle. That wrinkle relates to food families. Foods are grouped into families that are biologically related. For example, oranges are in the citrus family with grapefruits, tangerines, and lemons, among others. All the foods in the family share some common agents, agents we do not want the immune system to see every day. So, it is actually the whole family that needs to rotate, not just individual foods. A four-day rotation would not allow oranges one day, grapefruit the next, followed by tangerines on day 3, and then lemons on day 4. Instead, one day of the cycle would be designated as citrus-family day. On that single day, any member of the citrus family could be eaten; then there would be three days of no citrus until the cycle repeated. Some family groupings, like citrus, seem intuitive. But not all families are like that. Take the gourd family for instance. It includes cantaloupe, zucchini, pumpkin seeds, and others. That grouping is not as obvious as the one for citrus, so you need a little help. A book like *Allergy and Candida Cooking* by Sondra Lewis and Dorie Fink is very helpful for explaining the nuances of the rotation diet and giving extensive lists of foods and their families. When using a rotation diet, I have found that the task of assigning foods to different days of the rotation takes some time. But once that is figured out and posted in the kitchen, it becomes a useful aid for planning meals and making grocery lists.

A rotation diet has another benefit besides preventing new food sensitivities: it also helps you spot existing food problems. It has been my friend on several occasions. In each instance, Will was having a recurring symptom, seemingly unrelated to anything in particular. After a while, it would dawn on me that the symptom cycled—hmm, just like his foods. Bingo! In each instance, the rotation made it easy for me to zero in on the culprit, and it always made me feel clever. Yet, if it had not been for the rotation, who knows if I ever would have made the connection? Here is what the ARI parent ratings say about the rotation diet:

	Got Worse	No Effect	Got Better	Better: Worse Ratio	No. of Cases
Rotation Diet	2 percent	46 percent	51 percent	21:1	938

Low sugar diet

Sugar can be a real problem for those who struggle with yeast overgrowth. Carbohydrates, especially sugar, are the favorite food of yeast. In fact, it can catapult them to feverish heights of reproduction and overgrowth. I had a hard time appreciating this relationship until I actually did a simple experiment from a book.[34] I showed it to Will because I hoped it would help him understand why his sacrifice was so important. Now I barely remember Will's reaction; I was so engrossed in my own amazement.

This is what happened. I took a clear glass with half a cup of lukewarm water (nice and cozy, like the human gut). Then I cut open a little package of active dry yeast used for making bread. Though bread yeast is different from what lives in the gut, both need the same environment and have similar growth patterns. I poured the tame little grains of yeast into the water and gave them about three minutes to wake up. At first they floated, inert, on the water's surface. Over the course of the three minutes, some drifted gently to the bottom of the glass like lazy snowflakes. Then it was time to feed them. I sprinkled a table-spoon of sugar into the glass, an action that weighted many of the floating yeast down to the bottom. Not much happened for the first couple of minutes—but then the sugar hit its mark, and the energized yeast went wild. They foamed and frothed and beat their chests. They began leaping upward to the water's surface making the water cloudy and dense. A puffy, ever-thickening layer of foam formed at the water's surface. It was a scene of major food lust. Will turned up his nose in disgust at the noxious odor the yeast were pumping out. Eventually, the water cooled and the frenzy subsided. How bizarre, yet fascinating! This experi-ment helped me realize how much I had been underestimating the powerful effect of sugar on yeast.

At an earlier time over the Christmas holidays, I had let Will overindulge in sugary goodies and drinks. It took us a long time to regain the ground we lost in the gut. After seeing the yeast experiment, I could understand why. At a different time, I had not realized how much sugar is in fruit juice, nor was I taking notice of how much juice Will was drinking in his jars of fruit. Over time, we worked our way into major yeast overgrowth. This time again, regaining control was a lengthy, uphill battle. After that incident, I went back to some of my resources to reread what had been said about sugar and yeast overgrowth. It was a topic I had hoped to ignore, but I could not escape. For unfortunate people like us, yeast are the relentless, baying hounds on a fox chase. Sugar is the scent leading them straight to the fleeing fox.

And what did my resources say? They said to eliminate or limit sugars and starches when yeast is an issue. That included fruit juices, especially those con-taining apples or grapes. Pear juice is an exception since it does not seem to excite yeast as the others do. On labels of manufactured foods, sugar goes by many names. Some are rice syrup, maple syrup, honey, brown sugar, sucrose, glucose, fructose, and galactose. In addition, fruits contain a lot of natural sugar, which is the reason they are so sweet. They might need to be limited as well. While admitting that nothing is without its drawbacks, *Children with Starving Brains* recommends the sugar substitutes stevia and xylitol.[35] Furthermore, a gradual removal of sugar from the diet is recommended since stopping cold turkey can cause behaviors to temporarily worsen.

Yeast can ferment sugar into alcohol just as it does in the brewing of alcoholic beverages. Doesn't this make you wonder about children on the spectrum who exhibit "drunken" behavior or inappropriate "drunken" laughter, both symptoms of yeast overgrowth? Could it be the yeast are fermenting sugar in the diet to alcohol?[36] As you may have already guessed, a primary objective of a low sugar diet is to starve yeast. Additional tactics for yeast control will be discussed in the next chapter on gut flora. Yet, their effectiveness can be severely hampered if yeast are well fed by sugar in the diet.

In addition to feeding yeast, sugar also destabilizes blood sugar in many children. Sugary foods, as well as high-starch foods like potatoes and corn, pass through the digestive tract quickly and cause blood sugar to spike and then dive. Symptoms of low blood sugar can include poor cognitive function, irritability, tantrums, spaciness, tiredness, weakness, confusion, and inconsistent articulation. These problems can be alleviated by a diet low in sugar and starch. High-protein foods and high-fiber foods make better choices because they pass through the gut slowly. Eating small, frequent meals throughout the day also helps.[37]

Hats off to Will's fifth-grade autism teacher who figured out that Will's mid-morning or mid-afternoon episodes of irritability could be cured with a snack. Very perceptive of her, don't you think? Apparently, despite a big breakfast and lunch, Will's blood sugar would run low between meals, at least back then. Packing extra food in Will's lunch and asking teachers to allow a subtle snitch from it during the day ended the episodes. Will also had infrequent, seemingly random occurrences of evening irritability. After the insightful teacher voiced her suspicion, I realized the evening episodes occurred only in circumstances when Will could not help himself to a snack. It was an easy fix for risky situations to toss a piece of fruit in my purse or keep a big can of nuts in the car. I even gave Tutor Dear snacks to keep on hand. For a time, I had food stashed all over the place. Fortunately, the problem has since resolved.

Here is what the ARI parent ratings for autism say about a low sugar diet:

	Got Worse	No Effect	Got Better	Better: Worse Ratio	No. of Cases
Removed Sugar	2 percent	48 percent	50 percent	25:1	4,187

Yeast-free/mold-free diet (Candida diet)

The yeast-free/mold-free diet is also called the *Candida* diet, named after a particularly troublesome strain of gut yeast, *Candida albicans.* Consider giving this diet a trial if yeast overgrowth in the gut is a problem.[38] The diet avoids yeast in foods, but not for fear of them taking up residence in the gut. No, yeast are killed during baking and brewing. Even when eaten alive, they do not usually survive digestion. Rather, the diet avoids yeast because people with yeast problems in the gut are frequently sensitive to yeast in their food as well. In fact, they can also be sensitive to other foods closely related to yeast such as molds.[39]

Yeast and mold are just about everywhere in food, so it is nearly impossible to avoid them completely. Therefore, the diet focuses only on removal of foods that have the highest concentrations of yeast and mold. If improvement in symptoms results from a strict trial lasting 5-to-14 days, then you know the person needs to avoid dietary yeast and mold. However, if there is no improvement or results are unclear, the next step is to binge eat yeasty and moldy foods to see if there is a reaction. If one occurs, it will usually be within a few minutes to a few days after binge eating begins. If a yeast/mold problem exists, repeated variations of avoidance/binge trials can determine what level of yeast and mold is acceptable for this individual. Specific troublesome foods may be identified as well.

What foods contain yeast and mold? In a surprising number of ways, yeast and mold creep into the diet. For starters, they grow on the surfaces of fruits and vegetables, so they are present in your fruit bowl, as well as in fruit juices from contact with the skin. Dried fruits like raisins have loads of yeast that accumulate during the drying process. In addition, molds grow on the surface of grains and are ground into their flours. Yeast is intentionally added to baked goods to make them rise and is also present in fermented foods like alcoholic beverages and vanilla extract. Malt, a yeasty brewing product, appears in the ingredient lists of many manufactured foods. Vinegar, which is essentially spoiled wine, crops up in most condiments and sauces like ketchup and salad dressing. Milk and many cheeses contain yeast as well. Molds grow on beans and nuts during storage. When we eat a mushroom, we are eating a mold, a big one.

Autism: Effective Biomedical Treatments by Jon Pangborn and Sidney Baker provides details about trials and which foods to eat and avoid during a trial.[40] However, the gold standard for guidance and recipes is *Feast Without Yeast* by Bruce Semon, MD, PhD, and Lori Kornblum. Another yeast-free cookbook that contains valuable extras about yeast overgrowth, related symptoms, and a well-rounded approach to combating yeast and promoting health is *Allergy and Candida Cooking* by Sondra Lewis and Dorie Fink. Here is what the ARI parent ratings say about this diet:

	Got Worse	No Effect	Got Better	Better: Worse Ratio	No. of Cases
Candida Diet	3 percent	41 percent	56 percent	19:1	941

Specific carbohydrate diet (SCD)

Despite a trial of the GF/CF diet, some people continue to have unrelenting gut issues such as chronic diarrhea, yeast overgrowth, or gut inflammation. In fact, some may do worse on the GF/CF diet because of its increased use of rice and potatoes as substitutes for gluten and casein foods.[41] For them, SCD might just be the ticket. In origin, this diet was used for people with gut problems like irritable bowel syndrome, Crohn's disease, and ulcerative colitis, yet it is successful for many on the autism spectrum as well.[42]

SCD focuses on the trouble some people have digesting certain carbohydrates. Diarrhea, especially in children, can damage the gut wall impairing the ability to digest starches and complex sugars. When starches and complex sugars are subsequently eaten, they cannot be broken down as they would by a healthy gut. Instead, they are left to ferment in the gut where they may become a source of intestinal gas. As they travel through the tunnel, they serve as an invigorating smorgasbord for bad gut flora. Of all components in food, carbohydrates offer bad gut flora the richest supply of energy. This helps the bad flora to thrive, reproduce, and hit record levels of toxin production. As a result, the gut wall suffers further inflammation and injury. A vicious, self-perpetuating cycle is established in which the body's inability to digest incoming starches and complex sugars feeds the flora that further impair digestion. In addition, mucus used to protect the gut wall may appear in the stool.[43]

SCD breaks the vicious cycle by eliminating consumption of starches and complex sugars. The only foods eaten are those the body can easily digest and absorb leaving little behind for the bad flora. In this way, the body receives maximum nourishment, while bad flora starve. As the gut wall heals, bad flora and their toxins are reduced, gas and mucous production subside, and digestion and absorption improve.[44] SCD is a healing diet. Once the vicious cycle has been broken, SCD can be let go.[45]

SCD eliminates starches like potatoes and *all* grains (not just those containing gluten). It also removes complex sugars such as table sugar, corn syrup, and milk sugar (lactose). Only the simple sugars found in fruits and honey are allowed since they are already in simplest form and ready for absorption. The diet allows only "specific carbohydrates." A person on this diet primarily eats meats, fruits, and vegetables. Of any diet used in autism, the specific carbohydrate diet is the most restrictive and comes closest to the diet of our Stone Age ancestors.[46]

Many children starting SCD have a temporary one-to-three-week period where behaviors and bowel function get worse before they get better. This is due to the die-off of bad flora and the resulting flood of their toxins that the body has to off-load. If a person shows no improvement after a one-month trial of SCD, it is probably not going to help.[47]

Some of the best resources about SCD include:

O   *Breaking the Vicious Cycle* by Elaine Gottschall, BA, MSc. Its associated Web site, www.breakingtheviciouscycle.info, is an excellent aid that includes an index of legal and illegal foods, as well as support groups and other information.

O   *We Band of Mothers* by Judith Chinitz, MS, and Sidney Baker, MD, has a particularly practical chapter (Chapter IV) that discusses use of SCD in autism.

O   www.pecanbread.com contains a wealth of useful information.

Here is what the ARI parent ratings say about SCD:

	Got Worse	No Effect	Got Better	Better: Worse Ratio	No. of Cases
Specific Carbohydrate Diet	7 percent	24 percent	69 percent	10:1	278

Low oxalate diet

For some, gut or urinary problems persist despite use of the GF/CF diet. Such gut problems might include constipation, diarrhea, gas, and gut pain. Urinary troubles may involve frequent urination, urgent urination, genital pain, or a family history of kidney stones.[48] These would be reasons to take interest in the low oxalate diet. This diet should also be considered if an organic acid test (discussed in Chapter 26) shows a high level of oxalates.

What are oxalates? They are a natural substance that is irritating to body tissues. Beginning in the late 1980s—unrelated to autism—it was found that excess oxalates played a significant role in pain and burning in various body tissues. Different tissues were affected in different individuals. For some people symptoms occurred in the genitals, skin, rectum, or bowel. For others, it was the muscles, joints, or urinary tract (including the formation of kidney stones).

There are three primary ways oxalates get into the body. They come from:

1. certain plant foods in the diet

2. fungi, such as *Aspergillus*, that live in the gut

3. human metabolism.

Oxalates gain access to locations throughout the body when they are absorbed through the gut wall into the bloodstream. Generally, healthy tissues are resistant to the typical levels of oxalates present. However, high levels can cause trouble as the oxalates lodge at various sites. The low oxalate diet was developed to reduce oxalates in the body and has been a powerful force in pain relief for many oxalate-sensitive individuals.[49]

Around 2005, the low oxalate diet was first applied to children on the autism spectrum with encouraging success. Researcher Susan Owens found that the diet brought several forms of improvement to children with autism. The children in her study made progress in fine and gross motor skills, receptive and expressive language, cognition, sociability, and sleep. There were also reductions in rigidity, bed-wetting, and self-abusive behaviors. When tested, 84 percent of these children had higher-than-normal oxalate levels.[50]

Though nobody had thought of it before, it does seem reasonable to be suspicious of oxalates in relation to autism. Here are the reasons:

1. *Poor gut health.* Under normal gut conditions, only 1–2 percent of oxalates are absorbed into the bloodstream. However, that percentage can increase seven-fold in a digestive tract plagued by leaky gut, bowel inflammation, diarrhea, constipation, poor fat digestion, or low calcium.[51] These common problems of the autism spectrum can increase the level of oxalates in the bloodstream.

2. *Aspergillus overgrowth.* Overgrowth of bad gut flora is common on the spectrum. If the fungus *Aspergillus* is in overgrowth, there will be an associated increase in the level of oxalates it produces. If desired, the organic acid test (discussed in Chapter 26) can be used to test for fungi overgrowth. The level of fungi are indicated on the test by furandicarboxylic acid and hydroxymethylfuroic acid.[52]

3. *Excess mercury.* Children on the spectrum often have unusually high levels of mercury. Unfortunately, oxalates intensify the mercury

problem because the two substances have an extremely high attraction for each other. When they meet in the bloodstream, oxalates latch onto the mercury and hold onto it as they lodge in body tissues. That is not a good thing: we want mercury to exit the body, not dig in and cause injury.[53]

The traditional low oxalate diet uses a two-prong approach to reduce oxalates:[54]

1. *Take the citrate form of calcium with meals.* Calcium citrate binds with oxalates in the gut making them too large to pass through the gut wall. Thus, they remain in the gut and pass out of the body.

2. *Stop eating high-oxalate foods and limit intake of medium-oxalate foods.* Oxalates are found in plants, though their levels vary significantly from one plant to the next. A few of the worst offenders are peanuts, almonds, cashews, kiwi, and spinach. Also high are many berries, grains, beans, and other plant foods. Foods must be tested individually to determine their oxalate level.

An excellent resource for the low oxalate diet is *The Low Oxalate Cookbook—Book Two* by the VP Foundation. Besides offering low oxalate recipes, the book contains valuable information about oxalates, related health problems, and treatment. Most importantly, it includes extensive lists of low-, medium-, and high-oxalate foods. The word *autism*, however, does not appear in this book. To better understand oxalate issues and their treatment in autism, obtain a copy of the article "Oxalates Control Is a Major New Factor in Autism Therapy" by William Shaw, PhD. It is available at the Great Plains Laboratory Web site (www.greatplainslaboratory.com). In addition, you may want to join a Yahoo! group (trying_low_oxalates@yahoogroups.com) to email questions and receive information specific to use of the diet in autism.

Feingold diet

If hyperactivity or stimming are continuing problems while on the GF/CF diet, you may want to run a trial of the Feingold diet. Often, it reduces symptoms of impatience, inattention, poor sleep habits, hyperactivity, impulsivity, and aggression. If a child improves on this diet, it will usually take from three days to three weeks. A nonprofit organization called the Feingold Association (www.Feingold.org) helps families start and continue the diet. They offer a book called *Why Can't My Child Behave?* by Jane Hersey, which details the diet and the symptoms that commonly improve. In a nutshell, the diet eliminates manmade food colorings, artificial flavorings, and certain preservatives, as well as foods that contain a natural substance called salicylates. Salicylates, which trigger behavior and learning problems in some children, are found in almonds, tomatoes, cucumbers, and several fruits. After a few weeks of behavioral success with the diet, foods with salicylates can be added back one at a time to see if old behaviors return. Since food labeling is not always adequate or accurate, the Feingold Association researches brand name foods to determine which ones are okay for Feingold dieters and which are not. An extensive food list can be purchased from the Association at (800) 321 3287. You can also get the list by purchasing a membership that includes diet information, recipes, newsletter updates, and phone numbers to call for help with the diet.[55] Here is what the ARI parent ratings say about this diet:

	Got Worse	No Effect	Got Better	Better: Worse Ratio	No. of Cases
Feingold Diet	2 percent	42 percent	56 percent	25:1	899

WRAPPING IT UP

So there you have it: more dietary options than you probably ever wanted to think about. But try not to feel overwhelmed. Just take one step at a time. Though diets are not easy for us creatures of entrenched habit, they are of pivotal importance for combating autistic behaviors and physical symptoms. They form an important foundation on which all additional interventions are built. This chapter gave you a starting-point diet and some other worthy options to try later if appropriate. One word of caution. It is a sure bet that if you read two books about the same diet, they will contradict each other in the details. Try not to let that drive you crazy. Yes, contradictions are exasperating when you are already unsure of what you are doing. But resist the urge to pitch the whole diet out the window. Instead, make your own decision about whose advice to follow and march forward undeterred. You can always experiment with the other option later if you want. Also keep in mind that each of these diets has many devoted followers. They live these diets because they are rewarded with fuller lives. The diets offer hope. Your challenge is to figure out which one or combination of ones helps your individual child the most. It may not be easy, but it is well worth the effort. Now, it is time to leave discussions of food and move on to restoring healthy gut flora, the topic of the next chapter.

NOTES

1.   Chinitz and Baker 2007, p. 89.
2.   Pangborn and Baker 2005, pp. 2:33–34; McCandless 2007, p. 84.
3.   McCandless 2007, p. 90; Seroussi 2002, p. 210.
4.   Seroussi 2002, pp. 15, 214, 221; Lewis 2006, p. 83.
5.   Lewis 2006, p. 83; Seroussi 2002, p. 14.
6.   Seroussi 2002, pp. 14, 214; Lewis 2006, p. 83.
7.   Lewis 2006, p. 83; Seroussi 2002, p. 14.
8.   Seroussi 2002, pp. 14, 214.
9.   Ibid., p. 214.
10. Ibid.
11. Ibid.
12. Ibid., p. 14; Lewis 2006, p. 83.
13. McCandless 2007, p. 89.
14. Seroussi 2002, p. 210.
15. Pangborn and Baker 2005, pp. 2:33–35, 38; Fall and Urwick 2006, p. 88; McCandless 2007, pp. 43, 85–86; Lewis 1998a, p. 27.
16. Pangborn and Baker 2005, p. 2:41.
17. Seroussi 2002, p. 209.
18. Ibid., p. 210.
19. Pangborn and Baker 2005, p. 2:34; Seroussi 2002, p. 14; Lewis 1998a, p. 91; McCandless 2007, pp. 44, 86.
20. Lewis 1998b, p. 212.
21. Fall and Urwick 2006, pp. 87–88; Pangborn and Baker 2005, p. 2:38.
22. Seroussi 2002, p. 210; Shaw 1998, p. 127; Lewis 1998b, p. 203.
23. Lewis 1998a, pp. 58–59.
24. Pangborn and Baker 2005, pp. 2:38–39.
25. Seroussi 2002, p. 10; McCandless 2007, pp. 91, 106–107.
26. Zukin 1996, pp. 53–61.
27. Lewis 1998b, p. 198.
28. Pangborn and Baker 2005, p. 2:43.
29. Chinitz and Baker 2007, p. 93.
30. Shaw 2004, p. 8; Lewis 1998a, p. 41.
31. Usman 2006, p. 61.
32. Bock and Stauth 2007, p. 203.
33. Lewis and Fink 2005, p. 58.
34. Ibid., p. 11.
35. McCandless 2007, pp. 97–98.
36. Ibid., pp. 100–101; Pangborn and Baker 2005, p. 1:41; Shaw 1998, pp. 67–68, 74; Baker 2004, pp. 62–63.
37. Bock and Stauth 2007, pp. 23, 153, 237–41.
38. Matthews 2007, p. 124.
39. Shaw 1998, p. 66.
40. Pangborn and Baker 2005, pp. 2:15–24.
41. Chinitz and Baker 2007, p. 126.
42. Matthews 2007, p. 124; Usman 2006, pp. 57–58; McCandless 2007, p. 107; Gottschall 2004, pp. 4, 8, 43, 51–52.

43. Gottschall 2004, pp. 8, 17–19.
44. Ibid., pp. 6, 10, 16, 19–20.
45. Chinitz and Baker 2007, pp. 63, 92, 110, 170.
46. Gottschall 2004, pp. 8, 27; McDonnell 2006a, p. 90.
47. Pangborn and Baker 2005, pp. 2:27–28; Gottschall 2004, p. 68.
48. Usman 2006, p. 61; Matthews 2007, p. 124; Owens 2007, pp. 246–50.
49. VP Foundation 2005, pp. 3–4, 7–8, 14.
50. Shaw 2006, p. 1.
51. Owens 2006, p. 93.
52. Shaw 2006, pp. 2, 7.
53. Ibid., p. 6.
54. VP Foundation 2005, p. 6.
55. Hersey 1999, pp. 9, 15–17, 19–20.

Chapter 26

Common Gut Interventions: Gut Flora

WHAT THIS CHAPTER HAS IN STORE

This chapter discusses the benefits of restoring healthy gut flora and the interventions to get you there. The primary tools for evaluating gut flora are reviewed along with their strengths and weaknesses. Also covered are tactics for subduing yeast overgrowth, as well as ways to avoid or minimize the die-off reactions that sometimes occur. In addition, this chapter discusses replenishment of good bacteria and how to improve the gut environment so that a healthy population can be established. Finally, there are situations when it is appropriate to pursue bad bacteria; these situations and their treatment are described.

THE BENEFITS OF GETTING YEAST UNDER CONTROL

For a child with a yeast problem, conquering yeast can bring about miraculous healing. Improvements can range from increased concentration, eye contact, speech, and socialization to reduced hyperactivity, aggression, self-abusive behavior, and stimming. Alongside the GF/CF diet, subduing yeast is one of the most effective methods for relieving autistic symptoms. It should be a high priority in treatment of those on the spectrum.[1]

Take a look at the ARI parent ratings in Appendix B. Overall, the drug category's track record is not very impressive. The other categories prove superior by comparison. Yet it is intriguing to notice that the two highest-rated drugs (prescription medications Nystatin and Diflucan) are antifungals, another word for yeast killers. For a child with yeast overgrowth, antifungals can produce dramatic and sustained improvements in behavior.[2] The improvement does not occur because antifungals target behaviors directly but because they address the underlying misery that spawns those behaviors. Antifungals are tools for healing. Think of them as plugs that stop a leaky boat from sinking. Their approach is completely different from that of behavior-suppressing drugs. Those drugs do not attempt to fix the source of the problem at all; instead, they merely try to mask its impact. They hope to keep the leaky boat afloat by eternally bailing out the water.

ASSESSING GUT FLORA IN A PERFECT WORLD

In a perfect world, it would be simple to tally the numbers of each strain of good bacteria, bad bacteria, and yeast present in a person's gut. Their hundreds of exotic names would appear in a comprehensive list along with a head count for each type. With such accurate and complete information, it would be easy to pinpoint trouble spots and devise a plan of attack. Overpopulated strains of yeast and bad bacteria could be targeted with tailor-made agents most effective at killing those strains. And those good strains of bacteria having a low head count could be repopulated by giving specialized supplements of new ones. Well, so much for a perfect world. Now for the real world.

ASSESSING GUT FLORA IN THE REAL WORLD

Unfortunately, real-world tests are not as reliable and comprehensive as we would like. However, as long as you understand their limitations, they can still be helpful and offer input for your decision making. Keep in mind that you do not *have* to use lab tests. Another choice is to bypass tests altogether and simply treat for yeast to see what happens. If you get a good response, then you know overgrowth was indeed a problem. It is a different approach from what we are used to—treating a potential problem rather than a known problem—but it works well in this case. But back to the tests. If you opt for laboratory testing, the two most commonly used tests are the stool analysis and the urine organic acid test. Among other things, these tests take a look at both yeast and bacteria.

Stool analysis

Life is uncertain for bacteria and yeast living in the human gut. At any moment, as they war, feed, and reproduce, a barrage of passing food can sweep them away. Before they know it, they are part of the stool and dumped into the toilet, hardly a hospitable place. Yet, if we rescue them and give them a cozy home in a laboratory, we might be able to get them to grow. If they do, then we can take roll call to see who is there. That gives us the names of at least some of the organisms living in the gut back home. We can also take a head count of each type of bacteria present to get an idea of their population in the gut.

However, what does this tell us about organisms that do not grow for the test? Nothing really. We remain completely in the dark about their status in the gut. For all we know, they could have a large gut population or none at all. There are several possible reasons that an organism living in the gut does not grow in a stool analysis. A major disadvantage from the start is that the vast majority of gut bacteria do not need oxygen to live. In fact, many even die in its presence. Thus, only about half of oxygen-free bacteria can even be grown from stool in a laboratory.[3] As for yeast, if they are in their aggressive and invasive form, they are physically anchored to the gut wall, and pieces have to break away in order to end up in the stool for analysis.[4] Another complication is that the immune system may be trying to hamper the growth of yeast in the gut by coating them with IgA antibodies. If levels of these antibodies are high, they can keep yeast from growing in the laboratory, despite a troublesome overgrowth problem back home in the gut.[5] The point here is not to make any assumptions about organisms that do not grow in a stool analysis.

At best, a stool analysis reveals only the tip of the gut-flora iceberg, a piece of the picture, not the whole. Nevertheless, even with its shortcomings, a stool analysis can still provide useful input for decision making. The test offers a general idea of the gut-flora situation. And for any organism that does grow, we know it truly does live in the gut. Moreover, if that organism is harmful, we know which treatment is most effective to kill it.[6] Furthermore, if counts of good bacteria are low, we know to take steps to improve the gut environment for them and to replenish their populations with reinforcements.

A stool analysis evaluates more than just gut flora; it also studies the remains of what was once food. If excessive meat or vegetable fibers are found in the stool, we know to question digestion and absorption of these foods, and the same goes if fats or carbohydrates are found. Ideally, if the gut is operating effectively, we should not find much wasted nutrition in the stool. Besides assessing digestion and absorption, the test also looks for signs of gut inflammation and other indicators of intestinal health and immune status. As with most biomedical tests, the lab provides a paragraph of information for each test result that is outside its expected range. This information helps you interpret the finding and understand possible causes and treatments.[7] For additional information about stool analysis, as well as contact information for laboratories that offer the test, see Pangborn and Baker's *Autism: Effective Biomedical Treatments*, page 4:2.

Organic acid test (OAT)

Yeast, fungi, and bad bacteria living in the gut produce various byproducts known as organic acids. When these organic acids pass into the bloodstream, they are filtered by the kidneys into the urine. The organic acid test analyzes a urine sample to see how much of each byproduct is present. High levels of byproducts related to yeast, fungi, or bad bacteria indicate overgrowth.

This test assesses more than just bad gut flora; it also looks at organic acids produced by the body's own metabolism. In this way, it can detect certain vitamin deficiencies and trouble spots in key parts of metabolism. In addition, the test checks for several genetic disorders such as PKU, maple-syrup urine disease, and hyperoxaluria.[8] Attached to the lab results is information to help interpret any test values that are outside the normal ranges.

Not all organic acid tests give the same information. Some laboratories have developed special versions that are more helpful in cases of autism. A discussion of the test and recommended laboratories appears in *Autism: Effective Biomedical Treatments*, pages 4:10–13.

There is one more test that is worthy of mention. It does not evaluate gut flora specifically, but rather the whole of the digestive tract engine. Though it is not as pleasant as test results printed on crisp white paper, it has the enticing bonus of being absolutely free.

Crossing the line of polite conversation: Poop

A person does not have to know the teeniest bit about the inner workings of a car engine to recognize signs of serious trouble. Explosive back-firing and billows of black smoke from a tail pipe are clear signals that something is wrong. The same goes for the "engine" of the digestive tract—only its "exhaust" is called poop. Of course, you can substitute your favorite word, be it stool, number 2, doo doo, or caca. I will use *poop* since it is universally recognized without regard to race, religion, sex, or ethnic origin. Yes, discussing it completely lacks all sense of decorum and good manners. I must apologize for that. But, come on, now—*everybody* does it: the president, your date, and the intimidating person behind the big desk at every job interview. When we can't, we wish we could. If we can't stop, we wish we would. So when it comes to the health of the digestive tract, poop is something we simply must discuss. Whether you do lab tests or not, the toilet test or diaper review has valuable information to offer.

What are the rules for poop? It should make an appearance once a day, and should not be unusually large or exceptionally tiny like rabbit pellets; tiny signifies constipation. Its consistency should not be loose and watery, grainy, or soft like mashed potatoes. Nor should it be hard or hard to pass. Poop should not float in the toilet either. Floating indicates that fats are not being digested and absorbed. When left in the stool, they make it lighter than water, so it floats. The right color for poop is a reassuring shade of brown, not pale or black. Granted all poop stinks, but it should not be particularly rank and foul-smelling. That is a clue that bad gut flora are at work; most likely feasting on undigested, fermented food that is encouraging their overgrowth. Mucus or blood should not be visible in poop. When any of these poop rules are broken, the body is telling you there are problems with digestion, absorption, inflammation, foods, and/or bad flora.[9]

If your child has problems with his "exhaust," you may want to make an album of poop photos. Really. No kidding. Order them by date. In the margins, write notes and dates of various interventions, including dietary changes. In that way you can evaluate their impact on the "bottom" line. Now, don't look so horrified. I am not suggesting you send these photos out in your Christmas cards. It is just that sometimes a detective needs an evaluation tool like this. If so, make one. It can be very helpful. If necessary, bribe your kid with money, a Lego block, or whatever he cares about to enlist his cooperation. If you use a doctor, there may be times the doctor should take a look at the photos. After all, a picture is worth a thousand words. Besides, after what doctors see in medical school, what could gross them out?

The ultimate test for yeast

Though lab tests and bathroom observations sometimes show agreement, at other times they contradict each other. That means your organic acid test may indicate yeast overgrowth while a stool analysis done the same day does not; the reverse also occurs. Moreover, lab tests sometimes reveal yeast overgrowth, despite a good bathroom situation. In some cases, picky eating habits betray the presence of yeast, despite a lack of observable bowel symptoms.[10] So then what good are tests and observations? They can still be useful input, yet we have to be aware of their limitations. When they uncover a yeast problem, we need to listen. However, when they fail to find a problem, we must realize we still do not know with absolute certainty if an overgrowth exists—and if so, its extent.

However, there is a conclusive test that settles the question. The ultimate test is treatment. That means that you go ahead and treat for yeast whether you know it is in overgrowth or not. Then infer from the response you get whether there was a yeast problem. Agreed, it is unusual in this world to treat a problem that might not exist. However, when it comes to yeast, it is worth making an exception. Here is the reason: people on the spectrum typically have a serious lack of immunity to yeast.[11] Considering how common overgrowth is, the low risk of treatment, and the great potential to improve autistic symptoms, why not treat? When you have to live in the real world, this is as good as it gets. Treatment, not lab tests or bathroom observations, has the last word.[12]

APPROACH TO TREATING YEAST

Yeast can be a very stubborn foe to subdue. After all, no tyrant gives up his throne without a fight. We can wage war against yeast on three fronts. Simultaneously we use a low sugar diet, probiotics (good bacteria), and antifungals. For some individuals, restoring and maintaining good gut flora is easy; for others, it is quite difficult. In these cases, even after good flora is restored, ongoing efforts and vigilance must continue since yeast can be a persistent bully, bent on staging a comeback.[13]

Yeast offensive: Low sugar diet

Sugar is the favorite food of yeast. It helps them thrive and reproduce. By minimizing the supply of sugar in the diet, we take an important step toward taming yeast. If we ignore the sugar issue, the effectiveness of other efforts to kill yeast is reduced.[14] For more details on the low sugar diet, refer to the previous chapter on diets.

Yeast offensive: Probiotics

Probiotics are good bacteria themselves who have been manufactured into pills or powders. They are discussed in more detail later in this chapter. For now, just know that they exist and can be supplemented to bolster an ailing population in the gut. Since they fight yeast, they are our allies. They also fulfill a second important military objective—they fight bad bacteria, too. Ah, yes, the cunning bad bacteria. These opportunistic fellows would just love for us to launch a yeast offensive with a blind side toward them. With us eliminating their yeast enemies, they would get a chance to become the new king of the hill. However, we do not want bad bacteria, especially the treacherous Clostridia clan, running amuck in the gut, so we supplement probiotics. It is like rain on their parade and dampens their chances of seizing power. Recognize that if bad flora are well established, it is unlikely probiotics alone can restore healthy flora to the gut. But, if probiotics are given while bad flora are killed off, good flora can get a foothold and offer a brighter future in the gut.[15]

Yeast offensive: Antifungals

Antifungals are a critical part of the strategy to subdue a known or potential yeast problem. Just as antibiotics specialize in killing bacteria, antifungals specialize in killing yeast. But, first, it is important to discuss something called a die-off reaction. You are not going to like it, but you need to know about it anyway. So here goes.

DIE-OFF REACTIONS

When battling yeast with antifungals, dying yeast can release record amounts of toxins; so, even though you may be winning the war, a temporary stampede of toxins can make you think you are losing. The stampede causes what is known as a die-off reaction, a problem that can last for days. In the short term, the child may get worse before he gets better. For him, being a battlefield is no fun. But hang in there. Keep using the antifungal. The die-off reaction's message is loud and clear: it means yeast overgrowth is indeed a problem and you have found an antifungal that is effective against the strain(s) in overgrowth. That knowledge is valuable input for future treatment decisions. It will pay off to weather the temporary setbacks of a die-off reaction. Symptoms of die-off might be similar to that of flu such as fever, nausea, or body aches. There may be increased irritability, aggression, hyperactivity, stimming, extreme tiredness, regression, or worsening of any unwanted behavior. Sometimes die-off reactions are severe. But take heart. Though they are unpleasant, they are not harmful.[16]

AVOIDING OR MINIMIZING A DIE-OFF REACTION

In an effort to avoid or minimize a die-off reaction, begin the following steps for a couple of weeks prior to using an antifungal:

- Avoid sugar in order to reduce the food supply for yeast.[17] That will weaken them and some may die off.
- Avoid constipation because it keeps yeast toxins bottled up inside. Ways to combat constipation are described in Pangborn and Baker's *Autism: Effective Biomedical Treatments*, pages 1:30–34.[18]

In addition to these precautions, there is an over-the-counter product that can be used during a die-off reaction. It is called activated charcoal and has a tremendous ability to quench reactions, often within an hour. It is an inert, black substance available in capsules or tablets. Like a sponge, it harmlessly absorbs and neutralizes yeast toxins. Interestingly, activated charcoal has a long history of use in poison situations. In fact, a professor in 1831 stood before his distinguished colleagues at the French Academy of Medicine and drank a lethal dose of strychnine mixed with activated charcoal. By surviving the stunt, he proved his claim that activated charcoal is highly effective for absorbing poison. I would say he also proved he was a complete idiot, but that is beside the point. Activated charcoal is a worthwhile product to have on hand when battling yeast. In fact, activated charcoal can even work wonders for bad behaviors that are completely unrelated to die-off.[19]

For whatever purpose activated charcoal it used, do not take it with food, medications, or vitamins. It will indiscriminately soak up whatever it finds along its way through the digestive tract. To make sure that it will absorb the intended target (toxins), give it to a child who has not eaten in an hour; then have him wait another hour before eating. In a pinch, make do with a half-hour on either side of the activated charcoal ingestion. Give a capsule at the first sign of a suspected die-off reaction and repeat every four hours. The dose is about four pills per day. If die-off symptoms go away, the frequency of doses can be reduced accordingly.

If swallowing pills is a problem, capsules can be opened or tablets crushed for mixing in a little water. Though the mixture is tasteless, it is gritty. Since an unwilling child can make a worthy opponent, sometimes it pays to smuggle in the charcoal. In that case, skip the water. Instead, mix the powdered charcoal in a teaspoon or two of honey or undiluted grape juice concentrate, which is very sweet and dark enough to hide the black powder. This mixture can be drawn up into a syringe and squirted into the mouth if that would help.[20] Also be aware that use of activated charcoal may cause stools to appear black.

Again, I am not a doctor. I am merely repeating what doctors who follow the Defeat Autism Now! approach have written. For your own peace of mind and to further your self-education, I urge you to look up information in my references for verification or more details.

ANTIFUNGAL APPROACH TO CONQUERING YEAST

So, back to the use of antifungals to treat a known or potential yeast problem. In the real world, we may not know which strain of yeast in the gut needs killing. That is a problem since each strain is vulnerable to certain antifungals yet resistant to others. No matter how strong we might think a given antifungal is, it works only on certain yeast strains, not on all of them. How can we choose our weapon if we do not know the target?

Autism: Effective Biomedical Treatments recommends using a succession of specific, high-powered antifungals to get yeast under control initially. If the child shows improvement with one of the antifungals in the sequence, you know you have hit the target. Only if you complete the succession without any improvement can you conclude there was no yeast problem in the first place. In the practice of medicine, this is not an approach we are used to seeing, but the limitations of the real world do not leave us much choice.[21]

Now let's take a closer look at the process sometimes referred to as the "antifungal parade." There are six high-powered antifungals in the succession of trials. You may end up having to run a trial of each one; again, that entirely depends on the responses you get as you work your way through the sequence. During each trial, watch for clues that indicate whether you are hitting the target. Certainly a noticeable improvement in behaviors or physical symptoms is a sign of success. Even a die-off reaction means you are on the right track. Stay the course. Once the die-off phase passes, improvements will follow. If desired, earlier lab tests can be repeated to see if they show improvement in the yeast situation.[22]

Where it gets tricky is when there is *no* response during a trial. Does that mean yeast is not a problem? Or does it indicate that the yeast strains in overgrowth were not susceptible to the antifungal being used? You won't know which it is. Perhaps the next antifungal will be effective, so onward to the next antifungal in the sequence. Each time, you base your next step on the responses you observed in previous trials. Depending on the situation you may even return to an earlier antifungal, whichever one seemed to work best. Only this time you should use a higher dose for the trial or run the trial for a longer time period. The process is guided by trial and error.[23]

If you reach a point where you see benefits and feel that the yeast has been subdued, stop the succession of trials and pass into a phase of yeast prevention and watchfulness. Otherwise, continue the sequence. If the full sequence is completed without any improvement, then you know yeast was not in overgrowth in the first place. Even if that turns out to be the case, console yourself that it was still worth trying to treat for yeast. The potential gains justified the effort to find out for sure.

YEAST PREVENTION AND WATCHFULNESS

Let's say you conquered yeast, since that is often the case. Now what? People are used to fixing a medical problem and then being done with it. Broken bones and stitches work that way—but not yeast infection. A susceptibility often exists to recurrent episodes of yeast overgrowth. Sometimes a weak immune system may be the reason. At any rate, think of yeast as a boomerang that you throw away only to have it come back to whack you in the back of your head when you turn to walk off. Unfortunately, if yeast make a comeback, the ground gained earlier can be lost over time. Therefore, preventative measures and vigilance are the order of the day. Keep yeast at bay by rotating natural antifungals and remaining alert to signs of a return. Also continue other yeast-control measures, such as the low sugar diet and probiotics. Combating yeast is not a one-time-only treatment, but rather a long-term endeavor.[24]

THE ANTIFUNGAL SEQUENCE

This section will discuss several antifungals, both those in the sequence as well as others used in the prevention stage. The recommended succession of high-powered antifungals starts with a trial of an over-the-counter yeast product called *Saccharomyces boulardii*. It is followed by a trial of either Nystatin or Amphoteracin B, which are both prescription antifungals. No particular order applies to the four remaining prescription antifungals in the sequence: Diflucan, Nizoral®, Sporanox, and Lamisil. The references in note 25 at the end of this chapter provide recommendations by medical doctors for dosing and trial length.[25]

YEAST ASSASSINS

We have several yeast assassins in our arsenal. If the yeast strains in overgrowth do not respond to one of them, perhaps they will to another.

Saccharomyces boulardii. This antifungal is available over-the-counter at pharmacies and health food stores. As antifungals go, it is the favorite champion to start with, according to *Autism: Effective Biomedical Treatments.*[26] It is itself a yeast, though not a native of the human gut. Its battle cry is, "It takes one to kill one!" And killing gut yeast is its specialty. As a bonus, it helps heal the gut wall and restore good flora. It can also neutralize bacterial toxins and stimulate immunity.[27] For all these reasons, it is a highly favored good guy, despite its reputation for bad die-off reactions. When supplementation stops, it dawns on *Saccharomyces boulardii* that it does not belong in the human gut, so it passes out, perhaps in search of its natural environment, the surface of a lichee nut. No kidding—that really is where it prefers to live.[28]

Two-thirds of the people who try *Saccharomyces boulardii* respond to it. The following dosing strategy is recommended by Sidney Baker, MD, a cofounder of Defeat Autism Now! who has extensive experience treating yeast in children on the spectrum. Dr. Baker starts the first day with one capsule or portion of a capsule mixed in food or water. If all goes well, he says to work up to one capsule three times a day. Stay at that dose for 10–14 days. As long as treatment continues to go well, increase the dose to three capsules three times a day for another 10–14 days. If dramatic benefits result, you know yeast overgrowth has been a big problem. This knowledge may justify use of a more aggressive antifungal as the next step. Or if die-off was tolerable and good benefits are continuing, you may opt to wait for the situation to stabilize. Depending on the quality of the benefits, you can decide what to do from there. Though using *Saccharomyces boulardii* on a continual daily basis is not recommended, periodic use can be helpful.[29]

If a full trial of *Saccharomyces boulardii* goes by with no effect, it does not prove there is no yeast problem. It may only mean that *Saccharomyces boulardii* is not effective against the yeast strains in overgrowth. In this case, it is time to consider the next antifungal option.[30]

There are a few other bits of information about *Saccharomyces boulardii* that are helpful to know. For one, *Saccharomyces boulardii* is a living organism that will be useless if it dies before being consumed. Therefore, it is worthwhile to purchase it from a store's refrigerated section and keep it refrigerated at home. The organisms live longer that way; it is the same reason fishermen keep their bait worms in the refrigerator—worms forgotten in a tackle box go bad fast. Furthermore, given that *Saccharomyces boulardii* is a yeast, there is no point using it while also using antifungal drugs that will kill it. Lastly, be aware that a stool analysis cannot tell the difference between *Saccharomyces boulardii* and another strain of yeast that can live in the gut. Therefore, to eliminate any confusion about yeast overgrowth in test results, discontinue *Saccharomyces boulardii* about a month before a planned stool analysis.[31]

Nystatin. This is a prescription antifungal with a very long history of safety, though it can produce bad die-off reactions. It has been used in the U.S. for over 50 years and can be taken for long periods of time. Nystatin and its close cousin, oral Amphoteracin B, are not like most drugs that are absorbed into the body from the gut. Instead, they do their job while staying safely within the tunnel, "outside" the body proper. Eventually, they exit in the stool. Their safety and effectiveness make them the next antifungal to try after a trial of *Saccharomyces boulardii*. Some people benefit from Nystatin but later find that symptoms return when treatment stops. For such cases, treatment can safely continue for weeks to months. The downside of Nystatin and Amphoteracin B is that they are not as effective against severe yeast infections as the other prescription antifungals. If a three-week trial shows no effect, an increase in the dosage may be in order. After that, it is time to pursue other prescription antifungals.[32] Unfortunately, many yeast strains have grown resistant to Nystatin over the years. Therefore, oral Amphoteracin B may be a better choice since it has not been used as widely in the U.S. Both medications are best without food, so the yeast have nothing to hide behind.[33]

Other prescription antifungals. These yeast killers are absorbed into the blood-stream from the gut. They include Diflucan (and its generic fluconazole), Nizoral® (generic: ketoconazole), Sporanox (generic: itraconazole), and Lamisil (generic: terbinafine). Before the 1980s and the arrival of these medications, drugs to fight severe yeast infections were very toxic and known to cause liver damage. Physicians became suspect of all antifungals except Nystatin. This attitude continues to linger. Though liver concerns appear in the warnings of these medications, the risks are small. These medications have yielded huge benefits to thousands of patients. To be on the safe side, however, appropriate blood tests should be done periodically during treatment to monitor liver function. These drugs can be very helpful when the yeast are resistant to Nystatin or oral Amphoteracin B. They can also get at yeast in the deeper layers of the gut wall where Nystatin does not reach.[34]

Because a person stands to gain so much by fixing a potential yeast problem, *Autism: Effective Biomedical Treatments* recommends proceeding through a three-week trial of each of these medications in turn. You will either achieve success with a noticeable improvement in symptoms and behavior or complete all trials without any gains.[35]

Other over-the-counter natural antifungals. Numerous nonprescription antifungals are available. They include Lauricidin®, capryllic acid, oregano, grapefruit seed extract, pau d'arco, undecylenic acid (Undecyn®), aged-garlic extract (Kyolic), and olive leaf extract. Many combination products also exist such as Biocidin, Yeast Aid, or Candicyn.[36] Though natural antifungals can be very effective, severe cases of yeast overgrowth often require the medications of the recommended sequence. Once yeast is subdued, however, rotating natural antifungals can help keep it from staging a comeback.[37]

Candex. This is an over-the-counter brand whose style of attack is rather novel: it is a digestive enzyme that literally eats through the cell wall of yeast. Kind of original, don't you think? Digested yeast are less likely to release toxins, so the chance of a die-off reaction is reduced. For Candex to work well, it is important to give it on an empty stomach at least an hour away from food that might prevent contact between it and the yeast.

RESTORING HEALTHY GUT FLORA

Individuals have different capacities for renewal of good flora.[38] For some, bad flora stubbornly defies repair. As mentioned earlier, effective treatment includes antifungals, the low sugar diet, probiotics, and possibly treatment of bad bacteria. Now let's take a closer look at probiotics and how to assist them, as well as tests and possible treatment for bad bacteria.

Send in the good troops

Good bacteria are called *good* because of the helpful services they provide for us. There are many different strains each with his own special gifts to offer.[39] Good bacteria:

o   fight yeast and bad bacteria

o   plug holes in the leaky gut and alleviate food sensitivities

o   aid the immune system and work against germs that sneak in on food

o   support digestion by unlocking vitamins from food

o   produce vitamins for us like biotin and vitamin K

o   predigest certain sugars and proteins that are hard for us to break down

o   reduce the quantity of certain compounds in food that can cause intestinal discomfort

o   support absorption, metabolism, and detoxification

o   control gut inflammation.

On the autism spectrum, think of good bacteria like endangered wildlife in nature. Nature's endangered populations can be increased by releasing new animals into the wild. The same strategy works for good bacteria in the gut. We can replenish their populations by fortifying them with newcomers. Certain foods, like yogurt, which contains good bacteria, are often eaten for just this purpose. Probiotics are used in the same way. Unlike yogurt, however, they have the added bonus of offering much larger quantities of good bacteria and are available in dairy-free brands.[40]

Probiotics are tiny living organisms of different strains of good bacteria. They are grown on a food source where they eat, grow, and multiply until ripe for harvest. Then, they are packaged into pills or powders. For people who cannot swallow pills, the powders are handy for hiding in food or drink. When probiotics arrive at a favorable spot in the gut, they implant and get back to the business of multiplying and doing good deeds. Almost all children on the autism spectrum need probiotics, usually continuously. This is true even though probiotics do not typically generate dramatic benefits, nor do they single-handedly restore healthy gut flora. In a sick gut, much of the initial cleanup work requires other interventions to kill bad flora and create a more hospitable environment for good bacteria. Given these supports, probiotics are important to help bring the ailing gut back to health. They are particularly valuable after antibiotics have been used.[41]

Though probiotics are in a dormant state when manufactured, they are still alive. It is important for them to stay that way until they arrive at a suitable home in the gut. Refrigeration from manufacture to mouth helps keep as many of them alive as possible. Unfortunately, refrigeration does not stop them from dying, but at least it slows the death rate. Though there are exceptions, brands that say they do not require refrigeration tend to lack some of the most beneficial strains and have a lower census of live organisms.[42]

Some of the particularly beneficial strains used in probiotics are *Lactobacillus rhamnosus*, *Lactobacillus acidophilus*, *Bifidobacter bifidum*, and *Streptococcus thermophilus*. Some brands of probiotics make a name for themselves by offering a high dose of one of these "super" strains. But there are also advantages to brands that combine strains since they offer a wider range of special services than a single strain offers. Both single strain and combination types are useful.[43] To see which strains are included in any given brand, read the ingredient list on the container or package insert; often, the amount of each strain will also be listed, usually expressed as millions or billions of "live organisms," also called "colony-forming units" (CFU).

Over 100 brands of probiotics are offered by pharmacies, health-food stores, and Internet sources. Use of high-quality brands that contain large numbers of organisms is advised because they produce superior results. Though there are many good brands, a few of the ones recommended by doctors of Defeat Autism Now! include Culturelle®, Kirkman Pro-Bio Gold™, Klaire Labs' Ther-biotic line, Natren, and Primal Defense. Rotating among different brands can be helpful. When trying to restore balance to gut flora, the daily dose is 20–100 billion CFU. After balance has been achieved, a daily maintenance dose of 10–25 billion CFU is recommended. In high-potency brands that equates to one or two capsules. Even at high doses, probiotics are remarkably safe, so the more, the merrier.

In a few cases where the gut was severely inflamed, probiotics appeared to have increased the inflammation. To be on the safe side, start with small doses and gradually build up. If a child does not do well on one brand, switch to another. Also be aware that some brands are grown on dairy as a food source. These probiotics will contain a small amount of dairy, a fact that will be mentioned on the container or package insert. For dairy-sensitive children, choose dairy-free brands. Like many supplements, probiotics are discussed in detail in the supplements section of *Autism: Effective Biomedical Treatments*.[44]

Support our troops

Often when a species of animal wildlife is endangered, loss of habitat is the primary problem. The same goes for good bacteria in the gut. If living conditions in the gut are harsh, good bacteria will not survive, even if new populations are constantly arriving. This happens all too frequently on the autism spectrum. In such a case, a person may see no benefit from probiotics unless the doses are very high. His stool analysis may not find much good flora to report, and switching brands of probiotics does not help. Rather than waiting to see whether probiotics can take hold, take steps in advance to improve gut conditions for good bacteria.[45] Such steps include the following:

1. *Kill bad flora.*

2. *Address food sensitivity by making dietary changes.* This will reduce the negative impact of food reactions on the climate in the gut.

3. *Fight constipation.* If constipation is a problem, address it with some basic nutrients such as magnesium and vitamin C to improve regularity. For additional tips on coping with constipation, see *Autism: Effective Biomedical Treatments*, pages 1:30–34.

4. *Use digestive enzymes.* They can improve digestion and will be discussed in the next chapter.

5. *Use insoluble fiber.* It is a welcome food supply to good bacteria. Vegetables and beans are good sources. Or you may want to consider a daily tablespoon of ground flaxseed (from the grocery store), psyllium seed powder (from a health-food store), or cellulose powder (800 654 4432 or international 01 603 656 9778).[46]

6. *Use FOS (fructooligosaccharides).* FOS feeds good bacteria (particularly Bifidobacteria) without feeding yeast, salmonella, E. coli, or certain other bad bacteria. An exception is the bad bacteria *Klebsiella pneumoniae*; if you have a positive test for *K. pneumoniae* wait until after treatment to use FOS. FOS is a substance that exists in small amounts in a variety of fruits, vegetables, and grains, such as onions, asparagus, and bananas. The FOS molecule is too large to be used by the body, so remains in the tunnel to feed our friends. It is a fine, white powder that is half as sweet as sugar. Regularly taking a dose of 4 grams/day (i.e., one teaspoon/day) can help support populations of good bacteria. Some brands of probiotics include FOS as an ingredient; it will be listed on the container's ingredient list.[47]

7. *Normalize pH*. pH is a measure of acid/alkaline balance. Ideally, urine pH should be 7. A pH below 7 indicates the body is more acidic; above 7, more alkaline. Since much of the gunk that yeast produce are acids, they tend to make the body acidic, thus making it harder to restore good gut flora. You can test pH using pH paper available from pharmacies and pool-supply stores. It comes with a key showing different colors and their corresponding pH value. When pH paper is touched with urine, it changes color; the color can be matched to the color key to determine the numerical pH value. Due to the nature of the pH scale, there is a very large difference from one number on the scale to the next, so what might look like a small numerical difference really indicates a larger problem.

And what do you do if urine pH is much below 7 (acidic)? There are a few options. One is to take Alka Seltzer Gold, which can be ordered on the Internet. It is different from regular Alka Seltzer in that it contains only sodium and potassium bicarbonate, no aspirin. It can counteract a body's tendency to be too acidic. Take one–two tablets in water, three–four times a day, on a fairly empty stomach. Other options are to take the juice of one lemon or a tablespoon of apple cider vinegar.[48] The hard part is figuring out how to get these unsavory remedies inside your child.

8. *See a qualified gastroenterologist, if needed*. This specialist can evaluate intestinal factors and recommend treatments depending on the findings.

How do we know if clostridia bacteria is a problem?

Up to 500 different species of bacteria can live in the gut of a healthy person. The vast majority of these are the oxygen-free type, so only about half of them can grow in a laboratory from stool. That is a great disadvantage since some of them are top suspects in many toxic or immune reactions.[49] One such suspect is Clostridia. It represents a whole family of oxygen-free villains that are usually only present in small amounts. When in overgrowth, however, as they sometimes are on the autism spectrum, they can become quite troublesome.[50]

One particularly nasty family member is *Clostridium difficile*. It produces toxins that can actually peel the lining off the inside of the colon and lead to explosive, debilitating diarrhea.[51] Like the rest of its family, this malicious fellow will not grow from stool. However, a stool analysis can still be used to search for the specific toxin it produces. If the toxin is found, we know *Clostridium difficile* is living in the gut. Be aware that this test says nothing about the status of any other strains of Clostridia, only about *Clostridium difficile.*[52]

There is also a way to check for the Clostridia family in general. It involves a compound that Clostridia strains produce, including *Clostridium difficile.* The organic acid test can measure the level of this compound known as HPHPA or DHPPA (depending on the laboratory). It has been found to be much higher in the urine of autistic children than typical children. Those with a high level may exhibit extremely abnormal behavior.[53]

Fighting Clostridia bacteria

If a stool analysis finds a *Clostridia difficile* toxin or an organic acid test finds an unacceptably high level of HPHPA, prescription treatment is recommended. Since Clostridia are resistant to commonly used antibiotics, special high-powered antibiotics are required to kill them. These prescription drugs go by unfamiliar names like Flagyl (generic name is metronidazole), Vancomycin (generic: vancocin), and Gentamycin. Unfortunately, like all prescription antibiotics, these drugs also lay waste to the good bacteria in the gut. Nevertheless, sometimes it pays to wipe the slate clean and start over from scratch. Whenever a high-powered antibiotic is used, a prescription antifungal like Diflucan is used along with it. Otherwise, yeast would happily enjoy overgrowth as all their bacterial foes fall. A die-off reaction can occur as the dying Clostridia release toxins. To avoid the double intensity of combined Clostridia and yeast die-off, the start times of the antibiotic and antifungal are staggered by a few days. Once the gut flora slate has been wiped clean, large doses of probiotics are used to repopulate the gut. Sometimes Clostridia can be a real stinker to treat because it comes back after antibiotic treatment ends. It accomplishes this sly trick through use of reproductive spores that are very hard to destroy. They wait until the coast is clear of antibiotics and then hatch out so they can vie for another chance in the gut. However, with good fortune, heavy use of probiotics, particularly *Lactobacillus acidophilus* GG (brand name: Culturelle®), can fend them off.[54]

CHAPTER RECAP

By this point, you have been hit with a great deal of information about biomedical treatment in the gut. First, Chapter 23 described the common gut problems in autism. Chapters 24 and 25 described avoidance of foods responsible for intensifying autistic behaviors and physical symptoms. Now this chapter has discussed ways to evaluate the flora situation and restore it to health. Restoration included strategies for killing yeast, replenishing good bacteria, improving living conditions for good bacteria, and killing bad bacteria if appropriate. You have covered a lot of ground. Hang in there. You are close to finishing interventions in the gut. There are just a few more odds and ends that will be reviewed in the next chapter.

NOTES

1. Pangborn and Baker 2005, p. 2:12; Seroussi 2002, p. 215; McCandless 2007, p. 28; Shaw 1998, p. 147; Shaw 2004, p. 10.
2. Pangborn and Baker 2005, p. 1:44.
3. Ibid., p. 2:13; Baker 2004, p. 75; Hanaway 2006, p. 49.
4. Shaw 1998, p. 69.
5. Shaw 2004, p. 10.
6. Ibid.
7. McCandless 2007, p. 76.
8. Ibid., p. 74; Shaw 2006, p. 1; Shaw 1998, pp. 69, 141.
9. Pangborn and Baker 2005, p. 1:36; Mumper 2008b, p. 28; Kartzinel 2006, pp. 103–104.
10. McCandless 2007, p. 74; Baker 2004, pp. 68–69.
11. Shaw 2004, p. 10.
12. Baker 2006b, p. 80; Pangborn and Baker 2005, p. 2:12; Baker 2004, pp. 68–69, 71–72.
13. Pangborn and Baker 2007, p. 25.
14. McCandless 2007, pp. 97–98; Shaw 1998, pp. 74–75.
15. Shaw 1998, pp. 71, 73, 140; Pangborn and Baker 2005, pp. 5:50–51; McCandless 2007, pp. 98–99.
16. McCandless 2007, p. 98; Baker 2006b, pp. 71–72; Shaw 1998, pp. 75–76; Baker 2004, pp. 70–71; Pangborn and Baker 2005, pp. 1:23, 2:10.
17. McCandless 2007, pp. 97–98; Shaw 1998, p. 76.
18. Baker 2006b, p. 72.
19. Ibid., pp. 72, 79; Pangborn and Baker 2005, pp. 1:23, 2:10; Baker 2004, p. 70.
20. Baker 2004, p. 70; Baker 2006b, p. 72; Pangborn and Baker 2005, p. 2:10.
21. Pangborn and Baker 2005, pp. 2:12–13; Baker 2006b, pp. 71–72.
22. Shaw 1998, p. 139.
23. Baker 2006b, p. 72; Pangborn and Baker 2005, pp. 2:12–13.
24. Shaw 1998, pp. 104–105, 149; Semon 1998, p. 172; Shaw 2004, p. 10; McCandless 2007, p. 98.
25. McCandless 2007, p. 99; Baker 2006b, pp. 71–74; Pangborn and Baker 2005, pp. 2:8–14.
26. Pangborn and Baker 2005, p. 5:53.
27. James, M. 2006, p. 29.
28. Baker 2006b, pp. 72–73.
29. Ibid., p. 73; Pangborn and Baker 2005, p. 5:53.
30. Baker 2004, pp. 68–69; Pangborn and Baker 2005, p. 1:45.
31. Pangborn and Baker 2005, pp. 2:10, 5:53.
32. Baker 2004, pp. 69–70.
33. Baker 2006b, pp. 73–74; Pangborn and Baker 2005, pp. 2:8, 10–11; McCandless 2007, p. 99; Semon 1998, pp. 154–55, 172; Shaw 1998, pp. 85–90.
34. Shaw 1998, p. 88.
35. Pangborn and Baker 2005, pp. 2:11–13; McCandless 2007, p. 99; Baker 2004, pp. 70–75.

36. Shaw 1998, pp. 25, 82.

37. Ibid., p. 73; Crook 2001, p. 27; Pangborn and Baker 2005, p. 2:13; McCandless 2007, p. 98.

38. Pangborn and Baker 2005, p. 1:7.

39. Ibid., p. 5:52; Furlong and Hanaway 2006, p. 18; Furlong and James 2006, p. 25; M. James 2006, p. 29; McCandless 2007, pp. 93–94, 180–81.

40. McCandless 2007, p. 94; Bock and Stauth 2007, p. 264.

41. Bock and Stauth 2007, p. 264; Hanaway 2006, p. 53; McCandless 2007, pp. 93–95, 181; Pangborn and Baker 2005, pp. 1:45, 5:50–52.

42. Pangborn and Baker 2005, p. 5:51; McCandless 2007, p. 94.

43. McCandless 2007, p. 181; Shaw 1998, p. 72; Pangborn and Baker 2005, pp. 5:52–54.

44. Pangborn and Baker 2005, pp. 5:50–54; M. James 2006, p. 29; McCandless 2007, pp. 93–94, 180–81; Shaw 1998, p. 72; Kartzinel 2006, pp. 99–100; Bock and Stauth 2007, p. 264.

45. Pangborn and Baker 2005, pp. 5:50–51.

46. Baker 2004, pp. 52, 62–63.

47. Hanaway 2006, p. 53; Lewis and Fink 2005, pp. 46, 241, 254; Hidaka, Tashiro, and Eida 1991, pp. 67; Hidaka, Tashiro, and Eida 1987, pp. 427–36; Furlong and James 2006, p. 26.

48. Baker 2004, pp. 64–65; Shaw 1998, pp. 76–78.

49. Pangborn and Baker 2005, p. 2:13; Baker 2004, p. 75; Hanaway 2006, p. 49.

50. McCandless 2007, p. 100.

51. Gershon 2003, p. 149.

52. Shaw 1998, pp. 21, 26.

53. Shaw 2004, pp. 10–11; Baker 2004, p. 75; Mumper 2008a, personal communication.

54. Shaw 2004, pp. 10–11; Sandler *et al.* 2000, pp. 429–35; Pangborn and Baker 2005, pp. 2:13–14, 5:50–51; McCandless 2007, p. 100; Baker 2004, pp. 75–76; Shaw 1998, pp. 21, 24–26, 76, 148.

Chapter 27

Common Gut Interventions: Last But Not Least

WHAT THIS CHAPTER HAS IN STORE

This is the catch-all chapter for gut interventions that did not fall squarely into the earlier chapters about food or gut flora. Yet, these odds and ends are valuable interventions on the autism spectrum. They include digestive enzymes, supplements to heal the leaky gut, and secretin.

DIGESTIVE ENZYME SUPPLEMENTS

A fully functioning pancreas produces numerous types of digestive enzymes. These enzymes break down food into progressively smaller peptides and eventually into amino acids that can nourish the body. The task performed by each enzyme is very specific to a particular component in food. For example, the enzyme lipase acts only on fat, while lactase breaks down only milk sugar (lactose).

Unfortunately, in autism, a person's natural enzymes often fall short of doing a good job. Sometimes the problem is a pancreas that is not producing enough enzymes. In other cases, the problem stems from stomach acid that is too acidic. When such acid accompanies food into the small intestine, it hampers the enzymes working there. Whatever the problem or combination of problems, the effect is the same: enzyme activity is inadequate and digestion suffers. A stool analysis can be used to assess digestive capability in a given individual. The test does not evaluate enzymes directly but instead looks in the stool for any left-over fats, carbohydrates, or fibers of meat and vegetables. When excesses are found, inadequate pancreatic enzymes are a possible explanation.[1]

Fortunately, digestive enzymes can be manufactured into capsules from plant sources. When taken with food, they help break it down, so the body gets more nourishment from what is eaten. In addition, less undigested food is left in the tunnel to feed bad flora. Thus, improved digestion is a twofold victory: nutrition increases and bad flora go hungry. An added bonus is that enzymes can also reduce inflammation since fewer irritating peptides are left hanging around in the gut.[2]

Many enzyme formulations are available that target the special needs of the autism spectrum. The best formulations include a broad array of the enzymes that are known to be weak in children with autism. These include DPP4 (for casein and gluten), lipase (for fat), and lactase (for milk sugar). Also included are maltase, isomaltase, and palatinase for digestion of complex sugars and starch. Other enzymes are supplied as well. Try different formulations to find what works best for a given individual. Some recommended brands include Kirkman EnZym-Complete/DPP-IV™ or DPP-IV II Isogest® Formula, Klaire Labs' Vital-Zymes™ Complete, and a prescription enzyme called Pancrecarb®. Like probiotics, enzymes are usually given continuously.[3]

When determining the dose of enzymes, a person's weight or age is irrelevant. What matters is how much food needs to be digested. A large meal requires more enzymes than a small one. Enzyme bottles offer dosing guidance. Enzymes are given just before or at the beginning of each meal. If needed, capsules can be opened and sprinkled on the food.

It is a good idea to start slowly with enzymes. Begin with a small dose and work up as tolerated by your child. Some children's behaviors worsen temporarily before they show improvement. There might be an increase in irritability, hyperactivity, tantrums, stimming, or other inappropriate behavior or regression. There are a couple of possible explanations for this. For one, bad flora may now be going hungry; they might be causing a die-off reaction as they release extra toxins when they die. But take heart. The reaction does not usually last more than a week, and it confirms that enzymes are of benefit. Another potential explanation for a temporary setback when first taking enzymes is that the opioid effect had been playing a role. When DPP4 was given in the enzymes, the number of undigested opioid peptides was reduced, leading to opioid withdrawal. Withdrawal may last 5–10 days or longer in some cases. Since digestive enzyme supplementation and the GF/CF diet both have potential for a withdrawal reaction, do not start them at the same time. Begin the diet first. Then wait several weeks before bringing enzymes into the picture. In this way, you can avoid the intensity of a double withdrawal reaction.[4]

Though enzymes improve ailing digestion, they do not cure it. For this reason, enzymes are not an adequate substitute for dietary restriction. The benefits from enzymes alone are simply not as good as the results of a special diet. For example, when compared to the GF/CF diet, enzyme supplementation is only about half as effective. For maximum benefit, enzymes are used *in addition* to a restricted diet; the two work together, so that allowed foods get digested more thoroughly, as well as "illegal" foods eaten by accident.[5] Here is what the ARI parent ratings for autism have to say about digestive enzymes:

	Got Worse	No Effect	Got Better	Better: Worse Ratio	No. of Cases
Digestive Enzymes	3 percent	39 percent	58 percent	17:1	1,502

HEALING THE LEAKY GUT

Leaky gut enables the downward spiral to continue spinning out of control. Fortunately, the spinning can be reined in if the gut wall is restored to health with a nice, tight seal. An important first step in this process is removal of foods from the diet that irritate the gut wall. In addition, subduing overgrowths of bad flora is key; the wall cannot heal while under constant physical and toxin attack from yeast and bad bacteria. Certain nutrients can also be used to support health of the gut wall. L-glutamine, for example, is an amino acid that is deficient in many children on the spectrum who have chronic gut problems. When supplemented, L-glutamine is an effective healer of the leaky gut. It improves immunity by nourishing immune cells on the gut wall, and it benefits gut performance in general. Unfortunately, it also feeds yeast so should not be given until bad flora are safely under control. Supplementation is recommended at 1,000–4,000mg/day. Other gut-healing agents include N-acetyl glucosamine and DGL (deglycyrrhizinated licorice) among others. Some brands on the market feature these supplements individually, while others offer a combination. A couple of combination products include GI Repair Nutrients (by Vital Nutrients) and Permeability Factors (by Tyler). There are also supplements that target inflammation. The one mentioned most often is fish oil, which is available in liquid or capsules. Because unacceptably high levels of mercury are found in some fish and fish oils, take care to select a high-quality brand. Brands and dosing are discussed in Appendix C on nutrient supplementation. Gut-healing products can be found in pharmacies, vitamin and health-food stores, and on the Internet. If desired, the leaky gut test (intestinal permeability test) can be used to monitor healing of the gut wall. This test was described in Chapter 24.[6]

SECRETIN: A BREAKTHROUGH FOR THOSE WHO RESPOND TO IT

When special cells in the small intestine detect stomach acid arriving with incoming food, they secrete a hormone called secretin into the bloodstream. The secretin is a message that tells the pancreas to send into the small intestine both alkaline to neutralize the acid and digestive enzymes to break down the food.

Secretin also exists as a prescription drug that can be used during an endoscopy procedure to evaluate the pancreas' production of digestive enzymes. In 1996 when secretin was used in this way on a boy with autism, the secretin evoked profound improvement in the boy's physical and autistic symptoms. Beforehand, the boy was nonverbal, commonly zoned out, and plagued by chronic diarrhea. Within days of the secretin, he spoke for the first time in over two years. His eye contact improved, and he began sleeping through the night. His bowel movements became normal, and his facial tics vanished. It was a shocking event that inspired his mother, Victoria Beck, to reach out to others with autism in a book entitled *Unlocking the Potential of Secretin*. The discovery also sparked scientific research into secretin as a treatment for autism. Research yielded various explanations for why secretin improved the health and behaviors of certain autistic children. Regardless of why it works, secretin was found to be safe for treating autism.

Unfortunately, only a small subset of children have a significant response to secretin. Often these are children with loose stools and little or no language. Also, children aged 3–4 are more likely to respond than older children, with a few noteworthy exceptions. For those who respond to it, secretin has a profound effect on bowel function and autistic behaviors, at least temporarily. Dramatic improvements have been seen in sociability, language, and bowel movements.

Depending on the individual, these improvements fade after weeks or months. Thus, IV injections of secretin need to be repeated, perhaps every five or six weeks, based on the rate of relapse. This repetitive form of treatment is similar in concept to insulin injections used for people with diabetes: a substance the body fails to produce on its own is supplied from the outside as needed. There is also a cream-form of secretin that is absorbed through the skin. It can be used nightly or for a few nights a week.[7] Here is what the ARI parent ratings say about secretin:

	Got Worse	No Effect	Got Better	Better: Worse Ratio	No. of Cases
Intravenous Secretin	7 percent	49 percent	44 percent	6.3:1	468
Transdermal/ Cream Secretin	10 percent	53 percent	37 percent	3.6:1	196

SO WHERE ARE WE?

Our initial discussions of biomedical intervention in autism covered body chemistry and heavy-metal overload. Then the gut chapters described common gut problems and how to combat them through food, repair of gut flora, and a few odds and ends. Congratulations! You have covered a lot of territory. Now you are in the home stretch. Hang in there. You only have a couple of chapters left in this part. The first reviews problems and interventions for the immune system, while the next offers practical tips for doing biomedical intervention.

NOTES

1. Kartzinel 2006, p. 98; Shaw 1998, p. 133; Adams 2007, p. 16; Pangborn 2006b, p. 64.
2. Pangborn 2006b, pp. 62, 64; McCandless 2007, pp. 106–107.
3. McCandless 2007, p. 92; Pangborn and Baker 2005, p. 5:51; Pangborn 2006b, pp. 62–63; Bock and Stauth 2007, p. 266; Kartzinel 2006, p. 98.
4. Kartzinel 2006, p. 98; McCandless 2007, p. 92; Pangborn 2006b, pp. 64–65.
5. Pangborn 2006b, p. 69; McCandless 2007, pp. 43, 92, 106–107.
6. McCandless 2007, p. 179; Kartzinel 2006, p. 34; M. James 2006, p. 29; Seroussi 2002, p. 93.
7. Kartzinel 2006, p. 100; McCandless 2007, pp. 101–105; Jepson and Johnson 2007, p. 255.

Chapter 28

Common Immune System Problems and Interventions

WHAT THIS CHAPTER HAS IN STORE

The health of the immune system plays a key role in treatment of autism-spectrum disorders.[1] This chapter starts by describing a healthy immune system, as well as the weak version of it that is found on the autism spectrum. It also discusses what can cause such weakness and what to do about it.

THE IDEAL IMMUNE SYSTEM

The health of our immune system can make us or break us. Of any disease, AIDS makes the most vivid statement about the crucial nature of the immune system. We need that system to be strong, alert, discriminating, and effective.[2] An ideal immune system:

- identifies all foreign invaders accurately
- destroys invaders efficiently and rapidly
- prevents a second infection from the same invader through a keen memory (immunity)
- never injures its own body (autoimmunity).

EVIDENCE OF WEAK IMMUNE SYSTEMS ON THE AUTISM SPECTRUM

According to several studies, the immune system on the autism spectrum is far from ideal. Depending on the study, immune impairments are found in 30–70 percent of autistic patients.[3] There is a wide variety of impairments, which can include:[4]

- multiple infections, especially ear infections
- other bacterial or viral infections
- yeast overgrowth in the gut
- inhalant allergies
- food sensitivities
- chronic inflammation in the gut and elsewhere.

This is a list of mistakes the immune system is making; these mistakes tell us that something has gone awry in immune performance. At one time, the immune system may have been strong and capable, yet it has since grown weak and confused. In addition, children on the autism spectrum often have family histories of autoimmune disorders, especially in the mother. Examples of such disorders include rheumatoid arthritis, insulin-dependent diabetes (Type I), psoriasis, hypothyroid disease, lupus, and rheumatic fever. Such a family history suggests a genetic predisposition to weakness in immune-system performance. It sets a stage of vulnerability that, under certain environmental conditions, can lead to impaired immune function.[5]

SKEWING OF IMMUNE SYSTEM BALANCE

On one hand, when it comes to fighting off illness, the immune system on the autism spectrum is weak, yet, at the same time, it is hypervigilant and overreactive when faced with harmless substances like pollen or food. Doesn't that seem odd? How can it be both weak in one respect and overpowering in another?

The contradiction makes more sense if you understand that an immune system needs to have balance between two of its forces. Both of these forces work together to fight "dangerous outsiders"; however, each has a different approach. One force, called Th1, wages battle inside cells to protect against infection caused by bacteria, viruses, fungi, and cancer. Th1 is also important for defense against yeast overgrowth in the gut. The other immune system force, Th2, fights foreign invaders by using antibodies as its weapon.[6]

For illustration, say that you are a nation defending yourself against "dangerous outsiders." You face these enemies on two fronts, one on land and one at sea. The ideal distribution of your military force is to split it in half. With half on each front, you have a strong overall defense. This tactic works well until one day, for reasons beyond your control, some of your sea forces switch over to fighting on land. Now your defenses are out of balance. Two results occur. For one, you take a beating at sea where the forces are spread too thin. At the same time, the land forces are *too* strong. With too much time on their hands, these warriors go a step beyond defense. They begin to pillage, loot, and burn.

In a sense, a similar scene is playing out on the autism spectrum. The distribution of immune system forces are split unequally and are out of balance. Many battles are lost by the depleted Th1 forces fighting infection inside cells, resulting in illness, including an increased risk of yeast overgrowth in the gut. At the same time, the excessive Th2 forces who command the antibodies are picking on everybody, even harmless outsiders like pollen and food. An easy way to keep the Th1/Th2 forces straight is to remember that there are "2" many Th"2" forces for the body's own good. With immune balance out of sorts, immune performance becomes faulty or ineffective.[7]

CHARACTERISTICS OF AN OUT-OF-BALANCE IMMUNE SYSTEM

What is the impact of being out of balance? It reminds me of when I was a kid trying to skate on the frozen pond near our house. Timidly, I teetered out on wobbly ankles. My arms stuck straight out, swaying this way and that as I inched forward. What a delightful sight I must have been to my big brother Bernie, who had an evil streak when it came to little sisters. As he whizzed up from behind me on powerful blades, I went stiff with apprehension. With him, there was no telling what scheme was brewing. This time as he sailed by, he seized hold of my arm, and off we zoomed at harrowing speed. I braced as best I could for the inevitable that I knew was coming—the release. Actually, it was more like a launch. If Bernie was feeling "nice," he would merely send me sailing across the open ice. Otherwise, I would be aimed at the shoreline, maybe even a tree. Evergreens were the worst. As the moment of truth arrived, my arm received an extra vigorous fling, and I was catapulted free, hurling wildly into the unknown. Flailing madly, I tried to gain my balance. With a swoop forward and then a swoop back, I sailed out of control across the ice. As the shoreline loomed, I attempted to turn, dipping far to one side and then overcorrecting to the other. It was the ultimate experience of being out of balance, no thanks to Bernie—and it gives me tremendous sympathy for the immune system on the autism spectrum.

This system has been thrown out of kilter and is struggling to regain control. Though there is no single test for Th1/Th2 imbalance, the immune system's plight is still easy to recognize. There are observable signs that something has gone wrong.[8] They include:

1. *Inadequacy*. The immune system's attack on an enemy is ineffective. Thus, it loses many battles and illness results.

2. *Malfunction*. The immune system's attack is faulty in some way. Again, more battles are lost and illness results.

3. *Hypersensitivity*. The immune system's Th2 antibody forces overreact to harmless foreign substances like pollen and food. The result is allergy or sensitivity accompanied by physical or behavioral symptoms of its own.

4. *Inflammation ("bystander" injury)*. When a healthy immune system spots an invader, it launches a quick attack to destroy the invader and then withdraws so there is minimal injury to the surrounding body tissues caught in the crossfire. Think of the swelling, redness, pain, and warmth you feel when a cut gets infected. That is "innocent-bystander" injury to your tissues inflicted by your own immune system, not the invading organism. For an immune system, it is just as critical to know when to shut down an attack as it is to ignite one in the first place. Chronic inflammation can result when the immune system launches an overly vigorous attack, causing excessive bystander injury to the body's own tissues.[9]

5. *Autoimmunity (shoot-yourself-in-the-foot immunity)*. So as not to attract an assault from the immune system, invading organisms often try to disguise themselves as the body's own cells. It is an ingenious tactic. A wolf in sheep's clothing looks a lot like a sheep, right? It can get tricky for the immune system, particularly a weak one, to tell the difference from friend and foe. In a case of mistaken identity, the immune system can turn its gun barrels on innocent sheep: this is called autoimmunity. The body's tissues are being attacked and injured by the body's own immune system. Think of it as shoot-yourself-in-the-foot immunity. Different tissues may be injured in different people.[10]

A CLOSER LOOK AT INFLAMMATION

Inflammation is nearly universal on the autism spectrum.[11] Hardest hit are the gut and the brain. In 2005, researchers at Johns Hopkins University Medical Center performed autopsies on the brains of autistic children who had died in accidents. They found signs of brain inflammation in almost all of the children. The researchers believed the inflammation probably played a role in the children's autistic symptoms. Other studies have also found evidence of brain inflammation. Such inflammation and immune-system activity are similar to those found in other chronic brain conditions like Alzheimer's, Parkinson's, ALS (Lou Gehrig's disease), and HIV-related dementia.[12]

Widespread inflammation appears to be a common thread in many disorders. Examples besides the autism spectrum include eczema, hay fever, and food allergies. Inflammation also plays a significant role in bad gut flora, impaired immune function, and asthma. Through messengers of the immune system called cytokines, inflammation can spread from one part of the body to another. You see, cytokines regulate the intensity and duration of an immune response. Like errand boys, they carry messages between immune cells, as well as other systems of the body, especially the nervous system.[13] Some types of cytokine messengers spread news of alarm that incites inflammation. Others come by later to broadcast that the emergency is over so that inflammation can subside and unnecessary injury to tissues can be minimized. In autism, research shows that the levels of alarmist cytokines are abnormally high, while the levels of calming cytokines are abnormally low. So, say that one part of the body has inflammation, perhaps due to pollen inflaming the airway or a certain food inflaming the gut wall. The inflamed cells send out large numbers of alarmist cytokine messengers that travel throughout the body shouting alarm. Without a normal level of calming cytokines to regulate the immune response, inflammation can be triggered in distant areas such as the joints, the lining of the airways, the lining of the gut, and even the brain. In turn, each of these areas deploys its own inflammatory messengers, creating further inflammation. In fact, the findings of the Johns Hopkins brain-inflammation study suggest that the source of inflammation and immune activity in the brain is not located in the brain itself but comes from elsewhere as a result of circulating cytokines. The good news is that healing inflammation in one area can help resolve inflammation someplace else. For example, inhalant allergies in some people can be overcome by resolving root-cause inflammation that existed in their digestive tracts.[14]

IMMUNE-SYSTEM TESTING

Over the years, immune-system testing in hundreds of autism-spectrum children has revealed a wide variety of impairments, including a tendency toward production of antibodies that attack the body's own tissues (autoimmunity). Though having a general immune-system profile for autism is helpful, the test information didn't necessarily lead to specific treatment recommendations for the individuals tested. So, today, rather than testing each child, we treat based on the general profile. It works about as well as an individual portrait.[15] However, for some individuals immune-system testing is appropriate.

According to immunologist Jane El-Dahr, MD, of Defeat Autism Now!, an autism-spectrum child with recurrent infections should receive an immune evaluation by an immunologist. Those with eczema, chronic nasal symptoms, asthma, significant gut symptoms, or recurrent respiratory infections should receive an allergy evaluation for IgE inhalant and food allergies.[16] Now let's turn our attention to those factors that can weaken the immune system.

WHAT CAN WEAKEN THE IMMUNE SYSTEM?

The immune system has many foes that can sap its strength in various ways. For some individuals, a single, isolated foe is able to cause injury. For others, the collective action of several foes ganging up at once is what takes the toll on the immune system.[17] Thus, the timing of insults can be a deciding factor in how the immune system fares.[18] Keep in mind that 60–70 percent of the immune cells of the entire body are centered in the gut.[19] With the immune system and the gut so intimately entwined, trouble in one spells trouble for the other; they are inseparable.[20] Foes capable of weakening the immune system include:

- heavy metals and toxins (including mercury and other heavy metals in vaccines)
- antibiotic overuse
- childhood vaccines
- viruses
- bacteria
- fungi (including yeast overgrowth in the gut)
- nutritional deficiencies (this is particularly a hazard for picky eaters or those with digestion or absorption problems)[21]
- artificial substances in foods[22]
- foods to which the body is sensitive or allergic[23]
- pollen, mold, dust, and other foreign substances with allergy potential
- emotional stress (this depresses the immune system)[24]
- ultraclean environments.

Most of these have already been discussed in earlier chapters. But let's take a closer look at a few of them: antibiotic overuse, ultraclean environments, viruses, and childhood vaccines.

Antibiotic overuse can lead to inhalant allergies

Overuse of antibiotics, especially during infancy, contributes to skewing of the immune system toward the top-heavy, antibody side, Th2. By killing good bacteria in the gut, antibiotics can lead to yeast overgrowth. Not only do yeast produce toxins that can burden the immune system, they can also kick off the downward spiral of expanding woes in the gut and beyond—the topic of Chapter 23 (Common Gut Problems in Autism). In addition to the information presented in that chapter, the downward spiral can also contribute to *inhalant* allergies and sensitivity. This process has been shown in tests on mice, who became significantly more allergic to inhaled mold after taking antibiotics.[25]

Ultraclean environments

The human immune system evolved over millions of years combating foes in the environment. Germs that did not kill us made us more resistant and less prone to chronic problems later in life. Perhaps the immune system, like a muscle, gets a little stronger when it gets some exercise—and a little flabbier when it doesn't. Along that line of thinking, there is a hygiene hypothesis. It proposes that people who live in less clean, less hygienic environments are better able to develop balanced immunity with more resistance and are less likely to be sensitive to foreign substances like dust, mold, and animal hair.[26] Ultraclean environments, on the other hand, minimize opportunities for our immune systems to develop natural resistance as our ancestors did.

Take, for instance, the very unscientific survey of two sisters—Laura and me. As a kid, Laura always loved getting dirty. She seemed to revel in it, much to my mother's repeated displeasure. Take Laura any place and she could find a dirt pile or mud puddle in five minutes flat. I'd bet money on it. But perhaps my sister, besides being a human divining rod for dirt, was also a scientist testing the hygiene hypothesis. As far as allergies go, she has none—zip, zero, zilch. Clean little Miss Priss I, on the other hand, was the one always toting a Kleenex box and getting allergy shots. Perhaps the immune system appreciates a little exercise to make it strong and discriminating.

Viruses on the autism spectrum

Viruses are a significant problem for some children on the autism spectrum, yet not for others. For those with viral issues, antiviral treatments can bring about major improvements in autistic symptoms.[27] So be on the lookout for symptoms that clue you in to a problem with viruses. Symptoms include easy fatigue, warts, cold sores, visual issues like squinting, chronic gut problems, or regression after the MMR vaccine.[28] In addition, some children have high virus titers, especially for measles ("titers" are a measure of immunity to a disease).[29]

The MMR vaccine

When virus organisms are used in vaccines, they are either "dead" or "live". Both types provoke a response from the immune system that results in protection against the disease (immunity). However, live-virus vaccines produce stronger protection. Though their virus organisms have been weakened so should not be able to cause disease, live-virus vaccines are not considered as safe as dead-virus vaccines for people who are pregnant or have weak immune systems. Dead viruses are safer because they cannot reproduce and are thus incapable of causing disease.[30]

The MMR vaccine is three live viruses (measles, mumps, and rubella) rolled into one injection. It was added to the mandatory pediatric vaccine schedule in 1979. Before that time, each virus had its own separate vaccine. According to the Center for Disease Control (CDC), children should receive the MMR at 12–15 months of age and again at 4–6 years of age. In case you are wondering, the MMR does not contain the mercury-preservative, Thimerosal. It couldn't because the mercury would kill the live viruses.[31]

A pediatric gastroenterologist in England, Andrew Wakefield, MD, published a study in 1998 which has embroiled him in controversy ever since. He found measles virus in biopsies taken from the inflamed intestines of children with regressive autism. These children who had chronic diarrhea and abdominal pain had no known exposure to measles except through the MMR vaccine. The majority of them had become ill within 14 days after receiving this vaccine. Based on viral DNA comparisons, Dr. Wakefield believed the smoldering measles infections he found in these children was a unique disease process resulting from the MMR's live virus.[32]

Since Dr. Wakefield's initial study, numerous laboratory and clinical studies have emerged that support his findings. Vaccine-strain measles virus has been found in bowel tissue, blood, and cerebral spinal fluid. There is also research evidence that an inappropriate immune response to the MMR may trigger production of antibodies that attack brain tissue. These various studies suggest that vaccine-strain measles virus may have played a role in a subgroup of children with regressive autism and gut symptoms.[33]

The results of most population studies, however, have refuted a causal relationship between the MMR and autism. Many objections have been raised to these studies including bias, incomplete reporting of autism cases, and flaws in methodology. Since the MMR-autism debate has been a fiery one, it is worth taking a closer look at the population studies which encompass English, Danish, Japanese, and U.S. data.

ENGLISH DATA

Consider a 1999 published study by Taylor *et al.* that absolved the MMR of playing a role in autism. The study's authors wrote, "We hope that our results will reassure parents…and that they will help restore confidence in the MMR vaccine." Some have pointed out that these do not sound like the words of objective-minded scientists, especially considering that several of the authors were members of the UK's Public Health Department. In the study the research-ers had considered a possible MMR-autism connection from three angles. From the first angle, they found a clustering of parent concern about their child's development at a time that was six months after the MMR. However, the researchers decided to dismiss this finding, saying that its dependence on parent recall made the finding unreliable. A second finding was that the age of an autism diagnosis was no different between children who got their MMR before 18 months of age and those who got it after that age. And lastly the research team found that autism had begun its exponential rise a couple of years before the MMR was introduced in England in 1988. There was no sudden step-up after its introduction.[34] A study by Stott *et al.*, however, disagreed. These researchers pointed out that a significant number of children born before 1988 received the MMR in a "catch-up program." Taking this into account, their reanalysis of the data showed a clear relationship between the MMR's introduc-tion and a rising rate of autism.[35] The Taylor study has also been criticized for being an after-the-fact review of patient charts which made it dependent on the accuracy and completeness of record keeping. Indeed, only 41 percent of the cases identified in the study could be confirmed according to ICD-10 criteria. The study was also criticized for including many children who were too young to receive a diagnosis.[36]

DANISH DATA

A 2002 population study by Madsen *et al.* was the first to encompass data of an entire national population (Denmark—which introduced the MMR in 1987). The study compared children who had received the MMR to those who had not. The researchers found that, although a continual rise in autism rates appeared in the 1990s, there was no difference between the vaccinated and unvaccinated groups. Nor was there clustering of cases at any time after the MMR.[37] Critics of the study point out that three members of the research team were employees of the largest vaccine maker in Denmark. In addition, others who analyzed the Danish data came to different conclusions:

- Lauritsen *et al.* published an analysis that found a sudden increase in autism rates beginning in 1990 after the MMR was introduced.[38]

- Goldman and Yazbak reported a clear increase in autism rates after 1995. Concern was also raised that a large portion of Madsen *et al.*'s study population was too young to be diagnosed and many of these were even too young to get the MMR. The Madsen team had said this was accounted for with an "age-adjustment" factor, but the trustworthiness of their conclusion is entirely dependent on the accuracy of this factor. Without use of the factor, there is a statistically significant 45 percent increase in the risk of autism linked to the MMR.[39]

- Stott *et al.* published an analysis that looked at autism rates by date of birth rather than age of diagnosis. They found that annual growth in autism rates was relatively steady (-0.5%) in the years before introduction of the MMR. However, after that time, there was a sharp increase (14.8%) through the end of the study period in 1992.[40]

Many other studies of Denmark's data have investigated the MMR-autism issue from various angles. None have identified a link. At the same time, these studies have been widely criticized for bias, incomplete reporting of autism cases, and flaws in methodology.[41]

JAPANESE DATA

Japan's data is interesting because Japan is the only developed nation to introduce the MMR (1989) and later withdraw it (1993). The withdrawal was due to concern over meningitis cases linked to the *mumps* portion of the vaccine. While the MMR was used in Japan, vaccination rates dropped rapidly until the vaccine's withdrawal. Then the MMR was replaced by three separate vaccines given four weeks apart. A study published by Honda *et al.* concluded that the MMR could not cause autism since autism rates rose after the MMR's withdrawal.[42] However, Dr. Wakefield refutes this conclusion. He contends that the MMR is the near-biological equivalent of the three individual vaccines when spaced only four weeks apart. This idea is supported by studies that suggest exposure to viruses within several months or even up to a year during critical stages of development might still be close enough to cause a harmful combined reaction.[43] If this is the case, autism cases in Japan decreased due to declining rates of MMR usage but resurged as its biological equivalent gained popularity.[44]

U.S. DATA

○ A study by Geier and Geier on the VAERS vaccine data compared serious neurological events (including autism) that occurred within 30 days of the MMR versus the DTP vaccine. The DTP is an interesting comparison point since it was replaced by the DTaP vaccine due to its high risk of causing neurological events. Though the Geier team found immediate neurological events to be quite low, the events were significantly more frequent with MMR than DTP.[45] This study has been criticized for several reasons, the biggest of which is the unreliability of the VAERS data.[46] In addition, the study did not consider vaccine reactions beyond 30 days.[47]

○ A 2006 study by Richler *et al.* investigated whether a subgroup of autistic children with gut symptoms regressed at a time linked to the MMR. They compared autistic children who had regressed (i.e., lost developmental skills) to autistic children who had not regressed. Interestingly, they found that those who regressed:

  ○ had significantly more gut problems

  ○ showed abnormal signs of development before regressing

  ○ received their MMR at a younger age (14.3 months vs. 17.7 months)

  ○ developed autistic symptoms at a later age (19 months vs. 14.5 months)

  ○ had lower verbal IQ scores and more severe social problems.

The researchers did not find a significantly shorter time period between the MMR and the start of autistic symptoms.[48] They concluded that the MMR does not cause autism, though some say that conclusion is not clear from the data. Assuming the data are accurate, it more likely builds a case that autistic symptoms are not *immediate* after the MMR. Even if that is so, a question remains about delayed regression since we know that measles virus can be very destructive to the brain even years after the initial infection—eight years on average for subacute sclerosing panencephalitis (SSPE).[49]

THE MMR AND DEFEAT AUTISM NOW!

So can the measles virus in the MMR contribute to autistic symptoms in a vulnerable subgroup of autistic children? Many physicians of Defeat Autism Now! believe that Thimerosal-containing vaccines weakened the immune systems of susceptible children. As a result, when these children were later exposed to the concerned that the rising epidemics of autism-spectrum disorders, as well as allergies and asthma, are, in part, due to the increase in childhood vaccines. In addition, the timing and combining of vaccines is questioned. Are we injecting babies with disease-causing substances before their immune systems are mature enough to cope effectively? Is it really a good idea to give multiple, simultaneous vaccines? This practice launches several attacks against the immune system at the same time.[60]

WHAT SHOULD A PARENT DO?

Decisions regarding your child's vaccinations are very important. Even though there is a mandatory vaccine schedule, you do have choices. Stephanie Cave, MD, is a key resource within Defeat Autism Now! for information about children's vaccines. Dr. Cave treats over 2,000 autism-spectrum children in her Louisiana medical practice. She and Deborah Mitchell wrote a book in 2001 titled *What Your Doctor May Not Tell You About Children's Vaccinations*. I have a dog-eared, highlighted copy that I reach for whenever a vaccine issue arises regarding one of my children. The book answers many questions relating to a wide range of vaccine topics, including vaccine testing and vaccine ingredients such as Thimerosal, aluminum, and formaldehyde. The book contains excellent information about many specific vaccines and the diseases they are designed to prevent. Each disease is discussed, including how it is contracted, what its symptoms and treatment are, and who is most at risk. Each vaccine is described, including its level of effectiveness and potential side effects. Certain groups of people are identified who, for various health reasons, should not get a particular vaccine. Dr. Cave also gives practical recommendations for specific safety precautions regarding the timing and combining of vaccines and other relevant issues. In addition, the book discusses the CDC's plans for many future vaccines against several sexually transmitted diseases, respiratory syncytial virus (RSV), and dozens of other diseases.[61] Many of these new vaccines are being recommended for babies and children, 11–12 years of age typically. The book closes by discussing parents' rights and ways to request exemptions from vaccines if desired. In addition to her book, Dr. Cave regularly presents vaccine updates at Defeat Autism Now! conferences. Her most recent presentations, complete with audio and video, can be viewed on the Internet for free (www.autism.com).

BACK TO OUR STORY: WILL'S SIBLINGS

Something was eating at me. I had learned a great deal about heavy metals, vaccines, allergies, and the immune system in my quest to help Will. Now that

MMR, their immune systems could not stop the live measles virus from creating a low-grade infection. This infection contributed to autoimmunity (the body attacking itself), as well as inflammation, leaky gut, and other consequences of the downward spiral.[50] Many doctors of Defeat Autism Now! recommend using a separate vaccine for each component of the MMR and spacing them many months apart so the immune system is spared the simultaneous assault of three live viruses.[51]

Childhood vaccines

There was a time when parents lived with the realistic threat that some horrible, contagious disease like diphtheria or whooping cough (pertussis) could kill their babies and young children. The menace of a crippling disease like polio also loomed, keeping even President Franklin Delano Roosevelt bound to a wheelchair. Today, parents do not live in fear of these diseases. In fact, most of us don't even know what diphtheria is, though it killed 13,000 people a year in the early 1920s.[52] Today, we tend to forget what a truly significant achievement vaccines are. They enable us to expose the immune system to deadly or crippling germs in a safe, controlled situation. In response, a healthy immune system produces specially designed antibodies to fight those germs. Later, if the germs are encountered in real life, the body is prepared to stop them in their tracks—that's immunity. To determine a person's level of immunity, we can measure the level of antibodies in the blood for a specific disease. If its level or "titer" is high enough, we have immunity.[53]

But is immunity the *only* effect vaccines have on us? In truth, there is much that scientists don't know about how vaccines work in the cells and molecules of the body.[54] What research is now finding is that childhood vaccines can promote allergy and asthma. In a study conducted in England, vaccinated children were 14 times more likely to have asthma. They were 9.4 times more likely to have eczema, an allergic skin condition. Another study compared children who had been vaccinated for measles to those who had actually contracted measles and fought it off. Those who contracted measles had about 50 percent less allergic hypersensitivity such as food and inhalant allergies. Thus, many researchers have begun to consider vaccines a contributing factor to allergy.

Think about how the immune system naturally fights germs, say a virus, for instance. When the infecting virus gets inside the body's cells, the immune system's Th1 forces who fight inside cells lead an attack. However, when a child is vaccinated against a virus, his immune system may never launch a vigorous Th1 attack. As a result, the child's Th2 antibody forces may overdevelop, thus skewing the immune system. In this way, the artificial means used by vaccines to manipulate immunity can have the side effect of increased susceptibility to allergic disorders.[55]

It makes you wonder about the all-time high we are witnessing in the U.S. for childhood autoimmune disorders. They include juvenile rheumatoid arthritis, juvenile diabetes, pediatric asthma, pediatric Crohn's disease, and Guillain-Barré syndrome (progressive muscle weakness). In fact, in the U.S. and many other industrialized nations, autoimmune disorders have become the third leading cause of illness behind cancer and heart disease. Such observations bring vaccine-testing practices into question. Typically, study participants are observed only for hours or several days, only occasionally for a few weeks or longer. That is sufficient time to know if a vaccine causes injection-site swelling or fever, but not autoimmune responses, which can take months or even years to surface.[56]

A 2007 survey casts heavy suspicion on a relationship between childhood vaccines and both neurological disorders and asthma. In the hope of urging the CDC to conduct a full-scale study, a nonprofit group, Generation Rescue, sponsored a survey comparing vaccinated and unvaccinated children. The survey carefully mimicked the format of those performed by the CDC when assessing the nation's rates of neurological disorders like autism and ADHD. This survey of nearly 12,000 households in California and Oregon collected information from parents on 17,000 children from ages 4 to 7. Nearly 1,000 of these children were completely unvaccinated. The survey found that vaccinated boys were 155 percent more likely to have a neurological disorder than were unvaccinated boys. They were 224 percent more likely to have ADHD, and 61 percent more likely to have autism. Among girls, no association was found between vaccination and neurological disorders. A larger-scale study that included more girls may possibly have a different result. Nevertheless, vaccinated boys and girls were 120 percent more likely to have asthma than their unvaccinated counterparts.[57]

This survey underscores the importance of more research. It also raises an important question: are we overvaccinating our children? Think back to what you were doing in 1983. In that year, the only mandatory vaccines that U.S. children received were the polio vaccine, MMR (measles, mumps, rubella), and DTP (diphtheria, tetanus, and pertussis/whooping cough). The CDC schedule for these three vaccines required a total of ten injections by age 6. This situation contrasts sharply to the 2008 mandatory schedule of 36 injections of numerous vaccines. Table 28.1 shows a comparison of the 1983 and 2008 vaccine schedules. Our bodies of ancient design have never been confronted with such a wide variety of serious diseases at such young ages before. Many people are

Table 28.1 CDC mandatory vaccine schedule comparison [58, 59]

1983 Vaccine	Recommended age (in months)	2008 Vaccine	Recommended age (in months)
DTP	2	Influenza	Prenatal
OPV	2	Hep B	Birth
DTP	4	Hep B	1
OPV	4	DTaP	2
DTP	6	Hib	2
MMR	15	IPV	2
DTP	18	PCV	2
OPV	18	Rotavirus	2
DTP	48	Hep B	4
OPV	48	DTaP	4
		Hib	4
		IPV	4
		PCV	4
		Rotavirus	4
		Hep B	6
		DTaP	6
		Hib	6
		IPV	6
		PCV	6
		Influenza	6
		Rotavirus	6
		Hib	12
		MMR	12
		Varicella	12
		PCV	12
		Hep A	12
		DTaP	15
		Hep A	18
		Influenza	18
		Influenza	30
		Influenza	42
		MMR	48
		DTaP	48
		IPV	48
		Varicella	48
		Influenza	54

Total: 10 injections   **Total: 36 injections**

knowledge was making me wonder about my other sons, Allan and Lucas. They had drawn their genes from the same gene pool Will had. Each, in turn, had received the same mandatory vaccine schedule—Allan starting in 1991, Will in 1993, and Lucas in 1996. These were all years when U.S. children received a peak of mercury exposure through vaccines (1991 to roughly 2001). As babies and young children, all three boys received plenty of antibiotics for various infections, particularly ear infections. Yet only Will slipped onto the autism spectrum. Had Allan and Lucas gotten off scot-free as it appeared? Having learned that mercury is toxic to the immune system, I worried about Allan's and Lucas' histories of early childhood infections and their inhalant allergies of today. Should I discount their allergies since I had some myself?

Lucas' medical history especially bothered me. He was the only one of the three who had so many ear infections that tubes were implanted in his ears. Tubes were supposed to be the cure-all for ear infections, but, for Lucas, they were not. So, his pediatrician drew blood for an immune system test. It turned out Lucas' antibodies were low and his immune system was weak. That diagnosis explained the continuing ear infections, but no course of treatment was recommended. With a wrinkled brow, I crossed my fingers and hoped the infections would stop. Fortunately, they did.

But, now, many years later, they were nagging at me again. For some peace of mind, I emailed the Laboratoire Philippe Auguste in France (www.labbio.net) for a urinary porphyrins test kit. I was sure I would feel better if I just got Lucas tested for heavy metals; then I could put my nagging concerns to rest. So much for that idea. It backfired miserably. Lucas' indicator for pesticides and toxic chemicals was above the normal range, as was his level of mercury. The comment line at the bottom of the report read "mild mercury toxic effect." I felt sick. This was *not* making me feel better.

I couldn't help ordering another test, this time for Allan. I had to know what the test would say about him, too. Though Allan's mercury result was not out of range, it was at the extreme high end of the range. His comment line read the same as Lucas': "mild mercury toxic effect." I had found out the answer to my question, though I was definitely not happy about it. For whatever reasons, Allan and Lucas had fared better than Will, but they did not get off scot-free. Some level of accumulated mercury was present, even after all these years.

A BOOK LINKING AUTISM-SPECTRUM DISORDERS TO ALLERGIES AND ASTHMA

For me, it was the perfect time for release of a 2007 book about biomedical intervention called *Healing the New Childhood Epidemics: Autism, ADHD, Asthma, and Allergies.* It was the first book I had seen that linked the autism spectrum to allergies and asthma. The book was written by Kenneth Bock, MD, and Cameron Stauth. Dr. Bock is highly experienced in treating children using the Defeat Autism Now! approach. In fact, he is a frequent speaker at their conferences. His book begins by discussing the epidemic increases over the past 20 years in the "4-A" conditions, as he calls them. According to him, autism has skyrocketed a dramatic 1,500–6,000 percent (1 in 150–166 births); ADHD has increased by 400 percent; asthma by 300 percent; and allergies by 400 percent. Combined, these conditions affect 20 million children, which is nearly one-third of the total population of U.S. children. Moreover, peanut allergy, one of the most common life-threatening food allergies, has more than doubled since 1997. Two hundred people, many of them children, now die from food allergies each year.[62] Dr. Bock's book goes on to identify four fundamental changes in the environment of U.S. children that he believes have spawned the 4-A epidemics:[63]

○ a widespread increase in environmental toxins in food, water, and air in the past 20 years

○ inadequate dietary intake of nutrients that help the body remove toxins

○ the doubling in the number of childhood vaccines since 1991

○ reduced ability of children's body chemistry to detoxify their bodies.

The book's greatest offering is a healing program that targets all of the 4-As. It includes dietary change, nutritional supplements, detoxification, and medication as appropriate.

INTERVENTIONS TO IMPROVE THE HEALTH OF THE IMMUNE SYSTEM

So far, this chapter has discussed the poor health of the immune system on the autism spectrum, as well as some of the contributors to its decline. But what can we do about it? That is what we really want to know.

For some sound advice, let's turn to pediatric immunologist and international speaker Jane El-Dahr, MD. At the spring 2007 Defeat Autism Now! conference, Dr. El-Dahr asserted that the most important way to restore immune-system health is by doing all the other interventions in the biomedical approach because these interventions heal the immune system as well.[64] Some soothe the harassed immune system by avoiding substances that agitate it. Others, like certain nutrients, support it directly. Still other interventions help by confronting the immune system's enemies. They all work together to give the immune system a boost. The interventions include:

1. *Making dietary changes* (discussed in Chapters 24 and 25 of this book). Changes in diet can aid the immune system in several ways. The elimination of antagonistic foods pacifies the immune system. A low sugar diet starves yeast, which reduces yeast toxins that weaken the immune system.[65] And a rotation diet that regulates how often a food group is eaten can prevent arousal of the immune system.

2. *Healing the gut* (discussed in Chapters 26 and 27). Remember that 60–70 percent of the body's immune cells are in the gut. Since the gut plays a huge role in regulating the entire immune system, when we help the gut, we help the immune system.[66] Consider probiotics, for instance. Numerous studies have shown that, as they restore the gut, they also improve immune function in that area.[67] In addition, probiotics support the weak Th1 forces that fight inside cells and can help rebalance the skewed immune system.[68]

3. *Improving nutritional status* (discussed in Appendix C). Many nutritional supplements have already been mentioned. Some that are particularly important to the immune system are vitamins A, C, and D, glutathione (UltraGuy), methyl-B12, omega-3 fatty acids, and zinc.[69]

4. *Assisting body chemistry* (discussed in Chapter 18).

5. *Removing accumulated heavy metals and toxins* (discussed in Chapter 19).

6. *Minimizing exposures to heavy metals and toxins* (discussed in Chapters 20–22).

7. *Fighting the immune system's enemies* (viruses, yeast, bad bacteria, and parasites such as tapeworms or pinworms). If these foes are causing trouble, the immune system really appreciates an ally to help fight them. It may be appropriate to use antifungal, antiviral, antibiotic, or antiparasite medications. Antifungals and antibiotics were discussed in Chapter 26. Antivirals will be discussed later in this chapter.[70]

A SPECIAL LOOK AT TREATING INFLAMMATION

When treating inflammation, it is important to recognize and address each factor that may be contributing to it, such as:

o   *Food.* Food can be a major instigator of inflammation, especially if the diet is high in saturated fat and low in essential fatty acids.

o   *Infection.* Infection is a common cause of inflammation. Many on the autism spectrum have persistent inflammation especially in the gut.

o   *Childhood vaccines.* Vaccines can spark inflammation if they add to heavy-metal overload or cause low-grade infection such as that hypothesized in relation to the MMR vaccine.

o   *Stress.*

When targeting inflammation, eliminate as many of the sources of inflammation as possible. In addition, nutrients are some of the best anti-inflammatories. They include essential fatty acids, zinc, vitamin E, vitamin A, quercetin, pycnogenol, curcumin, and transfer factor.[71]

A SPECIAL LOOK AT TREATING VIRUSES

There is much that medicine does not know about viruses in general. Even less is known about their role in a complex disorder like autism. Despite this, interventions exist that can make a big difference for the subgroup of autism-spectrum children who struggle with viruses. Lifestyle factors are very important since susceptibility to viral infection increases with fatigue, a poor diet, a high-sugar diet, prolonged emotional or physical stress, and social isolation. Address matters of lifestyle as much as possible. Natural antiviral supplements can also be helpful. They include Lauricidin®, olive leaf extract, elderberry, and glutathione (UltraGuy), among others. Rotating through different ones as you use up each bottle can be helpful. Prescription antiviral drugs are also available; they include acyclovir, valacyclovir (brand name: Valtrex®), and famvir.

Here is what the ARI parent ratings for autism say about Valtrex®:

	Got Worse	No Effect	Got Better	Better: Worse Ratio	No. of Cases
Valtrex®	6 percent	42 percent	52 percent	8.5:1	65

In regard to the presence of measles in the gut lining that was first documented by Andrew Wakefield, MD, there is no specific treatment. Rather, the usual course of supportive biomedical interventions is followed, including anti-inflammatories and high-dose vitamin A (up to 25,000iu/day). High-dose vitamin A has been shown to help defend against acute measles infection. Its use requires the guidance of a qualified doctor for diagnosis, lab testing, and proper administration since vitamin A can be toxic at high doses.[72]

DIRECTLY TARGETING THE IMMUNE SYSTEM: IVIG

In addition to the biomedical interventions already mentioned, IVIG can be used to target the immune system directly.[73] Think of it as person-to-person antibody transfer. Antibodies (or immunoglobulins) produced by the immune system are extracted from the blood of human donors. Once processed, they can be given to another person through an IV. Use of IVIG, an expensive treatment, began in 1952 as a treatment for people with weak immune systems. It has had some success in autism. A 1999 study found IVIG benefited 4 of 10 autistic children, one markedly. In 2005, a study of 26 autistic children receiving IVIG every four weeks for six months found significant improvement in speech, hyperactivity, social interaction, and stimming. Unfortunately, 22 of the 26 children regressed within four months of discontinuing IVIG.[74]

Here is what the ARI parent ratings for autism have to say about IVIG:

	Got Worse	No Effect	Got Better	Better: Worse Ratio	No. of Cases
IVIG	10 percent	44 percent	46 percent	4.5:1	79

AN EYE ON THE FUTURE

If you would like to learn more about immune-system problems, testing, and treatment, turn to Chapter 8 of *Children with Starving Brains* by Jaquelyn McCandless, MD. Defeat Autism Now! conferences and publications offer more information as well. But even when you know everything there is to know, you will conclude that it is not enough. We could help our children more than we can today if we understood the immune system better and how it is impacted by environmental factors like vaccines, antibiotics, and other influences. We need knowledge that can only be uncovered by more research—research that is appropriate to our needs and unbiased by politics or industry. High on our agenda should be to motivate our government who mandates our vaccines to mobilize its energies and effectively manage its resources to get to the bottom of many vaccine issues. The ingenuity and know-how to help us are available. What we need is open-minded, capable leadership that acts in the best interests of our nation's children above everything else. Similarly, we need thoughtful investigation and appropriate regulation of the use of heavy metals, toxins, and food ingredients. Through discoveries of how environmental factors influence our children's developing bodies, we will be able to prevent and reverse many cases of autism-spectrum disorders.

NOTES

1. McCandless 2007, p. 188.
2. El-Dahr 2007b, p. 256.
3. El-Dahr 2006a, pp. 153–54.
4. Pangborn and Baker 2005, pp. 1:46–47; Adams 2007, p. 26; El-Dahr 2007b, p. 256; McCandless 2007, pp. 31–32, 41, 82–83; Jepson and Johnson 2007, p. 58.
5. McCandless 2007, pp. 17, 166; Cave with Mitchell 2001, p. 82; Usman 2006, p. 59; El-Dahr 2006a, p. 154; McCandless 2006b, p. 159; Comi *et al.* 1999, pp. 388–94; Sweeten *et al.* 2003, p. e420; Croen *et al.* 2005, pp. 151–57.
6. Bock and Stauth 2007, pp. 129, 168; Mumper 2007, p. 217; Kirby 2005, p. 67; Chinitz and Baker 2007, p. 45.
7. Kirby 2005, p. 67; Mumper 2007, p. 217; Bock and Stauth 2007, p. 168.
8. Pangborn and Baker 2005, p. 2:59; El-Dahr 2007b, p. 256.
9. Jepson and Johnson 2007, p. 56.
10. Pangborn and Baker 2005, pp. 2:37–38; Jepson and Johnson 2007, p. 57.
11. Chinitz and Baker 2007, p. 98.
12. Bock and Stauth 2007, p. 182; Jepson and Johnson 2007, pp. 58–59; Vargas *et al.* 2005, pp. 67–81; Zimmerman *et al.* 2005, pp. 195–201; Pardo, Vargas, and Zimmerman 2005, pp. 485–95.
13. El-Dahr 2006b, p. 156.
14. Bock and Stauth 2007, pp. 181–83; Jepson and Johnson 2007, pp. 51, 57–59, 95, 183.
15. Pangborn and Baker 2005, pp. 1:46–47.
16. Ibid., pp. 2:56–60, 4:18–19; El-Dahr 2007b, p. 257; Shaw 1998, p. 11.
17. Bock and Stauth 2007, p. 177.
18. McCandless 2007, p. 166.
19. Hanaway 2006, p. 51; Baker 2004, p. 96; McCandless 2007, p. 83.
20. McCandless 2007, pp. 83, 177.
21. Bock and Stauth 2007, p. 177.
22. Ibid., p. 179.
23. Ibid.; McCandless 2007, p. 177.
24. Bock and Stauth 2007, p. 180.
25. Ibid.; McCandless 2007, pp. 27–28.
26. Bock and Stauth 2007, pp. 180–81; Cave with Mitchell 2001, pp. 88–89.
27. McCandless 2007, pp. 26–27, 172–75.
28. Usman 2006, p. 63; Usman 2007, p. 143.
29. Levinson 2006a, p. 68; McCandless 2007, p. 32; Jepson and Johnson 2007, p. 85.
30. Cave with Mitchell 2001, p. 9.
31. Center for Disease Control and Prevention 2008b; Cave with Mitchell 2001, pp. 9, 15, 70, 208.
32. Wakefield *et al.* 1998, pp. 637–41; Jepson and Johnson 2007, pp. 65–66.
33. Jepson and Johnson 2007, pp. 82–86.
34. Taylor *et al.* 1999, pp. 2026–9.
35. Stott, Blaxill, and Wakefield 2004, pp. 89–91.
36. Jepson and Johnson 2007, pp. 67–70; Madsen *et al.* 2002, pp. 1477–82; Wakefield 1999, pp. 949–50; Altmann 2000, pp. 409–10.
37. Madsen *et al.* 2002, pp. 1477–82.
38. Lauritsen, Pedersen, and Mortensen 2004, pp. 1339–46.
39. Goldman and Yazbak 2004, pp. 70–5.
40. Stott *et al.* 2004, pp. 89–91.

41. Jepson and Johnson 2007, pp. 70–4.
42. Honda, Shimizu, and Rutter 2005, pp. 572–9.
43. Wakefield and Montgomery 2000, pp. 265–83; Wakefield and Stott 2005.
44. Jepson and Johnson 2007, pp. 75–6.
45. Geier and Geier 2003, pp. 203–8.
46. Zhou *et al.* 2003, pp. 1–24.
47. Jepson and Johnson 2007, pp. 77–8.
48. Richler *et al.* 2006, pp. 299–316.
49. Rima and Duprex 2006, pp. 199–214; Jepson and Johnson 2007, pp. 78–9.
50. Kirby 2005, p. 233; Pangborn and Baker 2005, p. 1:12; Bock and Stauth 2007, pp. 55–56, 181; McCandless 2007, p. 168.
51. McCandless 2007, p. 168; Bock and Stauth 2007, p. 394; Cave with Mitchell 2001, pp. 33–34, 295.
52. Cave with Mitchell 2001, p. 143.
53. Pangborn and Baker 2005, p. 2:61; Cave with Mitchell 2001, pp. 5, 7, 12.
54. Cave with Mitchell 2001, p. 24.
55. Bock and Stauth 2007, pp. 180–81.
56. Cave with Mitchell 2001, pp. 84–86.
57. Edelson 2007b, p. 1.
58. Center for Disease Control and Prevention 2008b.
59. Generation Rescue 2008.
60. Bock and Stauth 2007, p. 53; Cave with Mitchell 2001, pp. 8, 33–34, 84–85.
61. Cave with Mitchell 2001, pp. 14, 254.
62. Bock and Stauth 2007, p. 17.
63. Ibid., pp. 18–21.
64. El-Dahr 2007a, p. 255; McCandless 2007, pp. 176–77.
65. Shaw 1998, pp. 104–106.
66. Hanaway 2006, p. 51; Baker 2004, p. 96; McCandless 2007, p. 83.
67. McCandless 2007, pp. 94, 177, 180.
68. Bock and Stauth 2007, pp. 178, 264.
69. Ibid., pp. 178, 249; El-Dahr 2006b, p. 158; McCandless 2007, pp. 181, 187.
70. McCandless 2007, p. 177; Pangborn and Baker 2005, pp. 2:14–15.
71. Bock and Stauth 2007, pp. 182–83.
72. McCandless 2007, pp. 26, 116, 169, 175–77, 182–83; McCandless 2006d, pp. 242–43; Usman 2007, p. 143; James 2006b, p. 178; Bock and Stauth 2007, p. 251.
73. Adams 2007, p. 26.
74. Shaw 1998, pp. 11, 109–10; Adams 2007, p. 26; Pangborn and Baker 2005, p. 2:57.

Chapter 29

Practical Tips for Doing Biomedical Intervention

YOU HAVE COME A LONG WAY

Having journeyed through all the biomedical intervention chapters of this book, you have indeed come a long way. Congratulations. It was a great deal of information to wade through. I hope that you now understand the underlying physical problems that commonly harass children on the autism spectrum and have spotted those that match the symptoms in your child. If so, you have taken a huge step toward being able to help him. You stand in a position of power to intervene and possibly change the course of his life—and yours. To implement your new knowledge, this chapter offers practical tips to help you move forward. Tips relate to treatment priorities, use of a strong nutrient program, lab testing, record keeping and organization, and ways to self-educate and stay current on the rapid advances in biomedical treatment.

TREATMENT PRIORITIES

Autism is a word that describes a particular collection of behaviors. It is not the *cause* of anything. There are multiple causes of autism, and they can work together in various combinations to push a child over the edge. Since each child is his own unique genetic creation assailed by a unique combination of insults, we expect a unique expression of injury. It follows that there is no stringently defined sequence of interventions to go by when treating autism-spectrum disorders. Treatment priorities must be tailored to the needs of the individual. Yet, despite differences among individuals, many doctors using the Defeat Autism Now! approach find that almost all children improve when:[1]

o the inflamed gut heals

o the immune system is strengthened

- ○ abnormalities in body chemistry are addressed[2]
- ○ accumulated heavy metals are removed (if needed)
- ○ ongoing exposures to heavy metals and toxins are minimized.

First steps in treatment include removing troublesome foods from the diet, restoring healthy gut flora, and starting basic nutritional supplements (a supplement program will be discussed shortly). On the heels of these first steps come explorations in methyl-B12 shots and repair of detoxification chemistry with its links to inflammation. In some cases, infections such as viral infections need to be addressed as well. Some of these interventions require the assistance of a doctor. Keep in mind that, if the gut is a mess, other interventions will be less effective and more complicated, so success in the gut is a top priority.[3] Once these initial steps in treatment have been taken, there is no set course that all children should follow. The needs of the individual child, as well as his response to interventions, guide the next steps.

Some children respond dramatically to interventions with diet, antifungals, methyl-B12 shots, and various detoxification measures. Even so, most children need many kinds of intervention, some of which are applied simultaneously. Often, however, only one is introduced at time so that, if your child responds (for better or worse), you are sure of what caused it. Unless a longer time period is specified in the directions or by your doctor, wait a good week after introducing a change before making another change. If an intervention doesn't help after a reasonable period of time, discontinue it. Then wait to see if your child has a response to the stoppage before making any more changes.[4]

Some interventions are necessary only for a period of time as healing takes place. They can be discontinued after running trials to decide if they are no longer needed. On the other hand, some interventions are needed for the long run. Probiotics and yeast-control products are examples of interventions that may require long-term use by many children.[5]

USE OF A STRONG NUTRIENT PROGRAM

Taking a lot of different vitamins, minerals, and supplements is common in biomedical treatment because, due to a poor diet and/or poor digestion and absorption, almost all children with autism-spectrum disorders have deficiencies in various vitamins, minerals, fatty acids, and other nutrients. The majority of children, especially the younger ones, improve noticeably when they start a good basic nutrient program. Benefits surface within days to weeks; often these benefits include greater speech, more eye contact, and improved behaviors and sleep patterns.[6] See Appendix C for more information about nutrient supplementation, including doctor-recommended dosages and brand names.

TOLERANCE FOR UNCERTAINTY

When doing biomedical intervention, you have to get used to some level of uncertainty; it goes with the territory. Sometimes you treat for something, like yeast overgrowth, for example, when you don't know for certain that it is a problem. In addition, you cannot know in advance of doing an intervention what its effect will be. As for me, I am forever mulling over different questions. What should I try next? Should I call it quits on an intervention that is not paying off, or should I give it a little more time? Giving up can be a tough call. But, then again, you are unraveling a mystery, so you should expect some suspense. Besides, I have found that there is an upside to the uncertainties of biomedical intervention: they are much better than the kind of uncertainties I had before. Before trying biomedical intervention, when therapies, special education, and drugs couldn't turn the tide, I felt powerless; I lived at the mercy of a fickle, unpredictable gene. But not any more. Now I feel empowered. I have an opportunity to make a significant difference in my son's life and in mine, so I can accept whatever uncertainties biomedical intervention brings.[7]

EDUCATE YOURSELF ABOUT ANY INTERVENTION YOU ARE CONSIDERING

At the outset of any trial, whether diet, supplement, or drug, it pays to self-educate. You need to understand the intervention so that you know if it is a good fit for your child. And you need to determine your comfort level with the intervention. Some are more tried-and-true than others. As a result, you may choose to pursue some while bypassing others. Being educated also ensures you will do selected interventions correctly and give them their best chance of success.

The issues vary from one intervention to the next, but it pays to know what they are. For a simple intervention, take a couple of minutes to look it up in the index of this book or another biomedical book. For more complicated interventions like some of the diets, you may need to read a book or Web site on the topic. Learn from the example of my sister Laura who was once inspired by a can of silver spray paint to give her red bike a new look. Perhaps it was a good idea. The questionable decision was to lean the bike against the family station wagon to do the paint job. Laura sprayed only one side of her bike. Yes, indeed, it had a new look. As for the car, the proverbial Joneses had nothing on us. We drove the only vehicle in the neighborhood with the silver outline of a bike sprawled across our red side panel. It was one of those times that "Laura Anne!" rang throughout the house. But, as I said, painting the bike might have been a good idea. Had Laura taken the time to learn about proper painting practices, however, she could have kept herself out of a great deal of trouble. Similarly, when you get a good idea for an intervention, do yourself and your child a favor by taking the time to learn the rules.

Also, try to be strict about following the rules during the trial. With a dietary trial, don't cheat. With supplements and medications, don't miss dosages. Being strict gives your child his best shot at improvement and gives you the best chance of drawing the correct conclusion about whether the intervention is helping or not. Later, you can experiment with less strict variations if you like.[8] That said, don't drive yourself nuts trying to follow rules that are unrealistic in your particular situation. As always, stay within your limits whatever they are and don't become stressed over what you cannot do. Fanatical strictness has its place in certain instances, but often there is some leeway.[9] Doing an intervention mostly right is better than not doing it at all.

BOOSTING YOUR SELF-CONFIDENCE WITH BIOMEDICAL INTERVENTION

Reading about the experiences of other parents doing biomedical intervention can boost your confidence. If you feel you could use some encouragement, take a look at a book called *Recovering Autistic Children* by Stephen M. Edelson, PhD, and Bernard Rimland, PhD. The book contains 31 brief stories written by parents about their experiences with biomedical intervention. The book also provides a helpful table that identifies each child's symptoms before biomedical intervention began. By matching your child's symptoms to the symptom profile of one of these children, you may gain insight into which interventions may help your child. You may also be interested in the articles about specific treatments that are offered in the book.

Another option for boosting your confidence is to email a parent who has experience in biomedical intervention. Names and email addresses of such parents called "rescue angels" are available on Generation Rescue's Web site (www.generationrescue.org). Addresses are broken down by country, as well as states within the U.S., so you can ask questions of local parents who may be able to guide you to local resources.

OUR EXPERIENCE SO FAR

For my family, the first 18 or 20 months of biomedical intervention were the most exciting because the successes came quickly and were easier to see. What was hard back then was trying to learn so much so fast; it was overwhelming at times. Also, I worried too much about whether I was choosing the highest-payback interventions and if I was executing them exactly right. Now, three years later and over the course of many different interventions, Will's improvements surface more slowly and are not as dramatic. Sometimes his progress plateaus or even takes a minor setback, but these have been temporary. Overall, he improves at an encouraging rate. Often I cannot even put my finger on exactly why he is gaining ground. Is it due to a recent intervention or a longer-term one that is finally kicking in to a noticeable degree? I can accept the uncertainty as long as he continues to improve. In addition, many aspects of doing biomedical intervention are easier now. I understand its trial-and-error nature and have more self-confidence in what I am doing. I also adjust to change much more easily than I did initially and don't stress so much over doing every-thing perfectly. I have learned that often there is some leeway on various points.

What is hard now is the fear that I am running out of time. Yet I keep looking and learning, ever reading a new book or attending a Defeat Autism Now! conference. Then I get some ideas and try something new. We gain a little more ground, and I am encouraged. It is true what they say at the conferences: "Biomedical intervention is not a sprint. It is a marathon." You have to keep at it for the long haul.[10]

THE SCOOP ON LAB TESTING

There is much you can do in biomedical intervention without the use of lab tests if you have to. However, the advantage of tests is that they make your detective work easier, so you can act more quickly and with greater confidence. Tests are objective and can perceive things that are otherwise invisible. I found them par-ticularly exciting in the beginning because they discovered things about Will that no doctor had ever even looked for before.

Test kits and where to go for lab testing

Most biomedical testing is not available locally, but rather through mail-order labs that specialize in autism. These labs have various specialties, so often you use different ones for different tests. Parents receive test kits in the mail from the lab or from their health professional. The kit includes step-by-step instructions, as well as all the necessary supplies for specimen collection and return to the lab (usually by express mail). When tests involve collection of urine, stool, hair, or saliva, parents do everything themselves. It is like being in science lab back in middle school. However, for blood collection, the child and the kit must be taken to a local lab to have the blood drawn, processed, and mailed to the specialty lab. If you use a health professional, that person may already know where to go for lab testing. Some of the labs present at exhibit booths of Defeat Autism Now! conferences include:[11]

- Doctor's Data (Illinois)—www.doctorsdata.com; 800 323 2784 (U.S. and Canada), 0871 218 0052 (UK), 630 377 8139 (elsewhere)

- Genova Diagnostics (North Carolina)—www.gdx.net; 800 522 4762

- Genova Diagnostics Europe (Surrey, UK)—www.iwdl.net; +44 020 8336 7750

- Great Plains Laboratory (Kansas)—www.greatplainslaboratory.com; 888 347 2781

- Immunosciences Lab (California)—www.immunoscienceslab.com; 310 657 1077

- Metametrix (Georgia)—www.metametrix.com; 800 221 4640.

Most labs require the signature of a licensed health professional, which usually includes medical doctors, nutritionists/dieticians, nurse practitioners, chiropractors, or naturopaths.

Lab testing if you do not have a health professional

An Internet Web site that offers many tests including several of the ones used·in autism is offered by Direct Laboratory Services (www.directlabs.com). This site has a behind-the-scenes doctor who acts on your behalf to submit lab work to the appropriate lab. You should know that some doctors—perhaps most doctors—would be concerned about parents trying to interpret tests on their own. As far as prices on this Web site go, I have found them to be higher than what I have paid to the same labs for the same tests using Dr. Biomedical's signature. The Web site's test descriptions are brief, but it is easy to get more information. Take note of the lab where the test you are interested in will be processed, and then go to that lab's Web site (listed above) for more details about the test.

Learn about tests and the meaning of your results

Keep in mind that tests are not always completely reliable or able to tell us exactly what we want to know. Thus, they often guide treatment decisions rather than drive them. In earlier chapters, as you read about various tests, you saw that some were more reliable than others and that some are reliable only when they say "yes" but not "no" or vice versa. Once again, it pays to educate yourself about any test you are considering so that you understand its value and its limitations.

The best sources for learning about lab tests and the meaning of their results are:

○   an experienced biomedical doctor

○   the book *Autism: Effective Biomedical Treatments* by Jon Pangborn, PhD, and Sidney Baker, MD. Section 4 describes different tests and identifies the various labs that offer each one

○   the book *Children with Starving Brains* by Jaquelyn McCandless, MD. Chapter 4 discusses specific information about tests and labs

○   the labs' Web sites.

Before my involvement in biomedical treatment, I was never shown lab results, either for myself or my children. Rather, the doctor would comment on the results and then file them away in his or her files, giving me the impression that patients cannot understand results so there is no point in their seeing them. I have not found that to be the case in biomedical treatment. I can indeed learn what a test is telling me. In fact, it is quite valuable that I do since, ultimately, I am the one who decides treatment for my child.

Most specialty labs have helped me by providing Dr. Biomedical with two copies of the test results.[12] One is intended for me. There is something empowering about holding test results in my own hands where I can see and examine specific findings for myself. For each finding, the test shows what the normal ranges should be so that I can see if the result is high, low, or just right. And the lab typically provides pages of interpretive comments for any finding that is out of range. I may not understand everything they say, but I grasp some of it, and even more as time goes on. If I repeat a test at a later date, I find it very helpful to compare it line by line to earlier ones so I can gauge progress.

Organizing test results

For storing test results and related information, you may find it helpful to get a three-ring binder with index tabs. Depending on the tests you do, you might label your index tabs:

- o Food sensitivity tests
- o Stool analysis tests
- o Detoxification tests (e.g., urinary porphyrins tests or urine toxic-metals tests)
- o Red blood cell elements tests
- o Blood work (these are tests ordered by a doctor and performed at a local lab like LabCorp or Quest)
- o One-time tests (these are tests you have not repeated, so they don't need their own tab in the binder).

It is also helpful to have a tab for "Test paper work" where you keep the instructions that came in the lab kit, as well as a copy of the completed requisition form you mailed back to the lab with the specimen.

It is good when things are wrong

It can be traumatic when you first use tests to look inside the black box that is your child and find things wrong. But try to think of it in this way: bad test results are *good* news. You knew before taking the test that something was wrong, or you wouldn't have run the test in the first place. At least now you know *what* is wrong, and that knowledge empowers you. Finally, you will get a chance to fix the underlying problems, so physical symptoms and behaviors can improve. Focus on the exciting opportunities, rather than the heartbreak. You would have much more reason to be depressed if the tests showed everything was perfectly fine, because, then, you wouldn't have anything to do to help your child.

PARENTAL GUILT AND IF ONLYS

Before exploring biomedical intervention, many parents believe that their child's autism was due to unlucky genes—not something they could control. But once they begin to learn about biomedical intervention, their perspective changes. They might come to feel that their child's autism was due in part to factors that they could have influenced. This puts parents at risk for blaming themselves in some way when their child receives a bad test result. But you know what? I have found that feeling guilty drains my energy and distracts me from my goal. It makes me less effective to help my child. Besides, it is self-destructive and a waste of time, too. The same goes for pining away with "if only" I had done this or "if only" I had done that. Don't do that to yourself. It is none of my business, but the way I see it you love your child and you did the best you knew to do at the time, right? No ifs, ands, or buts. If nothing else, you have spent many hours reading this big, fat book in the hope of helping him, haven't you? Then let yourself off the hook. Your child is truly lucky to have you. Move forward and don't look back. You cannot do anything about the past anyway so keep your mind on the present.

BEING YOUR CHILD'S CASE MANAGER

As a parent, I am my son's "case manager," a sizable role. My other children, for example, have a running series of isolated medical events: a broken bone here, an ear infection there—not much of a "case" to manage. That goes for school, too. Allan and Lucas just go. For the most part, they do homework on their own. Oh sure, issues come up sometimes, but nothing that has an extensive history throughout the grade levels.

Will, on the other hand, cultivated a lengthy saga of interwoven events across the medical, emotional, educational, and therapeutic realms. As case manager, I am the only common denominator throughout his life. Teachers, doctors, therapists—they all change over time. Only the case manager can provide continuity. Managing all the issues and keeping track of important information as time goes by is a big job. Adding biomedical intervention into the mix makes the job even bigger. Thus, it helps to write things down and to be organized. Use whatever methods work for you, but here are a few that I have found helpful.

Use binders and computer files for information

When doing biomedical intervention, some information, like test results, comes to you from the outside; as described earlier, binders can be very helpful for organizing this kind of information. But there is also much information that is worthwhile for you to create on your own for future reference. Three-ring binders divided by index tabs work well for short, handwritten notes about such things as vitamin purchases. Other types of information lend themselves better to storage on a computer. The computer works especially well for information that keeps changing over time, such as a vitamin schedule. It is also handy when more lengthy information needs to be entered, such as notes about a doctor visit.

Helpful types of information you create yourself

No matter where you record the following types of information, they can be very helpful for managing biomedical treatment:

1. *Daily vitamin schedule and treatment plan spreadsheet.* These are my two favorite helpers to make my life easier and keep me on track. They are described in Appendix C about nutrient supplementation.

2. *Log of intervention changes.* Whenever anything in your child's treatment changes, jot an entry about it in the change log. Each entry describes a dietary change, the start or stoppage of a supplement or medication, a dosage change, or switch in brand names. An entry can include the date the change took effect and a description of the change, including dosage, brand names, time of day administered, and the reason for the change, if appropriate. As you see your child's response to various interventions, you will be able to look back and know exactly what you did and when. Over time the pages of entries form a history that comes in handy for various purposes.

3. *Log of responses to treatment.* Note how your child responds to various interventions, as well as the times he gets sick. Some people find that their needs are met by a simple log in which they write down behaviors or symptoms (good or bad) that are out of the ordinary. Others prefer to create checklists or more elaborate systems.[13]

4. *Log of purchase information.* It is easy to lose track of where you buy certain items used in biomedical treatment and what you paid for them. The purchase information log helps you to keep track of this information so it is easy to find it later when making repeat purchases or comparison shopping. Simply jot an entry in the log each time you buy something. Include relevant details such as purchase date, seller (store name or Web site), a description of the item, and its price.

5. *Doctor appointment information.* Keep a folder on your home computer that is named after the doctor. Give each file in the folder a name that includes the date of an appointment. Between appointments, as you think of questions or comments for the doctor, go to the file for the upcoming appointment and make an entry so you won't forget it. Take a print-out of the file to the appointment, and use it like a checklist as you talk to the doctor. Also take notes during the appointment. Many doctors will give you their visit notes for your files.[14] When you get home, type whatever notes you have collected into your computer appointment file so they are easy to refer to later if needed.

6. *List of future interventions.* As you learn about interventions that you want to try in the future, record them so you don't forget about them. Include a description of the intervention and where you learned about it. Review the list periodically. When you are ready to begin one of the interventions, you can look up the source you listed for details.

NEXT STEPS IN YOUR SELF-EDUCATION

As you continue to learn about biomedical intervention, there are two particularly helpful books to read. They have been mentioned many times before throughout this book, but their importance in this field bears repetition. They are:

○ *Healing the New Childhood Epidemics: Autism, ADHD, Asthma, and Allergies* by Kenneth Bock, MD, and Cameron Stauth

○ *Children with Starving Brains*, 3rd ed., by Jaquelyn McCandless, MD.

If you are a medical professional, consider *Changing the Course of Autism* by Bryan Jepson, MD, with Jane Johnson, a book written with health-care specialists in mind. It is not a treatment guide like the others. Rather, it compiles and organizes sound medical research that has been published in mainstream medical journals to form a comprehensive disease model for autism. The model presents autism as a disease of disrupted body chemistry that affects multiple organ systems such as the brain, the immune system, and the gut.[15] The book's intent is to change the way the illness is perceived so doctors will base their treatment decisions on scientific evidence rather than on historical opinions. Finally, even if you don't have time to read any of these books cover to cover, keep them on hand as references. Use their indexes to locate a specific topic of interest when needed.

Staying abreast of current biomedical news

Biomedical knowledge in autism is expanding rapidly. The Autism Research Institute (ARI) and Defeat Autism Now! are at the forefront and offer multiple ways to keep current:

1. *Defeat Autism Now! conferences.* Attend a conference in person or watch the free video presentations of conference speakers on your home computer (www.autism.com). You can also order conference syllabuses from ARI, which contain valuable articles in addition to the speakers' presentation slides.

2. *ARI's monthly e-newsletter.* This free email newsletter is produced by ARI parents and focuses on current events and news of interest to the autism community.

3. *ARI's quarterly newsletter,* the *Autism Research Review International.* This seven-page scientific newsletter features articles about autism-relevant research from around the world, as well as articles about biomedical treatment and related information. A yearly subscription is $18 in the U.S., $20 outside the U.S. Individual articles from past issues can be viewed for free on the ARI Web site using a handy index that includes topics such as aggression, the use of Ritalin, Asperger's, or seizures.

For more information or to subscribe to any of these, see ARI's Web site (www.autism.com).

SOLVING THE PUZZLE OF AUTISM

Autism-spectrum disorders are an extremely complex puzzle to solve. They are pervasive and seep into nearly every system of the body. Everywhere we look, we find a puzzle piece, often without knowing whether it is a cause or an effect. How can we grapple with the challenge of treating a disorder that reaches into almost every medical and biological discipline? The puzzle encompasses genetics, heavy-metal and toxin exposure, body chemistry, detoxification, the gut, inflammation, impaired nutritional status, the immune system, allergies, disease-causing agents like viruses, bacteria, and yeast, infections, vaccines, overuse of antibiotics, and, ultimately, the nervous system and the brain.[16] The challenge of autism seems overwhelming.

ARI and Defeat Autism Now! have long believed that, to treat autism, it is imperative that expertise across disciplines be pooled together. Speakers at Defeat Autism Now! conferences cross the gamut of disciplines: medicine, pediatrics, neurology, immunology, pharmacology, biochemistry, psychiatry, nutrition, neurobiology, and more. Bit by bit, as diverse experts pool their knowledge, they have been able to fit together many important pieces of the puzzle with ever-increasing momentum. As the image in the puzzle takes form, I am inspired with hope for improved prevention and treatment of autism-spectrum disorders. The experiences of many recovering children show that the challenge of autism is within our ability to treat. But to be successful, we must work together and think outside any box that threatens to contain and block our ingenuity. Solving the complex puzzle of autism *is* within our grasp. We can do it—and must—when so much is at stake—our children.

NOTES

1. McCandless 2007, pp. 30–32.
2. Mumper 2008a, personal communication.
3. Pangborn and Baker 2005, pp. 1:35–36, 2:1–3; McCandless 2007, pp. 31, 90; Binstock 2007b, p. 310; Baker 2006c, pp. 3–4.
4. Baker 2006c, pp. 3–4; McCandless 2007, pp. 32, 96.
5. Pangborn and Baker 2007, p. 25; Bock and Stauth 2007, pp. 249, 256.
6. Bock and Stauth 2007, pp. 247–49, 253–54; McCandless 2007, pp. 95, 106, 111, 115, 142, 144–45, 161.
7. Pangborn and Baker 2005, pp. 1:35–36.
8. Ibid., p. 2:15.
9. Chinitz and Baker 2007, p. 93.
10. Jepson and Johnson 2007, p. 185; Pangborn and Baker 2005, p. 1:11.
11. McCandless 2007, pp. 78–79.
12. Ibid., p. 79.
13. Ibid., p. 96; Pangborn and Baker 2005, p. 1:17.
14. Mumper 2008a, personal communication.
15. Jepson and Johnson 2007, pp. 6–9.
16. McCandless 2003, pp. 186, 210–11; Green 2006b, p. 187.

Chapter 30

Parting Thoughts, Farewell, and Best Wishes

I will leave you with a story from a family camping trip when I was about 12 years old. Under overcast skies, Laura and I struck out together along a deserted beach. We walked a while before getting the brilliant idea of digging a tunnel into a sand dune. About four feet apart, we each started burrowing straight into the side of a massive dune. I was in past my hips when we turned our tunnels inward to create the way-coolest arching passageway known to man. No doubt a shrine would be built to commemorate our illustrious achievement.

At the height of our excitement, just as our fingers touched in the pinnacle of the arch, my world went dark. The smashing weight of a ton of wet sand collapsed into my every pore. I began screaming to Laura to rescue me. Why wasn't she coming? I was completely helpless. My fingers, still curled about their last fistfuls of earth, were locked in place like a statue. I could not push backward with my arms; they were paralyzed by a crippling downward pressure. The entire length of my back and hips were riveted in place by the hungry dune. *What* was taking Laura so long? A terrifying thought seized me. I stopped screaming. From the other side of our tomb, Laura was screaming, too. A horrifying realization punched into my consciousness: we were *both* trapped. And we were going to suffocate if we did not get out *now*.

I began hurtling my legs wildly through space since they were all I had free. If I could just kick hard enough, maybe my arching back would raise the sand a precious difference. It was our only chance because, being shorter than I, Laura was probably completely buried. But, no, my violent kicks were not loosening the dune's grip. The forceful, pressing weight of the sand would not budge. I was much too far inside the clutching dune to save myself or my sister.

But, then, I kicked something or someone. What was that? I went limp, holding my breath and hoping against hope. Strong fingers clasped my ankles and heaved me out of the belly of the dune. Lo and behold, amid the fresh air and daylight was my big brother, Bernie. In all my life, I have never been so glad to see him as I was then. The very fellow who was usually trying to kill me, as many brothers do to their sisters, had actually saved my life—and Laura's, too. I was definitely nicer to the guy after this. It turns out that Mom and Dad had sent him looking for us. It was a miracle.

It would be many years before I found myself trapped in another dune. Only this time it was Will and I trapped in the suffocating sands of autism, robbed of light and air and freedom. Thank goodness for all those blessed heroes who helped pull us out! At the forefront are the Autism Research Institute and Defeat Autism Now! Also indispensable have been medical doctors, specialty laboratories, compounding pharmacies, and nutrient manufacturers. And where would we be without our dedicated and caring teachers and therapists, family and friends, Rich, Allan, Lucas, and a host of others? We owe a great debt to them all.

Will too is a hero. He has worked very hard. Day in and day out, he carefully follows his dietary restrictions. With fortitude, he endures the daily assault of pills, liquids, creams, and other intrusive but necessary and beneficial treatments. He submits to personal invasions for collections of lab specimens and other intrusions on his privacy. Always, he puts his best foot forward in the never-ending tide of therapeutic and educational efforts. Due to no fault of his own, he was swallowed by a dune. Yet, with help, he has risen up with resilience and courage to pick up the shattered pieces and fit them back together. He is one tough kid—dedicated, enduring, and ready with a smile.

Well, dear reader, seek out your heroes with care. Find the supports you need. Educate yourself. Learn to understand and appreciate that special child of yours. Focus on his strengths. And always remember that you have that *something* that makes all the difference in the world. You are the hero of your own story. And when you can, give back to the autism community in whatever way fits your time and talents.

Will and I wish you and your special child our very best. We hope this book has helped you, and you have enjoyed reading it. If not, blame Laura who always said I should write a book. What do little sisters know anyhow?

Will's Heroes Unveiled

Will has been blessed with many heroes. It is impractical to name them all. Those listed here are a tip of the iceberg, but a very precious tip indeed. In the book, you have known them by various aliases. Now is our opportunity to thank them in person from the bottom of our hearts. In order of appearance:

Hero Doctor
Mark G. Goetting, MD, Evansville, Indiana (Presently Portage, Michigan)

Teacher First
Michele Todd, Russellville, Arkansas

Talented Team who Diagnosed Asperger's Syndrome
Dennis Developmental Center, Little Rock, Arkansas, University of Arkansas for Medical Sciences

Chesterfield County Public School System
Midlothian, Virginia

Third-Grade Teacher During Crisis Move to Virginia
Riki Stone, Richmond, Virginia

Tutor Dear
Karen Tanner, Midlothian, Virginia

Dr. Biomedical
Mary N. Megson, MD, FAAP, Richmond, Virginia

Fifth-Grade Autism Teacher
Ashleigh Dirr, Midlothian, Virginia

Middle School Autism Teacher
Beth Beckman, Midlothian, Virginia

Middle School Psychologist
Kenneth Roach, MA, Midlothian, Virginia

ARI Parent Ratings of Behavioral Effects of Biomedical Interventions

ARI Publ. 34/Feb. 2008

PARENT RATINGS OF BEHAVIORAL EFFECTS OF BIOMEDICAL INTERVENTIONS
Autism Research Institute • 4182 Adams Avenue • San Diego, CA 92116

The parents of autistic children represent a vast and important reservoir of information on the benefits—and adverse effects—of the large variety of drugs and other interventions that have been tried with their children. Since 1967 the Autism Research Institute has been collecting parent ratings of the usefulness of the many interventions tried on their autistic children.

The following data have been collected from the more than 26,000 parents who have completed our questionnaires designed to collect such information. For the purposes of the present table, the parents responses on a six-point scale have been combined into three categories: "made worse" (ratings 1 and 2), "no effect" (ratings 3 and 4), and "made better" (ratings 5 and 6). The "Better:Worse" column gives the number of children who "Got Better" for each one who "Got Worse."

DRUGS	Got Worse[A]	No Effect	Got Better	Better: Worse	No. of Cases[B]
Aderall	43%	25%	32%	0.8:1	775
Amphetamine	47%	28%	25%	0.5:1	1312
Anafranil	32%	38%	30%	0.9:1	422
Antibiotics	33%	53%	15%	0.5:1	2163
Antifungals[C]					
Diflucan	5%	38%	57%	11:1	653
Nystatin	5%	44%	50%	9.7:1	1388
Atarax	26%	53%	22%	0.9:1	517
Benadryl	24%	50%	26%	1.1:1	3032
Beta Blocker	17%	51%	31%	1.8:1	286
Buspar	27%	45%	28%	1.0:1	400
Chloral					
Hydrate	41%	39%	20%	0.5:1	459
Clonidine	22%	31%	47%	2.1:1	1525
Clozapine	37%	44%	19%	0.5:1	155
Cogentin	19%	54%	27%	1.4:1	186
Cylert	45%	36%	20%	0.4:1	623
Deanol	15%	57%	28%	1.9:1	210
Depakene[D]					
Behavior	25%	43%	32%	1.3:1	1071
Seizures	11%	33%	56%	4.8:1	705
Desipramine	34%	35%	31%	0.9:1	86

DRUGS	Got Worse[A]	No Effect	Got Better	Better: Worse	No. of Cases[B]
Dilantin[D]					
Behavior	28%	49%	23%	0.8:1	1110
Seizures	15%	37%	48%	3.3:1	433
Felbatol	20%	55%	25%	1.3:1	56
Fenfluramine	21%	52%	27%	1.3:1	477
Haldol	38%	28%	34%	0.9:1	1199
IVIG	10%	44%	46%	4.5:1	79
Klonapin[D]					
Behavior	28%	42%	30%	1.0:1	246
Seizures	25%	60%	15%	0.6:1	67
Lithium	24%	45%	31%	1.3:1	463
Luvox	30%	37%	34%	1.1:1	220
Mellaril	29%	38%	33%	1.2:1	2097
Mysoline[D]					
Behavior	41%	46%	13%	0.3:1	149
Seizures	19%	56%	25%	1.3:1	78
Naltrexone	20%	46%	34%	1.8:1	302
Paxil	33%	31%	36%	1.1:1	416
Phenergan	29%	46%	25%	0.9:1	301
Phenobarb.[D]					
Behavior	47%	37%	16%	0.3:1	1109
Seizures	18%	43%	39%	2.2:1	520

DRUGS	Got Worse[A]	No Effect	Got Better	Better: Worse	No. of Cases[B]
Prolixin	30%	41%	29%	1.1:1	105
Prozac	32%	32%	36%	1.1:1	1312
Risperidal	20%	26%	54%	2.8:1	1038
Ritalin	45%	26%	29%	0.7:1	4127
Secretin					
Intravenous	7%	49%	44%	6.3:1	468
Transderm.	10%	53%	37%	3.6:1	196
Stelazine	28%	45%	26%	0.9:1	434
Steroids	35%	33%	32%	0.9:1	132
Tegretol[D]					
Behavior	25%	45%	30%	1.2:1	1520
Seizures	13%	33%	54%	4.0:1	842
Thorazine	36%	40%	24%	0.7:1	940
Tofranil	30%	38%	32%	1.1:1	776
Valium	35%	41%	24%	0.7:1	865
Valtrex	6%	42%	52%	8.5:1	65
Zarontin[D]					
Behavior	35%	46%	19%	0.6:1	153
Seizures	19%	55%	25%	1.3:1	110
Zoloft	35%	33%	32%	0.9:1	500

BIOMEDICAL/ NON-DRUG/ SUPPLEMENTS	Got Worse[A]	No Effect	Got Better	Better: Worse	No. of Cases[B]
Calcium[E]	3%	62%	35%	14:1	2097
Cod Liver Oil	4%	45%	51%	13:1	1681
Cod Liver Oil with Bethanecol	10%	54%	37%	3.8:1	126
Colostrum	6%	56%	38%	6.1:1	597
Detox. (Chelation)[C]	3%	23%	74%	24:1	803
Digestive Enzymes	3%	39%	58%	17:1	1502
DMG	8%	51%	42%	5.4:1	5807
Fatty Acids	2%	41%	56%	24:1	1169
5 HTP	13%	47%	40%	3.1:1	343
Folic Acid	4%	53%	43%	11:1	1955
Food Allergy Trtmnt	3%	33%	64%	24:1	952
Hyperbaric Oxygen Therapy	5%	34%	60%	12:1	134
Magnesium	6%	65%	29%	4.6:1	301
Melatonin	8%	27%	65%	7.8:1	1105
Methyl B12 (nasal)	15%	29%	56%	3.9:1	48
Methyl B12 (subcut.)	7%	26%	67%	9.5:1	170
MT Promoter	13%	49%	38%	2.9:1	61
P5P (Vit. B6)	12%	37%	51%	4.2:1	529
Pepcid	12%	59%	30%	2.6:1	164
SAMe	16%	63%	21%	1.3:1	142
St. Johns Wort	18%	66%	16%	0.9:1	150
TMG	15%	43%	42%	2.8:1	803

BIOMEDICAL/ NON-DRUG/ SUPPLEMENTS	Got Worse[A]	No Effect	Got Better	Better: Worse	No. of Cases[B]
Transfer Factor	10%	48%	42%	4.3:1	174
Vitamin A	2%	57%	41%	18:1	1127
Vitamin B3	4%	52%	43%	10:1	927
Vit. B6/Mag.	4%	48%	48%	11:1	6634
Vitamin B12 (oral)	7%	32%	61%	8.6:1	98
Vitamin C	2%	55%	43%	19:1	2397
Zinc	2%	47%	51%	22:1	1989

SPECIAL DIETS

	Got Worse[A]	No Effect	Got Better	Better: Worse	No. of Cases[B]
Candida Diet	3%	41%	56%	19:1	941
Feingold Diet	2%	42%	56%	25:1	899
Gluten- /Casein- Free Diet	3%	31%	66%	19:1	2561
Removed Chocolate	2%	47%	51%	28:1	2021
Removed Eggs	2%	56%	41%	17:1	1386
Removed Milk Products/Dairy	2%	46%	52%	32:1	6360
Removed Sugar	2%	48%	50%	25:1	4187
Removed Wheat	2%	47%	51%	28:1	3774
Rotation Diet	2%	46%	51%	21:1	938
Specific Carbo- hydrate Diet	7%	24%	69%	10:1	278

A. "Worse" refers only to worse behavior. Drugs, but not nutrients, typically also cause physical problems if used long-term.
B. No. of cases is cumulative over several decades, so does not reflect current usage levels (e.g., Haldol is now seldom used).
C. Antifungal drugs and chelation are used selectively, where evidence indicates they are needed.
D. Seizure drugs: top line behavior effects, bottom line effects on seizures
E. Calcium effects are not due to dairy-free diet; statistics are similar for milk drinkers and non-milk drinkers.

ARI Publ. 34 Asp/Feb. 2008

Note: The data below are based on cases identified as "Asperger Syndrome" N=1,297

PARENT RATINGS OF BEHAVIORAL EFFECTS OF BIOMEDICAL INTERVENTIONS
Autism Research Institute • 4182 Adams Avenue • San Diego, CA 92116

The parents of autistic children represent a vast and important reservoir of information on the benefits—and adverse effects—of the large variety of drugs and other interventions that have been tried with their children. Since 1967 the Autism Research Institute has been collecting parent ratings of the usefulness of the many interventions tried on their autistic children.

The following data have been collected from 1,297 parents who have completed our questionnaires designed to collect such information. For the purposes of the present table, the parents responses on a six-point scale have been combined into three categories: "made worse" (ratings 1 and 2), "no effect" (ratings 3 and 4), and "made better" (ratings 5 and 6). The "Better:Worse" column gives the number of children who "Got Better" for each one who "Got Worse."

DRUGS	Got Worse[A]	No Effect	Got Better	Better: Worse	No. of Cases[B]
Aderall	39%	26%	34%	0.9:1	186
Amphetamine	31%	28%	41%	1.3:1	113
Anafranil	19%	42%	39%	2.1:1	69
Antibiotics	35%	45%	20%	0.6:1	97
Antifungals[C]					
Diflucan	7%	38%	55%	7.8:1	56
Nystatin	8%	38%	54%	6.8:1	76
Atarax	35%	35%	30%	0.9:1	40
Benadryl	28%	51%	21%	0.8:1	184
Beta Blocker	10%	57%	33%	3.3:1	30
Buspar	19%	54%	27%	1.4:1	59
Chloral Hydrate	30%	57%	13%	0.4:1	23
Clonidine	22%	38%	40%	1.8:1	198
Clozapine	31%	50%	19%	0.6:1	26
Cogentin	25%	58%	17%	0.7:1	12
Cylert	32%	54%	14%	0.4:1	69
Deanol	0%	75%	25%		4
Depakene[D]					
Behavior	26%	39%	36%	1.4:1	70
Seizures	8%	60%	32%	4.0:1	25
Desipramine	25%	50%	25%	1.0:1	12

DRUGS	Got Worse[A]	No Effect	Got Better	Better: Worse	No. of Cases[B]
Dilantin[D]					
Behavior	22%	72%	6%	0.2:1	18
Seizures	20%	40%	40%	2.0:1	10
Felbatol	0%	100%	0%		4
Fenfluramine	11%	78%	11%	1.1:1	9
Haldol	35%	41%	24%	0.7:1	37
IVIG	14%	43%	43%	3.0:1	7
Klonapin[D]					
Behavior	11%	68%	21%	2.0:1	19
Seizures	0%	83%	17%		6
Lithium	18%	43%	39%	2.1:1	49
Luvox	26%	46%	28%	1.1:1	46
Mellaril	31%	33%	36%	1.2:1	36
Mysoline[D]					
Behavior	25%	75%	0%		4
Seizures	0%	100%	0%		3
Naltrexone	11%	33%	56%	5.0:1	18
Paxil	43%	25%	33%	0.8:1	89
Phenergan	30%	45%	24%	0.8:1	33
Phenobarb.[D]					
Behavior	40%	50%	10%	0.2:1	20
Seizures	20%	27%	53%	2.7:1	15

DRUGS	Got Worse[A]	No Effect	Got Better	Better: Worse	No. of Cases[B]
Prolixin	0%	78%	22%		9
Prozac	29%	32%	38%	1.3:1	177
Risperidal	22%	25%	53%	2.4:1	167
Ritalin	36%	30%	35%	1.0:1	400
Secretin					
Intravenous	6%	50%	44%	8.0:1	18
Transderm.	0%	50%	50%		8
Stelazine	27%	73%	0%		11
Steroids	41%	35%	24%	0.6:1	17
Tegretol[D]					
Behavior	31%	49%	20%	0.6:1	65
Seizures	26%	32%	42%	1.6:1	31
Thorazine	57%	33%	10%	0.2:1	21
Tofranil	25%	40%	36%	1.4:1	73
Valium	38%	43%	20%	0.5:1	40
Valtrex	0%	50%	50%		2
Zarontin[D]					
Behavior	38%	63%	0%		8
Seizures	0%	100%	0%		5
Zoloft	28%	28%	43%	1.5:1	99

BIOMEDICAL/ NON-DRUG/ SUPPLEMENTS	Got Worse[A]	No Effect	Got Better	Better: Worse	No. of Cases[B]
Calcium[E]	3%	61%	36%	14:1	191
Cod Liver Oil	5%	42%	53%	11:1	160
Cod Liver Oil with Bethanechol	0%	67%	33%		15
Colostrum	5%	56%	40%	8.5:1	43
Detox. (Chelation)[C]	7%	18%	75%	11:1	72
Digestive Enzymes	2%	36%	61%	25:1	161
DMG	11%	49%	40%	3.5:1	230
Fatty Acids	2%	33%	65%	29:1	133
5 HTP	5%	54%	41%	8.0:1	39
Folic Acid	8%	44%	48%	6.3:1	131
Food Allergy Trtmnt	3%	34%	63%	23:1	109
Hyperbaric Oxygen Therapy	9%	36%	55%	6.0:1	11
Magnesium	11%	74%	16%	1.5:1	19
Melatonin	6%	20%	75%	13:1	107
Methyl B12 (nasal)	20%	60%	20%	1.0:1	5
Methyl B12 (subcut.)	13%	25%	63%	1.5:1	8
MT Promoter	30%	30%	40%	1.3:1	10
P5P (Vit. B6)	12%	27%	62%	5.3:1	52
Pepcid	0%	56%	44%		18
SAMe	17%	67%	17%	1.0:1	12
St. Johns Wort	15%	73%	12%	0.8:1	26
TMG	21%	41%	38%	1.8:1	58

BIOMEDICAL/ NON-DRUG/ SUPPLEMENTS	Got Worse[A]	No Effect	Got Better	Better: Worse	No. of Cases[B]
Transfer Factor	7%	71%	21%	3.0:1	14
Vitamin A	6%	62%	32%	5.0:1	111
Vitamin B3	6%	43%	51%	8.2:1	81
Vit. B6/Mag.	5%	45%	50%	11:1	321
Vitamin B12 (oral)	0%	38%	63%		8
Vitamin C	2%	51%	46%	19:1	201
Zinc	4%	38%	58%	16:1	163
SPECIAL DIETS					
Candida Diet	1%	41%	58%	41:1	71
Feingold Diet	0%	45%	55%		96
Gluten-/Casein-Free Diet	3%	27%	70%	24:1	237
Removed Chocolate	1%	50%	49%	36:1	149
Removed Eggs	3%	61%	36%	11:1	125
Removed Milk Products/Dairy	2%	43%	56%	31:1	336
Removed Sugar	3%	48%	49%	14:1	207
Removed Wheat	1%	41%	58%	44:1	226
Rotation Diet	3%	37%	60%	20:1	65
Specific Carbohydrate Diet	3%	33%	64%	21:1	33

A. "Worse" refers only to worse behavior. Drugs, but not nutrients, typically also cause physical problems if used long-term.
B. No. of cases is cumulative over several decades, so does not reflect current usage levels (e.g., Haldol is now seldom used).
C. Antifungal drugs and chelation are used selectively, where evidence indicates they are needed.
D. Seizure drugs: top line behavior effects, bottom line effects on seizures.
E. Calcium effects are not due to dairy-free diet; statistics are similar for milk drinkers and non-milk drinkers.

Nutrient Supplementation

THE NEED FOR A STRONG NUTRIENT PROGRAM

Due to poor diet and/or poor digestion and absorption, almost all children with autism-spectrum disorders have deficiencies in various vitamins, minerals, fatty acids, and other nutrients. The majority of children, especially the younger ones, improve noticeably when they start a good basic nutrient program. Benefits surface in days to weeks. Often these include greater speech, more eye contact and improved behaviors and sleep patterns. Almost all children and adults need certain fundamental nutrients such as zinc, vitamin C, calcium, magnesium, and cod liver oil (valuable for its vitamins A and D and omega-3 fatty acids). Many need additional nutrients as well.[1] This appendix supplies information about nutrient supplementation including recommended dosages and where to find recommended brands. It also identifies excellent sources of additional information, as well as provides tips to help you stay on top of your program.

BEST RESOURCES OF NUTRIENT INFORMATION TAILORED TO THE AUTISM SPECTRUM

Two books written by doctors of Defeat Autism Now! contain a chapter that describes a nutrient program and dosing for children with autism-spectrum disorders. Both chapters are excellent, so take your pick:

- *Children with Starving Brains*, 3rd ed., by Jaquelyn McCandless, MD (Chapter 6, "Feeding the Starving Brain")
- *Healing the New Childhood Epidemics* by Kenneth Bock, MD, and Cameron Stauth (Chapter 18, "Supplementation Therapy").

An additional book that contains a section of in-depth information and dosing on numerous individual supplements is *Autism: Effective Biomedical Treatments* by Jon Pangborn, PhD, and Sidney Baker, MD (Section 5: "Nutritional Supplements for Autism"). This section is helpful if you want more information than the other two sources provide.

DOSAGE AMOUNTS

Table C.1 lists the most commonly recommended nutrients, as well as their daily dosages for autism-spectrum children. If you are used to the "Recommended Dietary Allowances" (RDAs), these dosages will seem high because RDAs are for healthy people, not for people with special health problems like autism. For purposes of healing, nutrients are needed at levels several times higher than RDAs.[2] Since supplements can have a strong effect on body function and behavior, start at a low dose and gradually increase over time based on your child's response.[3] Unless otherwise noted, the recommendations in Table C.1 come from *Children with Starving Brains*, 3rd ed., pp. 116–17.

Table C.1 Recommended daily dosage of vitamins, minerals, and supplements

Supplement	Recommended daily dosage	Comments
Vitamin A	2,500–5,000iu	Part may be cod liver oil.
Vitamin C	Up to 1,000mg	Better in divided doses taken 3–4 times/day since it does not stay in the body very long. Buffered form is tolerated better.
Vitamin D	1,000–2,000iu	2,000iu for children who do not get much sunlight, are dark-skinned, or breast fed. Otherwise 1,000iu.
Vitamin E	200–400iu	200iu under 5 years old. Otherwise 400iu. High gamma tocopherol is best.
B6	50–100mg	50mg under 5 years old. Otherwise 50–100mg. Activated P5P form preferred. Take with magnesium.
Calcium	1g or more	Divide in several doses during the day.
CoQ10[4]	30–200mg	Depends on whether powder, gel, or melt. Also depends on age, size, other treatments, and symptoms.
Digestive enzymes	See bottle label	Dosing is based on size of meal. See Chapter 27 for additional information.
DMG	125–750mg	125mg capsules or sublinguals 1–6/day. Take DMG or TMG but not both.
Folinic acid	800mcg	
Glutathione[5]	Cream (TD)	0.5ml applied twice a day (250mg/ml concentration). This concentration requires prescription.
	IV	Start at 200–300mg and work up to 600–800mg (1 time/week). Requires prescription.
	Oral	Unclear if giving by mouth is effective. Only use liposomal form. Take twice daily. See bottle or compounding pharmacy for dosing.

Table C.1 cont.

Supplement	Recommended daily dosage	Comments
Magnesium	200–400mg	Glycinate form is most absorbable.
Melatonin[6]	0.5–3mg	Give at night. Dose depends on age, size, other treatments, and symptoms.
Methyl-B12	Injections	750–2,500mcg (64.5mcg/kg) 2 times/week. Requires prescription. Daily injections help 40 percent of kids.
	Nasal spray	1–2 sprays daily or twice/week depending on response. Requires prescription.
Omega-3 DHA	250–500mg	
Omega-3 EPA	750mg	
Omega-3 GLA	50–100mg	
Probiotics[7]	10–100 billion CFU	20–100 billion CFU to restore healthy gut flora. 10–25 billion CFU to maintain health gut flora. Use high-quality, high-potency brands as described in Chapter 26.
Selenium	75–200mcg	75–150mcg under 5 years old. Otherwise up to 150–200mcg. High doses can be toxic but it is rare and unlikely.
TMG	500–2,000mg	Take DMG or TMG but not both.
Zinc	20–50mg	Up to 1mg/1b + 20mg if removing heavy metals with DMPS, DMSA, or EDTA. Picolinate form is most absorbable.

HIGH-QUALITY BRANDS AND WHERE TO FIND THEM

Some supplement makers cater to the specialized needs of the autism spectrum.[8] Their products:

- ○ come in numerous forms such as pills, chewables, liquids, powders, and creams to make them easier for parents to administer

- ○ omit potentially objectionable ingredients such as dairy, gluten, soy, and artificial colors and flavors. Read supplement bottles to verify that such ingredients are not used

- ○ are tailored to the most common deficiencies in autism and dosed appropriately for children. Super Nu-Thera or Nu-Thera by Kirkman are examples

- ○ use forms of nutrients that are preferred in autism such as the P5P form of vitamin B6, for example.

There are many good brands and products you may want to explore. Though there are too many to list here, a few product lines available at exhibit booths during Defeat Autism Now! conferences include BrainChild, Kirkman, Klaire Labs, New Beginnings, and Nordic Naturals. I have tried various products from each of these companies and been happy with them. Nevertheless, what is right for your particular child is something you will have to decide. Brand quality is particularly important for fish oils, which can contain mercury from fish if not adequately filtered. You may want to consider trying fish oil products from companies like Kirkman or Nordic Naturals, as well as specific brands such as Coromega, Eskimo-3, OmegaBrite, or ProDHA Jr.[9]

Your best chance of finding these and other high-quality brands locally is at compounding pharmacies and perhaps vitamin or health-food stores. There are also Internet mail-order stores such as Our Kids (www.OurKidsASD.com) and Wellness Pharmacy (www.WellnessHealth.com). They carry several quality brands, so you can save on shipping by ordering several products from one of them rather than from several different mail-order sources. Web sites abound for mail delivery of individual brands or products. They are easy to locate with a Google search on the specific product name or a brand name with the word *vitamin* (e.g., "Kirkman vitamin").

SUPPLEMENTS TAKE SOME TIME TO SHOW A RESPONSE

When a person responds to a drug, it is usually pretty fast, only hours to days. However, supplements tend to take longer. The response time varies depending on the particular supplement, as well as the individual. Consider vitamin B12 or melatonin, for example. One person who responds relatively quickly to one of these may show improvement within hours or days. However, for another person, it may take weeks to show improvement. Digestive enzymes and zinc are examples of supplements that may take even longer on average for a response, days to weeks. Longer still are vitamin A and calcium, which take weeks to months. As long as six months of vitamin E supplementation may be required to raise levels in the brain. Here is the point: don't throw in the towel too early. Give a supplement some time before deciding whether it helps.[10]

TIPS FOR KEEPING TRACK OF YOUR DAILY VITAMIN SCHEDULE

For me, it works well to have a different, weekly pill container for each time of day Will takes pills (e.g., breakfast, dinner, bedtime). Once a week, I fill all the containers following a "daily vitamin schedule sheet" that I keep with the vitamin bottles. You can create a vitamin schedule by hand or on a computer (a computer makes it especially easy to revise and reprint the schedule as needed). For each time of day your child gets vitamins, the vitamin schedule shows the vitamin's name and its dose. A schedule might, for example, have a breakfast list, dinner list, and bedtime list. Some supplements like powders, liquids, creams, and refrigerated items cannot go in the pill containers; so, on the vitamin schedule at the end of the breakfast list, for example, you might draw a line. Anything listed under the line is not in the pill container. I glance at that portion of the vitamin schedule each time I give Will his pills, so I don't forget anything. In fact, I tape a copy of just these "extra" items inside a kitchen cabinet, so it is handy to reference.

THE DAILY TREATMENT PLAN SPREADSHEET

When giving several supplements, each of which might contain multiple vitamins and minerals, it is easy to lose track of the total amount of each vitamin and mineral that your child is receiving. It can be hard to know if you are dosing at the right level, especially as the treatment plan changes over time. Creating a daily treatment plan spreadsheet helps you keep track of total daily dosages, so you can be sure they are within the recommended ranges. The spreadsheet also gives you a central place to record *all* the interventions you are currently using. This makes it an ideal tool to show your doctor (if you use one) at the start of each appointment. At a glance, he or she knows right where you are and can more effectively plot a course for what to do next.

It works well to create your plan on a computer spreadsheet, though it can be done on paper as well. See Figure C.1 for a portion of a sample spreadsheet that illustrates the idea. At the top of the spreadsheet, simply list any nonvitamin/mineral interventions you use, such as special diets, prescription medications, and miscellaneous supplements like digestive enzymes. The spreadsheet matrix itself follows next. Its first column lists the names of all the vitamins, minerals, or other supplements found in the ingredient lists of the supplements you use. There is also a column for "Recommended Daily Dose," whose values come from Table C.1 or other source. Next comes a "Total Daily Dose" column, followed by columns for the specific supplements you give your child. The column labels for specific supplements include the dose given each day such as one capsule or one teaspoon. A number in the Total Daily Dose column is the sum of all the numbers to its right. Once the spreadsheet is constructed, compare the values in the Recommended Daily Dose and Total Daily Dose columns to ensure you are giving the appropriate doses. Using the spreadsheet makes it much easier for you to see if you need to make any adjustments.

Non-Vitamin/Mineral Interventions:							
	GF/CF Diet						
	Digestive Enzymes Brand X (6 caps/day) (2/meal)						
	Probiotics Brand Y (1 cap/day)						
	Epsom Salt Baths (4x/week)						
Vitamin/ Mineral/ Supplement	Recommended Daily Dose	Total Daily Dose	Cod Liver Oil Brand X (4 softgels)	Multi-Vitamin Brand Y (2 caps)	Calcium Brand Z (2 caps)	Vitamin C Brand Y (3 tabs)	TMG Brand X (1 cap)
Vitamin A	2500-5000iu	5000iu	5000iu				
Vitamin C	Up to 1000mg	810mg		60mg		750mg	
Vitamin D	1000-2000iu	940iu	540iu		400iu		
Vitamin E	200-400iu	300iu		30iu			
Zinc	20-50mg	40mg		10mg			
Vitamin B6	50-100mg	50mg		50mg			
Omega-3 DHA	250-500mg	500mg	500mg				
Omega-3 EPA	750mg	500mg	500mg				
Calcium	1g or more	1.1g			630mg		
Folinic Acid	800mcg	800mg		400mcg			400mcg
Magnesium	200-400mg	400mg		100mg	300mg		
Selenium	75-200mcg	100mcg		25mcg			
TMG	500-100	500mg					500mg

Figure C.1 Daily treatment plan spreadsheet

NOTES

1. Bock and Stauth 2007, pp. 247–49, 253–54; McCandless 2007, pp. 95, 106, 111, 115, 142, 144–45, 161.
2. Garrison and Somer 1995, pp. 14–15.
3. Adams 2007, p. 10.
4. Bock and Stauth 2007, pp.276–77.
5. Mumper 2008a, personal communication; Autism Research Institute 2005, p. 8.
6. Bock and Stauth 2007, p. 269.
7. M. James 2006, p. 29.
8. McCandless 2007, p. 131.
9. Kartzinel 2006, p. 99; Hardy 2004, p. 238.
10. Pangborn and Baker 2005, pp. 2:6–7; Jepson and Johnson 2007, p. 197.

Interpreting the Urinary Porphyrins Test

The urinary porphyrins test measures the levels of substances called porphyrins that are found in urine. The various levels or patterns of different porphyrins indicate the body's levels of certain heavy metals (mercury, lead, arsenic, aluminum) and toxic chemicals (like PCBs and pesticides). In general, the higher the porphyrin levels, the more severe the autism.[1]

A valuable article explaining porphyrin testing and how to interpret results was written by Dan Rossignol, MD. The article, "The Use of Urinary Porphyrins Analysis in Autism," appeared in the April 2007 edition of *Medical Veritas*. In the article, Dr. Rossignol expresses a preference for a particular laboratory in France, Laboratoire Philippe Auguste (www.labbio.net), because:

○ its reference ranges that define "normal" on their test are based on their research findings in children rather than in healthy adults, which are used by most other labs

○ its lab machinery is calibrated to detect small variations in porphyrin levels, which can make a difference when evaluating children on the autism spectrum.

Dr. Rossignol's explanations refer to the format of the French test report. While the complete article is available from www.medicalveritas.com, a paraphrase of the test-interpretation portion of the article appears here. It is presented in the order that Dr. Rossignol follows when he evaluates test results. Depending on the specific lab results you are trying to interpret, drawing conclusions can be straightforward, quite confusing, or somewhere in between.

CREATININE

The first number Dr. Rossignol locates on a person's test results is the amount of creatinine. Creatinine itself is not a porphyrin, but its level indicates how accurate the porphyrin values on the test are. Ideally, Dr. Rossignol likes to see the creatinine level around 1,000 mg/l because:

○ if the level is less than 1,000 mg/l, the porphyrin values on the test could be falsely elevated

○   if the creatinine level is more than 1,000 mg/l, the porphyrin values could be falsely undervalued.

Children with autism often have lower creatinine levels than typical children, which makes interpretation of the test somewhat tricky. So, for autism, Dr. Rossignol is "generally happy" as long as the creatinine level is within 200–300 mg/l or so of the 1,000 mg/l ideal. In other words, 700–1,300 mg/l is acceptable to indicate reliability of the porphyrin values on the test. If the creatinine level is outside this range, one has to be careful with the interpretation. Sometimes it is worth repeating the test in the hope of getting a better creatinine result. However, in the case where creatinine is below the acceptable range, the porphyrin values are often so high that they remain quite high even after they are adjusted downward to account for false elevation. In this situation, heavy-metal overload is present despite the porphyrin levels being overstated.

COPRO (SHORT FOR COPROPORPHYRINS)

The next number Dr. Rossignol locates on the test is the copro level. It is a good indicator of overall toxic-metal burden in the kidney. Typically, if its level is higher than the laboratory's reference range, it is due to exposure to mercury, lead, and/or arsenic.

PRECO (SHORT FOR PRECOPROPORPHYRIN)

Preco is evaluated next. Its level is normally low in urine unless there is an elevated level of mercury in the body, so a preco level above the laboratory's reference range for preco indicates mercury exposure.

COMPARISON OF COPRO AND PRECO LEVELS

If copro and preco levels are both elevated above their respective reference ranges, Dr. Rossignol calculates the percentage that each one is elevated over its respective range. Comparing these two percentages indicates whether mercury is the only heavy-metal exposure or if other heavy-metal exposures are involved as well. According to Dr. Rossignol, one of the following determinations can be made:

○   If the preco percentage is higher than the copro percentage, mercury is predominant.

○   If the copro and preco percentages are about the same, it usually indicates mercury exposure.

○   If the copro percentage is higher than the preco percentage, then usually another metal is heavily involved, typically lead or arsenic.

PENTA (SHORT FOR PENTACARBOXY PORPHYRIN)

Penta is elevated with mercury exposure, though typically less elevated than preco.

HEPTA (SHORT FOR HEPTACARBOXY PORPHYRIN) AND URO (SHORT FOR UROPORPHYRINS)

When hepta and uro levels are elevated over their reference ranges, it is typically due to xenobiotic exposure such as PCBs, pesticides, and other toxic chemicals like dioxins. Arsenic and aluminum can also cause hepta and uro to be elevated.

RATIOS

So far, the only form of analysis presented has been to compare porphyrin test numbers to their respective reference ranges. However, if certain porphyrin numbers are combined into ratios, additional information becomes available. Dr. Rossignol's article discusses three ratios that come as part of the lab results from the French lab, Laboratoire Philippe Auguste. Each ratio is accompanied by a reference range. A word of warning is warranted: when children have been exposed to many different toxic metals and chemicals (mercury, lead, aluminum, arsenic, pesticides, PCBs, and others), the ratios can be tricky to interpret.

- *Preco/uro ratio* (helpful if preco is elevated). Since preco is elevated by mercury, but uro is not, making a ratio of them can help confirm that the preco elevation is real and not a false positive.

- *Preco/copro ratio*. If this ratio is elevated above its reference range, mercury is the predominant metal. If copro is elevated and the preco/copro ratio is lower than its reference range, another toxic metal like lead or arsenic is predominant.

- *Uro/copro ratio*. If this ratio is elevated, it confirms that the elevation in uro is real and not a false positive. It is also consistent with xenobiotics, arsenic, or aluminum exposure.

NOTE

1. McCandless 2007, p. 140.

Bibliography

Adams, J. (2007) *Summary of Biomedical Treatments for Autism.* ARI Publication 40. San Diego, CA: Autism Research Institute.

Adams, J., Levine, K. and Lin-Wen, H. (2006) "Mercury in First-cut Baby Hair of Children with Autism vs. Typically-Developing Children." *Proceedings of the Autism Society of America Annual Conference,* Providence, RI, July.

Altmann, D. (2000) "Autism and measles, mumps, and rubella vaccine." *Lancet 355,* 9201, 409–10.

American Psychiatric Association. (1994) *Diagnostic and Statistical Manual of Mental Disorders.* 4th ed. Washington, D.C.: American Psychiatric Association.

Ashwood, P., Anthony, A., Torrente, F. and Wakefield, A. (2004) "Spontaneous mucosal lymphocyte cytokine profiles in children with autism and gastrointestinal symptoms: Mucosal immune activation and reduced counter-regulatory interleukin-10." *Journal of Clinical Immunology 24,* 6, 664–67.

Attwood, T. (2006) "What Is Asperger's Syndrome?" In K. Simmons, *The Official Autism 101 Manual.* Alberta, Canada: Autism Today.

Autism Research Institute. (2005) *Treatment Options for Mercury/Metal Toxicity in Autism and Related Developmental Disabilities: Consensus Position Paper Feb 2005.* San Diego, CA: Autism Research Institute.

Baker, S. (2004) *Detoxification and Healing.* New York: McGraw-Hill.

Baker, S. (2006a) "Individuality." In Autism Research Institute, *DAN! Conference Proceedings Fall 2006.* San Diego, CA: Autism Research Institute.

Baker, S. (2006b) "Notes for Orphan Organ Lecture." In Autism Research Institute, *DAN! Conference Proceedings Fall 2006.* San Diego, CA: Autism Research Institute.

Baker, S. (2006c) "Summary for New DAN! Parents." In Autism Research Institute, *DAN! Conference Proceedings Fall 2006.* San Diego, CA: Autism Research Institute.

Baker, S., James, J. and Milivojevich, A. (2006) "Patterns of Thiol Chemistry in Autistic Children." In Autism Research Institute, *DAN! Conference Proceedings Spring 2006.* San Diego, CA: Autism Research Institute.

Barkley, R. (2005) *Taking Charge of ADHD.* New York/London: The Guilford Press.

Beck, V. (1998) *Unlocking the Potential of Secretin.* San Diego, CA: Autism Research Institute.

Bernard, S., Enayati, A., Roger, H., Binstock, T., Redwood, L. and McGinnis, W. (2000) *Autsim: A Unique Type of Mercury Poisoning.* Cranford, NJ: ARC Research. Accessed on 7/12/08 at www.safeminds.org.

Bernard, S., Enayati, A., Redwood, L., Roger, H. and Binstock, T. (2001) "Autism: A novel form of mercury poisoning." *Medical Hypotheses 56,* 4, 462–71.

Binstock, T. (2007a) "Autism, Metals, and the Mercury in Vaccines." In J. McCandless, *Children with Starving Brains*. 3rd ed. Putney, VT: Bramble Books.

Binstock, T. (2007b) "Intra-Body Toxins." In J. McCandless, *Children with Starving Brains*. 3rd ed. Putney, VT: Bramble Books.

Bock, K. and Stauth, C. (2007) *Healing the New Childhood Epidemics: Autism, ADHD, Asthma, and Allergies*. New York: Ballantine Books.

Bradstreet, J. (2006) "Simplified Evaluation and Treatment of Autism Using Biomarker Directed Algorithms." In Autism Research Institute, *DAN! Conference Proceedings Fall 2006*. San Diego, CA: Autism Research Institute.

Bradstreet, J., Geier, D., Kartzinel, J., Adams, J. and Geier, M. (2003) "A case-control study of mercury burden in children with autistic spectrum disorders." Journal of American Physicians and Surgeons 8, 3, 76–79.

Buie, T. (2003) "Examining GI Issues in Children with Autism and the Effectiveness of Traditional GI Medications." In Autism Research Institute, *DAN! Conference Syllabus Spring 2003*. San Diego, CA: Autism Research Institute.

Cave, S., with Mitchell, D. (2001) *What Your Doctor May Not Tell You About Children's Vaccinations*. New York: Warner Books.

Center for Disease Control and Prevention. (2008a) *What is the Prevalence of Autism?* Atlanta: Center for Disease Control and Prevention. Accessed on 1/6/08 at www.cdc.gov/ncbddd/autism/faq_prevalence.htm#whatisprevalence.

Center for Disease Control and Prevention. (2008b) *Childhood Immunization Schedule*. Atlanta: Center for Disease Control and Prevention. Accessed on 1/17/08 at www.cdc.gov/vaccines/recs/schedules.

Chinitz, J. and Baker, S. (2007) *We Band of Mothers*. San Diego, CA: Autism Research Institute.

Comi, A., Zimmerman, A., Frye, V., Law, P. and Peeden, J. (1999) "Familial clustering of autoimmune disorders and evaluation of medical risk factors in autism." *Journal of Child Neurology 14*, 6, 388–94.

Compart, P. and Laake, D. (2006) *The Kid-Friendly ADHD & Autism Cookbook*. Beverly, MA: Fair Winds Press.

Cordain, L. and Friel, J. (2005) *The Paleo Diet for Athletes*. Emmause, PA: Rodale Inc.

Croen, L., Grether, J., Yoshida, C., Odouli, R. and Van de Water, J. (2005) "Maternal autoimmune diseases, asthma and allergies, and childhood autism spectrum disorders: A case-control study." *Archives of Pediatrics and Adolescent Medicine 159*, 2, 151–57.

Crook, W. (1999) *The Yeast Connection Handbook*. Jackson, TN: Professional Books, Inc.

Crook, W. (2001) *Dr. Crook Discusses Yeasts and How They Can Make You Sick*. Jackson, TN: Professional Books.

Deth, R. (2006) "Methionine Synthase: The Redox Sentinel." In Autism Research Institute, *DAN! Conference Proceedings Spring 2006*. San Diego, CA: Autism Research Institute.

Deth, R. (2007a) "Update on Methionine Synthase, Adaptive Enzyme Functioning, Cobalamin, and Methylation of Phospholipids at the D4 Receptor." In J. Pangborn and S. Baker, *Autism: Effective Biomedical Treatments 2007 Supplement*. San Diego, CA: Autism Research Institute.

Deth, R. (2007b) "D4 Dopamine Receptors and Methionine Synthase in Human Cortex." In Autism Research Institute, *DAN! Conference Proceedings Spring 2007*. San Diego, CA: Autism Research Institute.

Deth, R. (2007c) "Oxidative Stress and the Metabolic Pathology of Autism." In Autism Research Institute, *DAN! Conference Proceedings Spring 2007*. San Diego, CA: Autism Research Institute.

D'Eufemia, P., Celli, M., Finocchiaro, R., Pacifico, L. et al. (1996) "Abnormal intestinal permeability in children with autism." *Acta Paediatrica 85*, 9, 1076–79.

Edelson, S. (2006a) "Following the vision of Dr. Rimland." *Autism Research Review International 20*, 3, 3.

Edelson, S. (2006b) "Stephen M. Edelson, Ph.D., named Director of ARI." *Autism Research Review International 20*, 3, 1.

Edelson, S. (2006c) "Why is Autism on the Rise?" In K. Simmons, *The Official Autism 101 Manual*. Alberta, Canada: Autism Today.

Edelson, S. (2007a) "Talk about recovery." *Autism Research Review International 21*, 1, 3.

Edelson, S. (2007b) "Survey: Vaccinated boys far more likely than other boys to have neurological disorders." *Autism Research Review International 21*, 2, 1.

Edelson, S. and Cantor, D. (1998) "Autism: Xenobiotic influences." *Toxicology and Industrial Health 14*, 4, 553–63.

Edelson, S. and Rimland, B. (2006) *Recovering Autistic Children*. San Diego, CA: Autism Research Institute.

Eggleston, D. and Nylander, M. (1987) "Correlation of dental amalgams with mercury in brain tissue." *Journal of Prosthetic Dentistry 58*, 6, 704–707.

El-Dahr, J. (2006a) "Inflammation and Disordered Immunity in Autism Spectrum Disorders." In Autism Research Institute, *DAN! Conference Proceedings Spring 2006*. San Diego, CA: Autism Research Institute.

El-Dahr, J. (2006b) "Inflammation from A to Z in ASDs." In Autism Research Institute, *DAN! Conference Proceedings Spring 2006*. San Diego, CA: Autism Research Institute.

El-Dahr, J. (2007a) "Immunologic Issues in Autism." In Autism Research Institute, *DAN! Conference Proceedings Spring 2007*. San Diego, CA: Autism Research Institute.

El-Dahr, J. (2007b) "Improving Immunity and Understanding Inflammation." In Autism Research Institute, *DAN! Conference Proceedings Spring 2007*. San Diego, CA: Autism Research Institute.

Faherty, C. (2000) *Asperger's…What Does It Mean to Me?* Arlington, TX: Future Horizons.

Fall, C. and Urwick, J. (2006) "Keeping It Simple: Starting a GF/CF Diet." In Autism Research Institute, *DAN! Conference Proceedings Fall 2006*. San Diego, CA: Autism Research Institute.

Feingold, B. (1975) *Why Your Child is Hyperactive*. New York: Random House.

Freedenfeld, S. (2005) "Recognizing and Removing Environmental Toxins for General Health." *Presentation at the DAN! Conference, Fall*, accessed on 1/15/06 at www.DANwebcast.com.

Furlong, J. and Hanaway, P. (2006) "Autism and the Gut: Finding the Source." In Autism Research Institute, *DAN! Conference Proceedings Spring 2006*. San Diego, CA: Autism Research Institute.

Furlong, J. and James, M. (2006) "Autism and the Gut: Finding the Source, Treating the Source." In Autism Research Institute, *DAN! Conference Proceedings Spring 2006*. San Diego, CA: Autism Research Institute.

Garrison, R. and Somer, E. (1995) *The Nutrition Desk Reference*. 3rd ed. New Canaan, CT: Keats Publishing.

Geier, M. and Geier, D. (2003) "Pediatric MMR vaccination safety." *International Pediatrics 18*, 2, 203–8.

Generation Rescue. (2008) *Vaccination Information*. U.S.A.: Generation Rescue. Accessed on 1/18/08 at www.generationrescue.org/vaccines.html

Gershon, M. (2003) *The Second Brain*. New York: Quill.

Goldman, G. and Yazbak, F. (2004) "An investigation of the association between MMR vaccination and autism in Denmark." *Journal of American Physicians and Surgeons 9*, 3, 70–75.

Gorman, C. with Hyde, M. (2001) *Less-Toxic Alternatives*. Texarkana, TX: Optimum Publishing.

Gottschall, E. (2004) *Breaking the Vicious Cycle*. Baltimore, Ontario, Canada: Kirkton Press.

Grandin, T., Rimland, B., Adams, J. and Edelson, S. (2006) "Advice for Parents of Young Autistic Children: Spring 2004." In K. Simmons, *The Official Autism 101 Manual*. Alberta, Canada: Autism Today.

Green, J. (2005) "Chelation Panel and Question/Answer Session." *Presentation at the DAN! Conference, Fall*. Accessed on 1/26/06 at www.DANwebcast.com.

Green, J. (2006a) "Overview: Detoxification through chelation therapy." *Autism Research Review International 20*, 1, 3.

Green, J. (2006b) "Environmental Chemicals and Autism." In Autism Research Institute, *DAN! Conference Proceedings Spring 2006*. San Diego, CA: Autism Research Institute.

Green, J. (2006c) "What Else Besides Mercury Is Injuring Our Children?" In Autism Research Institute, *DAN! Conference Proceedings Fall 2006*. San Diego, CA: Autism Research Institute.

Haley, B. and Small, T. (2006) "Interview with Dr. Boyd E. Haley: Biomarkers supporting mercury toxicity as the major exacerbator of neurological illness, recent evidence via the urinary porphyrin tests." *Medical Veritas 3*, 1, 921–34.

Halsey, N. (1999) "IVS Perspective on the Use of Thimerosal-Containing Vaccines." Presentation from *Workshop on Thimerosal and Vaccines*, Institute for Vaccine Safety, John Hopkins Bloomberg School of Public Health, August 11–12.

Hamilton, L. (2000) *Facing Autism*. Colorado Springs, CO: WaterBrook Press.

Hanaway, P. (2006) "Balance of Flora, Galt and Mucosal Integrity." In Autism Research Institute, *DAN! Conference Proceedings Fall 2006*. San Diego, CA: Autism Research Institute.

Hardy, P. (2004) "Essential Fatty Acids, Membrane Fluidity and Prostanoids." In Autism Research Institute, *DAN! Conference Proceedings Spring 2004*. San Diego, CA: Autism Research Institute.

Herbert, M. (2006) "Autism Biology and the Environment." In Autism Research Institute, *DAN! Conference Proceedings Fall 2006*. San Diego, CA: Autism Research Institute.

Hersey, J. (1999) *Why Can't My Child Behave?* Alexandria, VA: Pear Tree Press, Inc.

Hidaka, H., Tashiro, Y. and Eida, T. (1987) "Effect of fructo-oligosaccharides on intestinal microflora." *Nahrung 31*, 5–6, 427–36.

Hidaka, H., Tashiro, Y. and Eida, T. (1991) "Proliferation of bifidobacteria by oligosaccharides and their useful effect on human health." *Bifidobacteria Microflora 10*, 1, 65–79.

Holmes, A. (2001) *Autism Treatments: Chelation of Mercury.* Baton Rouge, LA: Self-published. Accessed on 12/29/07 at www.healing-arts.org/children/holmes.htm#results.

Holmes, A., Blaxill, M. and Haley, B. (2003) "Reduced levels of mercury in first baby haircuts of autistic children." *International Journal of Toxicology 22*, 4, 277–85.

Honda, H., Shimizu, Y. and Rutter, M. (2005) "No effect of MMR withdrawal on the incidence of autism: a total population study." *Journal of Child Psychology and Psychiatry 46*, 572–79.

Horvath, K., Papadimitriou, J., Rabsztyn, A., Drachenberg, C. and Tildon, J. (1999) "Gastrointestinal abnormalities in children with autistic disorder." *Journal of Pediatrics 135*, 5, 559–63.

Hu, L., Bernard, J. and Che, J. (2003) "Neutron activation analysis of hair samples for the identification of autism." *Transactions of the American Nuclear Society 89*, 681–82.

Jackson, L. (2002) *Freaks, Geeks and Asperger Syndrome: A User Guide to Adolescence.* London: Jessica Kingsley Publishers.

James, J. (2006a) "New Evidence and Implications of DNA Hypomethylation in Autistic Children." In Autism Research Institute, *DAN! Conference Proceedings Spring 2006.* San Diego, CA: Autism Research Institute.

James, J. (2006b) "New Evidence for DNA Hypomethylation and Increased Vulnerability to Oxidative Stress." In Autism Research Institute, *DAN! Conference Proceedings Fall 2006.* San Diego, CA: Autism Research Institute.

James, J. (2007) "Oxidative Stress and the Metabolic Pathology of Autism." In Autism Research Institute, *DAN! Conference Proceedings Spring 2007.* San Diego, CA: Autism Research Institute.

James, J., Cutler, P., Melnyk, S., Jernigan, S. et al. (2004) "Metabolic biomarkers of increased oxidative stress and impaired methylation capacity in children with autism." *American Journal of Clinical Nutrition 80*, 6, 1611–17.

James, J., Melnyk, S., Jernigan, S., Cleves, M. et al. (2006) "Metabolic endophenotype and related genotypes are associated with oxidative stress in children with autism." *American Journal of Medical Genetics Part B: Neuropsychiatric Genetics 141*, 8, 947–56.

James, M. (2006) "A Natural Approach to Healing the Gut in Autism." In Autism Research Institute, *DAN! Conference Proceedings Spring 2006.* San Diego, CA: Autism Research Institute.

Jepson, B. and Johnson, J. (2007) *Changing the Course of Autism.* Boulder, CO: Sentient Publications.

Kanner, L. (1943) "Autistic disturbances of affective contact." *The Nervous Child 2*, 3, 217–50.

Kartzinel, J. (2006) "Current Uses of Nutritional Supplements for Adjunctive Therapy in Children with Autism Spectrum Disorders." In Autism Research Institute, *DAN! Conference Proceedings Fall 2006.* San Diego, CA: Autism Research Institute.

Kavanaugh, L., Fraser, J. and Dietrich, F. (2006) "Recent evolution of the human pathogen Cryptococcus neoformans by intervarietal transfer of a 14-gene fragment." *Molecular Biology and Evolution 23*, 10, 1879–90.

Kirby, D. (2005) *Evidence of Harm.* New York: St. Martin's Press.

Krigsman, A. (2004) "Current Concepts in the Treatment of Autistic Spectrum Associated Enterocolitis." In Autism Research Institute, *DAN! Conference Syllabus Spring 2004*. San Diego, CA: Autism Research Institute.

Kushak, R., Winter, H., Farber, N. and Buie, T. (2005) "Gastrointestinal symptoms and intestinal disaccharidase activities in children with autism." *Journal of Pediatric Gastroenterology and Nutrition 41*, 4, 508.

Lauritsen, M., Pedersen, C. and Mortensen, P. (2004) "The incidence and prevalence of pervasive developmental disorders: A Danish population-based study." *Psychological Medicine 34*, 7, 1339–46.

Levinson, A. (2006a) "Reversing Autism…One Child at a Time." In Autism Research Institute, *DAN! Conference Proceedings Spring 2006*. San Diego, CA: Autism Research Institute.

Levinson, A. (2006b) "Understanding the Biomedical Approach and Making the Right Choices." In Autism Research Institute, *DAN! Conference Proceedings Fall 2006*. San Diego, CA: Autism Research Institute.

Lewis, A. (2005) "Using a biomedical and biochemical model to better understand and treat autism." *Advocate 1*, 18–21.

Lewis, L. (1998a) *Special Diets for Special Kids*. Arlington, TX: Future Horizons Inc.

Lewis, L. (1998b) "Dietary Intervention for the Treatment of Autism: Why Implement a Gluten and Casein Free Diet?" In W. Shaw, *Biological Treatments for Autism and PDD*. Overland Park, KS: self-published.

Lewis, L. (2006) "Dietary Interventions for Autism Spectrum Disorders." In Autism Research Institute, *DAN! Conference Proceedings Fall 2006*. San Diego, CA: Autism Research Institute.

Lewis, S. and Fink, D. (2005) *Allergy and Candida Cooking*. Coralville, IA: Canary Connect Publications.

Madsen, K., Hviid, A., Vestergaard, M., Schendel, D. *et al.* (2002) "A population-based study of measles, mumps, and rubella vaccination and autism." *New England Journal of Medicine 347*, 19, 1477–82.

Martin, N. (2006) "How to Deal Emotionally with Spousal and Other Relationships Around Autism." In K. Simmons, *The Official Autism 101 Manual*. Alberta, Canada: Autism Today.

Matthews, J. (2007) "Excerpt from *Nourishing Hope*." In Autism Research Institute, *DAN! Conference Proceedings Spring 2007*. San Diego, CA: Autism Research Institute.

McAfee, J. (2002) *Navigating the Social World*. Arlington, TX: Future Horizons Inc.

McCandless, J. (2003) *Children with Starving Brains 2nd Edition*. USA: Bramble Books.

McCandless, J. (2005) "Clinical use of methyl-B12 in autism." *Autism Research Review International 19*, 4, 3.

McCandless, J. (2006a) "How Chelsey Changed Our Lives." In S. Edelson and B. Rimland, *Recovering Autistic Children*. San Diego, CA: Autism Research Institute.

McCandless, J. (2006b) "Viral/Immune Issues and Treatments in ASD." In Autism Research Institute, *DAN! Conference Proceedings Spring 2006*. San Diego, CA: Autism Research Institute.

McCandless, J. (2006c) "Detoxification Panel—Evaluating and Treating Mercury Toxicity." In Autism Research Institute, *DAN! Conference Proceedings Fall 2006*. San Diego, CA: Autism Research Institute.

McCandless, J. (2006d) "Viral/Immune Issues and Treatments in ASD." In Autism Research Institute, *DAN! Conference Proceedings Fall 2006*. San Diego, CA: Autism Research Institute.

McCandless, J. (2007) *Children with Starving Brains*. 3rd ed. Putney, VT: Bramble Books.

McCarthy, J. (2007) *Louder Than Words*. New York: Dutton.

McDonnell, M. (2006a) "Gastrointestinal pathology and the use of SCD in ASD." In Autism Research Institute, *DAN! Conference Proceedings Fall 2006*. San Diego, CA: Autism Research Institute.

McDonnell, M. (2006b) "The Role of Diet in Autism." In Autism Research Institute, *DAN! Conference Proceedings Fall 2006*. San Diego, CA: Autism Research Institute.

Megson, N. (2000) "Is autism a G-alpha protein defect reversible with natural vitamin A?" *Medical Hypotheses 54*, 6, 979–83.

Mumper, E. (2005) "Autism from a Cellular Perspective." *Presentation at the DAN! Conference, Spring*. Accessed on 7/27/05 at www.DANwebcast.com.

Mumper, E. (2007) "Vicious Cycles in Autism." In Autism Research Institute, *DAN! Conference Proceedings Spring 2007*. San Diego, CA: Autism Research Institute.

Mumper, E. (2008a) Personal communication: email dated 29 January.

Mumper, E. (2008b) "The Crucial Role of Intestinal Health." In Autism Research Institute, *Defeat Autism Now! 2008 Spring Conference*. San Diego, CA: Autism Research Institute.

Myles, B. and Southwick, J. (1999) *Asperger Syndrome and Difficult Moments: Practical Solutions for Tantrums, Rage, and Meltdowns*. Shawnee Mission, KS: Autism Asperger Publishing Co.

Nataf, R., Skorupka, C., Amet, L., Lam, A., Springbett, A. and Lathe, R. (2006) "Porphyrinuria in childhood autistic disorder: Implications for environmental toxicity." *Toxicology and Applied Pharmacology 214*, 2, 99–108.

Neubrander, J. (2002) *Methyl-B12: Myth, Masterpiece, or Miracle?* Edison, NJ: Self-published. Accessed on 12/29/07 at www.drneubrander.com/Files/Methyl-B12;%20 Myth,%20Masterpiece,%20or%20Miracle.doc

Neubrander, J. (2006) "The Methylation Puzzle: Methyl-B12 et. al." In Autism Research Institute, *DAN! Conference Proceedings Spring 2006*. San Diego, CA: Autism Research Institute.

Owens, S. (2006) "What a Low Oxalate Diet Has Been Changing in Children with Autism." In Autism Research Institute, *DAN! Conference Proceedings Fall 2006*. San Diego, CA: Autism Research Institute.

Owens, S. (2007) "Low Oxalate Diet." In J. McCandless, *Children with Starving Brains*. 3rd ed. Putney, VT: Bramble Books.

Pangborn, J. (2006a) "Nutrition Panel Comments." In Autism Research Institute, *DAN! Conference Proceedings Spring 2006*. San Diego, CA: Autism Research Institute.

Pangborn, J. (2006b) "Digestive Deficiencies in Autism—Benefits of Digestive Aids." In Autism Research Institute, *DAN! Conference Proceedings Fall 2006*. San Diego, CA: Autism Research Institute.

Pangborn, J. (2006c) "Overview of the DAN! Biomedical Approach: A Message to Parents and Clinicians." In Autism Research Institute, *DAN! Conference Proceedings Fall 2006*. San Diego, CA: Autism Research Institute.

Pangborn, J. and Baker, S. (2005) *Autism: Effective Biomedical Treatments*. San Diego, CA: Autism Research Institute.

Pangborn, J. and Baker, S. (2007) *Autism: Effective Biomedical Treatments 2007 Supplement.* San Diego, CA: Autism Research Institute.

Pardo, C., Vargas, D. and Zimmerman, A. (2005) "Immunity, neuroglia and neuroinflammation in autism." *International Review of Psychiatry 17,* 6, 485–95.

Rapp, D. (1991) *Is This Your Child?* New York: William Morrow and Company, Inc.

Rea, W. (2007) "The Environmental Aspects of ASD." In Autism Research Institute, *DAN! Conference Proceedings Spring 2007.* San Diego, CA: Autism Research Institute.

Rhogam FYI (n.d.) *Thimerosal.* California: Einstein Law Inc. Accessed on 12/29/07 at www.rhogamfyi.com/thimerosal.html.

Richler, J., Luyster, R., Risi, S., Hsu, W. *et al.* (2006) "Is there a 'regressive phenotype' of autism spectrum disorder associated with the measles–mumps–rubella vaccine? A CPEA study." *Journal of Autism and Developmental Disorders 36,* 3, 299–316.

Rima, B. and Duprex. W. (2006) "Morbilli viruses and human disease." *The Journal of Pathology 208,* 2, 199–214.

Rimland, B. (1964) *Infantile Autism.* New York: Meredith Publishing Company.

Rimland, B. (2005) "Child's death due to drug error, not chelation." *Autism Research Review International 19,* 3, 1 and 3.

Rimland, B. (2006a) "Methylation: The Link Between Thimerosal and Autism?" In S. Edelson and B. Rimland, *Recovering Autistic Children.* San Diego, CA: Autism Research Institute.

Rimland, B. (2006b) "Chelation: The story behind the headlines." *Autism Research Review International 19,* 3, 3.

Rimland, B. (2006c) "Harvard researchers confirm GI/autism link." *Autism Research Review International 20,* 1, 4.

Rimland, B. (2006d) "Thimerosal again linked to neuronal death." *Autism Research Review International 20,* 1, 5.

Rimland, B. (2006e) "Viewing autism: Researcher says 'systemic' approach more valuable than 'genes/brain/behavior' approach." *Autism Research Review International 20,* 1, 7.

Rimland, B. (2006f) "High rate of gastrointestinal problems identified in autism spectrum children." *Autism Research Review International 20,* 2, 2.

Rossignol, D. (2007) "The use of urinary porphyrins analysis in autism." *Medical Veritas 4,* 1, 1276–81.

Sandler, R., Finegold, S., Bolte, E., Buchanan, C. et al. (2000) "Short-term benefit from oral vancomycin treatment of regressive-onset autism." *Journal of Child Neurology 15,* 7, 429–35.

Semon, B. (1998) "Treating Yeast in Children with Autism: Typical Results of Anti-Yeast Therapy." In W. Shaw, *Biological Treatments for Autism and PDD.* Overland Park, KS: Self-published.

Semon, B. and Kornblum, L. (1999) *Feast Without Yeast.* Milwaukee, WI: Wisconsin Institute of Nutrition.

Seroussi, K. (2002) *Unraveling the Mystery of Autism and Pervasive Developmental Disorder.* New York: Broadway Books.

Shattock, P. and Savery, D. (1997) "Autism as a Metabolic Disorder." In W. Shaw, *Biological Treatments for Autism and PDD.* Overland Park, KS: Self-published.

Shattock, P. and Whiteley, P. (2002) "Biochemical aspects in autism spectrum disorders: Updating the opioid-excess theory and presenting new opportunities for biomedical intervention." *Expert Opinion on Therapeutic Targets 6*, 2, 175–83.

Shaw, W. (1998) *Biological Treatments for Autism and PDD*. Overland Park, KS: Self-published.

Shaw, W. (2004) "Medical testing for autism, Asperger's syndrome and PDD." *Autism/Asperger's Digest Magazine*, July–August, 8–12.

Shaw, W. (2006) *Oxalates Control Is a Major New Factor in Autism Therapy*. Lenexa, KS: Great Plains Laboratory.

Shaw, W. (2008) *Porphyrin Testing and Heavy Metal Toxicity: Unresolved Questions and Concerns*. Kansas: Great Plains Laboratory. Accessed on 3/8/08 at www.greatplainslaboratory. com/porphyrin_gpllabcorp_vs_auguste_philippe%20_2_.pdf.

Stewart, K. (2002) *Helping a Child with Nonverbal Learning Disorder or Asperger's Syndrome*. Oakland, CA: New Harbinger Publications, Inc.

Stott, C., Blaxhill, M. and Wakefield, A. (2004) "MMR and autism in perspective: The Denmark story." *Journal of the American Physicians and Surgeons 9*, 3, 89–91.

Sweeten, T., Bowyer, S., Posey, D., Halberstadt, G. and McDougle, C. (2003) "Increased prevalence of familial autoimmunity in probands with pervasive developmental disorders." *Pediatrics 112*, 5, e420.

Taylor, B., Miller, E., Farrington, C., Petropoulos, M. *et al.* "Autism and measles, mumps and rubella vaccine: No epidemiological evidence for a causal association." *Lancet 353*, 9169, 2026–29.

Torrente, F., Ashwood, P., Day, R., Machado, N. et al. (2002) "Small intestinal enteropathy with epithelial IgG and complement deposition in children with regressive autism." *Molecular Psychiatry 7*, 4, 375–82.

U.S. Court of Federal Claims (2008) "Docket of Omnibus Autism Proceeding." *Autism Update—May 25, 2007*. Washington D.C. Accessed on 3/10/08 at www.uscfc.uscourts.gov/node/2718.

Usman, A. (2006) "Journey to Recovery...Finding the Way." In Autism Research Institute, *DAN! Conference Proceedings Spring 2006*. San Diego, CA: Autism Research Institute.

Usman, A. (2007) "Biomedical Individuality and Effective Treatment Strategies Using the DAN! Approach." In Autism Research Institute, *DAN! Conference Proceedings Spring 2007*. San Diego, CA: Autism Research Institute.

Vargas, D., Nascimbene, C., Krishnan, C., Zimmerman, A. and Pardo, C. (2005) "Neuroglial activation and neuroinflammation in the brain of patients with autism." *Annals of Neurology 57*, 1, 67–81.

VP Foundation. (2005) *The Low Oxalate Cookbook—Book Two*. Memphis, TN: Wimmer Companies.

Wakefield, A (1999) "MMR vaccination and autism." *Lancet 354*, 9182, 949–50.

Wakefield, A. and Montgomery, S. (2000) "Measles, mumps, rubella vaccine: Through a glass, darkly." *Adverse Drug Reactions and Toxicological Reviews 19*, 4, 265–83.

Wakefield, A. and Stott, C. (2005) "No effect of MMR withdrawal on the incidence of autism: A total population study." Austin, TX: Thoughtful House Center for Children. Accessed on 5/2/08 at www.thoughtfulhouse.org/pr/pr_030805072428.htm.

Wakefield, A., Murch, S., Anthony, A., Linnell, J. et al. (1998) "Ileal-lymphoid-nodular hyperplasia, non-specific colitis, and pervasive developmental disorder in children." *Lancet 351*, 9103, 637–41.

Wakefield, A., Anthony, A., Murch, S., Thomson, M. et al. (2000) "Enterocolitis in children with developmental disorders." *American Journal of Gastroenterology 95*, 9, 2285–95.

Walsh, W., Usman, A., Tarpey, J. and Kelly, T. (2002) *Metallothionein and Autism.* 2nd ed. Naperville, IL: Health Research Institute Pfeiffer Treatment Center.

Waly, M., Olteanu, H., Banerjee, R., Choi, S. et al. (2004) "Activation of methionine synthase by insulin-like growth factor-1 and dopamine: A target for neurodevelopmental toxins and thimerosal." *Molecular Psychiatry 9*, 4, 358–70.

Waring, R. and Klovrza, L. (2000) "Sulphur metabolism in autism." *Journal of Nutritional and Environmental Medicine 10*, 1, 25–32.

White, J. (2003) "Intestinal pathophysiology in autism." *Experimental Biology and Medicine 228*, 6, 639–49.

Zhou, W., Pool, V., Iskander, J., English-Bullard, R. *et al.* (2003) "Surveillance for safety after immunization: Vaccine Adverse Event Reporting System (VAERS)—United States, 1991–2001." *MMWR Surveillance Summaries 52*, 1, 1–24.

Zimmerman, A., Jyonouchi, H., Comi, A., Connors, S. et al. (2005) "Cerebrospinal fluid and serum markers of inflammation in autism." *Pediatric Neurology 33*, 3, 195–201.

Zukin, J. (1996) *Raising Your Child Without Milk.* Rocklin, CA: Prima Publishing.

Subject Index

Author Index